DECONSTRUCTING JESUS

DECONSTRUCTING JESUS

ROBERT M. PRICE

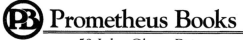
59 John Glenn Drive
Amherst, New York 14228-2197

Published 2000 by Prometheus Books

Deconstructing Jesus. Copyright © 2000 by Robert M. Price. All rights reserved. No part of this publication may be reproduced, stored in a retrieval system, or transmitted in any form or by any means, digital, electronic, mechanical, photocopying, recording, or otherwise, or conveyed via the Internet or a Web site without prior written permission of the publisher, except in the case of brief quotations embodied in critical articles and reviews.

Inquiries should be addressed to
Prometheus Books
59 John Glenn Drive
Amherst, New York 14228–2197.
VOICE: 716–691–0133, ext. 207.
FAX: 716–564–2711.
WWW.PROMETHEUSBOOKS.COM

07   6 5 4

Library of Congress Cataloging-in-Publication Data

Price, Robert M., 1954–
    Deconstructing Jesus / Robert M. Price.
        p.   cm.
    Includes bibliographical references and index.
    ISBN-13: 978–1–57392758–1
    ISBN-10: 1–57392–758–9 (cloth)
    1. Jesus Christ—Historicity. 2. Church history—Primitive and early church, ca. 30–600. I. Title.

BT303.2 .P75 2000
232—dc21   99–048140
                                                                             CIP

Printed in the United States of America on acid-free paper

This book is dedicated to

Darrell J. Doughty

Mentor, Friend, and Colleague in the Higher Criticism

CONTENTS

Introduction: Jesus Christ as the Effect of Christianity, Not the Cause   9

1. Reconstructing Christian Origins   21

2. The Jesus Movements   47

3. The Christ Cults   75

4. Messiah as Mishnah   97

5. The Lost Gospel   113

6. Sacred Scapegoat   169

7. The Cruci-Fiction?   213

8. The Historicized Jesus?   227

Conclusion: The Many Behind the One   265

Index   267

Scripture Index   275

Introduction

JESUS CHRIST AS THE EFFECT OF CHRISTIANITY, NOT THE CAUSE

The subject of this book is a rather abstract one. Though it deals with the very heart of the religion of a billion people, few of them even know there is an issue to discuss. For this book treats of the historical Jesus and whether we can know anything about him, whether even there is anyone to know about! Those billion Christians affirm the existence of Jesus Christ, the wonder-working man-god who died for sins and rose from the dead for them and their salvation. How do they claim to know these cherished facts? They were taught these things at their mothers' knees, or in catechism by clergymen. They would not think to question what they have thus learned, for it would seem to them the rankest disloyalty, as if one should think twice about one's patriotism. Many, however, would go beyond such pat certainty. "Bornagain" Christians, that is, evangelical pietists, filling the pews of most Protestant denominations and increasingly those of the Roman Catholic Church as well, do not rest content with believing inherited dogma. They see no advantage in taking one's religious convictions for granted this way. A faith analogous to one's ethnic background (to an extent that the two easily become synonymous) may become just as taken for granted. No, evangelical pietists insist, "God has no grandsons." One cannot inherit genuine faith but must personally opt for it. And this is what Billy Graham and his evangelistic brethren are trying to persuade people to do. Thus far, one can only applaud an apparent appeal for people to think for themselves.

But upon what ground is the certainty of such chosen faith, born-again faith, based? Apologists, defenders of the faith (with whose arguments I dealt at some length in a previous book, *Beyond Born Again*)[1] draw upon a great arsenal of arguments for the existence of God, the resurrection of Christ, and other major Christian tenets, but at bottom such polemics give the impression of being after-the-fact rationalizations of a position held ultimately on other, purely emotional and subjective, grounds. Faith, we are told, is "self-authenticating." The born-again pietist tells us that for him it is not a question of debating a theoretical proposition, but rather of celebrating a "personal relationship with Christ." It would be possible to question its reality, but entirely perverse—like entertaining the theoretical possibility that one's loving spouse is really a CIA agent assigned to spy on one, as in the movie *Total Recall*. What are the chances?

I believe there is less here than meets the eye. Again, in *Beyond Born Again*, I explored the meaning and possible referents of the phrase "having a personal relationship with Jesus Christ." Here let me just pause for a moment on the issue of self-authentication or self-evidence. John Calvin claimed that the believer in Christ enjoys such subjective reassurance; he called it "the witness of the Spirit," a term derived from 1 John 5:10 ("The one who believes in the Son of God has the witness in himself"). As the old chorus puts it, "You ask me how I know he lives? He lives within my heart!" Since Christians can frequently be heard reminding one another to quiet their doubts by falling back on "the witness of the Spirit" within them, it is apparent that this witness cannot be quite as self-authenticating as it sounds! Whence arise doubts in the first place?

Dubious claims of the self-evidence of this or that point are hardly unique to religious rhetoric. René Descartes's whole epistemology depended upon the supposed reliability of what seemed "clear and distinct" to the rational mind. As Richard Rorty summed up the position, traditional philosophy has imagined the human mind as "the mirror of nature."[2] The external world and objective truth are just *there*, hanging in metaphysical space, as it were, and the mind is a passive receptor for this truth. The truth is supposedly self-evident. But if this is so, why do equally acute truth seekers not arrive at the same conclusions? The pre-Socratic philosophers theorized about the origin and composition of the world, but they could not agree in the absence of better data, so Socrates turned from natural philosophy, such as Thales and Anaximander had practiced, to the introspective study of human nature instead. And great was his confidence (to hear Plato tell it) that clear thinking could penetrate the secrets of human nature, morals, epistemology, and a great many other things. Yet Socrates' opinions, and Plato's after him, were hardly beyond doubt. The Skeptics were a philosophical school that anticipated modern Agnosticism in every way. They banished all reliance on what seems self-evident with one mighty blow. They merely pointed out the fact that all of us have at one time or another been absolutely certain of something—which later proved erroneous. You were wrong then; how can you be so sure you're not wrong now? Everyone knows the feeling of having a bubble popped, and thinking, "Oh yes! I never thought of *that*!" So much for self-evidence.

But Descartes believed what was self-evident, what was clear and distinct to the mind, had to be true. So did his fellow Rationalists Leibniz and Spinoza. And they only repeated the sad spectacle of the pre-Socratics, since their supposedly infallible cogitations did not agree. David Hume began chipping away at the certainties of the Rationalists, pointing out that while we consider many things so self-evidently true that it would be insane to doubt them, they are in fact quite unprovable. Hume doubted we could prove there is an observing self, a feeling and sensing ego, a sequence of cause and effect, and so on. All these apparent realities which we think we experience are actually mere associations of ideas whose particular linkages we infer without proof. Jacques Derrida and Richard Rorty, among others, have taken up the weapons of unblinking analysis against such naive confidence in the supposedly self-evident. Derrida aims his guns at what he calls the "Presence Metaphysics" of traditional philosophical and theological thinking. We can always find the hidden tracks on the virgin snowfield if we look hard enough. We can always find the seams in the seamless garment if our lens is sharp enough. What seems basic, tacit truth, upon closer inspection, bears the telltale marks of composition. The sublimely simple is yet the product of a hidden process of relation. Derrida points to Freudian analysis to demonstrate that even "clear and distinct" knowledge of the self is anything but. The conscious self is but a carefully edited "authorized version" provided for our own "public consumption." Perception is twisted, at least refracted, in a thousand ways. Even the bare perception of "the present moment" is not a spontaneous reception of naked phenomena, but is rather a compounding of memory's echo and imagination's anticipation. The overlap of the two results in a scripted, preinterpreted "now" moment that only seems to have emerged from the time stream perfect and full-blown like Aphrodite rising from the waves.[3]

Just as presence may be deconstructed, so may the "experience" of Christ. Jesus Christ functions, for instance, in an unnoticed and equivocal way, as shorthand for a vast system of beliefs and institutions on whose behalf he is invoked. Put simply, this means that when an evangelist or an apologist invites you to have faith "in Christ," he is in fact smuggling in a great number of other issues. For example, Chalcedonian Christology, the doctrine of the Trinity, the Protestant idea of faith and grace, a particular nineteenth-century theory of biblical inspiration and literalism, habits of church attendance, and so on, are all distinct and open questions, or should be. And yet no evangelist ever invites people to accept Christ by faith and then to start examining all these other associated issues for themselves. Not one! The

Trinity, biblical inerrantism, for some even anti-Darwinism, are nonnegotiable. They say you cannot be genuinely "saved" if you do not toe the party line on these points. Thus for them, to "accept Christ" *means* to accept Trinitarianism, biblicism, inerrantism, creationism, and so on. All this, in turn, means that "Christ" has become a shorthand designation for this whole raft of doctrines and opinions, *all* of which one is to accept "by faith," on someone else's say-so. Christ has become an umbrella for an unquestioning acceptance of what some preacher or institution tells you to believe. Once the believer begins to "deconstruct" what "Jesus Christ" has come to denote in his particular religious community, he may discover that his primary religious allegiance has been utilized to manipulate him into transferring the same diehard loyalty to other secondary or tertiary issues, political and cultural.

But I have already anticipated that I intend to deconstruct "Jesus Christ" on a deeper level, one underlying believers' imaginary relationships with their Savior, himself largely an amalgam of Sunday School illustrations and Holman Hunt paintings, stretched rigid on the rack of christological dogma. What I do not propose to do is what an increasing ocean of books endeavor, namely reconstructing a historical Jesus from what scanty evidence remains to us. In what follows I hope to indicate why that is practically impossible and ill-advised.

I believe that every "Life of Jesus" book is that scholar's own Gospel of Jesus, his or her own Christology. Albert Schweitzer made it clear enough that the first quest of the historical Jesus (in the nineteenth and early twentieth centuries) was a piece of theology from start to finish, even though its practitioners were sincerely convinced of the purely historical character of their efforts. Liberal Protestant scholars wanted to deprive Orthodoxy of its Christ, which served as the warrant (much like the medieval forgery the Donation of Constantine, which pretended to guarantee church ownership of the Papal States in perpetuity) for all they did and said. If Jesus could, via the expedient of historical research, be made to mirror Enlightenment Modernist preferences, then Jesus would have switched sides. He would have been the flag, and liberals would have captured it from traditionalists and won the game. Liberals could then use Jesus as their secret weapon, their trump card, their ventriloquist's dummy, just like traditionalists always had. Thus it should have been no surprise, Schweitzer pointed out, that the "historical Jesus" emerged from every one of these historical plastic surgeries looking like the surgeon who operated on him.[4] Indeed the whole enterprise of stripping away the theo-mythological encrustations built up around Jesus is a theological shell game from the word go. It is a case of the "dangerous supplement" described by Jacques Derrida.[5] It is like the "noble savage" of the Enlightenment philosophes and, later, Claude Lévi-Strauss. They held up the Tarzan-like innocence of the noble savage, uncorrupted by the evils of human society, as a rebuke to their own culture. But of course the noble savage, the historical Jesus, Marx's primordial Golden Age of primitive communism, Reagan's America, and the feminist primitive matriarchy are all alike: They are not genuine *discoveries* of the past, as they claim to be (something possible only with the aid of H. G. Wells's time machine), but rather clever polemical *constructions*. Pretending to be unvarnished *nature*, or brute fact, they are really sophisticated creations of *culture* like the culture creations they are employed to debunk. They seem to lend an ancient pedigree to the views of those who create them. What at first seems to be a critique of (corrupt) culture from the standpoint of nature turns out instead to be a creation of counterculture from within the very culture being critiqued. The traditional creedal Christologies of Nicea and Chalcedon are theoretical concepts of Jesus Christ based on an interpretive selection of New Testament texts. Certain texts are chosen as central, given a particular interpretation, and used as criteria for excluding others from serious consideration, or to explain away other texts inconvenient for one's christological theory. How different a procedure is that followed by historical Jesus researchers? They, too, are making a selection of core texts, based on consistency, distinctiveness, multiple-attestation, and so on. From this database emerges a consistent, distinctive picture of Jesus, who is again invoked to debunk and judge the dogmas and policies of traditional Christianity. It was only once the Vatican moved to quash liberation theology that liberal Catholic John Dominic Crossan dropped his fascinating Post-Structuralist readings of the gospels[6] and took up the historical Jesus enterprise, fashioning a Jesus who would furnish a new pedigree for liberation theology by seeming to have presciently espoused it nineteen centuries ago.

So today's critical scholars engaged in the quest for the historical Jesus are themselves, at least implicitly, theologians advocating new religiously relevant Christologies, just like Arius, Athanasius, Eutyches, Nestorius, and the rest did in the old days. But to go back to where I began, they are no less similar to the naive pietists with their "personal relationship" to Jesus. Pietists like to speak of "accepting Jesus Christ as one's personal savior." The scholarly efforts to discover the authentic Jesus (as valuable and illuminating as many of them are) eerily recall this pietistic slogan. For has not every one of them manufactured a "personal savior," that is, one custom fitted to each scholar's own predilections and priorities? I do not mean to charge anyone with simple ventriloquism, but it is remarkable how few scholars come out the way Albert Schweitzer did: with a Jesus that embarrassed him.

Let me mitigate my judgment yet again. As a brief survey will suggest, many of the current historical Jesus options are quite plausible and make good sense of a number of gospel texts. None violates historical method. All are the product of serious and deep scholarship. But what these learned labors have yielded may be called an embarrassment of riches. There are just too many that make too much sense, and that fact, it seems to me, vitiates the compelling force of any one of them.

Nothing makes sense of all those gospel sayings about abandoning family and possessions, like the model of Jesus as a Cynic-like sage. Burton L. Mack, John Dominic Crossan, Gerald Downing, and others strongly defend this view. Or Jesus may have been a liberal Pharisee, somewhat along the lines of his predecessor Hillel, as Harvey Falk[7] argues, since virtually every one of the halachic judgments made by Jesus is paralleled in contemporary Pharisaic and later rabbinic thought. (Despite a somewhat uncritical treatment of the evidence both from the gospels and the rabbis, I think Falk's basic contention has much to be said for it.) On somewhat the same theme, Geza Vermes, an expert on the Dead Sea Scrolls and New Testament–era Judaism, makes Jesus a freewheeling and only loosely orthodox charismatic hasid typical in many ways of other popular Galilean holy men and miracle workers, such as Honi the Circle-Drawer and Hanina ben-Dosa. Like them, Jesus was said by pious legend to have called God *Abba* (Father), to have been blessed by an audible voice from heaven, to have bargained with demons who steered clear of him, and to have roused the ire of the religious establishment.[8] Again, Jesus might have been a magician (or exorcist/faith healer, if you prefer), as Morton Smith held.[9] The gospel depictions of Jesus healing the blind, deaf, and mute with spittle and mud fit right in with contemporary magical healing methods (as fulsomely attested in numerous surviving Hellenistic magic handbooks from the period[10]), as do his exorcistic techniques, once you correct for christological exaggeration. As in Jesus' baptism story, magicians embarked on their career after the visionary descent of a familiar spirit in the form of a bird, filled with the assurance that they had become sons of God.

Or the historical Jesus might have been a priestly zealot, fomenting (violent or nonviolent) revolution against the Roman occupation, assuring the poor that their vindication was near at hand, and warning the temple fat cats, lapdogs of Pilate, that their days were numbered. How else can we explain that it was the Roman authorities who killed Jesus, by crucifixion? If the Jewish Sanhedrin simply needed Pilate's permission to execute Jesus, why didn't they get it and stone him as a blasphemer? Maybe the Romans had their own reasons for putting this King of the Jews to death. In one form or another, the case for a revolutionist Jesus has been ably argued, with many variations on the theme, by Robert Eisler, S. G. F. Brandon, Hugh J. Schonfield, Hyam Maccoby, A. J. Mattill Jr., Robert Eisenman, Juan Luis Segundo, and John Gager.[11] And there is much to be said for it. A somewhat similar position is that of John Dominic Crossan, Richard Horsley, and Elisabeth Schüssler Fiorenza, who regard Jesus as a kind of first-century E. F. Schumacher or Mohandas K. Gandhi, a radical community organizer with surprisingly prescient proto-feminist views.[12]

Perhaps Jesus was an eschatological prophet, foretelling the imminent end of the age and urging repentance upon his people, like the late Menachem Mendel Schneerson, the Lubavitcher Rebbe, seeking to spark a national movement of repentance in order to hasten the coming of the Kingdom of God. Ben F. Meyer sees it this way, as does (with some modifications) E. P. Sanders.[13] Johannes Weiss, Albert Schweitzer, and Rudolf Bultmann pictured Jesus on a similar crusade, but appealing to individuals to repent and save themselves from a crooked generation, rather than marshaling the people as a collectivity.[14] Joachim Jeremias, Norman Perrin, Günther Bornkamm, and others added to this picture an element of rejoicing that the kingdom, as Jesus thought, had already begun to be realized among himself and his followers.[15]

And there are more. More "historical Jesuses." None, as unfamiliar as they may sound to the reader not acquainted with critical Jesus scholarship, is particularly far-fetched. All tend to center on particular constellations of gospel elements interpreted in certain ways, leaving other data to the side as spurious (of course, this is what all critical historians, writing about any subject, do). All appeal to solid historical analogies for the Jesuses they posit. None is impossibly anachronistic. What one Jesus reconstruction leaves aside, the next takes up and makes its cornerstone. Jesus simply wears too many hats in the gospels—exorcist, healer, king, prophet, sage, rabbi, demigod, and so on. The Jesus Christ of the New Testament is a composite figure. Today's historical Jesus theories agree in recognizing that fact, but they part company on the question of which might be the original core, and which the secondary accretions.

Speaking of historical analogies, history does yield other, similarly complex figures, but they, too, seem to be overlays. For instance, Apollonius of Tyana appears in Philostratus' third-century hagiography as a wandering neo-Pythagorean sage. But he is quick with a miracle, a healing, an exorcism. Was he, then, like the gospel Jesus, both a sage and a miracle-worker? Probably not, for it appears that Philostratus has sought to rehabilitate Apollonius, traditionally remembered as a wizard, into the more sophisticated image of a philosopher. Similarly, do we not have in the messianic revolutionist Theudas (43 C.E.) a dual figure? Josephus calls him "a magician," implying he combined the roles of wonder-worker and revolutionary king—like Jesus? But apparently not: Theudas did not have a career as a healer; his "magic" is simply a climactic wonder he promised as the sign of God's imminent deliverance. God would part the Jordan as he had for Joshua of old. Josephus, a Jewish collaborator with Rome, naturally sneered at this extravagant promise as mere magic, always a disparaging way to refer to the other fellow's supernaturalism. So even in other cases where we seem at first to encounter ancient Jesus-like complex figures, they, too, have undergone legendary or redactional modification, combination with other stereotypes originally alien to them.

The historical Jesus (if there was one) might well have been a messianic king, or a progressive Pharisee, or a Galilean shaman, or a magus, or a Hellenistic sage. But he cannot very well have been all of them at the same time. Attempts, such as Crossan's, to combine several of these portraits only demonstrate how arbitrary the procedure is. Most even of critical scholars studying Jesus are at least liberal Christians, and one suspects they cannot bring themselves to stop at agnosticism about the historical Jesus. "He might have been this, he might have been that. We don't know for sure." No, one suspects that even the radicals of the Jesus Seminar still need a single Jesus to function as a religious totem: "One Lord, one faith, one baptism" (Eph. 4:5). Thus they will choose one possible Jesus and promote him as the ideal for the church to follow. Or they will, like Crossan, preserve as many of the newly reconstructed Jesus slices as they can by gluing them into a new pie. But this will not work. And once one accepts that sad conclusion, the implications are striking indeed.

Later on, I will discuss the Apocryphal Acts of the Apostles. They all had in common some form of Docetism, a superspiritual, nakedly mythic view whereby Jesus Christ was a pure spirit, merely sporting the illusion of a fleshly body. This he needed in order to communicate with flesh-bound humans, but actual incarnation was out of the question, since many early Christians viewed the body as far too sinful for Jesus to have had one. So he only seemed (δοκεω) to. In this, he was like the Olympian gods who might appear in any of a thousand forms. Zeus appeared as a bull, a shower of gold coins, a swan, an old man, and so on. Athena might appear as a crone or a warrior maid. This meant that the gods were beyond gross bodies of flesh. Even so, in the Acts of John, Jesus appears in different guises to the brothers James and John in the very same moment. One sees him as a beardless youth, while the other beholds a graybeard sage. Then they rub their eyes and see two more different images! To John, Jesus appears differently at different moments. Scholars call this motif "the polymorphousness of the savior." Again, it is the hallmark of Docetism: to have many forms is to have no true form at all.

Now, obviously no modern scholar believes Jesus was a bodiless ghost. And yet the theological mytheme of docetic polymorphousness is surprisingly relevant to the contemporary discussion of the historical Jesus. Call it a parable. Because in the same way that a Jesus who could take so many forms so readily had no real form to begin with, we may say that a "historical Jesus" capable of being portrayed with nearly equal plausibility as a magician, a revolutionary, a Cynic sage, an apocalyptic prophet, and so on, has no true and certain form at all! The various scholarly reconstructions of Jesus cancel each other out. Each sounds good until you hear the next one. The inevitable conclusion is that even if there was a historical Jesus who actually walked the earth two thousand years ago, *there is no historical Jesus any more*! The original is irrecoverable, unless someone invents a time machine and goes back to meet Jesus as in Michael Moorcock's novel *Behold the Man*.[16]

Generations of Rationalists and freethinkers have held that Jesus Christ corresponds to no historical character: There never was a Jesus of Nazareth. We might call this categorical denial "Jesus atheism." What I am describing is something different, a "Jesus agnosticism." There may have been a Jesus on earth in the past, but the state of the evidence is so ambiguous that we can never be sure what this figure was like or, indeed, whether there was such a person. Among contemporary scholars, Burton L. Mack seems to me to come closest to this assessment in that he seems to conclude that we cannot penetrate behind the various Jesus figures shaped by the disparate Christian sects and cults to meet their own religious needs. In broad outline, *Deconstructing Jesus* will endeavor to follow the bold lead Mack has provided, while pushing his insights, and those of other historical Jesus scholars, further in Mack's direction. Specifically, in chapter 1, I will deal with the pioneering work of F. C. Baur, Walter Bauer, Helmut Koester, and James M. Robinson. In chapter 2, I subject Burton Mack's map of the early "Jesus movements" to positive but critical scrutiny and follow up in chapter 3 with a discussion of his taxonomy of the "Christ cults." Chapter 4 takes Jacob Neusner's important critical work on the attribution of sayings in the Mishnah and applies it to the historical Jesus question, while chapter 5 pursues the question of oral traditions underlying the gospels into a reconsideration of the much-debated Q Document, bringing to bear some neglected comparative source material. Chapter 6 takes up the revolutionary "scapegoating" theories of René Girard, applying them to Christian origins in a way Girard himself, surprisingly, shrinks from doing. Next, in chapter 7, I turn to the relevance of the ancient novels for understanding the crucifixion accounts of the gospels, and in so doing I attempt to clarify the recent suggestions of John Dominic Crossan, who, again, seems to tread only so far down a dangerous path he himself has marked out. The last chapter confronts head-on a question that will have popped up again and again in the chapters leading up to it, that of whether Jesus was a real historical figure or rather perhaps a myth historicized. There I will be taking up insights from Jerome H. Neyrey about the christological evolution implied in the Gospel of John. In the process, I think we will see how everything old is new again. We will find that some of the most radical conclusions of the skeptics of past generations, long ignored by mainstream scholarship, receive new and surprising support from today's scholarship. I contend that radical New Testament scholarship, while disdaining to share the journey with Bruno Bauer, Arthur Drews, and others, has at last come amazingly close to meeting them, like a mysterious stranger on the road to Emmaus, at the same destination.

NOTES

1. Robert M. Price, *Beyond Born Again: Toward Evangelical Maturity* (Eugene: Hypatia Press, 1993), especially chapters 5–7.

2. Richard Rorty, "Mind as the Grasp of Universals," in *Philosophy and the Mirror of Nature* (Princeton: Princeton University Press, 1979), pp. 38–44.

3. Jacques Derrida, "Qual Quelle: Valéry's Sources," in *Margins of Philosophy*, trans. Alan Bass (Chicago: University of Chicago Press, 1982), pp. 273–306; Jacques Derrida, "Freud and the Scene of Writing," in *Writing and Difference*, trans. Alan Bass (University of Chicago Press, 1978), pp. 196–231; Jonathan Culler, *On Deconstruction: Theory and Meaning after Structuralism* (Ithaca: Cornell University Press, 1982), pp. 92–95, 99.

4. Albert Schweitzer, *The Quest of the Historical Jesus: From Reimarus to Wrede*, trans. W. Montgomery (New York: Macmillan, 1968); cf., Alan Sherman: "And your spine! Oh, your spine looks divine! It's exactly like mine—now doesn't that seem strange?"

5. Jacques Derrida, "... That Dangerous Supplement," in *Of Grammatology*, trans. Gayatri Chakravorty Spivak (Baltimore: Johns Hopkins University Press, 1976), pp. 141–64.

6. John Dominic Crossan, *Raid on the Articulate: Comic Eschatology in Jesus and Borges*. (New York: Harper & Row, 1976); John Dominic Crossan, *In Parables: The Challenge of the Historical Jesus* (New York: Harper & Row, 1973); John Dominic Crossan, *Cliffs of Fall: Paradox and Polyvalence in the Parables of Jesus* (New York: Seabury Press, 1980).

7. Harvey Falk, *Jesus the Pharisee: A New Look at the Jewishness of Jesus* (Mahwah: Paulist Press, 1985).

8. Geza Vermes, *Jesus the Jew: A Historian's View of the Gospels* (Glasgow: Fontana/Collins, 1977).

9. Morton Smith, *Jesus the Magician* (New York: Harper & Row, 1978). See also John M. Hull, *Hellenistic Magic and the Synoptic Tradition*. Studies in Biblical Theology, Second Series 28 (Naperville: Alec R. Allenson, 1974); Stevan L. Davies, *Jesus the Healer: Possession, Trance, and the Origins of Christianity* (New York: Continuum, 1995).

10. Hans Dieter Betz, ed., *The Greek Magical Papyri in Translation*, 2d ed., vol. 1: Texts (Chicago: University of Chicago Press), 1992.

11. Robert Eisler, *The Messiah Jesus and John the Baptist*, trans. Alexander Haggerty Krappe. (New York: Dial Press, 1931); S. G. F. Brandon, *Jesus and the Zealots: A Study of the Political Factor in Primitive Christianity* (New York: Scribners, 1967); Hugh J. Schonfield, *The Pentecost Revolution: The Story of the Jesus Party in Israel, A.D. 36–66* (London: MacDonald, 1974); Hyam Maccoby, *Revolution in Judea* (New York: Taplinger, 1980); A. J. Mattill Jr., *Luke and the Last Things: A Perspective for the Understanding of Lukan Thought* (Dillsboro: Western North Carolina Press, 1979); Robert Eisenman, "Maccabees, Zadokites, Christians and Qumran: A New Hypothesis of Christian Origins" in *The Dead Sea Scrolls and the First Christians: Essays and Translations* (Rockport: Element Books, 1996); Robert Eisenman, *James the Brother of Jesus: The Key to Unlocking the Secrets of Early Christianity and the Dead Sea Scrolls* (Baltimore:

Viking Penguin, 1996); Juan Luis Segundo, *The Historical Jesus of the Synoptics*. Jesus of Nazareth Yesterday and Today, vol. 2, trans. John Drury. (Maryknoll: Orbis, 1985); John G. Gager, *Kingdom and Community: The Social World of Early Christianity* (Englewood Cliffs: Prentice-Hall, 1975).

12. John Dominic Crossan, *The Historical Jesus: The Life of a Mediterranean Jewish Peasant* (New York: HarperCollins, 1991); Elisabeth Schüssler Fiorenza, *In Memory of Her: A Feminist Theological Reconstruction of Christian Origins* (New York: Crossroad Publishing, 1984); Richard A. Horsley, *Jesus and the Spiral of Violence: Popular Jewish Resistance in Roman Palestine* (Minneapolis: Fortress Press, 1993).

13. Ben P. Meyer, *The Aims of Jesus* (London: SCM Press, 1980); E. P. Sanders, *Jesus and Judaism* (Philadelphia: Fortress Press, 1985); E. P. Sanders, *The Historical Figure of Jesus* (London: Penguin, 1993).

14. Johannes Weiss, *Jesus' Proclamation of the Kingdom of God*, trans. Richard Hyde Hiers and D. Larrimore Holland (Philadelphia: Fortress Press, 1971); Albert Schweitzer, *The Mystery of the Kingdom of God: The Secret of Jesus' Messiahship and Passion*, trans. Walter Lowrie (New York: Macmillan, 1950); Rudolf Bultmann, *Jesus and the Word*, trans. Louise Pettibone Smith and Erminie Huntress Lantero (New York: Scribners, 1958).

15. Joachim Jeremias, *The Parables of Jesus*, rev. ed., trans. S. H. Hooke (New York: Scribner's, 1972); Günther Bornkamm, *Jesus of Nazareth*, trans. Irene and Fraser McLuskey (New York: Harper & Row, 1960); Norman Perrin, *Rediscovering the Teaching of Jesus* (New York: Harper & Row, 1976).

16. Science-fiction writers have undertaken just such a quest for the historical Jesus, via time machine. See, e.g., William Hope Hodgson, "Eloi Eloi Lama Sabachthani," in *Out of the Storm: Uncollected Fantasies by William Hope Hodgson*, ed. Sam Moskowitz (New York: Centaur Books, 1980), pp. 77–108; Arthur J. Burks, "When the Graves Were Opened," in *Black Medicine* (Sauk City: Arkham House, 1966), pp. 90–110; Michael Moorcock, *Behold the Man* (New York: Avon Books, 1970).

Chapter 1

RECONSTRUCTING CHRISTIAN ORIGINS

THE MYTH OF THE EARLY CHURCH

Preachers love to give sermons that make the congregation feel pretty shabby compared to the shining example of the "early Church." "Oh to have been there, soaking up the waves of Pentecostal power! To have their love, their boldness, their sure grasp of apostolic truth!" Granted, today's churches are lukewarm, spiritually diffident, theologically confused. But was the early Church really all that different? Was there ever such a church as the early Church? Sooner or later you begin to suspect that what is true of Jesus is true of Christianity: If the historical Jesus has gotten lost behind the stained-glass curtain of the Christ of dogma, the early Church is equally mythical, equally a product of holy propaganda. The official histories of the Church (such as the Acts of the Apostles and Eusebius' *Ecclesiastical History*) are like those "authorized biographies" of Pat Robertson and Jerry Falwell. "Authorized" means "sanitized," "whitewashed." They wouldn't call it that unless there was something to hide and they had managed to hide it. We have to take saying 6 of the Gospel of Thomas as our motto: "There is nothing hidden that will not be revealed." But keep in mind: It is likely to be no easier getting back to primitive Christianity than it has been excavating the historical Jesus.

If you have never thought about this question, I'm sure you are experiencing a sense of déjà vu anyway. In recent years Americans have been forced to face the fact of our society's wide ethnic and cultural diversity. Some find it hard to admit that our country is not a narrow patch of one breed of flowers, but rather a luxuriant garden of different and equally beautiful blossoms. Once we do admit it and come to appreciate all the exotic beauty, we realize that we are the ones who benefit. We see there was never anything to fear. The Christian religion has the same lesson to learn, but is slower in learning it. Here's what I mean: Anyone can see that the Ku Klux Klan is a bunch of bigots, because they insist that only one variety of Americans is good. But the church can somehow get away with saying that only one kind of Christianity is good: traditional orthodox Christianity. Oh sure, there are differences between Protestant, Catholic, and Eastern Orthodox Churches, between Baptist, Lutheran, and Pentecostal. But then the KKK allows a bit of diversity, too, if you can call it that. You can be English, German, Irish, French, Dutch, Scandinavian, whatever, as long as you are white. The crime is being nonwhite. And for the respectable bigotry of mainstream Christianity the crime is being "unorthodox." How did Christianity come to look like a hate group? That's a long story.

DIVERSITY AND DENIAL

The story of how Christianity suppressed its early pluralism in favor of emergent catholic orthodoxy starts with another story, a parable found in Matt. 13:24–30. A farmer plants wheat in his field, looking forward to a fine crop at harvest time. But as soon as the stalks start to sprout, his farmhands bring him ominous news: Every other plant is not wheat but darnel weed! The farmer knows this is no accident. "An enemy has done this!" For centuries the official historians of Christianity have taken this parable to describe the way the church started out orthodox and then became infested with heresy. Christ had sown the field with the good seed of orthodox Christianity. But then he left the scene, returning to Heaven, leaving the farm in charge of the apostles and the bishops. But, to their horror, they soon discovered that Satan had slipped in and planted all sorts of false doctrines.

Since it is a question of farming, perhaps we need the advice of a couple of farmers. Two of the most important investigators of early Christianity were a pair of New Testament scholars, Ferdinand Christian Baur (1792–1860) and Walter Bauer (1877–1960). (Both last names are German for "farmer.") F. C. Baur and Walter Bauer[1] pretty much threw the traditional jigsaw puzzle up in the air and then reassembled the pieces. The result could be described with another parable (though I'm afraid you won't find this one in any gospel): It is as if a man sowed his field with all kinds of seeds at random. "Let a hundred flowers bloom!" he said. Soon the plants began to sprout, each different from the others, until one plant with long tendrils choked out all the others and filled the field with its own seedlings, and none other was left.

MANY LORDS, MANY FAITHS, MANY BAPTISMS

F. C. Baur was the first to notice how much of the New Testament only made sense once you realized there was a major conflict between two rival Christianities: one Jewish in orientation, led by Simon Peter; the other Gentile, led by Paul. The first kept the Jewish Law and saw Jesus as a nationalistic Messiah. The second saw the Law as passé and understood Jesus in an internationalized, "spiritualized" way. Most of the New Testament writings lined up on either side of this great divide, and the rest were part of a later effort to paper over the differences once the two factions had buried the hatchet and merged into catholic orthodoxy. Baur recognized, for instance, that Matthew's gospel directs its readers to observe strictly every last regulation of the Torah (Matt. 5:17–19) and condemns those ostensible Christians who don't (Matt. 7:21–23: "Depart from me, you who practice lawlessness!"). Paul and his followers must be in view here. The Epistle of James has Paul in its sights, too ("You fool! Do you want to be shown that faith apart from works is dead?" James 2:20, after which follows a refutation of Rom. 3:27–4:1–5 ff.) On the other hand, in Galatians and 2 Corinthians, Paul lambastes certain "super-apostles" who require Gentile, Pauline converts to "judaize" (2 Cor. 11:4–5, 13–15; Gal. 1:6–9; 2:14). Paul claims that they represent a false gospel message designed by Satan. Mark's gospel sides with Paul in affirming that Jesus swept away all kosher laws (Mark 7:19), an editorial comment that Law-loving Matthew clipped when he appropriated that section of Mark into his own later gospel (compare Matt. 15:17). Jewish Torah-Christians like Matthew venerated Peter and the Twelve, who obviously stood for the twelve tribes of Israel. Paul, as we have seen, had little regard for these men. Mark parallels Paul in this, too, portraying the disciples of Jesus as blithering idiots every chance he gets.[2] Baur placed Revelation, with its reverence for "the twelve apostles of the Lamb" (Rev. 21:14) and for the twelve "tribes of the sons of Israel" (Rev. 7:4–8; 21:12), in the column with Matthew and James, while the Gospel and Epistles of John, together with Hebrews, belonged more or less in the Pauline camp.

Representing the later stage of reconciliation were Luke's gospel and its sequel, the Acts of the Apostles, as well as 1 and 2 Peter. Acts parallels Peter and Paul, having each apostle preach the same message and perform identical miracles: miraculous jailbreaks (Acts 12:1–11; 16:23–26); healing by shadows or clothing (Acts 5:14–16; 19:11–12); raising the dead (Acts 9:36–42; 20:7–12); restoring the lame (Acts 3:1–8; 14:8–10); and squaring off with magicians (Acts 8:9–24; 13:6–11). The Twelve are honored, but so is Paul. And though Luke seems to put the Twelve on a slightly higher level, he spends most of his narrative on the perils of Paul. No fan of either figurehead, Peter or Paul, could read Luke's Acts and come away with his hostility to the other left intact. Likewise the pseudepigraphical Epistles of Peter present a Peter who in 1 Peter sounds like Paul (so much so, in fact, that many scholars today think the writer of 1 Peter copied from the Pauline Epistle to the Ephesians!), and in 2 Peter mentions Paul by name, calling him "blessed," so long as one doesn't interpret his writings in a heretical fashion (2 Pet. 3:15–16). Thus Luke-Acts and 1 and 2 Peter, Baur said, are "catholicizing" in their tendency, just as are the later church legends that make Peter and Paul a kind of dynamic duo, working together to found the church at Rome. Ditto for the whole notion that the Twelve fanned out across the known world preaching the gospel. Paul's letters make it pretty clear that he, not they, was the one and only apostle to the Gentiles (Gal. 2:7–9; Rom. 1:5, 14; 15:15–20). Later legend remodeled the Twelve, originally the governors of Jewish Christians in Palestine (Matt. 19:28: "You shall sit on twelve thrones, governing the twelve tribes of Israel"), in the image of the jet-setting Paul.

I believe much, even most, of Baur's reconstruction is still persuasive, as far as it went. There was, however, more to say, and Walter Bauer said a lot of it. He jumped up into the second century. By reexamining just about every scrap of evidence surviving from the period, Bauer uncovered a remarkable fact: It turned out that in several major segments of the Mediterranean world, the first kind of Christianity to set up shop and hang out the shingle was not what we know as catholic orthodoxy at all, but rather one or another variety of so-called heresy. On this or that frontier of Christian expansion, "Christianity" simply meant Marcionism, Ebionism, Encratism, Gnosticism. The resultant picture, of course, was antipodal to the traditional version of Eusebius, Constantine's apologist and pet theologian, whereby "heresy" had appeared only after the apostles had planted catholic orthodoxy all over the Roman Empire. Eusebius had it that the apostles had passed on the doctrine of Jesus to their handpicked successors, the bishops, who handed it on to their own successors, and so on into Eusebius' own time. The "heretics" he libeled as eccentrics and troublemakers who cooked up perverse and baseless views, leavening the lump of orthodoxy for want of anything better to do.

Walter Bauer began his demonstration of the artificiality of this scenario by focusing on Edessa, a major center of early Christianity in eastern Syria. He showed how the Chronicle of Edessa records as events of note the births or arrivals of Marcion, Bardesanes, and Mani before it ever gets around to mentioning the establishment of a church building by the first representative of orthodoxy. Eusebius himself has nothing to say of any early orthodox Christianity in the area, though he cannot help mentioning the early ministry of Bardesanes and the circulation there of the Diatessaron of Tatian (a compilation of Matthew, Mark, Luke, John, and a bit of Thomas into a single narrative), which Eusebius considered heretical. Justin Martyr and heresiologists tell us the embarrassing fact that the name "Christian" in Edessa was the exclusive property of the Marcionites, and that the apparently late-arriving orthodox had to be satisfied with being called "Palutians" after the first orthodox bishop Palut. In fact, this remained the state of affairs until the Muslim conquest! A note from contemporary Greater Armenia makes clear that "heresy" was in the vast majority in the region. In light of these facts, Bauer deduced that the famous apocryphal correspondence between King Abgarus of Edessa and Jesus (in which the king, having heard of Jewish plots on Jesus' life, invites him to take refuge in Edessa) must have originated as a spurious pedigree for apostolic orthodoxy in Edessa dating back already to the time of Jesus and his apostle Addai (Thaddaeus), whom he sent to Abgarus with his "Thanks, but no thanks" reply.

Helmut Koester has supplemented Bauer's argument here by locating the Thomas tradition (the Gospel of Thomas, Acts of Thomas, Book of Thomas the Contender, and so on) in eastern Syria. This means that the "heretical" tendencies in the region go back very early indeed, perhaps even to the apostle Thomas himself, who tradition says missionized the region.

In western Syria, Antioch especially, we see a similar picture. Antioch is already pictured as a major center of Christian mission activity in Acts and Galatians. Paul, Peter, and Matthew are all associated with Antioch. Whether they were representatives of what would later be known as catholic orthodoxy depends on how one interprets their writings (as well as which writings attributed to them one thinks are authentic!). The first postbiblical missions we know of in western Syria were those of the Gnostics Satornilus/Saturninus, Cerdo, and Menander. It is in this region also that we find the orthodox bishop Serapion in 190 C.E., condemning the widespread usage of the local favorite Gospel of Peter, which he deemed docetic and heretical. When we get to the Letters of Ignatius, which Bauer considered authentic (at least the seven so received today), we must infer that Ignatius' desperate pleading for the firm control by, and absolute obedience to, the bishop in each church denotes a power struggle against a flood of "heresies" (docetic and judaizing) which only an ironhanded authoritarianism could hope to quash. Similarly, the Epistle of Polycarp (which, again, Bauer considered authentic) laments that "the great majority" embrace Docetism. Ignatius writes to Polycarp, and not to all his brother bishops, but rather only to those who take his side in the struggle, implying a real diversity of views. In all this we need not infer a falling away from an early orthodoxy. It may just as well imply a first serious attempt of orthodoxy to establish the dominance that it would eventually secure.

In Asia Minor we need only look at some late New Testament writings to discover an early, pervasive presence of "heresy." The Book of Revelation (Apocalypse of John) depicts a struggle between two parties, neither of which would qualify as orthodox by later standards. John the Revelator represents a type of ascetical Christianity (it is only 144,000 "virgins who have not defiled themselves with women" who will be saved; Rev. 14:4), and his bitter enemies, to be found throughout the seven churches under John's jurisdiction, are the Gnostic sect of the Nicolaitans.

In Acts and the Pastoral Epistles (quite likely all the work of one author) we have the strategic admission made pseudonymously through the lips of "Paul" that "All Asia has turned against me" (2 Tim. 1:15) and that "after my departure savage wolves will come in among you, not sparing the flock" of the Ephesian church (Acts 20:29). In other words, these catholicizing sources make the best of the fact that Paul's ministry in Asia Minor was not succeeded by catholic orthodoxy. Of course the assumption is that Paul must have taught orthodox views, so Luke can only understand the state of things in his day (the second century) as the result of an apostasy from an imagined Pauline purity.

Egypt presents us with the same picture yet again. The first attested workers for Christ there were the Gnostics Valentinus, Basilides, Apelles, Carpocrates, and his son Isidore. Phlegon preserves a letter attributed to Hadrian noting that all Christian priests in Egypt worshipped Serapis, too! The leading gospels in Egypt, the Gospels according to the Hebrews and according to the Egyptians, as far as we can tell from their extant fragments, were Gnostic or heretical in color. Bauer could detect no trace of orthodoxy in Egypt until the third-century bishop Demetrius. But does not tradition make the gospel-writer Mark the first bishop of Egypt? Indeed it does, but like the Letters of Jesus and Abgarus, this legend seems to be but another spurious retroactive pedigree meant to fabricate an "orthodox" origin for Egyptian Christianity (assuming Mark and his gospel could themselves be judged orthodox!).

Bauer lived to see his portrait of Egyptian Christianity amply confirmed by the discovery in 1945 of the Nag Hammadi library,[3] a cache mainly of Gnostic gospels, epistles, tracts, and revelations, which revealed an astonishing diversity of Christian beliefs and origins the breadth of which not even Bauer had dared suspect! Who would have guessed that Sethian Gnostics had become Christians on the assumption that Jesus was the reincarnation of Seth or of Melchizedek? Or that Jesus was believed in some quarters to have been the reincarnation of "the Illuminator" Zoroaster? What makes this discovery all the more astonishing is that associated documents show the collection of leather-bound volumes to have been taken from the monastic library of the Brotherhood of Saint Pachomius, the first known Christian monastery. Apparently when the monks received the Easter Letter from Athanasius in 367 C.E., which contains the first known listing of the canonical twenty-seven New Testament books, warning the faithful to read no others, the brethren must have decided to hide their cherished "heretical" gospels, lest they fall into the hands of the ecclesiastical book burners. We may perhaps take that monastery as a cameo, a microcosm of Egyptian Christianity in the fourth century, diverse in doctrine, though soon to suffocate beneath the smothering veil of catholic orthodoxy.

How did catholic orthodoxy manage to dominate? Bauer saw Rome as central to this development. There is striking evidence for an early diversity of belief in the Roman church, including the traditions of Marcion and Valentinus being influential leaders there for a time (something absolutely impossible if Rome had then shared the same view of these archheretics as later orthodoxy would). The Shepherd of Hermas, a work once widely considered to be authoritative scripture, was the work of Hermas, the brother of Bishop Pius of Rome (died 154 C.E.), and it contains teachings scarcely characteristic of later catholic orthodoxy, especially as regards Jesus Christ. In it, Jesus is portrayed as an archangel, and the Holy Spirit is the first Son of God who intercedes with his Father to resurrect Jesus, his faithful host body, as the second Son of God! But eventually catholic orthodoxy prevailed in Rome, and thanks to the emerging myth of apostolic succession, the bishops of Rome, with their spurious pedigree of joint Petrine-Pauline foundation, pulled rank. Catholic orthodoxy spread next to Corinth via the circulation of 1 and 2 Corinthians and 1 Clement (and if Harnack was right, 2 Clement, too, possibly written by the Roman bishop Soter). These letters invoked the authority of Paul to combat factionalism and Gnostic heresy in Corinth. The Corinthian bishop Dionysius was in Rome's pocket and began writing his own antiheretical epistles to other churches. Roman influence soon extended to Hierapolis in Asia Minor (next door to the New Testament cities of Colosse and Laodicea), though it was by no means secure there. (I suspect that another major tool of Roman propaganda was the Epistles of Ignatius, which, like the earlier Tübingen School but unlike Walter Bauer, I regard as spurious: They depict the Syrian bishop being "extradited" to Rome for execution for no apparent reason, against a rival tradition that he was killed at home in Syria. The real point, I think, was to account for the fact that the Ignatian epistles were first received from Rome, not because Ignatius had been taken there and their delivery delayed, but rather because they were written there in a later generation.)

The strategy of the orthodox apologists was to defame instead of refute. Their mudslinging against the Arians and the Montanists, for example, is both comical and grotesque. They simply assumed theirs was the old, original faith, despite the fact that the Gnostics had their own claims to apostolic succession. Valentinus, for example, claimed to have received the teaching of Paul at the hands of the latter's disciple Theodas, while Basilides credited his teaching to Glaukias, the disciple of Simon Peter. Were orthodox claims necessarily better grounded than these latter? Both are equally likely fictitious. Eusebius and other heresiologists late-dated Marcion and other heretics and forged a "heretical succession" whereby it would appear that they all inherited their errors from one another along a narrow channel. The point of this was to make unorthodox ideas appear to be a late growth as well as the property of a few related eccentrics instead of the widespread credos of whole sections of Christendom. Likewise, Eusebius refers to a vast corpus of anti-heretical literature dating back to the second century, but he actually cites very little, implying he has falsely generalized from a very few specimens known to him (his method at many other points as well).

Why did Rome prevail? Why did Roman propaganda succeed? The orthodox had tighter organization. Among the heretics, the two movements who did organize into congregations, the second-century Marcionites and the third-century Manichean Gnostics, flourished all over the empire and beyond until they were exterminated within Rome's boundaries and died away slowly elsewhere. Most Gnostics, by contrast, existed as secretive cells within larger catholic congregations and were forced to leave or keep quiet. Gnostics in general were fissiparous and freethinking. They were not the type to forge and enforce a single orthodoxy. Encouraging individual spiritual exploration, they were not great institution-builders. Many banded together on the model of the ancient philosophical schools, circles of disciples gathered around a teacher. Such is not the stuff of mass movements. Also, catholic orthodoxy represented the lowest common denominator, stripped of both the subtleties and the drastic asceticism of the heresies. This meant it was easier for most people to grasp. Bauer might have appreciated the analogies provided today by the victory of fundamentalism in world Protestantism: Simple-minded dogmatism is always more popular (as Dean Kelly showed in his *Why Conservative Churches Are Growing*).

The theoretical constructions of Baur and Bauer, as wide-ranging and illuminating as they are, are each but pieces of a larger picture. Walter Bauer showed how catholic orthodoxy triumphed over rivals no younger than itself, while F. C. Baur had tried to explain the origin of catholic Christianity as the fusion of two prior factions (Judaizing, Petrine Christianity and Gentile, Pauline Christianity). The Pauline-Petrine compromise would then have become the victor over other Christian parties, like Gnostics and Encratites with whom Baur had been little concerned. Both Baur and Bauer seem to have underestimated the continuing importance of Jewish Christianity. It remained for other scholars, particularly Helmut Koester, James M. Robinson, and Burton L. Mack, to fill out the picture Baur and Bauer had painted in sure but broad strokes. We will shortly see how they did so, and then we will try to sharpen the focus even further.

ANOTHER JESUS, A DIFFERENT GOSPEL

You can imagine the sort of reactions the research of both Baur and Bauer called forth. There was, to put it mildly, near-universal hostility. Most simply stopped up their ears at the blasphemy (Acts 7:57). But, like the farmer in the gospel parable of the sower (Mark 4:2–9), Baur and Bauer found that the seed they had planted did occasionally take root and sprout. Inspired by the work of Walter Bauer, two contemporary scholars of the New Testament and Early Christianity, Helmut Koester at Harvard and James M. Robinson at Claremont, put together a collection of their research called *Trajectories Through Early Christianity*.[4] In it, they followed the hunch that the diversity Bauer had revealed in second-century Christianity must have grown out of a similar diversity in first-century Christianity. That idea by itself was not particularly new. After all, F. C. Baur had already traced out some of the faultlines in New Testament-era Christianity. But there was more to the map, and a great amount of new evidence had been discovered not only since Baur's time, but since Bauer's as well. To appreciate the reconstructions of Koester and Robinson, we must briefly survey the known types of second-century Christianity; then we will be able to appreciate the links Koester and Robinson traced from the second back into the first century.

Marcionism was a church founded by Marcion of Sinope in the early second century. Though Baur understood Paul to be the great spearhead of Gentile Christianity in the first century, I believe that we look in vain for any first-century Paulinism. The first Paulinist movement in early Christianity, in other words, the only one that a time-traveling Protestant might recognize some kinship with, was Marcionism. Marcionites believed that Paul was the only true apostle and interpreted him to mean that the Old Testament God was not the Father of Jesus Christ. The loving Father had not created human beings but later sent Jesus to adopt them as his children. Marcionites were radically ascetic and required celibacy of all baptized Christians. Marcion was very likely the first to collect the Pauline Epistles, and he made them the basis of the first known "New Testament," which he called the Apostolicon, adding a single gospel, an earlier, shorter version of Luke. He rejected the Old Testament as the scripture of Judaism. It was not that Marcion was anti-Semitic, or even anti-Jewish (charges often leveled at him by scholars today). Rather, he simply recognized that Judaism and Christianity were different, separate religions. Marcion went so far as to grant that the Old Testament was an accurate account of the dealings of the Hebrew God with his people. The prophecies of that scripture were reliable and true, even those predicting the Jewish Messiah, a Davidic king. It was just that, as Marcion read them, these prophecies had no reference to Jesus of Nazareth. One day the Messiah of Jewish expectation would come to liberate his people. But his people were not

Christians, and he would not be Jesus. Marcion granted the righteousness of the Old Testament God, but he saw it as the rough justice of an oriental despot, ruthless and inexorable. Jesus' divine father, on the other hand, would judge no one. Christians served him not out of fear but from love and gratitude.[5] It is plain that had Marcion's views prevailed as official Christian doctrine, the history of the relations between Christians and Jews might have been considerably different. Christians would not have had to pretend that Jewish scriptures were really teaching Christianity, not Judaism. Christians would not have felt compelled to covet and contest the role of Jews as the elect children of the Hebrew God.

Marcion's natural opponents were *Jewish believers in Jesus* as the True Prophet and Messiah. In their opinion, Jesus had come not to abolish the Law of Moses but only to purify it of forged interpolations. Jeremiah had long ago charged the "lying pen of the scribes" with falsifying the Torah (Jer. 8:8), adding spurious laws mandating bloody animal sacrifice, a thing God had never thought of when he gave the Ten Commandments on Sinai (Jer. 7:21–26). One faction of Jewish Jesus believers, the Ebionites ("the poor"), believed Jesus and Moses had founded different covenants of equal validity.[6] Many rejected the virgin birth of Jesus as a piece of pagan mythology, believing instead in "Adoptionism," that Jesus became the son of God at his baptism or his resurrection. They claimed the Twelve Apostles (whose number implies a close connection to the tribes of Israel) and the Heirs (surviving relatives) of Jesus as their greatest leaders. Paul they repudiated with a vengeance, cursing him as a false apostle and an antichrist because of his teaching that Jews need no longer keep the commandments of Moses. Their scriptures were the Hebrew Bible and the Gospels according to the Ebionites, to the Hebrews, and to the Nazarenes. All these were variant versions of a basic gospel more or less identical with our Matthew (though ours may be merely one among many versions, not necessarily the original from which the others stemmed, as is usually thought).

It is proper to regard Matthew's gospel as a community product, because, even though it appears to be, in large measure, one writer's rewrite of another's work (the Gospel of Mark), it is clear that often Matthew employed earlier materials from his community, some of which do not quite fit either his basic outline or his own theology. The community from which the Gospel of Matthew emerged has been much studied in recent years. Most scholars agree that the evidence points plainly to a rather conservative Jewish Jesus-community which was composed of Jews and Gentiles, proselytes to Judaism or at least to Jesus-Judaism. They felt obliged to keep the whole Torah, even to the least commandment of it (Matt. 5:17–19), but at the same time, they took a liberal interpretation of several controversial questions, such as sabbath observance and hand washing, while taking care to keep dietary laws. Like many later rabbis, they disdained the common "minimum requirements" version of religion and instead stressed a "higher righteousness," exalting the attitude of holiness that causes the truly pious to shrink in horror from sin and to nip it in the bud by strictly monitoring every thought and impulse (Matt. 5:20–48). While it was possible to do so, before 70 C.E., the Mattheans, or Disciples of the Kingdom of Heaven,[7] practiced sacrifice at the Jerusalem temple. But they resisted the increasing rabbinization of Judaism, repudiated the use of "rabbi" as an honorific title, and vilified the Pharisee sect, their more successful rival. After an initial indifference to Gentiles and Samaritans (Matt. 10:5) the community undertook a mission to the nations (Matt. 28:19–20), though whether Gentiles were in view or Diaspora Jews, we do not know.

These "Jewish Christians" would not have called themselves "Christians." That was a product of Gentile Jesus worship. Instead they would simply have attracted faction labels to themselves, some ascribed to them by Jews who did not accept their faith. These included Ebionites ("the Poor," a title appearing in Gal. 2:10 and often in the Dead Sea Scrolls), the Elchasites (named after the baptizing prophet Elchasai), and the Nazarenes/Nazoreans. Patristic sources tell us that the Nazarenes agreed with emerging Hellenistic-catholic Christianity in most respects, except that they believed that they as Jews still needed to keep the Torah, though Gentile Christians needn't trouble themselves. My guess is that these Nazarenes represented a compromise with Gentile Christianity, as F. C. Baur had once suggested, a kind of theological assimilationism.

Cutting across the lines of several other groups, *Encratites* ("self-controllers," or "the sexually continent") shared the belief that sin was at bottom sexual, and that salvation required celibacy, so as to undo the sin of Adam and Eve.[8] Baptism restored the primordial oneness of Adam before Eve was separated from him. With conventional gender roles canceled, the Encratites had women apostles and prophets, rejected traditional social and family structures, and embraced pacifism, vegetarianism, and egalitarianism. They eagerly awaited the Second Coming of Christ to destroy the fallen world order. In all these respects they were much like the American sect of the Shakers.

Gnostic Christians cherished secret, mystical teachings they believed had been passed on by Jesus to selected disciples.[9] Gnostics ("those in the know") believed themselves to be members of a higher race possessing a spark of divine nature, unlike the mass of humanity. They spun fantastically elaborate myths of the creation in which some lower godling had created the material world by mistake, kidnapping divine spirits from the realm of light to populate the earth and provide some semblance of order amid the chaos. Jesus had appeared in a phantom likeness of a human body in order to awaken the Gnostics to the secret of their true origin and destiny. They viewed their own role as seeking to redeem the unspiritual ones, much like the long-suffering Bodhisattvas of Mahayana Buddhism.

What happened to all this diversity? It seems like Encratism was domesticated by catholic Christianity and segregated off to the side in the form of the celibate orders of priests and nuns. But it wasn't for everybody. Ebionites and other "Jesus-Judaisms" lasted for several centuries[10] (contrary to F. C. Baur, who thought they were all swallowed up in a compromise with Paulinism). But as Judaism and Christianity grew further and further apart, each increasingly defining itself in opposition to the other, Jesus-Jews found themselves without a market share. Gentiles preferred Law-free Pauline or catholic Christianity, while Jews wanted nothing to do with the notorious name of Jesus, the new pagan idol. With Gnostics and Marcionites it was quite a different story. Once the Emperor Constantine chose catholic orthodoxy as the true Christianity, it was soon open season on the "heretics." ("Heresy," by the way, simply means "choice." It came to mean "thoughtcrime," implying it was blasphemy to presume to choose your own belief instead of swallowing what the bishops spoonfed you.) They got to work exterminating their rivals with fire and sword, burning their scriptures and their flesh alike.

THIS TREASURE IN EARTHEN VESSELS

In 1945, just a year before the discovery of the Dead Sea Scrolls, Egyptian shepherds accidentally unearthed the Nag Hammadi Gnostic texts. Remember, these had most likely been the library of the monastery of Saint Pachomius, deep-sixed once the monks read Saint Athanasius' Easter Encyclical of 367 C.E., requiring all true Christians to read only our present list of twenty-seven New Testament books and no others. Knowing the inquisitors would soon be making their rounds, the brethren buried leather satchels containing the manuscripts. Better buried than cremated!

The documents included all sorts of fascinating new gospels, revelations, epistles, treatises, you name it. They threw a whole new light on Gnosticism, even as they confirmed much of what the church heresy hunters had told us and much more that scholars had surmised. Reitzenstein had traced Gnosticism to Iranian origins; lo and behold, here was an apocalypse called Zostrianos (=Zoroaster, Zarathustra).[11] Did Gnosticism seem to many a radical form of Platonism? Here was a fragment of Plato's *Republic*. Was Gnosticism, at least in some of its branches, an outgrowth of Judaism? Nag Hammadi contained various revelations from or to ancient biblical figures such as Seth, Adam, and Melchizedek. Did Gnosticism have pre-Christian pagan roots akin to Hermeticism? Up popped Asclepius and On the Eighth and the Ninth, pure Hermetic tracts. Had the sect founder Dositheus, rival of Simon Magus, been, like him, a proto-Gnostic? There was a Revelation of Dositheus. It appeared that many of the theories had been correct at the same time. Gnosticism was not just a "many-headed heresy" as the church fathers called it; it was a doctrine with many roots as well.

But Koester and Robinson saw something else, equally important. Like paleontologists puzzling over newly unearthed fossils, they realized these strange-seeming gospels and epistles must somehow fit into an evolutionary sequence. Suppose gospels like the Dialogue of the Savior, the Gospel of Philip, and the Sophia of Jesus Christ were not wild mutations from our more familiar gospels, but rather earlier transitional forms on the way to our gospels.[12] And Koester and Robinson realized something else: These gospels must have been written according to the beliefs and the religious needs of real people. With a bit of educated guesswork, they might be able to reconstruct just what kind of Christian groups had written and used these texts as well as how they eventually developed into the kinds of Christianity that produced and preserved the canonical gospels.

THE QUOTES OF THE HISTORICAL JESUS

Koester and Robinson decided there must have been three different pregospel types which, in different combinations, eventually evolved into the kind of gospels we have in the New Testament canon. Each type had its own distinctive theological slant and appealed to a different group. One pregospel type was the Sayings Collection. They were like the Book of Proverbs, the Wisdom of Solomon, and the Wisdom of Jesus ben-Sirach. The only surviving gospel of this type is the Nag Hammadi Gospel of Thomas. But Matthew and Luke must have had access to another which scholars today call "Q" (for *Quelle*, "source," denoting the sayings source of Matthew and Luke). Still another may lie behind the linked set of sayings in Mark 9:33–50.

Whoever produced writings like these was interested in the teaching of Jesus, not so much his fate or his identity. These would, hypothetically, be the sort of people whose faith eventually developed into Gnosticism as they scrutinized the sayings ever more closely until they began to see secret truths within them. "These are the secret sayings which the Living Jesus spoke. . . . Whoever finds their meaning will not taste death." Much has been written about the Q Document, and I will explore the matter further in chapter 5.

GNOSTIC NEWS CONFERENCE

A second pregospel type was the *revelation discourse/dialogue*. We see this form most clearly in Gnostic works like the Pistis Sophia, the Dialogue of the Savior, the Book of Thomas the Contender and the Sophia of Jesus Christ, as well as catholic works like the Epistle of the Apostles. These writings are something like news conferences in which the Risen Jesus answers questions from the disciples, revealing great mysteries fit only for Gnostic ears. As Robinson pointed out, revelation dialogues are structured on a basic division between the pre-Easter time of ignorance and parable, and the post-Easter time of open revelation. These books are nonetheless quite diverse, because the line between ignorance and revelation could be moved, like the marker on a scale, to the left or the right.[13] Some such books have pushed the line way over to the right, like the Pistis Sophia, in which Jesus is shown still teaching only in cryptic parables for *eleven years* after the resurrection, after which he ascends into Heaven, then descends again in glory to impart open revelations in plain speech. This helps us to recognize what is going on in Acts 1:6, where the scene is Jerusalem forty days after the resurrection, and Jesus is teaching, but the disciples seem fully as obtuse as ever. "Lord, is it at this time you will restore independence to Israel?" Shaking his head in bemusement, Jesus tells them they will have to wait till the Holy Spirit arrives (at Pentecost) before all will become clear. Here, the ignorance/revelation line has moved from Easter over to Pentecost.

On the other hand, the canonical gospels tend to move the line back to the left. They move the line back into the earthly life and ministry of Jesus, along with his Messiahship, originally something else that had to wait till his resurrection. The most obvious case of this would be the Farewell Discourse of Jesus in John chapters 13–17. We are ostensibly listening to the pre-Easter Jesus as he tells the disciples that he cannot yet reveal the whole truth, since they are not up to receiving it. Soon the mysterious Paraclete will come to fill in the blanks. But it is really as the post-Easter revealer that this author pictures Jesus. This is why the Jesus of the Fourth Gospel sounds so little like the Jesus of the first three gospels. The reader is to take the hint from the author's wink in John 16:12–15: "I have yet many things to say to you, but you cannot bear them now. When the Spirit of Truth comes, he will guide you into all the truth; for he will not speak on his own authority, but whatever he hears he will speak. . . . He will take of mine and declare it unto you." So the setting in the earthly life of Jesus is really just a dramatic framework for the author to present the deeper teaching he believes he has received from the Paraclete. Here the line has been moved back to *before* the resurrection.

Darrell J. Doughty[14] suggests that Mark's gospel, which has so many mysterious features, would make a lot more sense if we read it as having a circular structure—if it started with the resurrection! That's why the book seems to end so abruptly at Mark 16:8, with the women fleeing from the tomb after a young man tells them Jesus will rejoin his disciples in Galilee. Mark wants the reader to look next at the only place there is left to look: the beginning. There we find the episode of Jesus' calling the disciples at the lakeside and the mysteriously immediate response: The disciples drop what they are doing and follow him. Doughty noticed how much sense this scene makes if we assume the disciples know him already. Think of how similar the scene is both to Luke's version in Luke 5:1–11 and to that in John 21:1–11, where it is explicitly a resurrection story! *This* is the reunion Mark's young man was talking about (Mark 16:7)! So once the Risen Jesus regains his disciples at the Sea of Galilee, the post-resurrection teachings begin. They continue throughout the Gospel of Mark.

Yes, this would mean that the whole of Mark's gospel, like John's, is really a frame for later teachings that have been placed in the mouth of the Jesus character. Again, the line has been pushed all the way over to the left, to the very beginning of the ostensible story of the earthly Jesus. No wonder scholars keep saying this or that saying sounds suspicious as a saying of the historical Jesus, more like a later saying from the early Christians. So even Mark can be understood as a revelation dialogue like Thomas the Contender, the whole thing backlit by Easter.

RIGHTEOUS RÉSUMÉ

A very different third type of pregospel was the *aretalogy*, a wonder-laden religious hero biography or saint's life. Literally, it means a list of "virtues" (*areté*) or great deeds. In the ancient Hellenistic world we find these written about Moses, Alexander the Great, Pythagoras, Empedocles, Apollonius of Tyana, and others. Most of these names are familiar; others are not. But in their day, many of them were held in much the same esteem in which Jesus is held today. Like Jesus, many of these others were believed to be the sons of God, miraculously conceived, their births announced by gods or angels.

> The soul of Pythagoras came from the realm of Apollo, either being a heavenly companion or ranked with him in some other familiar way, to be sent down among men; no one can deny this. It can be maintained from his birth and the manifold wisdom of his soul. . . . He was educated so that he was the most beautiful and godlike of those written about in histories. After his father died, he increased in nobility and wisdom. Although he was still a youth, in his manner of humility and piety he was counted most worthy already, even by his elders. Seen and heard, he persuaded everyone, and to those who saw him he appeared to be astonishing, so that, reasonably, he was considered by many to be the son of a god. (Iamblichus, *Life of Pythagoras*, 3-10)[15]

Like the Gospel of John, Iamblichus makes his savior a preexistent heavenly being. He was born the son of God, like Jesus in Matthew and Luke. We also think of Luke's story of the young Jesus when we hear how Pythagoras grew in wisdom and virtue (as in Luke 2:52) and proved himself in argumentation with the wisest elders (cf. Luke 2:46–47).

> The bride (Olympias, mother-to-be of Alexander), before the night in which they were to join in the bride chamber, had a vision. There was a peal of thunder and a lightning bolt fell upon her womb. A great fire was kindled from the strike, then it broke into flames which flashed everywhere; then they extinguished. At a later time, after the marriage, Philip saw a vision: he was placing a seal on his wife's womb; the engraving on the seal was, as he thought, in the image of a lion. The men charged with interpreting oracles were made suspicious by this vision and told Philip to keep a closer watch on his marital affairs. But Aristander of Telmessus said (the vision meant that) her husband had impregnated her, for nothing is sealed if it is empty, and that she was pregnant with a child whose nature would be courageous and lionlike. On another occasion, a great snake appeared, while Olympias was asleep, and wound itself around her body. This especially, they say, weakened Philip's desire and tenderness toward her, so that he did not come often to sleep with her, either because he was afraid she would cast spells and enchantments upon him, or because he considered himself discharged from the obligation of intercourse with her because she had become the partner of a higher being. . . . After the vision (of the snake), Philip sent Chairon of Megalopolis to Delphi (to inquire of Apollo's oracle there as to what the dream might mean). He brought an oracle to Philip from Apollo: Philip was henceforth to sacrifice to Zeus-Amon and worship that God especially. (Plutarch, *Parallel Lives of the Greeks and Romans: Alexander the Great*, 2:1-3:2)[16]

Note how, like Mary in Matthew, the holy mother is first suspected of immorality (Matt. 1:18–19). After she is vindicated, her womb is sealed, recalling Joseph's not "touching" her till the divine birth (Matt. 1:25). Philip's abstinence is not quite so complete, but the point is the same: Olympias is no longer really his. The prophetic oracle of the child's future greatness recalls that of Simeon in Luke 2:25–38. Here is another, cut from the same cloth.

> To his [Apollonius'] mother, just before he was born, there came an apparition of Proteus, who changes his form so much in Homer, in the guise of an Egyptian demon. She was in no way frightened, but asked him what sort of child she would bear. And he answered, "Myself." "And who are you?" she asked. "Proteus," answered he, "the god of Egypt." . . . Now he is said to have been born in a meadow. . . . And just as the hour of his birth was approaching, his mother was warned in a dream to walk out into the meadow and pluck the flowers; and in due course she came there and her maids attended to the flowers, scattering

themselves over the meadow, while she fell asleep lying on the grass. Thereupon the swans who fed in the meadow set up a dance around her as she slept, and lifting their wings, as they are wont to do, cried out aloud all at once, for there was somewhat of a breeze blowing in the meadow. She then leaped up at the sound of their song and bore her child, for any sudden fright is apt to bring on premature delivery. But the people of that country say that just at the moment of the birth, a thunderbolt seemed about to fall to earth and then rose up into the air and disappeared aloft; and the gods thereby indicated, I think, the great distinction to which the sage was to attain, and hinted in advance how he should transcend all things upon earth and approach the gods, and signified all the things that he would achieve. (Philostratus, *The Life of Apollonius of Tyana* I:IV-V. Conybeare trans. Loeb ed.)

Though the element of the holy mother surrounded by her maids in the open country is even closer to the nativity of Gotama the Buddha, this story shares with the gospel nativities the elements of a divine annunciation (Luke 1:26–38) and a heavenly portent (Matt. 1:2).

And, like Jesus, many ancient heroes were thought to have survived attempts by evil tyrants[17] to destroy them while still children and later to have performed miracles and exorcisms.

And when he [Apollonius] told them to have handles on the cup and to pour over the handles—this being a purer part of the cup since no one's mouth touched that part—a young boy began laughing raucously, scattering his discourse to the winds. Apollonius stopped and, looking up at him, said, "It is not you that does this arrogant thing, but the demon who drives you unwittingly," for, unknown to everyone, the youth was actually possessed by a demon, for he used to laugh at things no one else did and would fall to weeping for no reason and would talk and sing to himself. Most people thought it was the jumpiness of youth that brought him to do such things, and at this point he seemed carried away by drunkenness, but it was really a demon which spoke through him. Thus, when Apollonius began staring at it, the phantom in the boy let out horrible cries of fear and rage, sounding like someone being burned alive or stretched on the rack, and he began to promise that he would leave the young boy and never again possess anyone else among men. But Apollonius spoke to him angrily such as a master might to a cunning and shameless slave, and he commanded him to come out of him, giving definite proof of it. "I will knock down that statue there," it said, pointing to one of those about the Porch of the King. And when the statue tottered and then fell over, who can describe the shout of amazement that went up and how everyone clapped their hands in astonishment! But the young boy opened his eyes, as if from sleep, and looked at the rays of the sun. Now all those observing these events revered the boy, for he no longer appeared to be as coarse as he had been, nor did he look dis-

> orderly, but had come back to his own nature nothing less than if he had drunk some medicine. He threw aside his fancy soft clothes and, stripping off the rest of his luxuriousness, came to love poverty and a threadbare cloak and the customs of Apollonius. (Ibid., IV:XX)[18]

This story parallels at many points the gospel tale of the Gadarene demoniac (Mark 5:1–20). The demoniac is notorious for strange behavior, which the wonder-worker cures. Once the latter starts threatening, the demoniac tries to negotiate. When the demon leaves, there is striking visible evidence of it. The crowd is moved, and the former demoniac changes his attire and wants to follow the miracle-worker. There is no reason to suspect one story has been borrowed from the other. No, the point is that they are the *same sort of story*, part of the same fictional genre.

> A young girl seemed to have died in the very hour of her marriage, and the bridegroom was following the bier weeping over his unfulfilled marriage. Rome mourned also, for it happened that the dead girl was from one of the best families. Apollonius, happening to be present where they were mourning, said, "Put down the bier, for I will end your weeping for this girl," and at the same time he asked what her name was. The bystanders thought that he was going to give a speech like those which people give at burials to heighten everyone's sorrow. But he didn't; instead he touched her and saying something no one could hear, awakened the girl who seemed dead. And the girl spoke and went back to her father's house, just like Alcestis who was brought back to life by Heracles. And when the relatives of the girl offered Apollonius 150,000 silver pieces as a reward, he replied that he would return it to the child as a gift for her dowry. (Ibid., IV:XLV)[19]

This one is so close to the story of Jesus' raising up the deceased son of the widow of Nain (Luke 9:11–17) that one is sorely tempted to assume borrowing in one direction or another, but in fact such stories, of a healer interrupting a funeral to raise up someone from the very lip of the grave, were numerous in the Hellenistic world.

> Sostrata, of Pherae, had a false pregnancy. In fear and trembling she came in a litter to the sanctuary (of Asclepius) and slept there (expecting to receive divine guidance toward a cure). But she had no clear dream and started for home again. Then, near Curni she dreamt that a man, comely in appearance, fell in with her and her companions; when he learned about their bad luck he bade them set down the litter on which they were carrying Sostrata; then he cut open her belly, removed an enormous quantity of worms—two full basins; then he stitched up her belly and made the woman well; then Asclepius revealed his presence and bade her send thank offerings for the cure to Epidaurus [the main cult site]. (Epidaurus inscription, 4th century B.C.E.)[20]

Here we cannot help thinking of the famous story of the disciples on the road to Emmaus (Luke 24:13–35). A disappointed believer returns home after a fruitless pilgrimage to the holy city where he/she hoped for some great deliverance from the savior, but nothing happened. Never fear, the savior himself appears incognito as a traveler on the road and asks the cause of the sadness. Then the savior performs the desired miracle and reveals his identity. This pair of parallel stories may perhaps be judged too close for coincidence, but it hardly matters whether Luke has borrowed the Emmaus story from Asclepius or whether the two tales are so similar because they conform so closely to type, to a particular miracle story subgenre.

> At that time he (Pythagoras) was going from Sybaris to Krotona. At the shore, he stood with men fishing with nets; they were still hauling the nets weighed down (with fish) from the depths. He said he knew the number of fish that they had hauled in. The men agreed to do what he ordered, if the number of fish was as he said. He ordered the fish to be set free, living, after they were counted accurately. What is more astonishing, in the time they were out of the water being counted, none of the fish died while he stood there. He paid them the price of the fish and went to Krotona. They announced the deed everywhere, having learned his name from some children. (*Life of Pythagoras*, 36, 60f.)[21]

No one will miss the similarity to the Johannine story of the miraculous catch of fish (John 21:1–11). In my judgment we can be sure John has taken over a version of the Pythagoras story. Why? Simply because of the now-irrelevant survival of the exact number of fish. It has been retained (perhaps because someone felt, like modern commentators do, that the number must mean *something*) from a version where it mattered because the whole thing hinged on the hero correctly assessing the number of fish in the nets. That was the miracle in the Pythagoras version. There, the whole thing was done for the sake of freeing the poor fish: Pythagoreans were strict vegetarians. Christians were not, so it didn't occur to them that Jesus would free the fish. So the miracle shifted to Jesus providing the catch when the disciples had hitherto caught nothing. The exact number is irrelevant; we only need to know the nets were too heavy to drag in (John 21:6). We do not hear that anyone on the scene counted them. But the number survives nonetheless, and it is a very special number—special to Pythagoreans, that is. One hundred fifty-three, the number of fish in John 21:11, "happens" to be what Pythagoreans called a "triangular number"; in fact, the sixteenth triangular number. One hundred fifty-three is the sum of $1+2+3+4+5+6+7+8+9+10+11+12+13+14+15+16+17$. One hundred fifty-three is also what you get if you add as follows: $1+(1\times2)+(1\times2\times3)+(1\times2\times3\times4)+(1\times2\times3\times4\times5)$. Add together the cubes of the three digits in 153 and you get 153![22]

Some aretalogical heroes were remembered as being tried before a wicked tyrant and to have miraculously escaped to rejoin their disciples and then to ascend into the heavens. After this, a few supposedly appeared to their followers for a last good-bye.

> When he [Romulus] was holding a maneuver in order to review the army at the camp near the marsh of Caprea, suddenly a storm arose, with great lightning and thunder, and it veiled the king by such a dense cloud that his form was hidden from the troops; from that time Romulus was not on earth. The terrified Roman soldiers were finally quieted after the sunlight came back and restored calm and serenity following that hour of wild confusion. But, even so, they remained silent and sad for a long time, as if stricken by the fear of being orphaned, although they readily believed the senators standing nearest him who said that Romulus had been taken up on high by the storm. Then at first a few, then all, joyfully declared Romulus, the king and father of the city of Rome, to be a God, the Son of a God. (Livy, *History of Rome*, Book 1.16)[23]

As with Jesus' ascension, Romulus' figure is first obscured by a cloud (Acts 1:9), creating narrative suspense by opening the possibility that he may reappear, but he does not. The preternatural darkness is mirrored in Mark 15:33, and in Mark it is at this point, the darkness attending the crucifixion, that Jesus is acclaimed as the Son of God (Mark 15:39). The elements are reshuffled, but the parallels are clear nonetheless.

> "Romulus Quirites," he [Julius Proculus, a senator] said, "the father of this city, at the first light of this day, descended from the sky and clearly showed himself to me. While I was awed with holy fright, I stood reverently before him, asking in prayer that I might look at him without sin. 'Go,' he said, 'announce to the Romans that Heaven wishes that my Rome shall be the capital of the earth; therefore they shall cultivate the military; they shall know and teach their descendants that no human might can resist Roman arms.' He said this and went away on high."[24]

Here is an episode in which the ascended savior appears on earth soon after for the edification of his mourning followers and delivers, as Jesus does in Matt. 28:18–20 and Luke 24:45–49, a "great commission."

> Others again say that he [Apollonius] died in Lindus, where he entered the temple of Athene and disappeared within it. Others again say that he died in Crete in a much more remarkable manner than the people of Lindus relate. For they say that he continued to live in Crete, where he became a greater centre of admiration than ever before, and that he came to the temple of Dictynna late at night. Now this temple is guarded by dogs, whose duty is to watch over

the wealth deposited in it, and the Cretans claim that they are as good as bears or any other animals equally fierce. Nonetheless, when he came, instead of barking, they approached him and fawned upon him, as they would not have done even with people they knew familiarly. The guardians of the shrine arrested him in consequence, and threw him in bonds as a wizard and a robber, accusing him of having thrown to the dogs some charmed morsel. But about midnight he loosened his bonds, and after calling those who had bound him, in order that they might witness the spectacle, he ran to the doors of the temple, which opened wide to receive him; and when he had passed within they closed afresh, as they had been shut, and there was heard a chorus of maidens singing from within the temple, and their song was this. "Hasten thou from earth, hasten thou to Heaven, hasten." In other words: "Do thou go upwards from earth." (*Life of Apollonius of Tyana*, Book VIII, XXX)

This is one of the "apotheosis narratives" appealed to by Charles L. Talbert to show how Mark's empty tomb story would by itself be enough to establish for the ancient reader that Jesus had risen/ascended.[25] The heavenly choir plays the same role as the young man in the tomb in Mark 16:6–7, and the business about the doors supernaturally opening and closing is of a piece with the closed doors breached by the risen Jesus in John 20:19.

There came to Tyana a youth who did not shrink from acrimonious discussions, and who would not accept truth in argument. Now Apollonius had already passed away from among men, but people still wondered at his passing, and no one ventured to dispute that he was immortal. This being so, the discussions were mainly about the soul, for a band of youths were there passionately addicted to wisdom. The young man in question, however, would on no account allow the tenet of the immortality of the soul, and said: "I myself, gentlemen, have done nothing now for nine months but pray to Apollonius that he would reveal to me the truth about the soul; but he is so utterly dead that he will not appear to me in response to my entreaties, nor give me any reason to consider him immortal." Such were the young man's words on that occasion, but on the fifth day following, after discussing the same subject, he fell asleep where he was talking with them, and of the young men who were studying with him, some were reading books, and others were industriously drawing geometrical figures on the ground, when on a sudden, like one possessed, he leaped up still in a half sleep, streaming with perspiration, and cried out: "I believe thee." And, when those who were present asked him what was the matter; "Do you not see," said he, "Apollonius the sage, how that he is present with us and is listening to our discussion, and is reciting wondrous verses about the soul?" "But where is he?" they asked, "For we cannot see him anywhere, although we would rather do so than possess all the blessings of mankind." And the youth replied: "It would seem that he is come to converse with myself alone concerning the tenets which I would not believe." (Ibid., VIII: XXXI)

Here is a counterpart to the Doubting Thomas story of John 20:24–29, intended to serve the same literary purpose by making the reader, who was of course not present for the original appearances of the savior, into a character in the story, to whom the savior accommodates himself, vouchsafing a special "command performance" appearance to "him of little faith." If the reader cannot himself see his lord, at least he may rest content with the "fact" that a doubter like him had similar doubts allayed! The invisibility of the revealed savior to the bystanders is the same as in the Damascus Road epiphany of Jesus to Saul in Acts 9:7.

> Now as he [Moses] went thence to the place where he was to vanish out of their sight, they all followed after him weeping; but Moses beckoned with his hand to those that were remote from him, and bade them stay behind in quiet, while he exhorted those that were near to him that they would not render his departure so lamentable ... so they restrained themselves, though weeping still towards one another. All those that accompanied him were the senate [i.e., the seventy elders], and Eleazar the high priest, and Joshua their commander. Now as soon as they were come to the mountain called Abarim ..., he dismissed the senate; and as he was going to embrace Eleazar and Joshua, and was still discoursing with them, a cloud stood over him on the sudden, and he disappeared in a certain valley, although he wrote in the holy books that he died, which was done out of fear, lest they should venture to say, that because of his extraordinary virtue, he went to God. (Josephus, *Antiquities of the Jews*, book IV, chapter VIII, Whiston trans.)

This is probably not a spontaneous parallel; it seems likely that Luke, the only evangelist to narrate the ascension (Luke 24:50–53; Acts 1:9), has actually borrowed it from Josephus' account of Moses' assumption.

Some of these aretalogies, filled with adventures and marvels, surprises and narrow escapes, cross over the line between saintly biographies and ancient novels. The stories of Alexander and Apollonius of Tyana would be two of these. The latter is, of all the aretalogies, the closest parallel to our canonical gospels.

MIX AND MATCH

Koester's guess is that various groups of Christians gradually combined what they liked of each pregospel genre they had, the eventual result being our gospels. Each of the canonical gospels has a sequence of miracle stories and ends with the confrontation with a tyrant, a crucifixion, the discovery of an empty tomb, and a joyous reunion with the disciples. So the narrative outline comes straight from the aretalogy form. But, packed in here and there, like meat on the bones, our gospels have great numbers of parables and proverbs attributed to Jesus. These have been taken from sources like Q, which had nothing but such sayings. It was easy to combine these two types because Q already had a number of pronouncement stories, brief narrative introductions that set the stage for a saying of Jesus, making it come across like the punch line in a joke. People had gradually added these brief introductions in order to supply a context for the saying, so the reader or hearer would have some idea what the saying was about. It was a simple matter to insert these little stories in the framework of the aretalogy.

And the same goes for the revelation dialogue. You could attach one after the resurrection, considerably beefing up what would have been pretty much an anticlimax in the aretalogy. Or, as we have seen, you could make the whole story into a revelation dialogue, as John and Mark did. People did continue writing and reading the traditional three types of gospels. The Gospel of Thomas was another like Q, while Thomas the Contender and many others are pure revelation dialogues. The various Infancy Gospels (cf., Infancy Gospel of Matthew, Gospel of Thomas the Israelite, and so on) maintained the aretalogy form for some centuries. They offer no teaching but simply relate miracle after miracle done by Jesus when he was a boy. These were mostly comical, at least to modern ears, probably to ancient ones as well. In them the boy Jesus smites his uncooperative playmates, brings clay-model birds to life so as to evade a charge from the Junior Pharisee Scouts that he violated the Sabbath by sculpting, saves his bumbling dad some work by miraculously evening up the legs on a chair Joseph had mismeasured, and so on.

The various types of gospels came from different kinds of Christian communities. They are different plants and must have grown from different roots, different seeds. This was the implication of the studies of Koester and Robinson. Burton L. Mack[30] has taken up where these two left off. Concentrating on Q and Mark, Mack has tried to imagine the sorts of groups whose interests produced these documents. He assumes that whatever was important to the Q or Markan communities made its way into the documents and that nothing was preserved there that wasn't important to them. Thus we ought to be able to get a pretty good idea of the beliefs of each group from the gospel it produced; each gospel should supply an adequate theological portrait of the community that produced it. This might seem a risky assumption; maybe there were other aspects of their religion that they simply didn't have occasion to record in their books. Maybe so. But is there any reason to think so? Doesn't it stand to reason that, if someone were writing up a kind of charter document, a handbook, a constitution, an instruction book, or whatever, it would cover all major points? Otherwise, why write it? And, to put the sandal on the other foot, even if, for example, the Q community did have a belief in the resurrected Jesus that they didn't mention in Q—how would we know it? We could, of course, just assume they believed it just because we would like to think all the early Jesus groups believed in it. But that's just circular reasoning.

Mack carves up the turkey of early Christianity into several other groups (or families of groups) that would seem to correspond to various New Testament writings. His analysis is fascinating throughout, and usually quite convincing, though here and there I find I must take issue with his conclusions. In the next two chapters, I want to set out Mack's range of early Christianities, filling in some of the gaps and redrawing a few of the lines.

NOTES

1. Ferdinand Christian Baur, *Paul, the Apostle of Jesus Christ: His Life and Work, His Epistles and His Doctrine*, trans. Allan Menzies, 2 vols. (Edinburgh: Williams and Norgate, 1875); Ferdinand Christian Baur, *The Church History of the First Three Centuries*, trans. Allan Menzies, 2 vols. (Edinburgh: Williams and Norgate, 1878); Walter Bauer, *Orthodoxy and Heresy in Earliest Christianity*, ed. Robert Kraft and Gerhard Krodel, trans. the Philadelphia Seminar on Christian Origins (Philadelphia: Fortress Press, 1971).

2. Theodore J. Weeden, *Mark: Traditions in Conflict* (Philadelphia: Fortress Press, 1971).

3. James M. Robinson, ed., *The Nag Hammadi Library*. 3d rev. ed. (San Francisco: Harper & Row, 1988).

4. James M. Robinson and Helmut Koester, *Trajectories Through Early Christianity* (Philadelphia: Fortress Press, 1971).

5. R. Joseph Hoffmann, *Marcion: On the Restitution of Christianity. An Essay on the Development of Radical Paulinist Theology in the Second Century* (Chico, Calif.: Scholars Press, 1984).

6. Hans-Joachim Schoeps, *Jewish Christianity: Factional Disputes in the Early Church*, trans. Douglas R. A. Hare (Philadelphia: Fortress Press, 1969), p. 67.

7. I believe the title of the Gospel of Matthew is a pun based on the importance in the work of μαθηται, or *mathetai*, "disciples."

8. Peter Brown, *The Body and Society: Men, Women, and Sexual Renunciation in Early Christianity* (New York: Columbia University Press, 1988).

9. The best book on Gnosticism remains Kurt Rudolph, *Gnosis: The Nature and History of Gnosticism*, trans. Robert McLachlan Wilson, P. W. Coxon, and K. H. Kuhn (San Francisco: Harper & Row, 1983).

10. Georg Strecker, "On the Problem of Jewish Christianity," trans. Gerhard Krodel, in Bauer, *Orthodoxy and Heresy in Earliest Christianity*, pp. 241–85.

11. Andrew J. Welburn, "Iranian Prophetology and the Birth of the Messiah: The Apocalypse of Adam," in *Aufstieg und Niedergang der römischen Welt: Geschichte und Kultur Roms im Spiegel der neueren Forschung* (New York: Walter de Gruyter. 1972–1987), vol. II, 25, 4, 1988, pp. 4752–94, shows heavy Zoroastrian influence on the Apocalypse of Adam, a text which Robinson, "On the *Gattung* of Mark (and John)" (see n. 13), shows to share significant ancient mythemes underlying many New Testament texts.

12. Stevan L. Davies, *The Gospel of Thomas and Christian Wisdom* (New York: Seabury Press, 1983), pp. 16–17, and Helmut Koester, *Ancient Christian Gospels: Their History and Development* (Philadelphia: Trinity Press International, 1990), pp. 75–128, argue that the Gospel of Thomas was composed in the mid–first century or not long thereafter, making it earlier than the canonical gospels. Barbara Thiering similarly argues for a first-century date for the Gospel of Philip ("The Date and Unity of the Gospel of Philip," *Journal of Higher Criticism* 2, no. 1 [spring 1998]: 102–11).

13. James M. Robinson, "On the *Gattung* of Mark (and John)," in *Jesus and Man's Hope*, ed. David G. Buttrick, vol. 1 (Pittsburgh: Pittsburgh Theological Seminary, 1970), pp. 99–130; Pheme Perkins, *The Gnostic Dialogue: The Early Church and the Crisis of Gnosticism* (New York: Paulist Press, 1980).

14. Darrell J. Doughty, class lectures. Cf. Norman Perrin, "Towards an Interpretation of the Gospel of Mark," in *Christology and a Modern Pilgrimage: A Conversation with Norman Perrin*, ed. Hans Dieter Betz (Claremont: New Testament Colloquium, 1971), pp. 1–78.

15. Iamblichus, *Life of Pythagoras*, trans. David R. Cartlidge, in *Sourcebook of Texts for the Comparative Study of the Gospels*, David L. Dungan and David R. Cartlidge 4th ed. Missoula: Scholars Press, 1974), pp. 33–34.

16. Plutarch, *Parallel Lives of the Greeks and Romans: Alexander the Great*, 2:1–8:2, trans. Cartlidge, in *Sourcebooks of Texts for the Comparative Study of the Gospels*, pp. 7–8.

17. See Otto Ranck, *The Myth of the Birth of the Hero*, in *In Quest of the Hero*, ed. Robert A. Segal (Princeton: Princeton University Press, 1990), pp. 3–86.

18. Philostratus, *Life of Apollonius of Tyana*, trans. Dungan, in *Sourcebook of Texts for the Comparative Study of the Gospels*, p. 280.

19. Ibid., pp. 282–83.

20. Epidaurus inscription, 4th century B.C.E., trans. N. Lewis, in *Women's Life in Greece and Rome: A Source Book in Translation*, ed. Mary Lefkowitz and Maureen B. Fant (Baltimore: Johns Hopkins University Press, 1982), p.120.

21. Iamblichus, *Life of Pythagoras*, p. 55.

22. Dr. Crypton, "Mathematics in the Bible," *Science Digest* (May 1985): 78. Thanks to Richard L. Tierney for bringing this to my attention.

23. Livy, *History of Rome*, bk. 1.16, trans. Cartlidge, in *Sourcebooks of Texts for the Comparative Study of the Gospels*, pp. 155–56.

24. Ibid.

25. Charles H. Talbert, *What Is a Gospel? The Genre of the Canonical Gospels* (Philadelphia: Fortress Press, 1977), pp. 25–43.

26. Burton L. Mack, *A Myth of Innocence: Mark and Christian Origins* (Minneapolis: Fortress Press, 1991; Mack, *The Lost Gospel: The Book of Q and Christian Origins* (San Francisco: HarperSanFrancisco, 1993); Mack, *Who Wrote the New Testament? The Making of the Christian Myth* (San Francisco: HarperSanFrancisco, 1995).

Chapter 2
THE JESUS MOVEMENTS

THE Q COMMUNITY

Burton L. Mack believes that the simple fact of the Q Document should revolutionize our picture of the early Jesus movement. Why? The people who compiled the Q Document cannot properly be called "Christians" since Q never refers to Jesus by the title "Christ." Nor is there a word about an atoning death. Jesus' death is at most implied in the saying about taking up one's cross, joining Jesus on Death Row (Matt. 10:38; Luke 14:27). The usual inference is that the disciple is following a Jesus who is carrying his own cross, but the saying does not actually say so. And perhaps the inference is not necessary, since the image might possibly be akin to that in 2 Cor. 2:14, where the image is that of Jesus as a triumphant Roman general (!) leading a parade of captured rebels to their execution: living trophies of war. Those who follow Jesus are bearing crosses, but he is not!

And there is not a word in Q about the resurrection, either. This is not exactly Christianity as we think of it. The compilers of Q seem to have regarded Jesus much as several Greek philosophical schools viewed Socrates, as a martyred sage who set the pattern for fearless preaching of the truth. Lucian of Samosata (a second-century C.E. Syrian philosopher and humorist) wrote a lampoon of one Proteus Peregrinus (The Passing of Peregrinus) who he said had first been a Cynic, then a Christian, apparently a smooth transition. In this context Lucian calls Jesus "the crucified sophist."

Jesus is said to have lived in Galilee, a marginally Jewish territory which had been heavily Hellenized. Nazareth was in the middle of a dozen Greek cities. If Jesus had not been familiar with Greek popular philosophy, Mack, Downing, Crossan, and others reason, it would be a surprise.[1] We know of three Cynic apostles (wandering soapbox preachers) who lived in nearby Gadara: Menippus (first half of the third century B.C.E.), Meleager (first half of the first century B.C.E.), and Oenomaus (early second century C.E.), enough to establish the presence of a long-standing Cynic tradition in the region. Thus it should come as no surprise when we compare the Q sayings with the proverbs and pronouncements of the Cynics and discover striking parallels between them. Many of the sayings from both sources advise us to throw off the burdens of social respectability, family entanglements, and soul-killing mundane work. Do the birds and flowers bother with such trifles? Aren't you supposed to be smarter than them? Well, then, what are you waiting for?

Jesus is depicted in the gospels as a wanderer with no place to rest his head (Matt. 8:20/Luke 9:58). Perhaps this was the way the historical Jesus lived, perhaps not. But this is the way certain of his latter-day followers lived.[2] Did they imitate Jesus, who himself was like the Cynic itinerants? Or did they get the idea directly from the Cynics themselves, and then reimagine Jesus in their own image? It wouldn't be the first time, but who knows? The Cynics wandered the roads with only a bare minimum: a cloak, a bag, a staff, precisely the list presupposed in the Mission Charge texts (Matt. 10:5–15; Mark 6:7-11; Luke 9:1–5) which stem from this group.[3] Cynic and Christian itinerants both claimed that God had sent them to demonstrate to others the freedom of living under the spartan freedom of the kingdom of God ("the government of Zeus"). They aimed cynical barbs at traditional religion (like Mark 7:18–19; why bother with food-purity laws when it's all going to end up in the toilet anyway?). But they also blessed those who maltreated them.

They were the wandering "brethren" or "apostles" of Matthew's gospel, the Johannine Epistles, and the Didache (a late-first/early-second-century teaching manual attributed to the Twelve). Gerd Theissen[4] pointed out the obvious: If there hadn't been a group of Jesus people who actually lived out all those uncomfortable sayings about giving away possessions, turning the other cheek, leaving your home and family—how would those sayings ever have survived? What Christian does not squirm hearing them? Why didn't people let them get lost to history when they still had the chance, before there was a Bible to preserve them in? Because *somebody* wasn't afraid to put them into effect. To repeat such sayings would even be a way of boasting of one's own credentials.

Some people were pretty impressed with their teachings, and with their apostolic lifestyle. Others were not. Theissen[5] surmised that Paul had to square off against such "superapostles" in Corinth. They had (unverifiable) miracle stories and tales of visions and heavenly ascensions to share with the credulous. Dieter Georgi[6] suggested that the "letters of recommendation" Paul derides (2 Cor. 3:1–2) were growing resumes of miracles they allegedly performed. If, as Theissen says, Paul's opponents in Corinth were some of the itinerant prophet/apostles from whose circles the Q collection came, we can make a very interesting connection. A moment ago I said how the very preaching of the radical sayings of Jesus would have underlined the radical self-denial of the itinerants themselves. They were, in effect, aggrandizing themselves even as they preached self-denial. It could have been only a small step from this to claiming full-fledged miracles (done in the last village back). That is what the superapostles did. And this means that the aretalogy form may have developed later from the same group, the itinerant apostles, as the sayings collections.

Of course, I am implying that the first miracle lists starred not Jesus but the itinerant apostles themselves! This is by no means far-fetched. Take a look at the many Apocryphal Acts of the Apostles, some of which may well be earlier than the canonical Acts. In the Acts of Paul, of John, and of Thomas, the apostles are practically Christs in their own right, with their own miracles, their own martyrdoms, and even their own resurrections and empty tombs! And think of 1 Cor. 1:12, where Cephas, Paul, and Apollos are esteemed by some as full rivals to Christ himself! Once Jesus himself became the subject of an aretalogy like theirs, it would certainly be natural for the communities who supported the itinerant apostles, who memorized their (Q) sayings and their aretalogies, to combine the two, attributing examples of both to Jesus.

What I am trying to do here is to supply a few more connecting links between the pregospel forms (and their community origins) and the canonical gospels descended from them. Obviously, I think there are more connections to be made than scholars have made so far. Here is a matter I think Mack skirts: We can easily imagine that there would have been loose-knit guilds of wandering Jesus-Cynics (Theissen has described them convincingly), but Mack seems to want to reject this picture. Though emphatically arguing for the Cynic character of the Q sayings, at least those in the hypothetical earliest stratum, or earliest version, of the Q collection, he does not see them as stemming from a group of wandering preachers. He suggests instead that there were only settled communities of people who tried to live out a countercultural "social experiment." Hippie communes? Oneida? Most critical scholars don't even think the Jerusalem church, as shown in the opening chapters of Acts, really lived communally. More likely, Luke is trying to create a "myth of innocence" about a golden age of what Marx would later call "primitive communism." In other words, a myth of the "early Church" to use to scold later generations with.[7]

I follow Stevan L. Davies[8] in thinking that no settled communities could possibly have organized themselves on the principles of Q insofar as these required the renunciation of family, home, and property. Such sayings are fine for lone wolves and loose cannons—like the Cynic and Jesus movement itinerants. They are like hoboes sitting around the campfire in a train yard: a fellowship, not a community. Davies sees that there would have been communities of people who would gladly offer food and shelter to such itinerant holy men and listen to their teaching with reverence. But, like modern churchgoers, when they heard talk of celibacy, homeless wandering, and voluntary poverty, they must have silently tuned out. The best comparison would be the two-track salvation system of Buddhism. The monks alone have really embarked on the Eightfold Path to Nirvana. Life in the workaday world is too distracting for anyone but a monk to pursue enlightenment. But the laity can, by supplying the needs of the monks, gain enough merit to ensure a better reincarnation next time around (not exactly salvation, but not bad).

We see the same sort of fund-raising theology in Mark 9:41 and Matt. 10:41–42, where we are told that anyone who helps a prophet will receive a prophet's reward. Anyone who quails at the prospect of "letting goods and kindred go, this mortal life also" might jump at the chance of buying into the kingdom the easy way by offering a cup of cold water to one of the Jesus Bodhisattvas. That's all the "Q communities" had to do. And who do you think the itinerants had in mind when they exhorted their hearers to cash in possessions and give the proceeds to "the poor"? In case anyone in the congregation missed the point and started thinking of poor Lazarus in the gutter outside, he might be brought up short with another inspired saying: "The poor you always have with you. You can help them whenever the mood strikes you. But you will not always have me" (Mark 14:7). And let's not waste the ointment, shall we? The three hundred denarii would come in a lot more handy, to tell you the truth.

We know abuses like this occurred; the Didache warns congregations not to allow one of these freeloader prophets to hang around over half a week without getting a job. People began to grow more suspicious of these wildcard prophets. As the congregations became more institutionalized and bishops began to emerge, they were able to squeeze the old-time itinerants out. We have already seen Paul trying to convince the Corinthians to sever ties with the medicine-show apostles. 2 John 10 says to slam the door on them, too, though 3 John 10, apparently written by someone on the other side of the door, says not to. Matt. 25:31–46 warns readers not to neglect the needs of these gospel vagrants, the little brothers of the Son of Man. Similarly, the Didache warns about wandering prophets who tire of their vagabond existence and wish to settle down in the community: "And if he wishes to settle among you and has a trade, let him work for his bread. . . . But if he will not do so, he is trading on Christ; beware of such" (12:3, 5).

When Mack (with Theissen, Horsley, and others) refers to "the Jesus movement," preferring it to the anachronistic term "Christianity," I can never help thinking of the Jesus movement of the 1970s in America, a kind of fundamentalist neoprimitivism that attracted many disillusioned counterculture dropouts as well as suburban church teenagers. It is interesting to observe how some of the problems of the first-century Jesus movement resurfaced in its twentieth-century counterpart. The rude and intimidating itinerants were reborn in the Children of God movement of Moses David (a.k.a. Dave Berg). "Several days a week they would witness on the beach; then on Sunday, often as many as fifty of them would invade local churches, disrupt the services, read passages from the Book of Jeremiah predicting the doom of a nation and damn the shocked congregation and minister as hypocrites."[9] As for those who "trade on Christ," compare the modern Jesus movement's "gospel bum." "He is the person who travels around from one Christian [communal] house to another sometimes getting saved at each, but always getting a free meal and a place to sleep. 'It's not a bad life,' one young man named Rich told me, 'I just go from place to place, and if the Christians think you're saved too, they don't bug you. If one comes up and starts to lay a rap on me, I just pick up a Bible or close my eyes to pray. Sometimes I even talk in tongues, and they really think that's heavy.'"[10] These modern analogies, it seems to me, go a long way to put the meat on the theoretical bones of the historical reconstructions of Theissen and others. Their Q itinerants ring true, as does their pattern of collision with the emerging authorities of settled Christian communities.

I believe we can find in this conflict the implicit point of the story of Peter's confession in Mark 8:27–29, a story Mark himself created.[11] Jesus asks what the common people think of him. And the answers are wrong. What are those wrong answers? They all boil down to the notion that Jesus was a wandering prophet, a man with no possessions or home, like the Cynics, Elijah, or John the Baptist. But not for Mark, who refers to Jesus' "home" (Mark 2:15; 3:19b). Mark had no way of knowing what people thought of Jesus in Jesus' day; his story is not a historical report of a conversation between Jesus and Peter. But he did know that in his own day some made Jesus an itinerant prophet like the Cynics, and he didn't much like it. He has Jesus condemn it. We can even locate this hotbed of christological error: Caesarea Philippi, one of those Hellenized cities. Otherwise, why should Mark set the episode there? It is a lot like the letters of Jesus aimed at the seven churches of Asia Minor in the Book of Revelation (chapters 2–3). Jesus is made to condemn heretical goings-on in the writer's own time.

In Thomas' version (saying 13), the false estimates of Jesus are even more interesting. Jesus spurns the opinion of those self-styled believers who consider him "a wise philosopher." Bingo! A wandering Cynic. (Thomas also has Jesus reject the idea, widely held by many early Christians, that he was an angel in human form.)

So we can measure a growing tide of opposition directed to the Q itinerants. Such rejection is anticipated in the Markan Mission Charge (Mark 6:7–11; Matt. 10:5–15; Luke 10:10–12): "If any village will not receive you, shake the dust off your feet as a witness against them. I tell you, it will go easier for Sodom and Gomorrah on Judgment Day than for that place!" The Spirit would supply retorts to which no comeback line could be found (Luke 21:14–15). One of these was the threatening appeal to the Son of Man: "Anyone in this generation of sinners and adulterers who is too proud to heed me and my words, well, the Son of Man won't be too proud of him when he comes in judgment! Just wait!" (Mark 8:38). The Son of Man would wipe the tear from every eye (Rev. 7:17)—and the smirk from every face! Q specialists have spotted a whole second layer of Q sayings which really pour on this sort of angry invective.[12] That would seem to denote that a turning point had been reached: The itinerants were no longer popular, carried no more clout. Alms were drying up, doors being slammed in their faces as if they were Jehovah's Witnesses, which, come to think of it, they were!

THE PILLAR SAINTS AND THE HEIRS OF JESUS

Both of these groups seem to have been quite prominent in the early Jewish Jesus movement (they would not have used the term "Christianity"), and both of the leadership groups included James the Just, the brother of Jesus. But Mack is not quite sure of the difference between the two. I think we are talking about the same group before and after 70 C.E., after the fall of Jerusalem to the Romans and the *hijra* (flight) of the Jerusalem Jesus community to the city of Pella. While still headquartered in Jerusalem, chosen because of its biblical reputation as the Holy City of Zion, the leadership was known as the Pillars (Gal. 2:9), the community as "the saints of Jerusalem" (Rom. 15:31) or "the Poor" (Gal. 2:10—a name maintained by the Ebionite sect, a later survival of this group). The "Pillars," a term used in Islam for the five foundational religious practices, was used in Jerusalem for the three leaders James the Just, Simon Peter/Cephas, and John, son of Zebedee.

In Mark's gospel, the pair James and John are given the title Boanerges, which Mark tries to dope out as meaning "sons of thunder" (Mark 3:17), which, however, it does not seem to mean. John Allegro (*The Sacred Mushroom and the Cross*) suggested that the title derives from an old Sumerian name for Castor and Pollux, the heavenly twins, and that it means "upholders of the vault of heaven."[13] Anthony T. Hanson sees an allusion to Boaz and Jachin, the mighty pillars in Solomon's temple (1 Kings 7:21), symbolizing the pillars that supported the firmament (Job 9:6).[14] Cephas or Peter, "the Rock," would refer to the great foundation stone of the world, which scribal lore located beneath the temple. So to be called the Pillars indicated quite an exalted status. We can see the same sort of godlike veneration reflected in Thomas, saying 12, "The disciples said to him, 'We know that you will leave us. To whom shall we go?' Jesus said to them, 'Wherever you come from, you are to go to James the Righteous for whose sake heaven and earth were created.' " ("Wherever you come from" refers to the obligation of missionary apostles to check in with a report to James in Jerusalem, another measure of his importance.)

The three Pillars seem to have been an earlier authority structure, or else a higher one, than that of the Twelve. The Twelve are never mentioned in the gospels outside redactional narrative, rewritten sayings (Matt. 19:28. cf., Luke 22:30), editorial comments, or later fabricated sayings (John 6:70; Mark 14:12—not in Matthew or Luke at this point). The three figures James, John, and Peter, by contrast, are mentioned as a group or individually several times. The trouble is that the James mentioned as one of the disciples is James the son of Zebedee, brother of John. This James is said in Acts 12:1-2 to have been executed early on by Herod Agrippa I. Did James the Just take his place? Possibly, but there is some confusion over the fates of both of the brothers Boanerges. Papias, a bishop writing in about 150 C.E., said the two were martyred at the same time, in fulfillment of the prediction in Mark 10:39. Since other traditions have John live on for several decades (apparently to connect him with the very late Gospel of John), scholars have rejected Papias' tradition. But how do we know Acts' report of James' death (Acts 12:2) and the tradition of John living to a ripe old age in Ephesus were not legendary? Perhaps distinguishing "James, son of Zebedee" from "James the Just" was an attempt to create two characters out of one, so as to make all the traditions sound right. John had been split into two characters ("John the Elder" and "John, son of Zebedee") in order to preserve "John" as author of both the Revelation on the one hand and the "Johannine" gospel and epistles on the other. So maybe Mark thought of the James who belonged to the inner circle of Jesus as being one of the three Pillars. Roman Catholic scholars have usually identified the two.

As for the Heirs, these were the royal household of Jesus (and James), at least as they were seen in retrospect by the Jesus group descended from them. James the Just had probably always owed his prominence to the accident of his birth, functioning as the caliph, the successor of his famous brother, just as Ali, cousin and adopted son of the Prophet Muhammad, served as caliph of the Muslim community. James shared the mantle of Jesus with John and Peter as *Primus Inter Pares* (first among equals) as a sort of compromise with these two others who had been close associates of Jesus during his ministry and whose claims to leadership were not to be easily set aside. But after the fall of Jerusalem and the death of Peter some ten years earlier (or so tradition tells us), the only authority claim that still commanded any credibility was that of James, or rather the other surviving brothers of James and Jesus, since James, too, had been martyred. As the younger Hasmonean brothers took over leadership when Judas or Simon would fall in battle, and the descendants of Judas of Galilee took turns leading the revolution in succeeding decades, so did the brothers of Jesus and James take their turn at the helm. Simeon succeeded James. Collectively they were known as the Heirs. The desultory references to the mother and brothers of Jesus in the gospels (Mark 3:20–21, 31–35; John 7:1–7) must originally have been polemical shots aimed at this faction by rival factions who supported other apostolic leaders.

All Mack is sure of is that for the community of the Heirs and/or the Pillars, Jesus was remembered as their founder, that they kept the Jewish Law, and that they preached a gospel quite different from that associated with the name of Paul, whom they deemed a false prophet. Mack rightly suspects that the death of Jesus meant little more to them than it had meant to the Q community (and the itinerants). First, let us suppose that they at least knew of the death of Jesus. Jesus as their Messiah would have been more like Menachem Mendel Schneerson is to Lubavitcher Hasidic Jews today. My guess is that, like the partisans of Rabbi Schneerson, the community of the Pillars/Heirs would have located the resurrection of their Messiah not in the recent past but rather in the near future. Jesus would shortly rise as the beginning (the "first fruits," 1 Cor. 15:20–23) of the resurrection harvest; in other words, the beginning of the process, not some early anticipation of the resurrection happening years or decades or centuries in advance of it!

C. H. Dodd[15] once noted a set of interesting parallels between a number of New Testament passages dealing with Jesus' resurrection on the one hand and his second advent on the other, implying perhaps that the early Christians had not at first differentiated very clearly between the two. For instance, we find the motif of "seeing" Jesus in a climactic sense applied both to the resurrection appearances ("There you will see him," Mark 16:7, c.f., 1 Cor. 15:3–11) and to the Second Coming ("Every eye will see him," Rev. 1:7). Similarly, the motif of a reunion in which the vindicated Christ will eat and drink with his followers—after the resurrection (Acts 1:4 RSV;10:41) or at the Second Coming (Mark 15:25; Rev. 3:20; 19:9). Likewise the theme of the gathering together of Christ's elect: in the church (Matt. 18:20; 1 Cor. 5:4) or at the eschaton (Mark 13:27; 2 Thess. 2:1). Again, the royal investiture of Christ with universal dominion and power, derived from Daniel 7, is associated now with the resurrection (Matt. 28:16–18; Phil. 2:6–11), now with the Parousia (Matt. 25:31; Rev. 11:15). Dodd thought that these parallels implied an early stage when Jesus' vindication after death was spoken of in general terms that were interpreted variously as referring to a return to earthly life shortly after death and to a return to the earth from heavenly concealment, leading an angelic army in his train. In time, he reasons, each interpretation sharpened or produced various sayings, like the ones cited here, that crystallized and specified the manner of Jesus' return one way or the other.

Dodd tactfully refrained from exploring the revolutionary implications of his suggestion, but nothing forbids us. It seems to me that for such an ambiguity as he describes even to have been possible, the early believers must not have thought the resurrection of Jesus had already happened! Cerinthus, a Jewish-Christian Gnostic of the late first century, is said to have believed that Jesus' resurrection lay yet in the future. I would consider him no innovator, but a stubborn traditionalist. It is hard to see how such a view could ever have occurred to him in the first place if the prior and universal belief had been that Jesus had long ago risen from the dead.

William Wrede[16] demonstrated how Jesus was originally believed to have become the Messiah only upon his resurrection. Such an understanding is called "Adoptionism," and it certainly seems to be present here and there in the New Testament. For instance, Rom. 1:3–4, which seems to be a quotation from an earlier hymn or creed, says that Jesus had already been positioned for Messiahship, as he was "Son of David according to the flesh" but then was "declared Son of God by an act of power by the resurrection of the dead." Similarly, Acts 2:36 has Peter say to the Pentecostal crowds, "Let all Israel know for sure that God has made him both Lord and Christ, this Jesus whom you crucified." The logic is clearly that Jesus' installation as Messiah and Lord followed, ironically, the nation's repudiation of him. Again, in Acts 13:33, Paul is shown saying, "He raised up Jesus, as it is also written in the second Psalm, 'You are my son; today I have begotten you.' " Christian faith so closely associated Jesus' resurrection with his inauguration as messianic "son" that Acts 13:33 takes a prediction of the one as being fulfilled in the other.

John A. T. Robinson showed there is reason to believe that an even earlier view was that the Risen Jesus was *still* not the Messiah but would have to wait to receive the title at his Second Coming, when he would do the work of the Messiah, defeating the powers of evil, as described in the Book of Revelation. Robinson pointed to still another tantalizing fragment in Acts, this time Acts 3:19–21, "Repent, therefore, and return, that your sins may be wiped away, in order that times of refreshing may come from the presence of the Lord, and that he may send Jesus, *the Christ appointed* for you, whom the heavens must hold until the period of restoration of all things which God spoke about by the mouth of his holy prophets from ancient time."[17]

In either case, the point is that early Christians would have at first expected the *second* coming of Jesus—his *first* coming as the *Messiah*—in the near future. But time went by and he never showed up. Eventually they decided he must already have been the Messiah, but he must have kept it a secret. That's why pretty much nobody knew about it till the Resurrection, and, in turn, that's why some assumed he had become Messiah only as of the resurrection. This scenario, though criticized by many scholars (I suspect mainly because of its disturbing implications for traditional dogma), still seems pretty cogent. But the unseen implication of it is that, since resurrection and Messiahship go together as two sides of the same coin, if Jesus' future Messiahship was pushed from the near future back into the recent past, *so was his resurrection*. This explains why all the resurrection narratives depict Jesus appearing only to small groups of disciples in private, and why Mark has the women at the tomb say nothing about it to anyone. In other words, part of the messianic secret was the secret that Jesus had already risen from the dead, but the news was slow in leaking out: "You mean he *did* rise from the dead and we just didn't know it? Yeah . . . *that's* the ticket!"

Why does this make enough difference for me to be spending so much ink on the matter? Because one of Burton Mack's most important suggestions is that the resurrection gospel was a myth that fit the interests of some early Jesus groups but not others. It was the *product* of one faction of early Christianity, not the *foundation* of any sort of Christianity at all. Mack says that even critical scholars have been too long enchanted by the myth of the "Big Bang" model of Christian origins: Jesus rose from the dead (or at least the disciples experienced such a vision), and Christianity began to evolve in its various forms from that point. But this is what we must deconstruct. And I have been trying to explain how the resurrection doctrine may have resulted from a gradual process of rethinking on the part of a single faction of the Jesus movement. The Jesus movement was already on the scene in another form, several other forms. And not only were those forms not resurrection-centered; they may not even have been all that Jesus-centered.

But what if even this faction did not at first take for granted the death of Jesus? This is a hard question even to ask, because we are so used to thinking of the crucifixion as the necessary prelude to the beginning of Christianity. What else could a Jesus community have supposed? Let us remind ourselves of what else one particular Jesus community of no less than one billion members today supposes. Islam inherited from Christian converts in the seventh century C.E., who brought their own accustomed belief with them, the idea that Jesus had not even gone to the cross but had instead escaped and been whisked away to safety by God. These Arabian Christians must have cherished the belief for centuries; the long arm of Constantinian orthodoxy was not quite long enough to touch them out in the desert.

Muslims believe Jesus dwells in Heaven, awaiting his Second Coming, at which time he will destroy Dejjal, the Antichrist, with the breath of his mouth. But he has neither died nor risen, but only been "occulted," hidden away in safety by God until then. This is a familiar legendary motif, told in one form or another of King Arthur, Barbarossa, the Seven Sleepers of Ephesus, and Constans, the orthodox heir of Constantine, deposed by his evil

Arian brother Constantius. God would send Constans back to earth in the role of the Emperor of the Last Days.[18] And Shi'ite Muslims came to believe the same thing of their Imams, the inspired descendants of Ali and Muhammad. Here we touch on history, not just legend. The Shi'ites were a heterodox minority in Islam, and often persecuted. They were governed by the guidance of the current descendant of Ali, the Imam (teacher). The Imam would have been a constant target of the Sunni Muslim authorities; thus he reigned from concealment, his whereabouts unknown even to the Shi'ite faithful. He would communicate with them through a chosen representative, a messenger called the Bab, or the Gate, that is, to the hidden Imam. For instance, it would be the Bab who communicated the passing of each Imam, at which time the Imam's son would take over and go into hiding. When the twelfth Imam, Muhammad ibn-Hasan-al-Askari, had long fallen silent, but no report of his death came, a crisis occurred. He had no son to succeed him. Had God left the community without leadership? Impossible! So they decided the only thing they could decide: God had taken Muhammad ibn-Hasan-al-Askari into supernatural occultation, from whence he would one day return, along with Jesus, at the end of the age.[19] Until then, as usual, his revelations would arrive via the Bab, eventually a whole series of them. Now the Babs became figures of even greater power, since, in the absence of actual physical communication with secluded leaders, they took on more the role of prophets in their own right. In the nineteenth century, one Ali Muhammad proclaimed himself the Bab, then the Hidden Imam himself, returned. This was the beginning of what would come to be known as the Baha'i Faith.[20] And there have been plenty of other candidates for the position in Shi'ite history. Several of these were active in India, and it is claimed of some of these, as well as of their rival Hindu messiahs and avatars, that they did not die, escaping to heavenly concealment as well. Such docetic escapees include Birsa al Chalkad (d. 1900), Saiyid Ahmad (d. 1831), and Ram Singh (d. 1888).[21]

So Shi'ite Muslims believe that the same sort of supernatural occultation preserved both Jesus and Muhammad ibn-Hasan-al-Askari from the persecution of their enemies. There may be an element of truth here. It may indeed be that the community of the Pillars/Heirs only knew Jesus was no longer present. In a time of persecution, he had disappeared. Confident that God could not have abandoned him to the clutches of the wicked, they concluded that he was safe in hiding (cf. Matt. 14:13; John 7:1), communicating through his brother James, his Bab. Many gospel scholars have suggested that many powerful sayings attributed to Jesus, but which cannot really go back to him, were the work of Christian charismatic prophets who spoke in his name. The "I am" statements of John's gospel (John 4:26; 6:35; 8:12; 10:14; 11:25; 15:1) would be prime examples. And one of these is "I am the door" (John 10:9). Was this one originally a dramatic declaration of a Jesus-prophet in the Johannine community? Had he declared himself the Bab of Jesus? Something like this seems to be presupposed in that gospel, where the Beloved Disciple, reclining at the bosom of Jesus at the supper (John 13:23–25), reflects the Son himself, "who is in the bosom of the father" (John 1:18) and who "has made him known" (ibid.). That unnamed disciple is himself the voice of the Paraclete (John 16:7).

And now, I think, we find ourselves on the verge of solving an ancient puzzle involving James the Just. In the traditional/legendary account of James' martyrdom as related by the Jewish-Christian historian Hegesippus and quoted by Eusebius (book II, chapter 23), James was such a devout Jewish hasid that the temple authorities sought to enlist his aid in bringing the pesky Jesus-sectarians to their senses. They put him up on a high balcony and ask him, "What is the 'door of Jesus'?" It becomes obvious that James' true loyalties had been unknown to them. They go wild when he replies, "Why do you ask me concerning the son of man? He sits at the right hand of the Father." The whole scene is obviously modeled on the trial scene of Jesus himself. (John 18:21: "Why do you ask me? Ask those who heard me." Matt. 26:64: "You say that I am, but I tell you, hereafter you will see the son of man seated at the right hand of Power.") But I wonder if this assimilation to the gospel trial scenes is not a secondary overlay, attempting to conceal an earlier meaning. Or maybe the original meaning was no longer understood.

It may well be that originally the story had James reveal that he himself was the door, the Bab, of Jesus. "Why do you ask me concerning the son of man?" might have meant, "Why do you ask me about me?" As is well known, sometimes the Hebrew/Aramaic term "son of man" (*bar-enosh/bar-nasha*) was a humble way of referring to oneself, like "this humble person." Once Phil Donahue asked a Hasidic Jew about a rather delicate custom: Did Hasidic Jews really have sex through a sheet with a hole cut in it? Talk show hosts may have no sense of shame, but a pious hasid does. He responded in distress, "It is an outrage to humanity!" Phil seemed to think he was denying the whole idea, saying that such a practice would be outrageous. But he was really saying, "It is an outrage for you to ask anyone (me) such a question! It's no one else's business!"

Jesus wasn't available, but James was in easy clubbing distance. Thus his martyrdom. But was he following in his brother's footsteps? Does the story presuppose Jesus had died? Who knows? Maybe Jesus was just hidden away somewhere. Maybe this is even the original denotation of James' epithet, "the Lord's brother." As the living oracle of Jesus, maybe he deserved the same title of honor as "Judas Thomas," "Judas the Twin" brother of Jesus, since he was believed to be his image on earth.

If the community of the Pillars/Heirs did believe in the death of Jesus, how would they have understood his death? Robert Eisenman[22] makes a persuasive case for Jesus having been an armed, priestly Messiah-king like Menahem, scion of Judas of Galilee and leader of the Zealots. Jesus would have died fighting in (or as a result of) the raid on the temple (Mark 11:15–18). As Burton Mack points out, the story of Jesus "cleansing" the temple is either a piece of fiction, which is Mack's own option, or it is a garbled (or edited) report of an armed assault as Robert Eisler and S. G. F. Brandon maintained, because the temple area envisioned actually covered an extent of some thirty-five acres, the equivalent of thirty-four football fields! It would have contained thousands of pilgrims, innumerable livestock stalls, and money-changing booths.[23] And it was crawling with armed guards! One thing that couldn't have happened is our usual picture of a lone figure busting up a church rummage sale!

But do we have any other clues about the James wing of the Jesus movement? Perhaps we have a great deal more than we had thought. Again, I refer to the work of Robert Eisenman. It is his contention that the Dead Sea Scrolls have been dated a century too early (he is by no means alone in this belief, nor is it even a new opinion). They should be seen instead as first-century C.E. works stemming from the community led by James the Just, called "the Teacher of Righteousness" or "the Righteous Teacher" in the Scrolls. Not content with bare possibilities, Eisenman sets forth a series of remarkable links between the Scrolls and numerous James traditions inside and outside the New Testament. Further comparisons between the Scrolls, the New Testament, Hegesippus, Josephus, and the Clementine Homilies tend to implicate Paul as "the Spouter of Lies" who had betrayed the community by denying the Law within the community itself. All this sounds quite close to the depiction of Paul in Jewish-Christian writings of the second century. As anyone acquainted with the Scrolls will know, the Teacher of Righteousness is said to have been ambushed, betrayed, and done to death by a "Wicked Priest." The parallel Eisenman suggests with the plot of Ananus the High Priest to trap and kill James in Hegesippus' history is a far closer one than any suggested by those scholars who insist the ciphers of the Scrolls must by hook or by crook refer to the events of the Hasmonean kings and the Pharisees and Essenes of the first and second centuries B.C.E.

It is the absence of any mention of Jesus in the Scrolls that has made it impossible for most scholars to entertain anything like Eisenman's theory (though Jacob L. Teicher[24] did suggest, in a series of articles back in 1950s, that the Scrolls community were Ebionites, one branch of the so-called Jewish Christians). But what if I am right about James' prominence as the "Door of Jesus," the Bab connecting followers to Jesus the Hidden Imam? James would soon come to eclipse Jesus in the eyes of his followers. Or, as Schonfield suggested, it would have been quite natural for Jesus' followers to have regarded him in retrospect as the anointed king who resumed David's royal line, with James as his successor *as Messiah*, that is, Davidic king. Jesus would have receded to the status of a *Deus Absconditus*, a hidden God, whereas James was a living mouthpiece of divine truth. And once he was himself martyred, his centrality was assured.

Eisenman can be understood as reopening the door for the theory of Renan and others (a very popular theory in the eighteenth and nineteenth centuries and even today) that Christianity began as "an Essenism." The fourth-century heresy hunter Epiphanius of Salamis preserves these startling facts: first, that there was a pre-Christian sect called "the Nazoreans" (meaning "the Observers," of the Torah), and second, that the earliest Christians were called "Jesseans," which sounds like someone's attempt to disguise the name "Essenes" by trying to connect it with Jesse, David's father, and thus reinterpreting it as a reference to the messianic "son of David" motif. Eisenman suggests that terms like "Nazoreans," "Essenes," "Zealots," and others were all interchangeable tags for the blurry cloud of overlapping Jewish "heretics," sectarians, and "enthusiasts" in New Testament times. "Jesus the Nazorean" would have denoted "Jesus the Sectarian," "Jesus the Hasid," not "Jesus from Nazareth."[25]

Eisenman's theory would leave us with a creatively inchoate, unstable, and diverse "early Jewish Christianity" that was not particularly centered on Jesus. He may have been venerated equally with a gallery of saints and messiahs including John the Baptist, James the Just, Simon Magus, and Dositheus (the latter two being Samaritan gurus and miracle workers said to have been, like Jesus, disciples and self-appointed successors of John the Baptist). We may easily imagine a series of schisms occurring in this movement, dividing it along the lines of the partisans of the various patron saints: "I am of James!" "I am of the Baptist!" "I am of Jesus!" (precisely as in 1 Cor. 1:11–12, where Christ is only one among several factional totems).

Splitting off and hanging out their own shingle, the "Jesus-Shi'ites" ("partisans") would have become the basis of the various later "Jewish Christian" groups known to historians as the Ebionites, the Nazarenes, the Elchasites, even the Cerinthian Gnostics. Those who favored James the Righteous Teacher relegated Jesus to the status of James' forerunner, just as the Jesus faction subordinated the Baptist to Jesus. From the James faction came the Dead Sea Scrolls which exalt their Teacher as a new Moses, bemoan his tragic death, and look forward to his return at the end of days to even the score.

And let's not forget John the Baptist. New Testament scholars from David Friedrich Strauss onward have recognized in the gospels evidence that the sect of John continued on alongside the Jesus movement for decades. For instance, Mark preserves a story in which we learn that Jesus is well known to have discarded the pious practice of fasting, a practice shared by John the Baptist's disciples with the Pharisee sect (Mark 2:18). Luke's introduction to the Lord's Prayer depicts Jesus' disciples asking him to compose a prayer for them to repeat just as John the Baptist had composed a prayer used by his followers (Luke

11:1). One need not assume these two passages represent real events in the life of Jesus. Indeed, it seems they do not. As Bultmann pointed out, in episodes where Jesus is asked not about his own conduct but about that of his disciples, we are surely dealing with a story composed in the early Church to serve as a proof text in a debate about what the church ought to do. Likewise, since Matthew and Luke both derived the Lord's Prayer from Q but have different contexts for it, it is clear Luke's introductory scene is artificial. The historically secondary character of both these passages underlines all the more dramatically that a sect of John, attributing fasting and prayer customs to him, survived for many decades alongside Christianity, at least into the time of Mark and Luke.

Similarly, both Luke and John seem to be at pains to assure readers that John the Baptist was not himself the savior, despite the hopes of many that he might have been (Luke 3:15; John 1:6–7; 3:28–30). What could be the point of such protestations if not to rebut or win over those who held John to be the Christ, not Jesus? In the Clementine Homilies we hear a debate in which John's followers argue against Jesus and claim that John himself is the Messiah. "And behold, one of the disciples of John asserted that John was the Christ, and not Jesus: 'Inasmuch,' he said, 'as Jesus himself declared that John was greater than all men and all prophets. If therefore,' he said, 'he is greater than all men, he must without doubt be held to be greater than both Moses and Jesus himself. But if he is greater than all, he himself is the Christ' " (*Recognitions* 1.60.1)[26] There survives even today an Iraqi Aramaic-speaking baptizing community called the Mandaeans (Aramaic for "Gnostics"), though their preferred self-designation is "Nazoreans"! These people still curse Jesus as a false prophet and Antichrist (see 1 Cor. 12:3). They revere the Baptist as a true prophet, but their Messiah is a heavenly savior called Enosh-Uthra, the Angel Enosh. Enosh was the first man, the primordial human, in some ancient Hebrew creation myths, though in Genesis he has been elbowed aside by the similar figure of Adam. In short, Enosh Uthra is the Son of Man. How could a sect wind up glorifying John and cursing Jesus if it is not the result of ancient sectarian strife between two factions of a movement that had previously venerated both?

There were various Simonian and Dositheanr sects in antiquity, too, but they have long since perished. I am willing to bet that all were the centrifugal fragments of an original pre-Jesus Nazorean-Essene movement to which John, James, and Jesus the Nazorean had all belonged. That any of these names should have become exclusive figureheads of their own movements must be a later development. And here we have a plausible picture of a Jewish Jesus movement that had not been Jesus-centered and that did not begin with the Big Bang of Jesus' resurrection. Contrary to Bultmann's famous theory, it did not all begin with the Easter morning faith of the original disciples.

I will return to the subject of the Galilean Christianity of the Heirs after the fall of Jerusalem in chapter 4.

THE COMMUNITY OF ISRAEL

Mack seems to include this fourth Jesus movement (counting the Pillars and the Heirs of Jesus as numbers two and three), as he does the Q community, to provide some flesh and blood context in which to place another distinct group of gospel materials. Here he has in mind a particular linked series of miracle stories that occurs twice, almost side by side, in Mark. Paul Achtemeier was the first to draw attention to the puzzle.[27] It is hard not to notice, even on a casual read-through of Mark's gospel, that he has two versions of the miraculous multiplication of loaves and fishes (6:34–44; 8:1–9). What begins to emerge from closer scrutiny is a more extensive pattern. In both cases we start off with a miracle on the high seas (stilling the storm in 4:35–41; walking on the water during a storm in 6:45–51). Next we find sets of three healing miracles. The first sequence is the story of the Gadarene demoniac (5:1–20), the healing of the woman with the hemorrhage (5:25–34), and the raising of Jairus' daughter (5:21–23, 35–43). The second, parallel sequence is comprised of the healing of the blind man of Bethsaida (8:22–26), the exorcism of the daughter of the Syro-Phoenician woman (7:24b–30), and the healing of the deaf-mute (7:32–37). Each chain of stories concludes with a miraculous feeding story, the feeding of the five thousand in Mark 6:34–44, and that of the four thousand in Mark 8:1–10. The thing that strikes us first is perhaps the suspicion that a single basic sequence was passed on intact by means of a process of oral transmission which eventually allowed many of the details to change and develop, until there were (at least) two versions circulating by the time Mark encountered the tradition. They were different enough that he decided not to risk leaving either set out. Like a modern fundamentalist faced with a set of biblical contradictions, Mark may have assumed similar events happened twice. At any rate, the mere fact of the doubling of the story chain is highly significant, since it allows us to gauge the kind of variation and evolution that was possible in the oral tradition.

But Achtemeier was perceptive enough to recognize that there had to be even more to it. There must have been some special significance to someone having threaded these particular miracle tales together, and for a whole series of someone elses to keep them linked in the process of repetition, since most gospel vignettes seem to have floated around one by one. The keen-eyed Achtemeier pointed out the general similarity between the twin miracle sequences he had discovered and the Signs Source, the numbered series of seven miracles used by John as the narrative skeleton of his gospel.[28] Robert Fortna, leading expert on the Signs Source, followed by Mack, went a bit further and suggested that the Signs Source was yet a third, somewhat reshuffled and augmented version of the same miracle sequence Achtemeier found twice in Mark. As this is hardly evident at first sight, let me briefly explain the equivalencies.

Right off the bat, it is obvious that John shares the sea miracle and the feeding of the multitude with Mark. He has 5,000 fed in common with Mark's first miracle sequence (John 6:10), while in John the sea miracle is walking on the water (6:19) as in Mark's second sequence rather than stilling the storm as in Mark's first. There are no exorcisms in John to match those of the Syro-Phoenician woman and the Gadarene demoniac, but John's story of Jesus' remote-control healing of the royal official's son (4:46–54) is a tradition-variant of Q's story of Jesus' healing at a distance of the Roman centurion's son (Matt. 8:5–13/Luke 7:1–10). This tale, as Bultmann pointed out, seems in turn to be a variant version of the story of the Syro-Phoenician woman (in Mark's second sequence)! John's story of Lazarus' resurrection (chapter 11) parallels the story of Jairus' daughter from Mark's first sequence, while John's episode of the man born blind parallels Mark's blind man of Bethsaida, from his second sequence.

Burton Mack agrees with Achtemaier that the particular miracles involved seem to echo, more than most other gospel miracles, the wonders performed by Moses and Elijah (and his double, Elisha). The two sea miracles recall Moses' parting the sea (Exod. 14), while the pair of feeding miracles mirror Moses' feeding the Israelites in the wilderness with manna and quails (Exod. 16; Num. 11:4–15, 18–23, 31–32) and Elisha's miraculous multiplication of food in 2 Kings 4:1–7 and 4:42–44. The Gadarene demoniac episode (Mark 5:1–20), with its sending of a herd of "Gentile" swine off the cliff into the sea, symbolizes Moses' (and then Joshua's) blitzkriegs overrunning the Canaanites, as does Jesus' initial disdain for the Canaanite woman (Mark 7:27). The shamanistic healing techniques Jesus uses on Mark's blind man (Mark 8:23) and deaf-mute (Mark 7:33–34) and on John's blind man (John 9:6) recall the sympathetic magic employed by Elisha to revive the son of the Shunammite woman (2 Kings 4:32–35). The raising of Jairus' daughter (Mark 5:35–42) recalls the same miracle of Elisha's (1 Kings 7:17–24). When Jesus sends the blind man to wash in the pool of Siloam in John 9:7, we think of Elisha sending Naaman the Syrian to wash away his leprosy in the Jordan in 2 Kings 5:10. The patient attention shown by Jesus to the woman with the hemorrhage (Mark 5:32–34) parallels Elijah's and Elisha's patronage of the widows of Israel and Zarephath (1 Kings 17:8–16; 2 Kings 4:1–7).

Moses and Elijah had been active in watershed periods in the history of Israel, Moses during the time of national formation, the consolidation of the Twelve Tribes, their liberation from Egypt, and their forging a covenant with God, Elijah during the decisive contest between God and Baal for the allegiance of Israel. What would it have meant to preserve a sequence of miracles recalling (or based on) those of Moses and Elijah? Mack suggests that the Jesus community behind these miracle sequences saw themselves as something of a renewed Israel and remembered Jesus as the one who called them into being as such. In his supernatural feats he was replaying the events of the Exodus as well as those of Elijah, who, despite his great wonders, was supported by only a tiny remnant of loyal worshippers of the God of Israel. Mack sees this community as a set of groups of Jews who would never have considered themselves a holy people before, and who gratefully marveled that Jesus had thought it worth gathering and tending a herd of such mangy lost sheep. Their new self-esteem struck them as no less a redemption than that of the Exodus.

I find Mack a bit unconvincing at this point. His portrait of the "Community of Israel" smacks of the liberal Protestant romanticizing of the poor. His Jesus sounds like a first-century Jesse Jackson leading the crowds of sinners and tax collectors in a chant of "I am—some*body*!" There has to have been more to it than this.

The major clue is the view of Jesus presupposed in these stories, the "Christology," if you will. Namely: Jesus is pictured like a new Moses or a new Elijah, but, pointedly, *not a new David*. And since the miracles happen in Galilee, I think we have a good case for locating the community who cherished such a foundation saga in Galilee and Samaria, where the concept of a Davidic Messiah cut no ice at all. These were the old regions that had constituted the Northern Kingdom of Israel. And after the harsh rule of Solomon, Israelites in the north had decided they'd given the dynasty of David more than a fair chance. They served notice that the honeymoon was over, and so was the marriage (1 Kings 12:1–20). From there on in, the biblical history went on in two parallel lines, one for the Kingdom of Israel in the north, the other for the Kingdom of Judah in the south. And it was only the southerners who eagerly awaited the revival of their monarchy by a new heir to David's throne. On the contrary, upstairs in Israel, the prospect of a new Davidic king would have been bad news, not good. They had dreams of the future, too, but their eager hopes were of a different sort. They read in Deuteronomy that God would one day send a prophet like Moses (Deut. 18:15–16). They read in Malachi that God would send them Elijah again just before the great and terrible Day of the Lord (Mal. 4:5). And neither of these figures had a thing to do with the House of David. Samaritans had developed their belief in a Mosaic prophet to the point where he had become a kind of Mosaic Messiah, called the Taheb, the restorer. He is the revealer whom the Samaritan woman expects (John 4:25, 29, 42)—and whom she believes she encounters in the person of Jesus!

We can now begin to guess the identity of the mysterious "Community of Israel" required by Mack's analysis. In fact, they fill a long-vacant hole rather nicely. We have finally stumbled upon the identity of L. E. Elliott-Binns's hypothetical "Galilean Christianity."[29] Elliott-Binns felt sure that the old north-south rivalries of the Old Testament would have lingered on into the period of early Christianity. There must have been a Galilean Christianity quite different from the Judean version centered in Jerusalem. But he was at a loss to sketch in any details for the simple reason that our New Testament stems from the Jerusalem group, just as our canonical Old Testament stems from the priestly scribes of Jerusalem. We can only guess what a northern, Israelite Bible might have looked like; likewise, we are left to sheer speculation about what form early Christianity may have taken in the north.

But let's not throw in the towel too quickly. After all, the northern "E" document, the Ephraimite, Elohistic Epic, was preserved among the traditions of Judah. Deuteronomy, the reform manifesto for Judean worship and society, was based on prophetic preaching originally given in the northern shrine of Shiloh, though edited to fit the southern context. In the same way, it seems no less likely that several northern Jesus traditions would have crept into southern gospels. We can spot them if we know what to look for. These chains of Moses- and Elijah-like miracles would be an important puzzle piece. Fortna repeatedly draws attention to the purpose of the compiler of the Signs Source, preserved in John 20:30–31: "Many other signs Jesus performed in the presence of the disciples which are not written in this book; but these are written that you may believe that Jesus is the Christ, the Son of God." This version of the miracle sequence was, then, supposed to convince the reader of Jesus' Messiahship—or so the redactor thought. No doubt the redactor believed in Jesus' Messiahship for other reasons and then sought to press the miracle sequence into service for evangelistic proof. But in and of themselves, it is important to note, not one of the miracles has anything particularly messianic about it! Being a miracle worker and being King Messiah have no obvious connection. Instead, as we have seen, the inherent thrust of the stories is to parallel Jesus with Moses, Elijah, and Elisha, northern and nonmessianic heroes. The redactor of the Signs Source version of the miracle chain may have thought his collection of miracles proved Jesus to be the Messiah, but would not most readers more naturally have concluded, with the crowds in Mark 8:28, that Jesus was Elijah returned?

Similarly, there is that otherwise baffling episode in which we listen in on Jesus refuting the southern notion that the Messiah must be a descendant of King David (Mark 12:35–37). It would make perfect sense as a bit of polemic aimed from up north in Galilee or Samaria, by Jesus people who rejected any notion of a Davidic Messiah. Mark has preserved it for us, not because he himself rejected the (Davidic) Messiahship of Jesus (he didn't—Mark 10:47–48), but simply because it was a controversy story showing Jesus trouncing his opponents. Mark didn't much care what the issue under debate was, as long as he could show Jesus silencing the scribes. But in the process he has told us more than he wanted to.

Rabbinical lore records the belief, held by some Jews, that there would be a pair of Messiahs, one from the south, the Messiah son of David, and one from the north, the Messiah son of Joseph (=the leading Northern tribes, Ephraim and Manassah). Some scholars have suggested that for Jesus to be called Joseph's son in the gospels is a later misinterpretation of Jesus' title as the Galilean Messiah. Just as "Jesus the Nazorean" need not refer to having roots in Nazareth but may instead imply membership in the pious Nazorean sect (see Acts 24:5), "Jesus son of Joseph" may be a messianic title. My guess would be that, once the southern idea of Jesus as a descendant of David caught on, someone tried to reinterpret his northern messianic identity, reinterpreting the epithet "son of Joseph" by making Joseph refer to the immediate, if adoptive, father of Jesus, instead of his remote ancestor, whose prophetic dreams promised him that the sun, moon, and stars would one day bow before him (Genesis 37:9).

The Transfiguration narrative (Mark 9:2–8), which obviously compares Jesus with Moses and Elijah, not with David, would fit in here. And the Good Samaritan parable (Luke 10:29–37) must reflect northern sympathies, as must Thomas saying 60, about the Samaritan carrying the lamb, whereas the anti-Samaritan sentiments of Matthew's Mission Charge (10:5) must stem from Judean circles.

We also begin to take a second look at all those scenes set in Galilean synagogues where Jesus is shown disputing with the Pharisees and tying them in knots. Our archaeological evidence, as Mack notes, gives no hint of there having been synagogues in Galilee in the first century. Nor does the pious Pharisee movement seem to have existed there until after 70 C.E., when Jews were forced out of Jerusalem and headed north. Before that, the scribes had only taunts for Galilee, calling it "Galilee of the Gentiles," denying that any prophet could appear there, calling a biblical ignoramus a Galilean ("Are you from Galilee, too? Search the scriptures and you will see that no prophet is to rise in Galilee." John 7:52), calling it "Galilee, who hatest the Torah." One rabbi, having lived there for a year or so, bemoaned, upon his return, that in all the time he had sojourned there, only once did anyone so much as ask him a single question about the Torah. Not exactly Pharisee turf, then—till decades after Jesus. Likewise, the use of the term "rabbi" for scribes and teachers seems to have become current only toward the end of the first century C.E. And yet already in Mark, Jesus is called "Rabbi," and is debating with Pharisees in Galilean synagogues! What we seem to have here is an anachronistic reading back of the circumstances of religious debate in late first-century Galilee into the time of Jesus. We see the same thing all over the text of the Koran, where the stories of Noah, Abraham, and Moses look startlingly like certain episodes in the life of the Prophet Muhammad! They seem to have had to endure the same opposition from unbelievers, even the same hecklers' jibes, as the Prophet!

I suspect that the controversy stories, which seem to delight at least as much in Jesus' rhetorical prowess as in the actual legal opinions he renders, represent the defensive reaction of the "Community of Israel" against the intrusion of Pharisaic, scribal Judaism having arrived from the south in the wake of Jerusalem's destruction. For the Galilean Jesus people, and for Galilean Jews in general, the arrival of the self-appointed experts in the Law of God, with little patience for Galilean legal laxness, would have been a lot like the arrival of the haughty priestly Exiles in Jerusalem under the leadership of the high-handed Ezra and Nehemiah, who presumed to dictate to the locals and to rebuff their leaders as heretics and half-breeds. History repeated itself, only this time the holier-than-thous (as they were at least perceived) were going *into* exile, not coming back from it.

This would also account for the outrageously unfair portrayal of the Pharisees and their views in some gospel controversy stories, where the Pharisees are blamed for inhumane opinions attested nowhere in rabbinical writings (more about this in chapter 4). Galileans probably neither knew nor cared what the fine print of the Torah said. All they cared about was lampooning straw men, always an easy victory to win. For the record, Burton Mack would credit these controversy stories to the next group on the list, not this one, but there might very easily be a good bit of overlap, as we will shortly see.

THE SYNAGOGUE REFORM MOVEMENT

Jewish synagogues ("meeting halls") grew up in the Diaspora, i.e., in the Jewish communities scattered thickly about the Mediterranean world. It is estimated that there were twice as many Jews living outside the Holy Land as within it. They could make pilgrimage to the Jerusalem temple only so often, and they needed some kind of local Jewish magnet to prevent them from becoming totally assimilated to the Hellenistic culture about them. Hellenistic Jews had already grown rusty on their Hebrew, Greek becoming their first language as new generations were born into the cosmopolitan world of the Roman Empire. For them the Hebrew Bible had become a closed book, and various Greek translations, especially the Septuagint Bible (so named for the committee of seventy scholars who legend held to have translated it) were produced to meet their liturgical needs. It was a period of massive social dislocation. There were "Diaspora" communities of every imaginable Asian race and ethnicity, and, in order to maintain their unique cultural identity, most of them formed various voluntary associations, like a local Slavonic Hall or Italian-American Association or Black Student Union today. Synagogues were part of this trend, and one can expect that religious debates raged there over questions no one in the Holy Land would even have raised.

There were both ultrazealous Jews who raised high walls between themselves and outsiders, as Hasidic Jews do today, and Jewish communities which had so largely assimilated to Hellenism that they dropped literal observance of the Law altogether! Philo of Alexandria warned the latter not to carry things so far, but others blamed him for the trend, since he himself taught that the Bible was only read right when you read it as an allegory symbolizing the truths of Platonic and Stoic philosophy. Diaspora Jews in Rome and North Africa did not mind mixing their worship of the Hebrew God with that of Dionysus, Zeus, and Attis, as the designs of ancient synagogue mosaics and burial sarcophagi demonstrate.[30] They figured these were just different names for the same divine beings, a conveniently ecumenical attitude guaranteed not to alienate one's neighbors, and a nearly universal opinion at the time among Greeks, Romans, Egyptians, and others.

Amid this great ferment, the introduction of one more pinch of theological spice, the faith of some Hellenized Jews in the prophet-sage Jesus, made waves, but not tidal waves. Just enough distance was created between Jesus Jews and other Jews to produce an agenda for intra-Jewish debate. Mack sees Jesus as something like a Hellenized Galilean Cynic sage functioning in a largely already-Hellenized context. And indeed the Book of Acts tells us there were Hellenistic (Greek-speaking) synagogues in Jerusalem itself, and that they were the setting for theological debates among fellow Jews over the teachings of Jesus and their implications for traditional Jewish practice (Acts 6:13–14). This is a striking irony: the existence of Greek-speaking synagogues in the Holy Land for the sake of Jews who had moved to the Holy Land only to find they could not "assimilate" there! They had become too Greek to fit in! Who could need a synagogue in Jerusalem itself? It sounds like having an American embassy in Washington, D.C. Hellenistic synagogues in the Holy Land were something of a "home away from one's home away from home"!

Religious change is most often occasioned by cultural change, and those who had been through the culture-shock of Jewish survival in the Diaspora would be a ready audience for new and Hellenic-leaning liberal ideas from the sophist Jesus. Mack attributes to the Hellenistic synagogues the bulk of the gospel pronouncement stories, for two reasons. On the one hand, Jesus Jews in this social context would have had occasion to debate with Pharisees and their sympathizers on points of religious law, arguing for a looser, freer view. The conservatives would have dismissed them as "seekers after smooth things." So the content of the pronouncement stories, especially the controversy stories, would have suited them. On the other hand, the form would have been natural for them, too. Mack has demonstrated how the gospel pronouncement stories fall into the same literary type as the Greek *chreia*, a brief introductory setting leading up to a pithy and/or humorous saying by the sage, who thus outwits his critics.

The crucial question is, who would have been prepared to tell such stories? People with a Greek education, that's who. It was a standard school exercise to compose new pronouncement stories starring a famous philosopher as a way of showing an understanding of his philosophy. "What would Socrates or Epicurus say if someone asked him thus and so?" Whether or not the pronouncement stories of the gospels actually contain authentic sayings of the historical Jesus is a different question. Even if they do, we have to ask: Who would have related those sayings in this particular form? Because the form is culture-specific. Pronouncement stories are a Hellenistic product. So the old idea that these stories were the stock-in-trade of Aramaic-speaking Jewish disciples of Jesus from the early days is ruled out—unless, of course, those disciples were semi-Hellenized Galileans who followed a Jesus who was more than a little like Diogenes, more like Meleager than Elisha.

But then, why should we not place the pronouncement stories back among the Q communities? If we divide these, as I suggested above, into settled communities of sympathizers on the one hand and the itinerant sages on the other, it all falls into place. We can imagine the sages issuing terse proverbs, aphorisms, and fortune-cookie preachments, as well as humorous diatribes. But Q contains quite a number of pronouncement stories, and if these are scholastic exercises, I wonder if we do not owe them instead to the settled communities of Q supporters. After all, where are you going to have a school for children except in a settled community of some kind? And of course this scenario would fit the very existence of a compilation of sayings and pronouncement stories like Q. The point of such wisdom collections is, after all, to preserve such valuable wisdom when it is in danger of being forgotten because such sages are no longer as common as they once were. Q would be a later fossil of the "Cynic" Jesus movement. And since the Greek *chreia* was a kind of thumbnail memorial of a thinker from the more or less distant past, the presence of them in Q means it must have been compiled by the later, settled adherents of the once-numerous Jesus itinerants. There is no particular reason not to identify these settled communities of latter-day readers of Q with Mack's Synagogue Reform movement. It would neatly fit the pattern of sectarian evolution: After an initial period of radical repudiation of the parent religion, the sect becomes increasingly assimilated to its worldly surroundings, and the old "worldly" considerations begin to make belated sense after all, rather as a child grows up and sees the wisdom of his parents long after the fact. And yet the sect members cannot simply surrender their old ideals, so they accommodate them. They water them down. Even so, the Q communities would eventually have given up the romantic delusion of Jesus radicalism and settled for "Christian Realism." They would have sought accommodation with the synagogues they had earlier ridiculed. Once there, they would have stood up for the liberal Judaism of the gospel pronouncement stories, though no longer for the sectarian radicalism of the itineracy sayings.

The same thing happened with eighteenth-century Hasidism. It began as a charismatic movement that repudiated the dead letter of scripture in favor of magnetic *rebbes* who personally incarnated the Torah. But in time, their youthful enthusiasm having cooled a bit, they returned to the Torah scrolls and wound up becoming super-keen scholars and keepers of the Law, as witness Hasidism today. Even so, we must picture the Q communities, tired of the self-arrogating oracles of holy freeloaders, finally closing the doors to shut out the noisy fulminations on the coming vengeance of the Son of Man. Older and wiser, they sought for ways they could hold on to some basic insights garnered from the Q sages which now substituted for the tiresome Q sages themselves. With Q in hand, they reapproached the synagogue communities, keeping mum until their membership was established in good standing. Then they began to try to leaven the dough with some of the still-pungent sayings of the Jesus prophets and sages. Or perhaps their nonconforming practices aroused anxious comments from others, a "weaker brother, stronger brother" scenario (cf., Rom. 14:1–15:6) as the Q people would have no doubt viewed it. And the answers they gave, that they imagined Jesus would have given, became part of Q. As Bultmann saw long ago[31] this is why in the gospels Jesus' critics protest not his own practice but that of his disciples: "Why do *they* do what is unlawful on the Sabbath?" (Mark 2:24). "Why do *your disciples* eat with hands unwashed?" (Mark 7:5). "The disciples of John and the Pharisees' disciples fast, but *your disciples* do not fast" (Mark 2:18).

Martin Noth noticed the same sort of thing in the Moses stories in Exodus, Leviticus, and Numbers: When Moses has the spotlight, why are the apparently superfluous elders of Israel, or secondary characters like Nadab and Abihu, mentioned at all? It must be because the stories were originally about them, Moses being added only later, in order to beef up the clout of the story. The telltale clue is that one pre-Moses story survives in nearly its original form. In Exod. 5:15–19, it is not Moses and his doppelganger Aaron (himself a later interpolation intended to inject priestly interests into what must at first have been solo Moses stories) who fearlessly confront Pharaoh, but rather the unnamed foremen of the Israelite slaves. Moses and Aaron are anxiously waiting out in the hall: "Well, what did he say?"[32] In the same way, Bultmann surmised that the mention of the disciples' practice, when it is ostensibly Jesus who is attacked, tips us off that the original target of the legalists' wrath was not Jesus but the early Christian community who fabricated the tale.

No one would criticize a set of theoretical categories like Burton Mack's because reality may turn out to be a bit more messy. An "ideal type" such as he is proposing is intended as a sort of dictionary definition, or a set of coordinates. Mack does not claim to have definitively mapped the landscape of early Christianities. He only means to indicate the kind of thing that must have been going on in order to give rise to the literary materials we have learned to distinguish in the New Testament. Thus what I say here is not intended to refute him, only to remind us that the reality was less cut-and-dried than any theoretical model makes it look. So I see a good bit of possible overlap between those groups Mack calls the Community of Israel, the Q Community, and the Synagogue Reform Movement.

NOTES

1. F. Gerald Downing, *Cynics and Christian Origins* (Edinburgh: T. & T. Clark, 1992), pp. 146–47.

2. Gerd Theissen, *Sociology of Early Palestinian Christianity*, trans. John Bowden (Philadelphia: Fortress Press, 1978), pp. 10–15.

3. It has often been objected that the Christian itinerants in view must be distinguished from Cynics because of the gospel prohibition of the very items the Cynics allowed themselves: cloak, pouch, sandals, staff. But given the general similarity, this seems absurd, a case of the old stand-by apologetics device of "the differences are greater than the similarities." In fact, it ought to be obvious that the gospel prohibitions are themselves nitpicking attempts to distinguish Christian itinerants from their Cynic competitors, since the two were otherwise so similar as to be easily confused by the public.

4. Gerd Theissen, "The Wandering Radicals: Light Shed by the Sociology of Literature on the Early Transmission of Jesus Sayings," in *Social Reality and the Early Christians: Theology, Ethics, and the World of the New Testament*, trans. Margaret Kohl (Minneapolis: Fortress Press, 1992), pp. 33–59.

5. Gerd Theissen, *The Social Setting of Pauline Christianity: Essays on Corinth*, trans. John H. Schütz (Philadelphia: Fortress Press, 1982), pp. 28–35.

6. Dieter Georgi, *The Opponents of Paul in Second Corinthians*, trans. Harold Attridge et al. (Philadelphia: Fortress Press, 1986), p. 244.

7. Ernst Haenchen, *The Acts of the Apostles: A Commentary*, trans. Bernard Noble, Gerald Shinn, R. McL. Wilson (Philadelphia: Westminster Press, 1971), pp. 233–35. See also Robert L. Wilken, *The Myth of Christian Beginnings: History's Impact on Belief* (Garden City: Doubleday Anchor, 1972); Norman Cohn, *The Pursuit of the Millennium: Revolutionary Millenarians and Mystical Anarchists of the Middle Ages*, rev. ed. (New York: Oxford University Press, 1972), pp. 187–97.

8. Stevan L. Davies, *The Revolt of the Widows: The Social World of the Apocryphal Acts* (Carbondale: Southern Illinois University Press, 1980), p. 36.

9. Michael McFadden, *The Jesus Revolution* (New York: Harper & Row, 1972), pp. 89. Cf., also Glenn D. Kittler, *The Jesus Kids and their Leaders* (New York: Paperback Library, 1972), pp. 54, 180–81, 209.

10. McFadden, *The Jesus Revolution*, p. 173–74. Cf., Lowell D. Streiker, *The Jesus Trip* (New York: Abingdon Press, 1971), p. 38; Jack Sparks, *God's Forever Family* (Grand Rapids: Zondervan Publishing House, 1974), pp. 62–64.

11. Gerd Theissen, *The Miracle Stories of the Early Christian Tradition*, trans. Francis McDonagh (Philadelphia: Fortress Press, 1983), p. 171.

12. The same sort of frustrated retreat from missionizing to sour-grapes doomsaying can be observed quite clearly in the Nag Hammadi text The Book of Thomas the Contender.

13. John M. Allegro, *The Sacred Mushroom and the Cross* (New York: Bantam Books, 1971), pp. 100–101. One need not subscribe to Allegro's inferences about the connection of this epithet to a hypothetical Soma cult among early Christians to appreciate his linguistic contribution on the meaning of "Boanerges."

14. Anthony Tyrrell Hanson, "The Foundation of Truth: I Timothy 3:15," in *Studies in the Pastoral Epistles* (London: SPCK, 1968), pp. 5–20.

15. C. H. Dodd, *Historical Tradition in the Fourth Gospel* (New York: Cambridge University Press, 1963), pp. 413–20.

16. William Wrede, *The Messianic Secret*, trans. J. G. C. Greig (Altrincham: James Clarke, 1971).

17. John A. T. Robinson, "The Most Primitive Christology of All?" in *Twelve New Testament Studies*. Studies in Biblical Theology 34 (London: SCM Press, 1962), pp. 139–53.

18. Cohn, *Pursuit of the Millennium*, pp. 29–36.

19. Abdulaziz Abdulhussein Sachedina, *Islamic Messianism: The Idea of the Mahdi in Twelver Shi'ism* (Albany: State University of New York Press, 1981).

20. Ignaz Goldziher, *Introduction to Islamic Theology and Law*, trans. Andras Hamori and Ruth Hamori. Modern Classics in Near Eastern Studies (Princeton: Princeton University Press, 1981), p. 246.

21. There is a whole Valhalla of such Mahdis in Stephen Fuchs, *Rebellious Prophets: A Study of Messianic Movements in Indian Religions* (New York: Asia Publishing House, 1965).

22. Eisenman, "Maccabees, Zealots, Christians and Qumran."

23. Robert W. Funk and the Jesus Seminar, *The Acts of Jesus: The Search for the Authentic Deeds of Jesus* (San Francisco: HarperSanFrancisco, A Polebridge Press Book, 1998), p. 121.

24. Jacob L. Teicher, "The Dead Sea Scrolls—Documents of the Jewish-Christian Sect of Ebionites," *Journal of Jewish Studies* 2, no. 2: 67–99; "The Damascus Fragments and the Origin of the Jewish Christian Sect," *Journal of Jewish Studies* 2, no. 3: 115–43; "Jesus in the Habakkuk Scroll," *Journal of Jewish Studies* 3, no. 2: 53–55; "The Teaching of the Pre-Pauline Church in the Dead Sea Scrolls," *Journal of Jewish Studies* 3, no. 3: 111–18; "The Teaching of the Pre-Pauline Church in the Dead Sea Scrolls—II," *Journal of Jewish Studies* 3, no. 4: 139–50; "The Teaching of the Pre-Pauline Church in the Dead Sea Scrolls—III," *Journal of Jewish Studies* 4, no. 1: 1–13; "The Teaching of the Pre-Pauline Church in the Dead Sea Scrolls—IV," *Journal of Jewish Studies* 4, no. 2: 49–58; "The Teaching of the Pre-Pauline Church in the Dead Sea Scrolls—V," *Journal of Jewish Studies* 4, no. 3: 93–103; "The Teaching of the Pre-Pauline Church in the Dead Sea Scrolls—VI," *Journal of Jewish Studies* 4, no. 4: 139–53; "Jesus' Sayings in the Dead Sea Scrolls," *Journal of Jewish Studies* 5, no. 1: 38–40; "The Habakkuk Scroll," *Journal of Jewish Studies* 5, no. 1: 47–59. Though J. Randall Price, *Secrets of the Dead Sea Scrolls* (Eugene: Harvest House, 1996), p. 374, dismisses Teicher's along with Cecil

Roth's and G. R. Driver's theories as "long-refuted" and "laid to rest," this only means that those committed to a rival paradigm mounted some arguments, whether weak or strong, against their competitors and moved on.

25. In the gospels Jesus is sometimes called "the Nazarene," sometimes "the Nazorean," though no translations known to me reflect the difference. It is an important one, though, because "Nazorean" ("observer" or "guardian," i.e., of the Torah) seems clearly to denote a sect label, while "Nazarene" seems to embody a subsequent misunderstanding or redefinition. Christians could no longer imagine their Lord had himself been simply a "believer" like themselves, so they inferred that his famous epithet had denoted he had hailed from Nazareth.

26. Robert E. Van Voorst, *The Ascents of James: History and Theology of a Jewish-Christian Community*. SBL Dissertation Series 112 (Atlanta: Scholars Press, 1989), p. 64.

27. Paul J. Achtemeier, "Toward the Isolation of Pre-Markan Miracle Catenae," *Journal of Biblical Literature* 89 (1970): 265–91; "The Origin and Function of the Pre-Markan Miracle Catenae," *Journal of Biblical Literature* 91 (1972): 198–221.

28. Rudolf Bultmann, *The Gospel of John: A Commentary*, trans. G. R. Beasley-Murray, R. W. N. Hoare, J. K. Riches (Philadelphia: Westminster Press, 1971), pp. 6–7; Robert T. Fortna, *The Gospel of Signs: A Reconstruction of the Narrative Source Underlying the Fourth Gospel*. Society for New Testament Studies Monograph Series 11 (New York: Cambridge University Press, 1970); Fortna, *The Fourth Gospel and Its Predecessor: From Narrative Source to Present Gospel* (Philadelphia: Fortress Press, 1988).

29. L. E. Elliott-Binns, *Galilean Christianity* (Studies in Biblical Theology 16, Naperville: Alec R. Allenson, Inc., 1956), pp. 25, 34–35.

30. Richard Reitzenstein, *Hellenistic Mystery-Religions: Their Basic Ideas and Significance*, trans. John E. Steely. (Pittsburgh: Pickwick Press, 1978), p. 176 ff.

31. Rudolf Bultmann, *History of the Synoptic Tradition*, 2d ed., trans. John Marsh (New York: Harper & Row, 1968), pp. 16–19 ff.

32. Martin Noth, "Figures Alongside Moses," in *A History of Pentateuchal Traditions*, trans. Bernhard W. Anderson (Englewood Cliffs: Prentice-Hall, 1972), pp. 175–88.

Chapter 3
THE CHRIST CULTS

By choosing the terminology "Christ cults," Burton Mack means to differentiate those early movements that revered Jesus as the Christ from those that did not. For the Synagogue Reformers, the Q people, and the Community of Israel, Jesus need not have been the Messiah in any Jewish sense at all. If the Pillars and Heirs communities saw Jesus as the Messiah or the Messiah-elect, they saw the role in strictly nationalistic Jewish terms. But starting with his sixth category, Mack considers the communities for whom Jesus as a teacher (and even as a miracle worker) was of no importance at all, and who may not even have been aware of such a Jesus tradition. For them his role as a savior of one kind or another was pivotal. And the title "Christ" came to denote this. Outside of Palestine, this Greek equivalent of "messiah," i.e., Anointed One, rapidly became the proper name of a divine savior. After all, outside the Holy Land, and among Gentiles, traditional Judaism counted for little or was eclipsed by other religious traditions.

Mack is perhaps not quite clear about what would constitute a Christ cult. Or at least he seems to me to obscure some important distinctions between what would appear to be significantly different subtypes of Christ movements. I will subdivide his Christ cult category to pick up some of these differences.

THE JESUS MARTYR CULT

One might with equal justice call this group the "Other Sheepfold" (cf. John 10:16) or the "Son of God fearers." Here Mack tries to provide an environmental niche for Sam K. Williams's brilliant reconstruction of probably the earliest version of the atonement doctrine.[1] How did the death of Jesus ever come to be considered the remedy for the sins of the human race, especially in view of the terrific logical and moral difficulties attending the doctrine? There have been some dozen major attempts to explain how the cross saves, and why it is necessary at all. Why cannot God just forgive sinners and leave it at that?

Sam Williams, whose argument Mack capably summarizes, reasons that the earliest Jewish Jesus people had no thought of Jesus' crucifixion availing for anybody's sins. They were Jews; Judaism had always had perfectly adequate ways of dealing with sins, both moral and ceremonial. The idea of Jesus' death as a sacrifice must have first arisen when Jesus Jews, probably Hellenistic ones, were faced with the conundrum of Gentiles, pagans, wanting to be baptized into the Jesus movement. Forgiving their moral lapses was no problem: God had always been perfectly willing to bless righteous Gentiles so long as they kept to the basic short list of Noahic commandments (Genesis 9:4–6). He never expected them to trouble themselves to keep the special customs and rituals of Judaism, so he didn't hold it against them that they didn't. But there was a barrier. Gentiles could not enter into the worshipping community of Israel because they dared not draw near the Divine Presence reeking of ritual impurity. Ham sandwiches were nothing to condemn Gentiles to Hell over, but they did bar them from entering his courts with praise.

This is the same problem that kept great numbers of Gentiles on the margins of the Jewish synagogues all over the Mediterranean world. There was great interest in Judaism and its noble ethical monotheism. Many pagans liked that. But to become a member in good standing, there was the little matter of circumcision to be dealt with, that and some 612 other commandments. For Jews, none of this was a problem; they had been born into the culture that these commandments defined. The implicit cultural rules of any people are equally complex—and equally invisible to any member of that culture. But the thought of having to try to adopt the mores of a different culture is quite daunting. So few of these Gentiles actually took the step of full conversion. Most remained on the periphery, where they were welcome to attend synagogue and hear the scriptures read and preached. They were called the God-fearers, i.e., the pious Gentiles, the noble pagans. It was not biblical morality they quailed at; no, that is what attracted them. It was the *ritual* boundary that loomed above them like the Berlin Wall.

It was among such people that missionary Christianity made such terrific headway in the early decades. The not-quite-Jewish God-fearers greeted

Pauline preaching with great joy. Such a Torah-free gospel seemed ideally suited for them (and that's just what critics said it was: a watered-down, more marketable version that made conversion too cheap and only a halfway measure—the same way Hindu gurus look askance at Transcendental Meditation in the West, a McDonald's trivialization of the genuine article). Here was a way to embrace what they liked about Judaism, to consider themselves truly a part of Abraham's children, and yet without all those nuisance regulations! Jesus was important to them not so much as a teacher, but as their ticket into the House of Israel. Here's how it worked.

Hellenistic Jesus Jews thought back to their community's proud tradition of martyrdom, how old Eleazer (2 Macc. 6:18–31; 4 Macc. 5 and 6) and the seven brothers and their mother (2 Macc. 7; Heb. 11:35) had all yielded up their lives rather than renege on the Laws of God when pagan tyrants had tried to force them to do so. These saints had died not as a punishment for sin—God forbid!—but as witnesses to righteousness. But they knew that the sinner's death can mitigate his guilt before God, and they prayed to God with their last breaths that he might consider their righteous deaths an atonement, an expiation counted toward the sins of fellow Jews whose backsliding had invited these terrible persecutions (2 Macc. 7:37–38; 4 Macc. 6:27–29). It was the old "righteous remnant" ideology with which the sixth-century B.C.E. priestly aristocrats explained why it was they who had been deported and not the idolatrous populace whose sins had called forth the Babylonian conquerors in the first place (Isa. 53).

Well, come to think of it, Jesus had died for no sins of his own, perish the thought. So is it possible God was willing to accept his martyr death as an expiation for the accumulated ritual impurities and abominations of the unwashed, shrimp-eating pagans? Sure, that had to be it! "Otherwise Christ died to no purpose" (Gal. 2:21). So the difference Jesus made to the Godfearers was to let them into at least one form of Judaism, Hellenized Jesus Judaism, as full-fledged members.

(The Epistle to the Galatians seems to have been written to address such a group whose members later began to feel conscience pangs, to suspect that something so easily won could not be worth much. It was like wondering if you really deserved the job, or whether you got it because of racial preference quotas, especially if your colleagues assume the latter and don't bother hiding their contempt. You'd feel the need to prove yourself. That's one reason a number of Nation of Islam members abandon Farrakhan's faith once they learn about historic Islam: They want the real thing. And so the Galatians had after all decided to make it official and at least get circumcised.)

Jesus' martyr death had become a red carpet for Gentile God-fearers to take their place among the clans of Judah. "Once you were no people, but now you are God's people" (1 Pet. 2:10a). Burton Mack calls this form of faith in Jesus a Christ cult. But I beg to differ. There is nothing about the theory of Jesus' death rehabilitating the unclean heathen that depends on or follows from his being a messiah or a Christ. Nobody made Eleazer or the seven brothers Christs. Both the Jewish category of religious martyrs and the Greek category of the noble death of a hero on behalf of his homeland were good enough on their own. Calling such a martyr-hero the Messiah would only have confused the issue.

Thus I would place Sam Williams's reconstruction of the early atonement theology among Hellenistic mission-congregations who organized themselves into their own synagogues parallel to the Jewish synagogues they had previously attended. They could not have continued in the same synagogues unless they were run by Hellenistic Jesus Jews, which is always a possibility. But if we are to reckon with anything like the picture Acts gives of Jesus missions in the Hellenistic synagogues, cases, in other words, where the Jesus Jews were propagandists from outside, then we will have to envision schismatic rival Jesus synagogues forming alongside the parent bodies. And this is not because the traditional Jews had a crazed antipathy to Jesus as Acts depicts, but rather simply because unless the synagogue leaders themselves accepted the Jesus-atonement doctrine, they could not in good conscience allow the God-fearers more access than they had already given them. The God-fearers' own new belief did not make it so. In this case, in order to enjoy the new advantage Jesus' death had provided ("Through him we have gained access to this grace in which we stand. . . ." Rom. 5:2), the God-fearers would have to set up their own parallel synagogues, which we may imagine having a good deal of resemblance, not to today's Protestant fundamentalist "Jews for Jesus" organization, but rather to present-day Reform Judaism.

Such a community could very well have generated the Epistle of James, written in the name of a great Jewish-Christian authority, and full of mixed Jewish and popular Stoic maxims, and with but an obligatory tip of the hat to Jesus, who would really have made little substantive difference for such a group. We might wonder if it is also such a group that comes in for criticism in the Book of Revelation as "those who say they are Jews and are not, but are a synagogue of Satan" (2:9). They are imagined still to partake of their old heathen ways, eating meat sacrificed to idols and patronizing temple prostitutes ("priestitutes," we might call them), all on the assumption that once Jewish purity regulations go, the whole thing's gone. (The logic is familiar enough: If Jesus eats with sinners, then he must have become one of them!—Mark 2:15–17; Matt. 11:19.)

If this group of "Son of God fearers" does not really fit the "Christ cult" rubric, is it even to be classed as a separate Jesus movement? Possibly, but then again, it would be no surprise to find them sharing worship with Mack's Synagogue Reform movement, if we imagine the debates being conducted between the two types of synagogues rather than within a single congregation. The God-fearers would certainly have had the Greek education to create the pronouncement stories or *chreias*. They could have been the later Q communities, too, since even the earliest layer of Q as Mack divides it up (following Kloppenborg) already contains the saying "Not even in Israel have I found such faith!" (Matt. 8:10/Luke 7:9). The Roman centurion to whom Jesus refers is a model portrait of a Gentile God-fearer. And remember that the second-century satirist Lucian of Samosata called Jesus "the crucified sophist," implying Jesus was recalled as no less a philosopher for having also been revered as a martyr. A Q community with Gentile God-fearers as members would certainly have viewed it that way.

Nor is it difficult to imagine this Jesus martyr cult as one with, or overlapping, the Community of Israel, once we recall how both Samaritans and Galileans traditionally bore the stigma of being only marginally Jewish (like Herod the Great, a professing Jew, but really a no-good Idumean/Edomite). If they had internalized this southern Jewish scorn, they would have felt much like the "halfway covenant" God-fearers on Greek soil. They would have welcomed the new understanding of the death of Jesus, as Sam Williams describes it. They would have seen Jesus as "the Prophet like Moses," and Moses had once offered to have his own name erased from God's book if only it could save his semipaganized people (Exod. 32:32). They might have been able to accept the Jewish estimate of themselves if in the same moment they were provided with a way of removing that taint.

In fact, to view the Community of Israel as including a significant percentage of God-fearers from "Galilee of the Gentiles" (Matt. 4:9) would make it much easier to accept Mack's characterization of that group as rejoicing over a new or renewed sense of Israelite identity. We would have the missing piece of this particular puzzle. Mack had a good idea of what it would look like (the self-esteem business) but hadn't yet found it. Here it is.

If the Jesus martyr cult does not qualify as a Christ cult, what does? First we have to try to supply a couple more transitional forms in the fossil record of early Christian evolution. One of these, the *Gnostic Christ cult* of the Syrian apostles, will somewhat overlap the Q community and some of its later developments. The other, the *Kyrios Christos cult*, is barely mentioned by Mack, and he never really distinguishes it from what I am calling the martyr cult of Jesus. And yet it is one of the most important of all.

THE GNOSTIC CHRIST CULT

Walter Schmithals[2] noticed various puzzling inconsistencies in the several New Testament uses of the term "apostle," as well as certain patterns to those inconsistencies. In short, he began to suspect that either traditional New Testament scholars had confused various names and ideas that were originally distinct, or the ancient writers and editors of individual New Testament writings had. In short, he wound up totally dismantling and rebuilding the concept and history of the term "apostle." Schmithals systematically examined all the hitherto suggested possible origins of the Christian idea of the apostles and finally traced it down to Syrian Gnosticism.

On the one hand, Schmithals showed how, once you bracket a couple of mistranslations (Mark 6:30 refers back to 6:7 and should be translated "the ones sent out returned to Jesus," not "the apostles returned to Jesus") and textual corruptions (someone has added "whom he also named apostles" to Mark 3:14: "he appointed twelve"), Matthew, Mark, and John never refer to "the apostles," but only to "the Twelve," or, at most, "the twelve disciples." Even the Twelve, Schmithals argues, are a group of authorities originating in the early church that was subsequently read back into the time of Jesus in order to give them greater clout. But the idea of the apostolate was not even in view here. The picture of an official and exclusive college of twelve apostles emerges only in early catholic writings from about 125 C.E. onward, and this includes the two-part work Luke-Acts. Schmithals agrees with John Knox[3] that Luke-Acts in its present, canonical form, is a response to Marcion in the mid–second century. Marcion, like the evangelist Mark, had written off the Twelve as dunces who grossly misunderstood Jesus. He accepted Paul as the only genuine apostle: Why had Jesus appeared to him after the resurrection except to find someone who could succeed where the Twelve had failed, in grasping the truth of his gospel? Marcion compiled the Apostolicon, a canon consisting of a single gospel (probably an earlier, shorter version of our Luke) along with the ten epistles ascribed to Paul at the time (lacking 1 Timothy, 2 Timothy, and Titus, the so-called Pastoral Epistles, which were no doubt subsequently written against Marcion, attempting to create an orthodox "counter-Paul"). The success of this theological Sputnik, a distinctively Christian Testament, spurred the emerging Catholic Church to reply with its own New Testament canon, which included an expanded, "catholicized" Luke followed up by an Acts which co-opted Paul by pairing him with Peter and subordinating him to "the Twelve Apostles." The Twelve Apostles, then, are a later churchly construct, just like the notion of the apostolic succession of bishops. But at first the office of an apostle had entered Christian circles from a very different source. Both "apostle" and "Christ" had meant something quite different.

Schmithals went on to sketch the origin of the apostle idea in the circles of early, pre-Christian Gnosticism. Gnosticism was later assimilated with Christianity, giving us both Gnosticized Christianity (including the idea of Jesus as an incarnation of a heavenly Christ-being) and Christian Gnosticism (like that represented in many of the Nag Hammadi texts, where Jesus is portrayed as a Gnostic teacher on the model of Valentinus, Markos, or Simon Magus). But in Gnosticism, before it began to crossbreed with Christianity, the Christ was not identified with any particular historical figure, at least with none from the recent past. The Revealer/Redeemer was identified instead with some ancient figure (Seth, Adam, Enosh, Melchizedek, and so on), or with some personified abstraction (e.g., Dame Wisdom in Proverbs, Wisdom of Solomon, Sirach; Manda d'Haye, "Knowledge of the Life," in Mandaean scripture), who in turn was supposed to be symbolic of the Primordial Human, the ανθρωπος. Like Gayomard, the first human in Zoroastrian myth, or the androgynous Adam of rabbinical speculation, the Primordial Human contained the souls of all future men and women in itself.

The ανθρωπος was a being of pure spirit and light. But somewhere along the line it had plunged into the shadow-world of loathsome matter and has been held prisoner ever since, long ago having forgotten its true identity. It exists now only in the form of a myriad of divine sparks scattered throughout the material world. It can become self-aware again only insofar as individual human beings who happen to possess the spark can be awakened to that fact. The Gnostic Revealer is the Gnosis (divine self-knowledge) awakened within the Gnostic himself or herself. Thus the savior and the saved are one and the same, and we can speak of a "Redeemed Redeemer." For Gnostics, the Christ, the Son of Man, is the spiritual nature of the elect, the Gnostic elite. Think of the connection made in 1 John 2:27 between revealed knowledge and anointing: "The anointing which you received from him abides in you, and you have no need that anyone should teach you; as his anointing teaches you about everything, and is true. . . ." There is nothing about nationalistic Jewish messianism here; we are in a different world altogether, one in which Gnosticism's Christ existed as a Transcendental Aion or Spiritual Power. This Christ was buried in the material world and would rise as more and more of his sundered shards awakened and, in so doing, reassembled the severed Body of the Christ, the Primal Man.

If it seems to be strained special pleading to suggest that the term "Christ" could have meant something unconnected with Jewish messianism, one only need remind oneself that already in the Pauline Epistles, "Christ" is nothing but the surname of Jesus (or sometimes the pronomen). As Werner Kramer shows, there is not one single instance in the Pauline Epistles where "Christ" seems to or needs to be a reference to the Jewish messiah.[4] This is the basis for Lloyd Gaston's bold statement, "For Paul, Jesus is neither a new Moses nor the Messiah."[5] I am not suggesting Paul was implying anything particularly Gnostic in his usage of "Christ." All I mean is that he could use it without any hint of Jewish messianism, and so could others, who might have filled the term with a different significance altogether.

In the understanding of the Gnostic Christ cult, who would qualify as an apostle? An apostle would be anyone who awakened to his or her true Christ-identity and experienced the urgency to spread this word of salvation to the rest of the lost sheep. The Gnostic mystagogues like Simon Magus, Valentinus, and Markos apparently considered themselves the visible "incarnations" of the Christ. But their point was hardly that *they* were Christ and *you* were *not*. Just the opposite. "Everyone who is of the truth hears my voice" (John 18: 37). It was much the same later with the Sufi mystic al-Hallaj, tortured and killed for the blasphemy of *hullul*, claiming to be God incarnate. He went about proclaiming "I am the Truth!" "I am God!" all the while meaning that God was all there was, and that al-Hallaj had renounced the brazen illusion that he had any separate existence alongside God.[6] No, his whole point was not that he was God in some sense in which others were not, but that he was God simply because everyone is. He had just awakened to the truth and was telling others. His knowledge made him a Christ and an apostle of God, for the two, in Gnostic terms, are synonymous.

We need not go outside the parameters of Gnosticism to show that such a Christ concept is no mere construct of Schmithals. But it may be worth noting that, as at so many points, this Gnostic idea finds a striking parallel in Mahayana Buddhist thought. Just as each Gnostic mystagogue was himself the Christ, the only "incarnation" of Christ that made any difference, the Bodhisattvas were all believed to follow the same path as Prince Siddhartha once had, through countless reincarnations through the Ten *Bhumis* (stages) on the way to full Buddhahood. But they viewed Siddhartha Gotama not as Western scholars do, as the single historical Buddha and the founder of Buddhism, but rather as merely one of at least twenty-six past and future Buddhas, all of whom are the subjects of fabulous legend. It was not that the other Buddhas and Bodhisattvas were following in his footsteps; rather, Siddhartha Gotama had simply trodden the same path all Bodhisattvas tread. And each alike was a manifestation of the eternal Buddha-Nature.[7] Once one awakens to the fact of one's own Buddha-Nature, one becomes both redeemer and redeemed. Just as in Gnosticism.

To make Jesus a Gnostic Redeemer in some exclusive sense was a hard adjustment for Christian Gnostics to make, and many of them did not quite make it. Some made Jesus just one of the previous temporary manifestations of the Christ, and for some, Jesus had himself been more recently superseded by Simon Magus or Mani. (Again, this was the way Mahayana Buddhism incorporated Siddhartha Gotama into a larger framework, pointedly denying his uniqueness.) Some Gnostics allowed a certain priority to Jesus as the historically revealed Christ, but they were tempted toward Docetism, denying that in this case the Revealer had really touched down in human history. (Again, Mahayana Buddhists had done precisely the same thing, making the earthly appearances of all the Buddhas mere apparitions of the Nirmankya, the "Transformation Body," without physical substance.) But when Jesus was given some measure of centrality, it meant that he himself would be considered *the* Apostle, the one sent from the heavenly realm of light to enlighten poor mortals. His earthly lieutenants, commissioned to relay that message, were not considered "apostles." But where there was no attempt to focus the role of Christ and ανθρωπος exclusively in the individual person of Jesus, the several previous and subsequent preachers of the *gnosis* (γνωσις) all alike qualified as "apostles," sent ones. In this sense Mani and Muhammad could both call themselves "apostles."

Schmithals concludes that the Gnostic idea of the Christ-Apostle had been adopted by Paul along with various items of Gnostic theology and terminology, only he had tried to use such conceptuality to express a faith centered upon Jesus Christ. Many who knew the Gnostic gospel in something like its pristine form took exception to Paul's syncretism. In Corinth Paul ran afoul of "superapostles" (2 Cor. 11:5) who could, without any hint of inconsistency, say both "I am of Christ" (i.e., part of the Heavenly Adam-Christ) and "Jesus be damned!" (Compare 1 Cor. 1:12 with 1 Cor. 12:3.) To curse Jesus was to deny Paul's claim that Jesus was uniquely and exclusively the Christ. (Beside the Corinthian curse of Jesus we may place the Zen saying, "If you meet the Buddha on the road, kill him"—because the only real Buddha is the Buddha-Nature, the gnosis, inside you.) To these Corinthian Gnostics, the Jesus Paul offered them must have seemed a veritable antichrist, a usurper of the saving Christ-identity that all Gnostics had as their inalienable birthright and the key to their salvation.

And yet Paul still considers himself an apostle. He is still using the original Gnostic term, even though he has had to squeeze Jesus into the system. But whether Paul embraced the Syrian Gnosticism or not, Schmithals's researches would in any case delineate for us the basis of a pre-Jesus cult of the Christ, one in which the Christ had nothing in particular to do with Jesus the Nazorean. And eventually it could be found alongside some form of Hellenized Jesus movement, I would guess the Jesus martyr cult, in Corinth.

Earlier I mentioned Gerd Theissen's identification of the Corinthian superapostles as some of the itinerant Q preachers, Jesus-Cynics. Would Schmithals's identification of the superapostles contradict Theissen's? Not at all. If we look at Theissen's earlier discussion of the "itinerant charismatics" we see that Theissen perceives how the references these people made to the Son of Man, either as a personified threat of revenge, or as the heavenly authorizer of their preaching, seemed to function less as an appeal to a famous historical predecessor, Jesus the Nazorean, than as the invocation of an ideal counterpart to themselves.[8] The Son of Man was something like many scholars take John's "Beloved Disciple" to be: an idealization of the faithful disciple. I submit that here we are contemplating something very close to Schmithals's picture of a multitude of wandering "apostles" (both Theissen and Schmithals make their itinerants the same as the apostles of the Didache) who themselves embodied their Christ/Primal Man/Son of Man. Neither group's ministry presupposes a previous historical founder, a historical Jesus Christ. Both groups, then, were probably the same group.

And, further, I submit that only on this understanding of the Corinthian superapostles do we have any hope of doing justice to the striking fact that some of the factions viewed Cephas, Paul, and Apollos as on the same footing with Christ himself, much as the Empress Julia Domna is said to have kept a chapel adorned with statues of Jesus, Abraham, Orpheus, and Apollonius of Tyana, a veritable pantheon of "Ascended Masters."

How does the Theissen-Schmithals conception of wandering Gnostic apostles fit with that of the Q tradition stemming from the itinerants? Rather well, as a matter of fact. Helmut Koester had already tagged the sayings collection pregospel type as the seed for Gnosticism. The Q-like Gospel of Thomas was certainly a favorite of Valentinian Gnostics and Manicheans, because they believed they had attained the gnosis required to "find the meaning" of these "secret sayings" and thus escape death.

How would there ever have been enough continuity, or even similarity, between a Gnostic Christ cult and any type of Jesus movement for the two of them to wind up cheek by jowl in the same meetings, as in Corinth? Or, to ask a related question, how would the sayings of the Divine Wisdom/Heavenly Christ have attracted the name "Jesus" for a character in pronouncement stories? The major consideration here is that sometimes the primordial Revealer figure in pre-Christian Gnosticism, as Schmithals shows, was an abstract personification like "Wisdom" or "Knowledge of the Life" or "The Anointing/Anointed." Might "Jesus," which means "salvation," have been originally such a personification?

The Gospel of Matthew, though in its present form it obviously assumes a historical Jesus, draws attention to the theological character, implicitly the titular character, of the name "Jesus." "You shall call his name Jesus, for he shall save his people from their sins" (1:21). Only two verses later, Matthew grafts into his narrative a text from Isaiah, "and his name shall be called Emmanuel." If we did not take for granted that the baby will be named Jesus, we would be surprised to discover the holy child is not henceforth called "Emmanuel Christ," or some such. But the parallel between the two divine namings, one mandated by an angel, the other by a prophecy, further underlines the symbolic theological significance of the name Jesus. That "Jesus" might once have been a title of a god, only later concretized into the personal name of a historical founder of Christianity, was sometimes argued by Arthur Drews[9] and other advocates of the Christ-Myth theory. But the argument was little heeded since it seemed to have little going for it but the bare possibility. However, I would suggest that Schmithals's parallels with Gnostic personifications of the principle or knowledge of salvation give the theory real credibility. I am not trying to say that there was a single origin of the Christian savior Jesus Christ, and that origin is pure myth; rather, I am saying that there may indeed have been such a myth, and that if so, it eventually flowed together with other Jesus images, some one of which may actually have been based on a historical Jesus the Nazorean. The old Christ-Myth theorists took for granted a single-root origin theory, just as orthodoxy did; it just chose a different candidate for the root.

By far the strongest piece of evidence for an early use of "Jesus" for a mythic figure is the so-called Kenosis hymn quoted in Phil. 2:6–11. M. Couchoud[10] long ago pointed out a startling detail never even mentioned in the great number of exegetical studies of the passage. What he was alone in noticing was the fact that the hymn has the exalted Christ being rewarded for his humiliation by the bestowal of the name of "Jesus." "Therefore he was highly exalted and given the *name* that is above every *name*, that at the *name Jesus* every knee should bow and every tongue confess that *Jesus* Christ is Lord, to the glory of God the Father." Exegetes universally take for granted that the "name that is above every name" is the title *Kyrios*, "Lord." But *Kyrios* is not a name. "Jesus," on the other hand, is.

The sense of the passage is also evident from the appositive parallelism between the two members, "at the name Jesus every knee should bow" and "every tongue should confess that Jesus Christ is Lord." Specifically, bowing the knee at the name of Jesus on the one hand, and swearing fealty to him, on the other, are equivalent. Neither reading fits conventional orthodoxy very well; for a man already named Jesus to receive the title *Kyrios* would suggest Adoptionism, but for the heavenly Christ subsequently to receive the name Jesus implies something even stranger, namely that the form of the salvation myth presupposed in the Philippians hymn fragment did not feature an earthy figure named Jesus. Rather, this name was a subsequent honor. Here is a fossil of an early belief according to which a heavenly entity (perhaps already called Christ, like the Valentinian Christ-Aion) subsequently received the cult name Jesus. In all this there is no historical Jesus the Nazorean. Nor, as Couchoud pointed out, could there be, since all the gospel tales of the wandering Jesus are at once revealed as later fabrications, taking for granted the naming of the savior as Jesus and reading it back anachronistically into his period of earthly servitude. (Is it possible, we might speculate, that the savior's name originally had been Emmanuel, attested in the christological fossil Matt.1:21?)

And eventually, Jesus, the martyred sophist whose death gave Gentiles access to the true Judaism, might have been identified with Jesus Christ the exalted Aion.

THE KYRIOS CHRISTOS CULT

The ancient Mediterranean world was hip-deep in religions centering on the death and resurrection of a savior god. Usually these religions and their rites measured the yearly renewal of nature. The imagery of death and resurrection might symbolize the withering of vegetation in autumn and winter and its restoration in spring and summer. Or it might stand for the waning of daylight till the Winter Solstice and its gradual waxing thereafter. Or perhaps the planting (death and burial) of the seed and its sprouting (resurrection). All were variations on the one theme. But the myths of each such god supplied the motivation for the fate and triumph of the savior, one that made sense in the native context.

One of the oldest we know of, the myth of Aleyan Baal, had the warrior god venture battle with the death monster Mot, who devoured him. His consort Anath bewailed his death and determined to enter the netherworld to bring her lover forth again. She did. And, thus raised from the dead, he took the divine throne beside his father El as Lord ("Baal") of gods and mortals. Dumuzi, or Tammuz, was his Babylonian counterpart. He, too, died and went to the netherworld, from whence his lover Ishtar rescued him, dying and rising herself in the process! Both these divine pairs were notoriously worshipped in Israel, much to the distress of certain prophets like Zechariah (12:11) and Ezekiel (8:14). The Song of Songs is most naturally interpreted as the liturgies of Ishtar and Tammuz.[11]

Osiris of Egypt, an ancient divine king who taught agriculture to the Egyptians, was betrayed and murdered by his brother Set (the desert god). Isis his queen bewailed the death and went forth, accompanied by her attendant maidens, to weep and to search for the body. Once she found it, she managed to revive Osiris in a kind of double resurrection. Osiris himself entered into the netherworld as its supreme judge and ruler, but not until he had fathered upon Isis a son, Horus/Harpocrates, his own earthly reincarnation, who grew up to take revenge on the wicked Set.[12]

Attis was a Phrygian godling, either the son or the lover (or both) of the cave goddess Cybele. One day he betrayed her, marrying a mortal princess. Cybele appeared at the event like the witch at Sleeping Beauty's birthday party and scattered the guests. Attis fled and, in remorse, castrated himself and bled to death. Cybele wept and contrived to raise him from the dead. Adonis betrayed Aphrodite, who sent a vicious boar to gore him to death, but she thought better of it and revived him. On Crete, Dionysus suffered the same fate and lived again.

In the Orphic myth, Dionysus, in his avatar as Zagreus the Hunter, had been dismembered and eaten by the Titans. Zeus wiped them out and consumed the heart of baby Zagreus, giving rebirth to him as the more familiar

Dionysus of Thebes. Mithras died on the shortest day of each year but was reborn on the next day.

Originally all these myths were rehearsed yearly in rites intended either simply to commemorate the change of seasons, or actually to facilitate the change.[13] At this stage of the game, either the king/chief himself was put to death and "raised" in the form of his replacement, a new consort for the queen, or else some hapless surrogate died as "king for a day," whereupon the real king returned to the throne. Eventually a new inner significance to the myth was "discovered" by those elite few for whom the external ceremonies of an agricultural faith were spiritually unsatisfying. These people were familiar with the ritual passage from childhood to adulthood, at which time they had been educated about the rituals of their people and declared qualified to participate in them.[14] Was it possible, they wondered, to undergo yet a further stage of initiation to a still greater maturity? Was it possible for them to participate in the god's death and resurrection in some way, and so gain an immortality like his? Sure it was. And the Mystery Religions were born. The Mystery cult would be the esoteric core of a traditional religion whose exoteric concern was the renewal of the fields in the spring. But with the great social dislocations of the Hellenistic age, great numbers of people found themselves trying desperately to maintain an ethnic/cultural identity in a radically pluralistic society. Like the Jews, who created the synagogue as a magnet for maintaining their heritage, other groups transplanted their religions, too. Only since they did not share a social religion with their new neighbors, the old exoteric dimension fell away, leaving only the esoteric Mystery rituals. These were still kept secret from outsiders, but anyone could become an insider, seeking redemption and finding it in their sanctuaries. And anyone could be a member of more than one such religion at the same time, probably suspecting that the various deities, all so similar to one another, were different names for the same savior.

The rituals which allowed the initiate to share the saving trial and triumph of the savior varied greatly from cult to cult, but most had this element in one form or another. For instance, whereas Mithras had wrestled a great bull to the death (originally symbolizing the supplanting of Taurus by Perseus in the precession of the equinox[15]), the Mithraist undertook a ritual shower in the blood of a disemboweled bull (or, if he couldn't afford it, a lamb). Brother, have you been washed in the blood?

Attis converts would be swept up in the ecstatic dances of the devotees and would feel impelled to castrate themselves, pitching the severed testicles into the lap of a silver image of Cybele. General mourning, both for Attis and for their own manhood, would follow, culminating in the ritual interment of an effigy of Attis crucified to a pine trunk. On the third day he would be proclaimed gloriously risen from the dead: "Rejoice, you of the mystery! For your god is saved! And we, too, shall be saved!"(Firmicus Maternus, *The Error of the Pagan Religions* 22:1)[16] Similarly, burial inscriptions for the believers in Osiris assure the mourner, "As Osiris died, so has N_ died; and, as Osiris rose, so shall N_ rise." His devotees would partake of a sacramental meal of bread and beer, symbolizing his body and blood. The (female) Maenads of Dionysus would recapitulate the death of their Lord by going into a frenzy and ripping live animals limb from limb.

Entering into these rituals initiated the process of an inner spiritual transformation into a divine and immortal being. Worship was often ecstatic, as the gathered congregation worshipped their *Kyrios*, their Lord, or their *Kuria*, e.g., the Lady Isis or the *Magna Mater*. We have copies of written invitations to sacramental banquets held in honor of the gods, e.g., "Pray come dine with me today at the table of the *Kyrios* Serapis." It is no doubt such social events which trouble Paul in 1 Cor. 8–11, where he admits that indeed "there are gods aplenty and *Kyrioi* aplenty" (1 Cor. 8:5), but seems to need to remind his Corinthian Christians that "for us there is but one God, the Father, who created all things, and one *Kyrios*, through whom all things were made" (1 Cor. 8:6).[17]

It is very hard not to see extensive and basic similarities between these religions and the Christian religion. But somehow Christian scholars have managed not to see it, and this, one must suspect, for dogmatic reasons. Those without such a Maginot Line mentality have less trouble. John Cuthbert Lawson[18] recounted how, during a trip to rural Greece, he attended a Passion play. As the local man acting the role of Jesus was being brought into the tomb on Good Friday evening, Lawson was startled at the manifest anxiety of an old peasant woman beside him. On his asking the cause of her distress, she blurted out, "Of course I am anxious; for if Christ does not rise to-morrow, we shall have no corn this year." One might venture to say that it was her very lack of scholarly sophistication that enabled her to recognize what was really going on.

Conservative scholars and Christian apologists have never been at ease even recognizing the existence of the dying-and-rising-god motif in non-Christian Mystery Religions, much less their relevance for Christian origins. As apologists are merely spin doctors for a theological party line, their aloofness to the dying-and-rising-god mytheme is scarcely surprising and one is hard-pressed to take their disdain seriously, any more than the ancient attempts of Justin Martyr and Firmicus Maternus to discount such parallels as Satanic counterfeits. But in recent days, the apologists' agenda has received significant support from an unexpected quarter. Jonathan Z. Smith, in his *Encyclopedia of Religion* article on "Dying and Rising Gods,"[19] seeks to explode the whole notion, dismissing it as an artificial composite of elements taken out of context from the religions in question. Since Smith, an excellent scholar, is rightly taken quite seriously, I believe a slight digression is called for: In my view, Smith's criticisms are unjustified, and to ignore the importance of the dying-and-rising-god mytheme in Christian origins is to short-circuit our understanding of that subject.

Smith's first error is his failure, as I see it, to grasp the point of an "ideal type," a basic textbook definition/description of some phenomenon under study. As Bryan Wilson has reminded us, an ideal type is not some box into which all the various instances of the phenomenon must fit snugly. If that were the nature of an ideal type, the scholar would find himself either trimming away the rough edges of particular phenomena (in this case redeemer myths) or building his box big enough and shapeless enough to fit everything in. And since this would serve no descriptive purpose, Smith, finding that there are significant differences between the so-called dying-and-rising-god myths, abandons any hope of a genuine dying-and-rising-god paradigm. For Smith, the various myths of Osiris, Attis, Adonis, and the others, do not all conform to type exactly; thus they are not sufficiently alike to fit into the same box—so let's throw out the box! Without everything in common, Smith sees nothing in common. But an ideal type, as Wilson points out, is rather a yardstick abstracted from the admittedly diverse phenomena; it represents a general family resemblance without demanding or implying any absolute or comprehensive conformity. Indeed the very lack of conformity to the type by a particular myth would serve as a promising point of departure for understanding its special uniqueness.

Smith's error is the same as that of Raymond Brown, who dismisses the truckload of comparative religion parallels to the miraculous birth of Jesus:[20] This one is not strictly speaking a virgin birth, since the god fathered the child on a married woman. That one involved physical intercourse with the deity, not overshadowing by the Holy Spirit, and so on. But, we have to ask, how close does a parallel have to be to count as a parallel? Does the divine mother have to be named Mary? Does the divine child have to be named Jesus? Here is the old "difference without a distinction" fallacy.

Smith tries to pry apart the dying-and-rising-god mytheme into disparate components: disappearing and reappearing deities on the one hand and dying (but not rising) gods on the other. Adonis, he says, is never said to have died, but only to have undertaken a bicoastal lifestyle, splitting the year cohabiting with two romantic rivals for his attention, Aphrodite and Persephone. To winter with the latter, he must head south to Hades. And then, with the flowers, he pops up again in the spring, headed for Aphrodite's place. This makes him not dead? But what does it mean to say someone has descended to the netherworld of the dead? Enkidu did not deem it quite so casual a commute "to Hell and back" as Smith apparently does: "He led me away to the palace of Irkalla, the Queen of Darkness, to the house from which none who enters ever returns, down the road from which there is no coming back." One goes there in the embrace of the Grim Reaper. Similarly, Pausanias: "About the death of Theseus there are many inconsistent legends, for example that he was tied up in the Netherworld until Herakles should bring him back to life" (*Guide to Greece*, I:17:4).[21] Thus, to abide in the netherworld was to be dead, even if not for good.

Aleyan Baal's supposed death and resurrection does not pass muster for Smith because the saga's text has big holes in it "at the crucial points." Mischievous scholars may like to fill them in with the model of the resurrected god, but Smith calls it an argument from silence. Is it? Even on Smith's own reading, the text actually does say that "Baal is reported to have died" after descending to the netherworld. There he is indeed said to be "as dead." Anath recovers his corpse and buries it. Later El sees in a dream that Baal yet lives. After another gap Baal is depicted in battle. What is missing here? Smith seems to infer that in the missing lines it would have been discovered that Baal was the victim of a premature burial, that the report of his demise, like that of Mark Twain, was premature. But does Smith have any particular reason to be sure about this? And even if his guess were to prove correct, it seems evident that a premature burial and a rescue via disinterment is simply a variant version of the death and resurrection, not an alternative to it.

Baal's variant self in Syria, Hadad, is even less prone to dying according to Smith, since Hadad is said merely to sink into a bog for seven years. He is only sick, but when he reemerges, languishing nature renews itself. Smith says, "There is no suggestion of death and resurrection." Nor any hint of ritual reenactment of the myth. What about Zech. 12:11, where we read of inconsolable ritual mourning for Hadad-Rimmon? What are they mourning? And even if one were to deny that seven years of submersion in a bog is as good as death, the difference would be, again, only a slight variation in a natural range for a widespread mytheme. We see the same variation among the Nag Hammadi and other Gnostic texts as to whether the Redeemer took on flesh. Some deny he did. Others say he did, but it was a condescension, and the savior stripped off the flesh shroud as soon as he got the chance. Some ascribe to Jesus a fleshly body but an apparent death. Others have a real death, but only of the human Jesus, once the Christ-Spirit has fled back to heaven. They are all equivalent versions, simply reflecting different choices from the menu of options. The differences are within a definite range along the paradigmatic axis, and the story is the same along the syntagmic axis.

Osiris, Smith admits, is said even in very ancient records to have been dismembered, reassembled by Isis, and rejuvenated (physically; he fathered Horus on Isis). But Smith seizes upon the fact that Osiris reigned henceforth in the realm of the dead. This is not a return to earthly life, hence no resurrection. But then we might as well deny that Jesus is depicted as dying and rising since he reigns henceforth at the right hand of God in Heaven as the judge of the dead, like Osiris. And the long constancy of the mytheme of Osiris' resurrection, from the ancient pyramid inscriptions to the Hellenistic period, ought to make us wary of Smith's constant suspicion that later, Christian-era mentions of the resurrections of Attis, Adonis, and the rest must be late innovations. In the case of Osiris, which we can trace, it is certainly no innovation. Why must Smith assume it was a late addition to the myth in the other cases? It is a fundamental methodological error to assume that a phenomenon must have arisen just shortly before its earliest attestation.

What about Tammuz, an ancient god so familiar to ancient Israelites that his name graces one month of the Jewish calendar to this day? Smith describes how scholars early speculated from the fragmentary Tammuz texts that he had been depicted as dying and rising, though the evidence was touch-and-go. Subsequently more textual evidence turned up, vindicating their theories. Shouldn't this tell Smith something? Namely that the dying-and-rising-god paradigm may not be a bad heuristic device to interpret fragmentary texts? But he quibbles even here. Though the new material makes unambiguously clear that Tammuz's lover Ishtar herself also dies and rises, Smith passes this by virtually without remark and picks the nit that Tammuz is "baaled out" of death for only half the year while someone else takes his place. Death, Smith remarks, is inexorable: The most Tammuz could get is a six-month furlough. The case is parallel to that of Adonis, but there Smith denied a half-year return from Hades meant a real death, whereas with Tammuz he says it means no real resurrection.

Why does Smith adopt the program of Christian apologists? I suspect it is part of his root-and-branch campaign to undo the theories of his great predecessor James Frazer. In any case, the viability of the dying-and-rising-god mytheme seems to me unimpeached. There was such a myth making the rounds. It is extant in several versions as we have seen. But did it exist before Jesus and Christianity? If not, may the borrowing have been in the opposite direction? Might the Hellenistic Mystery Religions have borrowed the resurrection doctrine from increasingly successful Christianity, as a top-rated sitcom swiftly garners imitations? Smith zeroes in on Attis, where the explicit mentions of his resurrection date from the Christian era (though they are not there mentioned *as* innovations). But as Vermaseren[22] has shown, we do in fact possess a pre-Christian pottery depiction of Attis dancing, the traditional posture of his resurrection. But it seems to me that the definitive proof that the resurrection of the Mystery Religion saviors preceded Christianity is the fact that ancient Christian apologists did not deny it! Only so would they have reached into left field for the desperate argument that Satan *foreknew* the resurrection of Jesus and counterfeited it *in advance*, so as to prejudice pagans against Christianity as a mere imitative also-ran, which is just what they thought of it.

Richard Reitzenstein and Wilhelm Bousset were two scholars who did manage to grasp the relevance of these ancient faiths for the study of early Christianity. Their conclusion was a simple and seemingly inevitable one: Once it reached Hellenistic soil, the story of Jesus attracted to itself a number of mythic motifs that were common to the syncretic religious mood of the era. Indeed, as people familiar with the other Mystery Religions came to embrace the Christian savior, it would have been practically impossible for them not to have clothed him in all the accouterments of his fellow *Kyrioi*. If Jesus was a savior, then he was *ipso facto* to be considered a dying and rising god whose immortality one might share through participatory sacraments.

And we need not only think of the situation as Reitzenstein did, still picturing a process of individuals breaking with their old religion and accepting a new one instead. Since the Mystery Religions made no exclusive claim and begrudged no member his simultaneous membership in a parallel Mystery, we must assume that many early Christian "converts" had no thought of abandoning Mithras, Isis, Attis, or Dionysus. Why should they? Hippolytus, in his *Refutation of All Heresies* (V, 7:3-10:2), preserves the Naasene exegesis of a still-earlier Hymn to Attis, in which we hear that the Savior Jesus is the same as Adam or Attis or Adonis. (Adam and Eve had long been identified with Attis and Cybele, presupposing the ancient version of the Eden myth echoed in the Nag Hammadi texts, that Eve was a goddess and created Adam.)

What was the danger Paul perceived in the case that one "weaker in faith" should observe another Christian partaking in an idol's feast (1 Cor. chapter 8)? The "weaker brother," Paul implies, is "weak" precisely for not grasping that Christ is the only real *Kyrios*. He would take the example of a Christian eating from the communion table of Serapis as confirming his assumption that a Christian might be a Mithraist or anything else he had the fees to pay for. What Paul apparently faced in Corinth in these instances was the practice by Christians of what Max Müller called "kathenotheism," the worship of several gods, but one at a time. With the gates thus open, we would be amazed not to find a free flow of older "pagan" myths and rituals into Christianity. For instance, it is only under the influence of Dionysus (whether in Greece or even in Palestine) that Jesus bequeaths his devotees a sacrament of his body, the body of grain, and his blood, the blood of the grape (Mark 14:22–25). Only so is he the True Vine giving vitality to his branches (John 15:1–6), does he turn water into wine (John 2:1–10). As Jesus the Corn King, his winnowing fan is in his hand (Matt. 3:12), he is slain while the wood is still green (Luke 23:31), yields up his life like the planted seed (John 12:24), and is buried in a garden (John 19:41).

And we need not think that these Corinthians had fallen from some purer version of Christian orthodox truth. No, what we are seeing in the Pauline warnings against syncretic kathenotheism is the *beginning* of the process to exclude the other faiths as rivals and counterfeits of Christianity. But the barn door was, as usual, shut after the horse had got out (or rather, in!).

A Christ religion modeled after a Mystery cult *is* a Mystery cult, a Christ cult worthy of the name. This is what we expect Burton Mack to be talking about when he talks about Christ cults. As we have seen, he usually has in mind what I have called the Jesus martyr cult. But I do see a connection. We have to presuppose some sort of previous Jesus or Christ religion already in operation before elements of other religions could become mixed with it. And in Europe and Asia, the best candidate would probably be the Jesus martyr cult. It was already based on Jesus' suffering and death. There is, however, no reason to think the Jesus martyr cult involved any sort of belief in the resurrection of Jesus, except maybe in the future, at the general resurrection.

In fact, the resurrection idea does not seem to fit the martyrdom idea. What kind of a martyrdom is it when someone dies only for a couple of days? This is not exactly the supreme sacrifice. Thus the resurrection has its natural home in a different context, that of the myth of the dying and rising god who represents the temporary death of nature, soon to be revoked. Accordingly, in this context, the designation "Christ" probably denoted "the Risen One," reflecting Isis' anointing of the dead Osiris, which restored him to life. It is this anointing which we glimpse behind Mark 16:1 and 14:8.

The priority of the Jesus martyr cult to the *Kyrios* Christos cult means, in sociological terms, that the first Jesus adherents were the God-fearers on the margins of the synagogue, and that those attracted from the ranks of the Mysteries represented a second wave, as the Gentilized Jesus-Judaism became available to a broader section of the populace than would ever have given the time of day to synagogue Judaism. The Mystery cultists became God-fearers on the margin of the Jesus martyr cult, just as the Jesus martyr cultists had once been positioned at the border of Judaism. Then the Mystery cultists joined, reasoning that they weren't losing an old savior, they were only adding a new one. Jesus Adonis, Jesus Dionysus was the result.

What would the Gnostic Christ cult have made of the *Kyrios* Christos cult? The point of the two systems was not really the same, but the Gnostic Christ cult and the *Kyrios* Christos cult could no doubt coexist peacefully. Both envisioned "Christ" as a divine being appearing on earth for the salvation of mortals. Both understood salvation in terms of divinization. Both enjoyed secret rites. And both may easily have practiced baptism, the Gnostics seeing it as a spiritual resurrection in much the same terms as the *Kyrios* Christians.

NOTES

1. Sam K. Williams, *Jesus' Death as Saving Event: The Background and Origin of a Concept*. Harvard Dissertations in Religion 2 (Missoula: Scholars Press, 1975).

2. Walter Schmithals, *The Office of Apostle in the Early Church*, trans. John E. Steely (New York: Abingdon Press, 1969).

3. John Knox, *Marcion and the New Testament: An Essay in the Early History of the Canon* (Chicago: University of Chicago Press, 1942).

4. Werner Kramer, *Christ, Lord, Son of God*, trans. Brian Hardy. Studies in Biblical Theology no. 50 (Naperville: Alec R. Allenson, 1966), pp. 212–13.

5. Lloyd Gaston, *Paul and the Torah* (Vancouver: University of British Columbia Press, 1987), p. 33.

6. Louis Massignon, *Hallaj: Mystic and Martyr*, trans. Herbert Mason. Mythos series. Bollingen Series 48. Abridged ed. (Princeton: Princeton University Press, 1994); for a shorter account of Al-Hallaj and his martyrdom, see Robert Payne, *The Holy Sword: The Story of Islam from Muhammad to the Present* (New York: Collier Books, 1962), pp. 199–221.

7. Har Dayal, *The Bodhisattva Doctrine in Buddhist Sanskrit Literature* (New York: Samuel Weiser, 1978); Leslie S. Kawamura, ed., *The Bodhisattva Doctrine in Buddhism*. Papers presented at the Calgary Buddhism Conference, September 18–21, 1978 (Waterloo, Ont.: Wilfrid Laurier University Press, 1981).

8. Theissen, *Sociology of Early Palestinian Christianity*, pp. 27–29.

9. Arthur Drews, *The Christ Myth*, trans. C. Delisle Burns. 3rd ed. Westminster College-Oxford: Classics in the Study of Religion (Amherst, N.Y.: Prometheus Books, 1998), pp. 51–63.

10. M. Couchoud, "The Historicity of Jesus: A Reply to Alfred Loisy," *The Hibbert Journal* 37, no. 2 (1938): 193–214.

11. Marvin H. Pope, *Song of Songs: A New Translation with Introduction and Commentary*. Anchor Bible. 7C (Garden City: Doubleday, 1977), pp. 145–51.

12. Roland Guy Bonnel and Vincent Arieh Tobin, "Christ and Osiris: A Comparative Study," in *Pharaonic Egypt: The Bible and Christianity*, ed. Sarah Israelis-Groll (Jerusalem: Avigness Press, 1985), pp. 1–29.

13. Mircea Eliade, *The Sacred and the Profane: The Nature of Religion*, trans. Willard R. Trask (New York: Harcourt, Brace & World, 1959), pp. 68–115.

14. Arnold Van Gennep, *The Rites of Passage*, trans. Monika B. Vizedom and Gabrielle L. Caffee (Chicago: University of Chicago Press, 1960).

15. David Ulansey, *The Origins of the Mithraic Mysteries: Cosmology and Salvation in the Ancient World* (New York: Oxford University Press, 1991).

16. Firmicus Maternus, *The Error of the Pagan Religions*, trans. Clarence A. Forbes. Ancient Christian Writers no. 37 (New York: Paulist Press, 1970), p. 93.

17. Wilhelm Bousset, *Kyrios Christos: A History of the Belief in Christ from the Beginnings of Christianity to Irenaeus,* trans. John E. Steely (New York: Abingdon Press, 1970), pp. 119–52.

18. John Cuthbert Lawson, *Modern Greek Folklore and Ancient Greek Religion: A Study in Survivals* (Cambridge: Cambridge University Press, 1910), p. 573.

19. Jonathan Z. Smith, "Dying and Rising Gods," in *The Encyclopedia of Religion.*, vol. 4, ed. Mircea Eliade (New York: Macmillan Publishing Company: 1987) pp. 521–27.

20. Raymond E. Brown, *The Birth of the Messiah: A Commentary on the Infancy Narratives in Matthew and Luke* (Garden City: Doubleday, 1977), p. 523.

21. Pausarias, *Guide to Greece*, trans. Peter Levi (Baltimore: Penguin Classics, 1971), p. 48.

22. Maarten J. Vermaseren, *Cybele and Attis: The Myth and the Cult*, trans. A. M. H. Lemmers (London: Thames and Hudson, 1977), pp. 119–24.

Chapter 4
MESSIAH AS MISHNAH

ANACHRONISMS AS EVIDENCE

The gospels portray Jesus as in conflict with "the Jews," "the scribes," and "the Pharisees," implying Jesus was opposed to a monolithic "normative" Judaism—which did not yet exist! The Mishnah, a codification of scribal commentary on the Torah compiled by the end of the second century C.E., shows that the process of consolidating various earlier schools of thought and local, even idiosyncratic traditions of observance (e.g., in a certain village, of a certain scribe and his disciples) was a later endeavor beginning at Yavneh, the northern Palestinian town where, with Roman permission, Rabbi Johannon ben-Zakkai organized a new, postwar Sanhedrin empowered to adjudicate purely religious issues.

When, as recently, some Christian scholars[1] have been willing to notice these anachronisms, it is difficult enough for them to draw the unwelcome inference that the gospel traditions in question must be removed from consideration as evidence for the historical Jesus. But, as R. G. Collingwood pointed out,[2] what seemed to be evidence for A and proved not to be, may yet become evidence for B. Anachronisms do not tell us about the time in which they are ostensibly set, but they do provide evidence about the period from which they actually stem. And as yet New Testament scholars have not shown much interest in asking what the gospel anachronisms *do* tell about their own *Sitz-im-Leben*. I will suggest that infosar as the various gospel data reflect post-Jesus formative Judaism they provide new clues as to the dynamics of the formation of the gospel tradition itself.[3] To see this, we need to pursue what parallels we can find between gospel pericopae and their Mishnaic counterparts, between the emerging gospel sayings tradition and the emerging rabbinical sayings tradition.

Let me not risk seeming to minimize the pioneering efforts of such great Christian scholars as Rudolf Bultmann, Joachim Jeremias, Harald Riesenfeld, and Birger Gerhardsson.[4] These all understood very definitely that the rabbinic/scribal tradition might provide important clues for understanding the sayings traditions compiled in the Synoptic gospels. But these treatments all suffered from the retrojection (then universal) of Mishnaic Judaism into the first century C.E. Bultmann took controversy stories from the Mishnah as analogies and exemplars for the apophthegms (or pronouncement stories, "paradigms," or *chreia*) of the first-century Christian movement, some of these even going back substantially to the historical Jesus. Bultmann, though quite skeptical as to the authenticity of many of these *hadith* of Jesus, did not doubt that they were authentically Jewish (Christian) and early.

Riesenfeld, Gerhardsson, A. H. McNeile,[5] and others sought to combat Bultmann's more rigorous skepticism by appealing instead to the imagined mode of oral transmission of rabbinical tradition. Pointing to the acclamation of a disciple of Yohannan ben Zakkai as "a plastered cistern that loses not a drop" (*Aboth* ii. 8), these apologists objected that Bultmann had neglected to take into account the high standards of faithful oral tradition prevailing among the rabbis. If the rabbinical analogy held good, they reasoned, then the form critic must reckon with a process whereby "Rabbi Jesus" carefully drilled his pupils "line upon line, measure upon measure" until they got it right. And if they did, then the gospels ought to be a good deal more accurate than Bultmann supposed.

Never mind that Riesenfeld and Gerhardsson begged the central question of whether, even granting the existence of such a circle of faithful memorizers, the gospels' traditions stemmed from them or from anyone and everyone else who thought they remembered what Jesus had said or, by God, what he *ought* to have said! A more serious problem was that, as I have anticipated, Riesenfeld, Gerhardsson, and the others simply took for granted the Jewish apologetic view that normative Yavneh Judaism existed and prevailed already in first-century Palestine, not to mention the blithe confidence of precritical Jewish scholars/apologists that all the business about verbatim transmission and attribution of this saying to that sage was literally true. Whereas these Christian scholar-apologists thought to call to their aid Jewish scholars with an analogous apologetic agenda to dislodge the skepticism of Bultmannian form-critics, imagine their surprise when Jacob Neusner realized that Bultmannian "skepticism" provided just the methodological rigor that Mishnaic criticism had been lacking! Neusner showed that when the compilers/redactors of the Mishnah (and other charter documents of rabbinic Judaism) took the trouble to ascribe a particular saying to a particular name, there had to be some reason in terms of the redactional aims of the document itself.[6] Neusner was no longer willing to assume that such attributions meant much diachronically (actually going back in history to Rabbi X); no, instead they must derive their meaning synchronically: as it were, two-dimensionally along the picture plane of the particular document. Not that Neusner was concerned with the fallout of all this rethinking for Christian apologetics, but it is worth noting that the goal of Riesenfeld and the others in citing rabbinical parallels is completely subverted by Neusner's higher-critical revolution.

And yet I wonder: Perhaps we ought to take the premise of Riesenfeld and Gerhardsson seriously, but as corrected by Neusner. That is, maybe we *can* understand the Jesus tradition through the categories of rabbinic tradition, but as corrected by Neusner's explanation of how the latter actually worked. In speculating along these lines, we will be going beyond Neusner's own published reflections on the gospel traditions,[7] informative as they are. If any light can thus be shed, we will have only further corroborated the worth of Neusner's paradigm by showing its utility for "predicting" results in adjacent fields of study. (Similarly, it would be of great interest to see Islamic specialists apply Neusner's methodological insights to the study of the *hadith* of the Prophet Muhammad.)

Neusner reasons that the gospels exist to promote the distinctiveness of a unique individual, Jesus Christ, and thus have a hagiographic focus impossible for the Jewish tradition, which sought instead to exemplify righteous behavior *for* the community (in general) as well as *by* the (authority of the) community (of sages). Jewish tradition neither depended upon nor fostered individualism. Thus, while material existed for rabbinical gospels—i.e., wise sayings, miracle tales, and martyrdoms—none was ever written. There is no gospel of Hanina ben-Dosa or of Eliezer, though there might have been. The exaltation of the heroic individual authority of Jesus is somewhat analogous to that accorded in some circles to Eliezer. But, Neusner reasons, Christians simply elected to go much further, and along a different way, to exalt the unique charismatic authority of an exceptional individual whose name would come to have the same authority in Christianity as the Torah would in emerging normative Judaism.

GEMEINDETHEOLOGIE

Gerhardsson and Riesenfeld sought, by appealing to the idea of a rabbi's disciple as "like a plastered cistern that loses not a drop," to overthrow Bultmann's idea of a community of anonymous sages and prophets whose words became appropriated for Jesus, but the implication of factoring in Neusner's work may be to reinforce Bultmann after all! If we explore the possible analogy between the gospel sayings tradition and the Mishnaic tradition as Neusner has explained it, we would have to reckon with a piously anonymous gospel tradition whereby the prophets or sages from whom the traditions stemmed would, perhaps ironically, not be remembered by name for their contributions (at least not at the subsequent stage of collection formation). In the emerging gospel tradition all such sayings would be attributed to "Jesus," who had in the Christian community become homologous in function to "Torah" (or "Moses" as metonymous for the Torah) in the Jewish community. In both cases, the rule would be much like that which Hermann Hesse attributed to his futuristic magisterium of scholars in *Magister Ludi/The Glass Bead Game*: "We moderns . . . do not even speak of major personalities until we encounter men who have gone beyond all original and idiosyncratic qualities to achieve the greatest possible integration into the generality, the greatest possible service to the superpersonal. If we look closely into the matter we shall see that the ancients had already perceived this ideal."[8] Hesse's narrator lists several examples, though the Mishnaic sages are not among them, perhaps because the character of the Mishnaic tradition was not sufficiently clear until Neusner's work.

Though Neusner is willing to take at face value Christian generalizations that the gospel pericopae function primarily to glorify Jesus as Messiah (or Son of God, and so on), this is a (Christian, christological) overgeneralization. In fact, New Testament critics know that much in the gospels does not attempt in the first instance simply to glorify Jesus. Form criticism shows how "useful" the various miracle, exorcism, and pronouncement stories were for governing and informing Christian conduct. For example, it looks like Mark drew upon miracle healing stories employed as evangelistic propaganda, not mere self-referential hagiography, while Matthew further recycled Mark's miracle stories, making them into lessons of faith and answered prayer.[9] Jesus himself is more the presupposition than the focus of the individual pericopae. Thus the gospels in large measure share the Mishnah's anonymous collective, communal authority. "Jesus" is a kind of authoritative fiction like "Moses our rabbi."

Granted, on the surface the gospels do seem to present us with the central authority of Jesus as a charismatic sage, but there may be both more and less than meets the eye here. The closest analogy in the Mishnah to the sort of "maverick Jesus versus the Establishment" opposition the gospel tradition presents us with is the opposition between Eliezer ben Hyrkanus (a Pharisee whose career spanned the destruction of the temple) and the assembled sages of Yavneh. This is true even to the point of the repeated miraculous vindication of Eliezer by signs and heavenly voices! His opinions are nonetheless rejected, the sage himself excommunicated. And God is displeased at the excommunication, first attempting to destroy Rabban Gamaliel, who presided at the excommunication, by a tidal wave, from which he is dissuaded, then killing him anyway in answer to Eliezer's prayers for vindication!

How can the Mishnah possibly record all this and yet still hold that Eliezer was in the wrong? Such stories would seem to flow most naturally from the disgruntled partisans of Eliezer, but they do not. The problem was not so much with the specific opinions of Eliezer, many of which were in fact accepted, and none of which was spoken ill of even when not accepted. Nor was Eliezer deemed a heretic or even wrong! Just the reverse! God himself agreed with him! The opposition is between the consensus of the sages and the "loose canons" of charismatic authority, of which Eliezer serves as a symbol. The opposition is that between dogmatic claims of individual figures (and their partisans) and the authority of the community. (Precisely the same cleft would open up in formative Islam between the *ijma* (consensus) of the *ulemma*, doctors of the law, and the inspired Alid Imams: Who had the authority to interpret the Koran? From this disagreement arose the split between Sunni and Shi'a Islam.)

This is also why we can never be sure if the Mishnah is accurately attributing the right opinion to the right sage. One story has Akiba falsely attribute Eliezer's sayings to others after his excommunication, so that either the sayings may be allowed to continue without being disqualified by association with the heretic, or they may win their way on their own merit, not riding the coattails of charismatic authority. New Testament critics are at home with the notion of anonymous individuals attributing their own sayings to Jesus (or their pseudepigraphical books to other ancient worthies) so as to lend them weight they would otherwise lack. But as Neusner shows, it is, ironically, just the opposite tactic that enhances the clout of a saying in the Mishnah, since the authority there is anonymous and communal (as of a timeless revelation self-evident to all, to all the sages anyway).

Thus also, when particular names are tagged on to sayings in the Mishnah, it is a function of dissent and disharmony. A name attached to a saying marks it as a deviant oddball view, literally the idea of a "heresy," the opinion of one who has drawn attention to himself by the effrontery of *choosing* for himself rather than bowing to the authority of the community. A particularly clear case is to be found in one of the two talmudic references to Christian halakhah, where Eliezer gets a reputation for heresy for having accepted the opinion of Jesus of Nazareth, told him by Jacob of Kefar-Sechania, to the effect that the offering of a prostitute to the temple treasury, though filthy lucre, can nonetheless be used to buy a toilet for the high priest! Here is the ultimate case of an individual attribution denoting heresy! The legal opinion was reasonable enough, but the "Jesus" tag placed it along a heretical trajectory, outside the authority of the community. To remain faithful to the community is to eschew the fruits, and thus the roots, of alien authority.

Sometimes, granted, a sage's words are simply cited in the Mishnah with the force of scripture. It can be assumed (as in the case of the Prophet Muhammad) that his example or opinion proceeds from a thorough imbuement of Torah and so may be trusted (1 Cor. 7:25: "I have no commandment from the Lord, but I give an opinion as one who by the mercy of the Lord is trustworthy"). Agehananda Bharati provides an Indian parallel, that of Sri Ramakrishna, who "told many a parable, either of his own making or out of local folklore, but they were certainly not Vedic, as he claimed. Quite often he preceded these tales with the words *bede ache*, 'it says in the Veda'; and I think the reason why even the most learned didn't object was that they tacitly granted him the status of a Veda-maker, a rishi, on a par with the original compilers of the Veda. They did this because they were satisfied with his statements about the [mystical] experiences he was having all the time."[10]

Does not such a focus on an individual, despite his saintliness, or rather *because* of his saintliness, run against the grain of the Mishnah's tendency toward collective anonymity? Actually not: This spotlighting is often because the sage's word must be harmonized with that of another sage or with a particular scripture passage, which is of course also named. The point is that the sage and his saying, as the individual scriptural book, are relevant *as* an individual contribution *only insofar as there is a problem assimilating it to the larger whole*. Once the harmonization is effected, it doesn't matter who said it and its irritating individuality is thankfully lost.

The story of Eliezer's excommunication itself, not a historical datum, is a piece of such after-the-fact Mishnaic harmonizing. It is Eliezer's standing as a charismatic authority in his own right "with whom the Law always agrees" that needs to be put down, not necessarily the specific opinions he held. And this urgency betrays the later perspective. The excommunication is a purely narrative symbol for the later adjustment of the authority predicated of him. It is thus exactly analogous to the flogging of Enoch-Metatron by the interpolating scribe of 3 Enoch, who meant by this means to discourage and rebuke excessive veneration (as it seemed to him) of the transfigured patriarch.[11]

PESHER AND PALIMPSEST

Once we understand that the secondary attribution of Christian prophets' and sages' sayings to Jesus caused their individual identities to be forever lost, as in the Mishnah, a number of seeming anomalies in the gospel tradition are seen to make new sense. For example, reams of learned discussion have wrestled with the numerous third-person "Son of Man" sayings attributed to Jesus in the gospels (e.g., "When the Son of Man comes, will he find faith on earth?"). Bultmann, H. E. Tödt, and Ferdinand Hahn[12] all argued that Jesus must have predicted the Son of Man as a distinct eschatological figure subsequent to himself. This conclusion created a number of theological shockwaves, but in turn it was jeopardized when Norman Perrin, Maurice Casey,

Geza Vermes, and others showed how Jesus could not have used "Son of Man" as an eschatological title, that it must have arisen via Christian messianic midrash, applying Psalm 110, Dan. 7, and Zech. 12 to Jesus after the fact.[13] This only made the whole mess more inexplicable: If the Son of Man sayings began as Christian Christology, why do Christian texts depict Jesus seeming to refer to the Son of Man as someone else? Gerd Theissen solved the problem (to my satisfaction) by means of a simple Copernican turning around of the telescope: The Son of Man sayings were first understood as spoken *about* Jesus but *not* spoken *by* Jesus.[14] Theissen turned Bultmann's solution on its head: It was the "he" that represented Jesus, not the "I." The "I" represented the (now-anonymous) prophet. The Mishnaic-like tendency to subsume all individual sagely pronouncements to the anonymous collectivity would have resulted in the incongruity that "Son of Man" predictions originally spoken about Jesus by Christians were put into the mouth of Jesus himself!

It would also explain the fact, often noted by apologists for an "implicit Christology" hinted at by Jesus himself, that Jesus did not preface his sayings as the prophets did ("Thus saith the Lord . . .") but rather with "Amen, I say unto you. . . ."[15] What we ought to see is that it is the very attribution of the saying to Jesus by the evangelists/tradents that is the equivalent of the ancient prophet attributing his oracle to the Lord. The attributer is the evangelist; it is the evangelist, not Jesus, who is the counterpart of the old-time prophet. Jesus does not correspond to the prophet but to the Lord! The ascription of the saying to Jesus allows the dubious authority of some early Christian sage to recede behind the Torah-like clout of the Lord Jesus. The "implicit Christology" in such sayings is not that of Jesus himself, but rather of the gospel writer. As Neusner says, the ascriptions must be understood synchronically within the document—i.e., redactionally, not diachronically, going back to Jesus.

Note also the gospel sayings that "whoever hears you hears me" (Luke 10:16) and that "a disciple is not greater than his teacher" (Matt. 10:24–25), both of which would surely encourage, even demand, the humble deferral of any original voice to the larger "Jesus" tradition. "Jesus" is the community, as the "Body of Christ" (1 Cor. 12:12 ff; Eph. 4:16–17) language also ought to suggest.

As to the fear of individual authorities fragmenting the house of Israel, we have the same concern in 1 Corinthians where the several advocacies of Paul, Cephas, Apollos, and Christos threaten to split the community. 1 Cor. 1:12–13 seeks to subsume all the rest to Christ. The Apocryphal Acts, despite superficial orthodox redaction, preserve the earlier picture[16] in which all the apostles were alike Christs, cut from the same cloth, each "Acts" serving as the "gospel," the divine "aretalogy" for a wonder-working apostle who was the real object of faith. Even the later orthodox Christological patina which has, at a crucial point in each Acts, the ascended Jesus appear onstage *in the physical likeness of the eponymous apostle* (whether Paul,

Peter, Andrew, John, or Thomas) gives away the original game. But eventually Jesus Christ won out over his exactly identical "Thomas twins."

As Neusner intimates, however, with the rise of saint worship[17] this Christocentric monolithicity broke apart again. Calvin understood the phenomenon in exactly these terms when he tried to suppress the Catholic saints in favor of Jesus, who had become lost in the shuffle and relegated to the also-ran status of a minor saintlet.[18] Just as in 1 Corinthians!

It is striking that one of the two places in the Talmud where a point of Christian halakhah is adduced (by a "philosopher," i.e., a heretic), the source is not specifically Jesus, but rather the *"evangelion,"* the gospel itself which speaks in the first person! "I, the Gospel, am not come to take away from the Law of Moses but to add to the Law of Moses" (*Shabbat* 116 a, b). Thus a Jewish account easily recognizes and depicts the gospels not as accounts of a unique individual but as a body of sayings/rulings analogous to the Mishnah.

But might it not still be feasible to remove the anachronistic "Jesus versus normative Judaism" framework of the controversy stories and to make them derivative of actual exchanges of opinions between Jesus and individual scribal colleagues as some have suggested?[19] With Burton Mack, there is a multitude of reasons to say no.

First, these exchanges teem with anachronisms. Jesus expresses the opinion that a vow to dedicate one's property to the temple at the expense of one's family forces a breach of the commandment to honor one's parents, and hence, presumably, ought to be considered null and void (Mark 7:11–13). Leaving aside the telling fact that Jesus is made here to cite the Greek Septuagint of Isaiah to prove his point (the Hebrew would not really apply), there is another problem with the saying going back to Jesus, namely that the same opinion was remembered as an innovation, and a controversial one, credited to Eliezer ben Hyrkanus, a later figure. It is thus not an issue that had been hotly debated before Eliezer's time, e.g., by Jesus and the scribes. The Mishnah has no trouble having Eliezer adopt a view first propounded by Jesus when it wants to. Had Eliezer adopted the view from Jesus' halakhah, this would have provided all the more reason for the sages to disdain it, but of this we hear nothing. Such a double attribution is reminiscent of the double attribution of the conquest of Jerusalem first to Joshua and then to David. It seems more likely that the attribution to the earlier figure is the later version.

Ironically, it does *not* work the other way around, as some apologists have suggested, that a question of halakhah is rightly attributed to Jesus (at least to some pre-70 C.E. Christian) if it deals with a point of temple protocol, like the coin in the fish's mouth (Matt. 17:24–27, a blatant legend in any case), which treats of the two-drachma temple-upkeep tax. Likewise the "Render unto Caesar" pericope (Mark 12:14–17), which does give the impression of being a serious bit of casuistical halakhah. Paying a Roman tax entails no religious compromise since, as the very presence of money changers at the temple demonstrated, such "filthy lucre" (because of its idolatrous inscription) could not be rendered to God (i.e., could not be used to purchase sacrificial animals) anyway. Apologists for the saying going back to Jesus or the pre-70 church maintain that such niceties (as they view them) would be utterly moot after the fall of the temple. But no, for the simple reason that Pharisees like Eliezer assumed the temple would soon be rebuilt (as perhaps it *was* under Bar Kochba![20]), whereupon all these questions would be anything but moot. Of course it was in exactly analogous circumstances that the Holiness Code, Ezekiel, and the Levitical Codes were drawn up—*sans* temple!

Second, we cannot overlook numerous gospel caricatures of Judaism: Jesus is shown combating opinions (or appealing to opinions in a circumstantial *ad hominem* fashion) which are unattested for Judaism. As to the case of healing on the Sabbath, repeatedly broached in all four gospels, the scribes prohibited only the professional practice of a medical doctor for pay in routine cases. Emergency relief was licit, as was, explicitly, "healing by word" as Jesus did. If anyone ever gave him grief over the issue, we never hear of them in Jewish tradition.

In the course of these gospel controversies, Jesus assumes that his opponents routinely have enough compassion to allow someone to extricate a poor beast from a pit into which it has fallen, Sabbath or no Sabbath (Luke 14:1–6; Matt. 12:10–14). But we hear only the rule, both among the rabbis and at Qumran, that the animal must be fed there and rescued later.

Regarding leniency on the Sabbath in general, Jesus is made to quote a commonplace: "The Sabbath was made for man, not man for the Sabbath" (Mark 2:27). Compare another rabbinic version: "The Sabbath is delivered unto you, not you unto it." Even the Sabbath day's journey, far from being a bit of restrictive legalism, was instead a piece of casuistical *stretching* of the law. Granted, no one expresses such an opinion unless there are stricter opinions to oppose with it. But the point is that to focus on Jesus as if the sentiment were unique to him is to caricature Judaism.

Christian scholars and feminists still do the same thing, quoting Rabbi Eliezer out of context to the effect that a man should sooner teach his daughter harlotry than teach her the Torah. In fact he was saying it would be better not to instruct her in the Torah if one's goal (as his opponent suggested) was to allow her to circumvent the proof of adultery. If that's the goal, then you might as well go the whole way and teach her the tricks of the prostitution trade while you're at it! Was Jesus a feminist, the scribes misogynists? No.

Third, in the gospel controversy stories the criterion to settle halakhic questions is simply the authority of Jesus.[21] Jews, obviously, would not accept such an argument, so these stories cannot stem from actual Jesus-scribes debates: "Because I *say* so, is why!" They presuppose a Christian context. Even when it is not just Jesus pulling rank—"The Son of Man is Lord of the Sabbath," (Mark 2:28)—or a rule miracle,[22] the logic often sounds good only to a cheering Christian doting on Jesus: "Which is legal on the Sabbath: to do good or to do evil? To save life or to kill?" One might as well imagine the ancient Ammonites' and Moabites' assessments of the Israelite theory of their national origins (Gen. 19:30–38)!

We must note, however, that these controversy stories do sometimes employ scripture prooftexts, attributing them to Jesus (Mark 2:25–26). Does this attest an earlier stage in which Jesus himself offered such arguments to fellow scribes, as sparring sages do in Mishnaic anecdotes? No, they can be shown to be secondary. First, again, Mark 7's prooftext only works in the Septuagint version of Isa. 29:13. Second, the issues there (washing pots, and so on, when returning from the *Gentile* marketplace) arose only in Diaspora Judaism. Third, Matthew has added some prooftexts to Mark (Matt. 12:5–7), indicating the trend to add them.

While one might have expected a natural shift from scripture quoted by Jesus to Jesus himself being appealed to as the prooftext, as Christology grew higher, what we see reflected in the evidence is rather a debate over traditional legal and purity rules within the Christian community (e.g., Rom. 14–15). "The Pharisees in the Gospel who oppose Jesus are, for Luke, prototypes of the traditionally Jewish Christians (like the Pharisees in Acts 15:5). . . . Jesus' Pharisaic opponents in the Gospel *stand for* traditionally Jewish Christians."[23] Since both sides of intra-Christian debates appealed to Jesus (even to supposed sayings of his) other criteria must be sought out to settle the point. Thus Matthew augmented Jesus by the citation of scripture. Likewise, à la Matt. 5:17–19, to have Jesus quoting scripture was to have Jesus endorse scripture over against Christian antinomians.

Fourth, as Bultmann pointed out long ago, the fasting, hand-washing, and Sabbath gleaning stories all have the scribes/Pharisees objecting not to Jesus' own practice but that of his disciples. Thus the issues arose in the early church, not in the time of Jesus.

Then there are broader historical anachronisms that seem to vitiate the gospel controversy stories: Generally, the whole depiction of Jesus preaching in "their" synagogues is anachronistic, as there were virtually no synagogue buildings in Galilee till late in the first century C.E., after the flight of Pharisees and other refugees into Galilee (which "hated the Torah"). Luke even has a Gentile (a clone of his Cornelius character, Acts 10:1–4 ff.) praised for bankrolling the construction of one synagogue (Luke 7:5). Apologist Howard Clark Kee admits this one is a problem but maintains that, otherwise, in gospel usage "synagogue" need mean no more than "assembly" or "meeting."[24] But is this really likely? Mark has Jesus stop preaching "in" synagogues because the crowds are too large, presumably, for *buildings* to accommodate. Hence he *assembles* the Jews at the seaside or in the open. Would there be "rulers of the synagogue," like Jairus, if the synagogue in view were merely someone's porch? How about "the seat of Moses" and the "chief seats in the synagogues" in Matt. 23:2, 6? Just someone's Naugahyde couch?

Neusner speaks of the tendency to anachronistically "rabbinize" earlier figures, as some traditions do Eliezer. This surely has happened with Jesus when he is called Rabbi, a term we are told only *began* to take on titular use sometime in the second century C.E.[25] Matthew tells his "scribes discipled unto the kingdom of heaven" (Matt. 13:52) not to be called Rabbi or Abba (Matt. 23:8–9), since these are the practices of a competitor type of Judaism. Thus the titles are *already established*, and Matthew wants his people to *break with convention* on the point!

Many doubt that the gospels' picture of Pharisees in Galilee is any more to be trusted than their picture of rabbis or synagogues there in Jesus' day, since the spirituality of Pharisaism was the extension of temple purity codes into the *surrounding* homes of the pious. Jerusalem, then, was where the action was for the Pharisees, not Galilee. The picture of Jesus debating with scribes and Pharisees coming down from Jerusalem seems to me to reflect scenarios like Gal. 2:12 and Acts 15:1. The implied *Sitz-im-Leben* would seem to be something like that described in Rom. 14–15, Acts 15, in Antioch as described in Gal. 2, and in the critical interface implied in the Matthean redaction (Matt. 15:17) of Mark 7:19 (on the point of whether Jesus declared all foods clean). Thus these materials seem to me not to represent a stage along the trajectory of Hellenistic Jewish Christianity emerging from Hellenistic Judaism, but rather the interstice between Hellenistic Jewish/Judaizing Christianity and Gentile God-fearer, ex-Jewish antinomian Christianity (including those Paul mentions, 1 Cor. 7:18, as wanting to undo circumcision).

These conflicts also might easily belong to Galilee, after Judaic Christians took refuge there following the fall of Jerusalem. We may picture a take-charge attitude on the part of the expatriate Jerusalemites toward the indigenous half-Christians much like that which alienated the people of the land and the Samaritans from Ezra and Nehemiah some centuries before. In chapter 2, I discussed the possibility of Galilean Christianity being identical with what Burton Mack calls the Community of Israel, one of the early Jesus movements. Now let me return to the question of Christianity in Galilee, to ask what may have happened after the exodus of the Pillars/Heirs community from Jerusalem and their arrival in Galilee.

GALILEAN CHRISTIANITY

Catholic and other traditionalist scholars try mightily to explain away Epiphanius' evidence that the Nazorean and Ebionite sectarians of Kochaba and

Nazareth considered themselves direct heirs of the Jerusalem church.[26] It should be recognized that this evidence extends Walter Bauer's thesis[27] *into Palestine itself*: The earliest "Christianity" attested for this important region, as with Edessa, Egypt, and Asia Minor, is what would later be branded "heretical." It changes nothing to point out that the Ebionites and others were preceded by James and the Heirs and thus must have been later, heretical Johnny-come-latelys, since this is just the point at issue: What besides Eusebian apologetics would allow us to assume[28] that hypothetical earlier Galilean Jewish Christians like James must have been "orthodox"?

I suggest we might be able to trace three major stages of so-called Galilean Christianity. First, we can envision a period of renown of Jesus as a charismatic hasid in Galilee. Geza Vermes shows how well many of the most characteristic gospel images of Jesus comport with the tradition of charismatic Galilean holy men. Vermes may jump the gun and prematurely historicize when he derives an hasidic Jesus from gospel legends, which match hasidic legends of Honi the Circle-Drawer and Hanina ben-Dosa. All we can say, though all we need to here, is that Jesus was *remembered* in such ways, denoting his veneration in popular hasidic circles.

It may be from this period that the Mark 6:1–3a pericope stems, where Jesus gets a warm reception as a local boy made good. The original point seems to be to provide a credential list for the relatives (i.e., the dynasty) of Jesus, whom parasitic writers tell us had clout in the Galilean villages of Kochaba and Nazareth. However, we must bear in mind that if the group of Jesus' relatives fled into Galilee or the Decapolis only after 70 C.E., the Markan story may reflect the attempt to fabricate or reinforce a Galilean pedigree for them once they got there.

Second, we may suspect a period of unsuccessful Christocentric preaching in Galilee by missionaries from Jerusalem. This reaction is reflected in Mark's addition of 6:3b–6, where the admiration of Jesus' countrymen is arbitrarily turned to hostility. What we must suspect here is an "updating" of the original version à la Gen. 27:40b, which contradicts 27:40a. Isaac's testament to Esau originally legitimated the Jewish annexation of Edom in David's time, but afterward, when Edom broke away (cf., Ps. 2:1-3), this had to be taken into account, "predicted," too, no matter what a mess it made of the original story. So now the Galilean "rejection" of Jesus had to be prefigured in Jesus' own time (exactly equivalent to Mark 4:12; 1 Pet. 2:7–8).

From this period also stem the prophetic denunciations of the Galilean towns Capernaum, Chorazin, and Bethsaida (Matt. 11: 20–24; cf., Rev. 3:14–22: These tirades are not from the historical Jesus but rather from flame-eyed prophets zealous for his reputation, speaking in his name) preserved in Q, in the later Christianizing stratum.[29] Wherein lay their sin? Had the Galileans turned away from an earlier faith in Jesus? No, they had never had any christological faith in Jesus as the Christ in the first place. For them he was a charismatic hasid, and that was enough: an exorcist, lax in legal exactitude, on familiar terms with God. But this was by no means enough for later orthodoxies (cf., the attacks of Epiphanius of Salamis and others on Nazoreans and Ebionites for their "merely human" Christologies and continued observance of the Torah).

As we have already seen in chapter 2, Mark has set 8:27–30 conspicuously in the villages around Caesarea Philippi, taking the occasion to blast what he deemed inadequate local Christologies of the region: Jesus as Elijah (and not a particularly eschatological one, either);[30] Jesus as an Israelite prophet; Jesus as John the Baptist raised from the dead. No one in Caesarea Philippi had it so much as occur to him that Jesus might be the Messiah! Why? Again, because northerners would have had no desire for a Davidic Messiah. Instead they looked for a Prophet like Moses, or the returned Elijah, or a Messiah ben-Joseph. And such a faith would have been considered as heretical by Jerusalem Christianity as the Samaritans and the "Torah-hating Galileans" were by the scribes of Jerusalem. I am guessing that Mark 8:27–30 reflects such antipathy to nonchristological Jesus movements in Galilee.

The third period of Galilean Christianity would have been that inaugurated by the Hegira of the Jerusalem church to Pella in the Decapolis in response to the oracle of Jesus, mentioned by Eusebius, of the impending fall of the city. Originally this oracle will have been the repeated doom cry of the Nietzschean mad prophet Jesus ben Ananias (Josephus, *Jewish War* 6:300-309), tipped off to Jerusalem's doom by the death of James the Just, the bulwark whose removal meant trouble.[31] The oracle would then have been rewritten and attributed to the Christian Jesus in the form of the Little Apocalypse of Mark 13.

As various scholars have surmised,[32] the flight to Pella tradition is meant to function as a foundation legend for the Pella church, trying to claim for itself the status of the Jerusalem church of the Pillars in exile. Right enough, but this needn't mean they did not actually make such an exodus. Perhaps only the oracular direction to do so need have been the legendary element. Otherwise it might have seemed like cowardice. I see the Pella tradition as legitimizing a Christian version of the Yavneh reconsolidation, with Simeon bar-Cleophas taking the place of Johannon ben Zakkai as presiding over the new Sanhedrin. This is why both are likened to Moses, another "exodus" lawgiver, both of them dying at age 120 as Moses did. I think the commission of Simeon Cephas, confused with Simeon bar-Cleophas in early Christian tradition,[33] as the foundation stone with the keys of halakhic binding and loosing stems from the election of Simeon bar-Cleophas to the throne vacated by his brother James the Just. It is in this third period that we might most probably look for the *Sitz-im-Leben* of the evolution of the gospel sayings tradition along parallel lines with that of the Mishnah, stemming from the Yavneh Sanhedrin.

I am tempted to regard the story of the Gadarene Demoniac (Mark

5:1–20) as yet another competing foundation legend for the Pella (Decapolis) church/sanhedrin, one aimed at meeting the objection of it being on pagan soil, as well as possibly defending their Jewish credentials against charges of cowardice in the Roman War. It also establishes an alternate link of apostolic succession. First, note that in this tale Jesus himself ordains a non-Twelve disciple to go and preach his glories (Mark 5:19) some forty years before the arrival of the Jerusalem interlopers in Galilee and the Decapolis in the wake of the fall of Jerusalem.[34] Second, Jesus drives out the Romans symbolically in the form of unclean swine possessed of (Roman) "legions" of demons.[35] Thus, Jesus had sanctified and fumigated the Decapolis area, so that it was not unclean territory (overcoming one of the major problems Brandon saw with the historicity of the Pella Hegira tradition, that Pella in the Decapolis would have been an improbable place for pious Jews to seek shelter.)[36] The Mark 5:1–20 story, as I read it, evidences embarassment over just that point.

So Jerusalem-style Christianity got into Galilee the same way and at more or less the same time Jerusalem-style Pharisaism did, after the fall of Jerusalem in 70 C.E. And it is there that we may imagine the gospel sayings tradition to have formed by the gradual assimilation of earlier Christian sayings to the collective and anonymous authority of "Jesus Christ" in much the same way and for much the same reason that the rabbinical sayings tradition was forming elsewhere at pretty much the same time: to provide each religious community with a retrojected pedigree seeming mythically to stem from "of old, from ancient days." Given the uncertain present in the aftermath of the fall of Jerusalem, the stability of the future would be anchored in a newly secured sacred past. And in that sacred time were located the authority, on the one hand, of the Mishnah, and on the other, of the Messiah.

NOTES

1. E.g., Burton L. Mack, *A Myth of Innocence: Mark and Christian Origins* (Minneapolis: Fortress Press, 1991), pp. 193–207.

2. R. G. Collingwood, *The Idea of History* (New York: Oxford University Press, Galaxy Books, 1957). "The enlargement of historical knowledge comes about mainly through finding how to use as evidence this or that kind of perceived fact which historians have hitherto thought useless to them" (p. 247).

3. Collingwood, *The Idea of History*: ". . . the assertions they make are by no means uniformly trustworthy, and indeed are to be judged more as propaganda than as statements of fact. Yet this gives them an historical value of their own; for propaganda, too, has its history" (p. 260).

4. Rudolf Bultmann, *History of the Synoptic Tradition* (New York: Harper & Row, 1972); Joachim Jeremias, *The Parables of Jesus* (New York: Scribners, 1954); Harald Riesenfeld, *The Gospel Tradition and its Beginnings: A Study in the Limits of 'Formgeschichte'*

(London: A. R. Mowbray, 1957); *The Gospel Tradition* (Philadelphia: Fortress Press, 1970); Birger Gerhardsson, *Memory and Manuscript: Oral Tradition and Written Tradition in Rabbinic Judaism and Early Christianity* (Uppsala and Lund: C. W. K. Gleerup, 1964); Gerhardsson, *The Origins of the Gospel Tradition* (Philadelphia: Fortress Press, 1979).

5. A. H. McNeile, *An Introduction to the Study of the New Testament*, 2d ed., revised by C. S. C. Williams (London: Oxford University Press, 1953), p. 54.

6. E.g., Jacob Neusner, *In Search of Talmudic Biography: The Problem of the Attributed Saying*. Brown Judaic Studies 70 (Chico, Calif.: Scholars Press, 1984).

7. E.g., Jacob Neusner, *Why No Gospels in Talmudic Judaism?* Brown Judaic Studies 135 (Atlanta: Scholars Press, 1988).

8. Hermann Hesse, *Magister Ludi/The Glass Bead Game*, trans. Richard and Clara Winston (New York: Bantam Books, 1970), p. 4.

9. Heinz Joachim Held, "Matthew as Interpreter of the Miracle Stories," in *Tradition and Interpretation in Matthew's Gospel,* ed. Günther Bornkamm, Gerhard Barth, and Heinz Joachim Held (London: SCM Press, 1963), pp. 275–95.

10. Agehananda Bharati, *The Light at the Center: Context and Pretext of Modern Mysticism* (Santa Barbara: Ross-Erikson, 1982), p. 78.

11. Hugo Odeberg, ed. and trans., *3 Enoch, or The Hebrew Book of Enoch* (1928; reprint, New York: Ktav Publishing House, 1973), pp. 85–86.

12. Bultmann, *History of the Synoptic Tradition*, pp. 122, 136–37; *Jesus and the Word* (New York: Scribners, 1958), pp. 30–31; H. E. Tödt, *The Son of Man in the Synoptic Tradition* (Philadelphia: Westminster Press, 1965), p. 295; Ferdinand Hahn, *The Titles of Jesus in Christology: Their History in Earliest Christianity* (New York: World, 1969), pp. 21–27.

13. Norman Perrin, *A Modern Pilgrimage in New Testament Christology* (Philadelphia: Fortress Press, 1974); Maurice Casey, *Son of Man: The Interpretation and Influence of Daniel 7* (London: SPCK, 1979); Geza Vermes, *Jesus the Jew: A Historian's Reading of the Gospels* (London: Fontana/Collins 1977), pp. 160–85.

14. Gerd Theissen, *Sociology of Early Palestinian Christianity*, pp. 24–30.

15. Joachim Jeremias, *New Testament Theology: The Proclamation of Jesus* (New York: Scribners, 1971), pp. 35–36.

16. Walter Schmithals, *The Office of Apostle in the Early Church* (New York: Abingdon, 1969), pp. 198–217 ff.

17. Peter Brown, *The Cult of the Saints: Its Rise and Function in Latin Christianity* (Chicago: University of Chicago Press, 1981).

18. Calvin, *Reply to Sadolet*: "Thy Christ was indeed worshipped as God and retained the name of Saviour; but where he ought to have been honoured, he was left almost destitute of glory. For, spoiled of his own virtue, he passed unnoticed among the crowd of saints, like one of the meanest of them." In J. K. S. Reid, trans., *Calvin, Theological Treatises*. Library of Christian Classics. (Philadelphia: Westminster Press, 1965), p. 247.

19. Harvey Falk, *Jesus the Pharisee: A New Look at the Jewishness of Jesus* (Mahwah: Paulist Press, 1985).

20. Leibel Reznick, *The Mystery of Bar Kokhba: An Historical and Theological Investigation of the Last King of the Jews* (Northvale, N.J.: Jason Aronson Inc., 1996), pp. 65–76.

21. Mack, *A Myth of Innocence*, p. 203.

22. Gerd Theissen, *The Miracles of the Early Christian Tradition* (Philadelphia: Fortress Press, 1983), pp. 106–11.

23. Jack T. Sanders, *The Jews in Luke-Acts* (Philadelphia: Fortress Press, 1987), pp. 95, 96.

24. Howard Clark Kee, "Early Christianity in the Galilee: Reassessing the Evidence from the Gospels," in *The Galilee in Late Antiquity*, ed. Lee I. Levine (New York: Jewish Theological Seminary and Cambridge: Harvard University Press, 1992), p. 9. Watch Overman squirm: " 'The seat of Moses' is a symbolic expression of authority. The actual seat as part of the synagogue architecture develops later." J. Andrew Overman, *Matthew's Gospel and Formative Judaism: The Social World of the Matthean Community* (Minneapolis: Fortress Press, 1990), p. 47.

25. Overman, *Matthew's Gospel and Formative Judaism*, p. 46. The apologetical attempt of Overman to sidestep the implications for gospel dating strikes me as comical: "The Gospels reveal a general, honorific, and nontechnical understanding of the term."

26. Sean Freyne, *Galilee from Alexander the Great to Hadrian, 323 B.C.E. to 135 A.D. A Study of Second Temple Judaism*. University of Notre Dame Center for the Study of Judaism and Christianity in Antiquity 5 (Wilmington, Del.: Michael Glazier, and University of Notre Dame Press, 1980), p. 350. Gerd Lüdemann, too, rejects the link, but distances himself from those who do so on theological apologetical grounds: *Opposition to Paul in Jewish Christianity* (Minneapolis: Fortress Press, 1989), p. 213.

27. Walter Bauer, *Orthodoxy and Heresy in Earliest Christianity*, ed. Robert Kraft and Gerhard Krodel, trans. the Philadelphia Seminar on Christian Origins (Philadelphia: Fortress Press, 1971).

28. As do Ray A. Pritz, *Nazarene Jewish Christianity* (Jerusalem: Magnes Press/Leiden: E. J. Brill, 1988), who can actually speak of "Trinitarianism" in such a context, p. 108, and Freyne, *Galilee*, p. 350.

29. In fact, since these towns were decimated in the war with Rome, the denunciations of them must rather be seen as gloating, or, if one wishes to dignify it, as examples of the *mathnaa* form used by the Koran, warning sinners to repent lest the disastrous fate of heathen cities like Irem overtake them as well (e.g., 89:5).

30. Vermes, *Jesus the Jew*, p. 90.

31. Robert Eisenman, *James the Brother of Jesus* (New York: Viking, 1997), pp. 193, 357–58, 949, 959–60.

32. S. G. F. Brandon, *The Fall of Jerusalem and the Jerusalem Church* (London: SPCK, 1951), pp. 172–73; Freyne, *Galilee from Alexander the Great to Hadrian*, p. 250.

33. Eisenman, *James the Brother of Jesus*, p. 816.

34. The point is exactly parallel to that of the legend of the Holy Grail, which seeks to provide an independent apostolic (i.e., pre-Roman Catholic) foundation for British Christianity by Joseph of Arimathea, understood as Jesus' uncle commissioned to take the Grail to Britain. See Arthur Edward Waite, *The Hidden Church of the Holy Graal: Its Legends and Symbolism* (London: Rebman LTD, 1909), book 7, "The Holy Graal in the Light of the Celtic Church," pp. 433–68.

35. Theissen, *Sociology of Earliest Palestinian Christianity*, pp. 101–102.

36. Brandon, *The Fall of Jerusalem and the Jerusalem Church*, p. 169.

Chapter 5

THE LOST GOSPEL

THE Q QUESTION

Scholars have always felt that with Q they were especially close to the historical Jesus. In the heyday of the two-document hypothesis that Matthew and Luke had both separately incorporated both Mark's gospel and Q into their own, Mark shared the honors with Q. Scholars tended to grant Mark priority as being more likely historical than Matthew or Luke. And one can at least show that at several points Mark's theological conceptions are earlier and less sophisticated (or less extravagant) than those of Matthew and Luke, because the changes the two later gospels made to their source, Mark, are easily seen. But then William Wrede (Schweitzer's "thoroughgoing skeptic")[1] showed how Mark was far from being a cut-and-paste compiler, much less a reporter. Wrede discerned a complex pattern of theological rewriting already evident in Mark. In fact, compared with Mark, the later writers who used him seem *less* sophisticated on some points, such as Mark's elaborate "messianic secret" theme which they appear not to have picked up on.

This left Q as the best candidate for a pregospel look at the historical Jesus. Burton Mack certainly thinks so. Indeed, he believes that the historical Jesus revealed by the Q gospel is so different from the Jesus of Christian dogma as to necessitate the root-and-branch rejection of the latter as debunked by the former.[2] Of course, that is nothing new; it was pretty much the same way the original liberal Protestant questers viewed the matter. What is new, however, is the portrait of Jesus that emerges from the careful work of Mack, John Kloppenborg, Leif E. Vaage, and others on the "stratigraphy" of Q.[3] For it turns out that Q is not simply a pristine, untracked snowfield either. Like Mark, the Q source seems to have undergone theological retooling. But Mack and his fellow Q-questers are reasonably confident they can peel back the subsequent layers and reach back to the original sayings collection they call Q1.

Along with F. Gerald Downing, Leif E. Vaage, and others, Mack sees Q as essentially a collection of sayings and anecdotes reflecting the ancient popular philosophy of Cynicism, founded by Antisthenes of Athens and Diogenes of Sinope in the generation after Socrates. Cynics were irreverent radicals who moved from place to place without family, home, or possessions, preaching, often with sarcastic invective, their message of the excellence of living in accordance with nature's plan. One need fear no thief if one has no property. One need not bother with jealousy or with domestic drudgery if one has no marriage. Government, private property, clothing, and especially money, are all artificial conventions concocted by people too clever for their own good. God's will for the creation is revealed clearly enough for all to see in the freedom of the birds of the air and the beasts of the field who have no jobs or kings or worries. Nothing unnatural can be good, and nothing natural can be bad. Cynics blessed those who cursed them and loved their persecutors. Some were ascetics, others were libertines, heedless of the condemnations of the bourgeois. They preached the government of Zeus (the Kingdom of God), living in accord with nature by simple common sense. They urged their hearers to let goods and kindred go, and wander through the wide world. They lived by begging and of course encouraged generosity.

Mack and his colleagues have shown that beneath the present text of the reconstructed Q can be discerned an original collection divided into seven thematic sections, none of which includes anything about the authority of Jesus or threats of eschatological judgment to come. Subsequent layers of Q include predictions of the coming of the apocalyptic Son of Man, but no Q sayings refer to the earthly Jesus as the Son of Man or Messiah. No Q saying from any stratum ever mentions Jesus' death, much less his resurrection. So Q would seem to have been only subsequently Christianized, and never nearly so thoroughly as Mark.

Mack reasonably asks why the compilers of Q would have left out all mention of the saving life, death, and resurrection of Jesus had they believed in these things. And we must assume they recorded what they believed to be of importance about Jesus. We have no evidence of the Q community believing anything they did not record, obviously. We have no right simply to assume that the Q compilers also believed the same doctrines as we find, for example, in the Epistle to the Romans, *if they do not say so*. There is simply no ground to assume that all early Jesus followers believed the same things.

Just the opposite: The minimally christological Q counts as strong evidence that at least this quarter of early Christianity (if that is even the proper word for the Q community) had no particular doctrine about Jesus or Christ at all. Q (especially Q1) implies a radically multiform early Christianity.

The power of Burton Mack's case is such that he has managed to convince the great proponent of the Christ-Myth theory in our day, George A. Wells, to abandon the ground he defended for so long. Wells now significantly qualifies his own argument to the effect that, while there was a Cynic-style sage named Jesus underlying Q1, this shadowy figure did not give rise to the full-blown mythic Christ of the gospels, and that we must look elsewhere for the antecedents of the latter.[4] And Mack would agree. We will be asking in what follows whether Mack's thesis, as plausible as it is, is necessarily strong enough to prevail over Wells's original viewpoint. But it will take a while to get there.

Mack's estimate of the (non)theological proclivities of Q might be said to receive a kind of corroboration from a neglected source: the Islamic Agrapha, or Sufi Sayings of Jesus. There are scores of aphorisms and apophthegms attributed to Jesus among the writings of the Sufi ascetics. Here is a community of wandering ascetics, much like that loose alliance of itinerant charismatics posited by Gerd Theissen, taking Jesus as their example and attributing their sayings to him. In this Q-like material, Jesus is frequently addressed "O Spirit of God," which denotes not the divine nature of Jesus (impossible in Islam), but rather his unworldliness and itinerant asceticism, as Mary Douglas's anthropological-sociological analysis of "spirit" language would also confirm. She notes,[5] on the basis of her characteristically exhaustive crosscultural research, that religious groups who devote a great deal of attention to things of the body, namely, dietary restrictions and sexual rules— especially celibacy, distinctive dress, and so on—are thereby reflecting their openness, or lack of it, toward the outside world. Invariably, kosher laws exactly mirror intermarriage rules. The wider the options in the one case, the wider they will be in the other. The amount of control over the openness of the literal bodily orifices is an indicator of the social openness of the group to interaction with outsiders. The one fits hand in glove with the other, so that, for instance, if you cannot eat many foods, or foods prepared a certain way, your dining with those who do not observe these strictures will be accordingly limited. (This was the issue of controversy over Peter's preaching to Cornelius in Acts 10–11: It necessitated his eating and staying with Gentiles, threatening his hitherto-strict observation of the kosher laws.) A group with tight strictures on such behavior has erected high walls against outsiders, "the world." The alienation from those without matches the solidarity with those within. In Douglas's terms, such a group (e.g., the Dead Sea Scrolls sect, Hasidic Jews, and the Amish) has a "strong group" identity because of its "high grid" of rules governing belief and behavior. In such a group, then, attention to the body signifies both the regulation of the physical bodies of the individual sect members and the defensive perimeter of the social "body" of the sect itself. Everything will be different when "spirit" language predominates. The body suffers in contrast, literally and physically by ascetical self-mortification, and socially by the increased preoccupation with individual spirituality and asceticism on the part of the individuals in the group. The classic example would be those monasteries, as in Late Antique Egypt, where Christian ascetics banded together in the loosest of "communities" but really constituted a league of hermits. Such fellowships would count as "weak group" but "high grid." A strong sense of self-definition serves in such a case to alienate members both from the outside world and from fellow members of the group. The Q itinerants would fit such a sketch, as would the ancient Cynic preachers and the Sufis of Islam. Thus their Jesus is the "Spirit of God," and his sayings, like those in Q and the Gospel of Thomas, presuppose and inculcate such a radical lifestyle.

SUFI Q

I propose to make a few observations about the Sufi-preserved sayings of Jesus and their relevance to the Q question. I have drawn on various secondary sources for them, primarily reproducing them from the collection and the translation of D. S. Margoliouth, professor of Arabic at Oxford, as they appeared in *The Expository Times*, 1893–1894. As it turned out, Margoliouth had inadvertently omitted several sayings from his main source, Al-Ghazali's *Revival of the Religious Sciences*; I have filled them in from other secondary sources, including Javad Nurbakhsh's *Jesus in the Eyes of the Sufis* and T. J. Winter's translation of *Remembrance of Death and the Afterlife*, book 40 of Al-Ghazali's larger work.[6] I have retained Margoliouth's numbering, adding the sayings drawn from Nurbakhsh and Winter with lowercase letters attached at their proper place in the sequence from Al-Ghazali. I believe these sayings will prove more relevant to the consideration of the Q question than has generally been realized. One thing to keep in mind will be the controversial Criterion of Dissimilarity, so christened by Norman Perrin, but a staple of form criticism before and after him.[7] The idea is that a saying attributed to Jesus is more likely to be authentically his if it contrasts with the beliefs or practices of both contemporary Judaism and the early Church. Though one need not suppose Jesus to have held nothing in common with either the religious community into which he was born or that to which he gave rise, the goal of the Criterion of Dissimilarity is to weed out sayings that may have been borrowed from Judaism (on the assumption that "if it sounds good, Jesus must have said it") or that may have been ascribed to Jesus by inventive Christians eager to authorize their own viewpoints (on the assumption that "if it's true, Jesus would have said it"). Though you might lose some genuine sayings this way, you would be left with a core of material you could with some confidence attribute to Jesus that ought to represent his most distinctive message. The results of applying this criterion to the tradition have been surprisingly ambiguous, Perrin himself applying more than a bit of wishful thinking. But I think it will be a worthwhile exercise to invoke the dissimilarity principle here on the assumption that, given the Muslim identity of the Sufi transmitters of the sayings, any apparent non-Islamic element might mark the saying as pre-Islamic and thus at least possibly to be traced back to the historical Jesus.

1. Jesus asked Gabriel when the Hour was to come. Gabriel answered: He whom thou askest knows no better than he who asks. (Castalani, *Commentary on Bukhari*, i. 163.)

We at once think of Mark 13:32, "But of that day and that hour no one knows, not even the angels in heaven, nor the son, but only the Father." But there is a significant difference: In Mark, Jesus himself is the revealer and yet qualifies his revelation; there is one vital piece of data to which even he is not privy. In the Sufi version Jesus is no longer the revealer, Gabriel is, and it is his divine knowledge that is qualified. Note that in Mark 13:32 "the angels" in general are mentioned, but in the Sufi version Gabriel is specified, he who brought revelation to Daniel (Dan. 9:21–22), to Mary (Luke 1:26 ff), and later to the Prophet Muhammad. What we have to ask is whether this saying represents an Islamicization of Jesus, to make him more human, less divine, analogous to the Prophet Muhammad as a "mere" recipient of revelation rather than a supernatural revealer in his own right. It might be so, but on the other hand, we must wonder if perhaps in this case oral tradition has preserved an earlier version of a saying which was later rewritten as we find it in Mark, where it seems to represent a backtracking from a high Christology: "the Son" might have been expected to have had infallible knowledge of the eschaton, and yet he did not, since "this generation" passed away without seeing the fulfillment of his predictions. Perhaps Mark had resorted to the early saying, now preserved only in the Sufi tradition, to correct the embarrassment in the Markan Apocalypse (chapter 13), but he had to rewrite it in light of the higher Christology of the church in his own day, leaving us the strange spectacle of Jesus the clueless revealer.

2. Jesus said: The world is a place of transition, full of examples; be pilgrims therein, and take warning by the traces of those that have gone before. (Jacut's *Geographical Lexicon*)

This saying presupposes the wandering lifestyle of the early Christian charismatic itinerants, as do several sayings in the Gospel of Thomas and the Q collection. As the Sufis included many wandering mendicants, the saying might have been coined by them, or simply passed on from their pre-Christian or Christian predecessors.

3. Jesus said, Be in the midst, yet walk on one side. (Baidawi, *Commentary on the Koran*, p. 71, Constantinople ed.)
The reference to "walking" again recalls the itineracy of ascetics.

4. In the sermons of Jesus, son of Mary, it is written: Beware how ye sit with sinners. (Zamakhshari, *Commentary on the Koran*, p. 986)
William Morrice quips: "as if Jesus wrote sermons."[8] But the same might be said of the Sermon on the Mount, a distinct collection of sayings already in Q. Zamakhshari would seem to have drawn the saying from a larger collection. This, as we will see, may be quite significant.

5. Jesus said: I have treated the leprous and the blind, and have cured them; but when I have treated the fool, I have failed to cure him. (*El-Mustatraf*)
As we see in the Gospel of Thomas, Jesus has been identified with the literary personification of Wisdom.[9] Jesus speaks here as Lady Wisdom does in Proverbs chapter 8, or as Jesus/Wisdom does in Thomas, saying 28: "Jesus said: I took my stand in the midst of the world and in flesh I appeared to them. I found them all drunk, I found none among them athirst. And my soul was afflicted for the sons of men, because they are blind in their heart and do not see that empty they have come into the world; empty they seek to go out of the world again. But now they are drunk. When they have shaken off their wine, then they will repent." The saying, however, does presuppose the gospel tradition of Jesus as a miracle worker and thus is probably not so early as some would make the prechristological Q.

6. God revealed to Jesus: Command the children of Israel that they enter not my house save with pure hearts, and humble eyes, and clean hands; for I will not answer any one of them against whom any has a complaint. (*El-Hadaic El-Wardiyyah*, i. p. 27.)
Though the sentiment recalls Matt. 5:23–24, it is even closer to Isa. 1:10–17. We might even suspect that this Sufi saying and Matt. 5:23–24 are independent examples of the tendency of early Christians to misattribute, or to reattribute, familiar scriptural material to Jesus in a slightly different form.

7. Jesus said: *Whoso knows* and does and teaches shall be called great in the kingdom of heaven. (Al-Ghazali, *Revival of the Religious Sciences* i. 8)
Here is an abridged version of Matt. 5:19 ("Whoever then relaxes one of the least of these commandments and teaches men so, shall be called least in the kingdom of heaven; but he who does them and teaches them shall be

called great in the kingdom of heaven"), already itself a redactional creation aimed at Paulinist anti-Torah libertines. But the Sufi version has dropped the specific reference to Torah commandments, no longer the issue in a later set of circumstances, with the result that the point of the saying is made more general, along the lines of James 1:22 ("But be doers of the word, and not hearers only, deceiving yourselves"). Again, we are later than the conjectured date for a prechristological Q.

The marked words in this saying provide "catchwords," mnemonic pegs on which the next saying depends for its sequence, a pattern we will observe throughout the rest of the Sufi sayings considered here.

7a. Jesus said: "God has declared that those who observe the canonical devotion will be saved, while those who perform supererogatory worship, will be drawn close to him." (Ibid., 78, Nurbakhsh)

Let no one dismiss this saying as late, since the language of canonical—that is, traditionally prescribed—religious duties need imply no more than the Jewish Torah commandments, while the "works of supererogation" may refer to acts such as that assigned the rich young ruler by Jesus: The man had already done what the Torah commanded, hence already had assurance of the salvation he sought (cf. Luke 10:28, "Do this and you will live"), yet he felt the need for devotion above the strict stipulation of the commandments (Matt. 19:16–20). This Jesus fulfilled by telling him to renounce all worldly attachments and join him (Matt. 19:21).

8. Jesus said: Trees are many, yet not all of them bear fruit; and fruits are many, yet not all of them are fit for food; and *sciences [or kinds of knowledge, or things known] are many, but not all of them are profitable.* (Ibid., i. 26)

The marked words match the motif marked in saying 7 dealing with teaching and knowledge. It was this general relation of theme that led to the juxtaposition of the two sayings in the collection used, and followed in its original sequence, by Al-Ghazali, the source of all the rest of the Sufi sayings to follow.

This saying may have been intended as a warning against "vain philosophy" à la Col. 2:8, and thus it is easy to propose an Islamic *Sitz-im-Leben* for it: We need only think of the influx of alien philosophical ideas in the days of the Abassid Caliphate headquartered in Damascus. It was in large measure against this new tide of "orientalization" and sophistication that the Sufis reacted in their return to the primitive simplicity of the early days in Mecca. But then again the same reservations would have been held by the Christian monks of Syria who were a great influence upon Sufism.

We might trace the saying back even further, though, since it may easily be read as inculcating encratite asceticism. This early Christian movement, especially strong in Asia Minor in the second century C.E., regarded the sexual encounter between Adam and Eve as the primordial sin through which death entered the world. Salvation required not only Christian faith and baptism but also celibacy. They were quite similar to the American sect of the Shakers. In such a framework, it would be the fruit of the Tree of Knowledge of Good and Evil (i.e., sex) which proved unprofitable. This was the one fruit tree of Eden forbidden to the first couple.

9. Jesus said: *Commit not wisdom* to those who are not meet for it, lest ye harm it; and withhold it not from them that are meet for it, lest ye harm them. Be like a gentle physician, who puts the remedy on the diseased spot.
According to another version:
Whoso commits wisdom to them that are not meet for it, is a fool; and whoso withholds it from them that are meet for it, is an *evil-doer*. Wisdom has rights, and rightful owners; and give each his due. (Ibid., i. 30)

The theme of "committing wisdom" to others links this saying with numbers 7 and 8 above.

The subject of saying 9 is esoteric spiritual wisdom or doctrine. It is always a risk sharing it: One must keep mum around the impenetrably orthodox lest they put one to death for heresy. On the other hand, one bears heavy responsibility for withholding the truth from those ripe to hear it. One has no right to deprive them of spiritual nourishment for fear of one's own safety. This concern led many Middle Eastern sects, like the Druze, to embrace what is called the doctrine of dissimulation. One may deny one's faith in times of persecution so as not to tempt persecutors to the sin of murder. Since they cannot be expected to understand the higher knowledge, it will be the Gnostic's own fault if he gets himself into trouble. The Sufis certainly had reason to fear: One of their greatest, the mystic al-Hallaj, was crucified for proclaiming "I am the Real [i.e., God]," something the pantheistic Sufis understood but your average Muslim in the street did not.

And yet the saying may easily be pre-Sufi. Claims of esoteric knowledge are much older than Sufism. Thomas saying 13 knows the danger: "Now when Thomas came to his companions, they asked him, What did Jesus say to thee? Thomas said to them: If I tell you one of the words he said to me, you will take up stones and throw at me; and fire will come from the stones and burn you up." I suspect the same concern lies behind Matt. 7:6, "Do not give sacred things to dogs; and do not throw your pearls before swine, lest they trample them under foot and turn to attack you."

9a. Jesus said: Do not hang jewels around the necks of swine. Wisdom is finer than gems, and those who do not value it, are worse than swine. (Ibid., 172., Nurbakhsh)

If this saying were found in the gospels, no doubt it would read: "They do not hang jewels upon the necks of swine, and yet he who values not wisdom is worse than a swine." The point would be that even a worldly man values gems enough not to waste them on swine, whose appearance cannot be enhanced by them, and yet the worldling is himself a swine since he fails to realize the superior value of wisdom to jewelry!

The saying owes its place in the sequence to the fact that someone recognized a kinship between it and the gospel aphorism "Do not cast your pearls before swine," which is a good summation of the point of the preceding saying immediately above.

10. Jesus said: *Evil scholars* are like a rock that has fallen at the mouth of a brook; it does not drink the water, neither does it let the water flow to the field. And they are like the conduit of a latrine which is plastered outside, and foul inside; or like graves, the outside of which is decorated, while within are dead men's bones. (Ibid., i. 49)

This saying has been joined to number 9 above based on the common occurrence of "scholars" here and the communication of wisdom, or miscommunication of it, anticipated in saying 9. The variant version of saying 9 contains an explicit reference to "evildoers," anticipating "evil scholars" here.

The saying is obviously another version of a pair of Q sayings against the Pharisees and/or Jewish scribes. Matthew and Luke have used them both, each in his own words, and in a different order. Matt. 23:13, 27: "But woe to you, scribes and Pharisees, hypocrites! because you neither enter yourselves, nor allow those who would enter to go in." "Woe to you, scribes and Pharisees, hypocrites! for you are whitewashed tombs, which outwardly appear beautiful, but within they are full of dead men's bones and all uncleanness." Luke 11:52, 44: "Woe to you lawyers! for you have taken away the key of knowledge; you did not enter yourselves, and you hindered those who were entering." "Woe to you! for you are like graves which are not seen, and men walk over them without knowing it." It is hard to know which version is closer to the Q original, since Luke has the redactional tendency to flatten poetry into prose, while Matthew tends to make the prosaic more poetic. Has Luke added the "key of knowledge" metaphor? Thomas also has it (saying 39: "The Pharisees and the scribes have received the keys of knowledge, they have hidden them. They did not enter, and they did not let those enter who wished"). Thomas has added another to the same saying: "Woe to them, the Pharisees, for they are like a dog sleeping in the manger: neither does he eat nor does he allow the oxen to eat" (saying 102). In the same way, the Sufi version adds the image of the boulder blocking the flow of water.

11. Jesus said: How can he be a *scholar who*, when his journey is unto the next world, *makes for the things of this world*? How can he be a scholar who *seeks for words in order to communicate by them, and not to act according to them*? (Ibid., i. 50)

This saying's reference to the "scholar who . . . makes for the things of this world" follows up "evil scholars" in the preceding saying.

11a. Jesus said: One who teaches higher knowledge and does not practice its wisdom, is like a clandestine adulteress whose swelling condition betrays her to shame. Such a person who does not act on the precepts he knows, will be shamed by the Lord before all creation on the Day of Judgment. (Ibid., 188, Nurbakhsh)

One must locate the arising of this logion among the ranks of teachers, and aimed at their own fraternity, whether originally Syrian Christian monks or Sufis. The simile of the adulteress includes both the elements of one's life speaking louder than one's words and of public exposure. (Given the great number of adulterers liable to be exposed on Judgment Day, one may at least hope to be relatively anonymous, lost in the shuffle.)

12. God said unto Jesus: *Exhort thyself, and if Thou hast profited by the exhortation, then exhort others; otherwise be ashamed* before me. (Ibid., i. 52)

The notion of a sage entrusted with words of wisdom but possibly not taking them seriously in his own case provides the link between this saying and number 11 above. Beyond this, we might observe how this saying reflects the idiom of the Koran in which revelations are ascribed not to Muhammad himself, but to his Lord. Allah addresses the Prophet, "O Muhammad, say, . . ." In the gospel tradition, Jesus is not shown telling people what God told him.

13. Jesus said: If a man send away *a beggar* empty from his house, the angels will not visit that house for seven nights. (Ibid., i. 77)

We can readily recognize here the interests of the wandering mendicants whose missionary vicissitudes also form the subject matter of the Q Mission Charge (Matt. 10:5 ff; Luke 9:3 ff). The point of saying 13 is pretty much the same as Matt. 10:12–13: "As you enter the house salute it. And if the house is worthy, let your peace come upon it; but if it is not worthy, let your peace return to you." The visiting angels are the protectors, keepers of peace over the house.

13a. It is recounted that Jesus once went into the desert to *pray* for rain. When people gathered round, he said to them: Whoever has sinned, must go back. Everyone went away, except one man. Jesus turned to this man and asked him: Have you never sinned? The man replied: By God's Name, I know nothing of sin. Indeed, one day I was saying my prayers, when a woman passed by. My eye happened to fall upon her, so I plucked it out and cast it behind her. Jesus then told him to pray. As soon as he began, clouds proceeded to gather. Rain began to fall—and a goodly downpour it was! (Ibid., ii., p. 437)

The anecdote is connected to the next saying by the simple fact that this one involves prayer, and that one *is* a prayer.

Strikingly, Jesus is not himself the hands-on miracle worker in this story, but rather more the broker of the miracle, seeming to know, as his question to the crowd implies, how the miracle is to be wrought: through the agency of a righteous saint whom he will ferret out. (Cf. James 5:16b–18, "The prayer of a righteous man has great power in its effects. Elijah was a man of like nature with ourselves and he prayed fervently that it might not rain, and for three years and six months it did not rain on the earth. Then he prayed again, and the heaven gave rain, and the earth brought forth its fruit.") And yet Jesus is "in charge," and thus the story fills a gap: E. A. Harvey,[10] seeking to highlight Jesus' supposed uniqueness among legendary thaumaturges, contends, "The most common miracle attributed to holy men of his time and culture was that of procuring rainfall. . . . But this is something never credited to Jesus." Never say never.

14. The *Prayer* of Jesus: O God, *I am this morning unable to ward off what I would not, or to obtain what I would. The power is in another's hands. I am bound by my works, and there is none so* poor *that is poorer than I.* O God, make not mine enemy to rejoice over me, nor my friend to grieve over me; make not my trouble to be in the matter of my faith; make not the world my chief care; and give not the power over me to him who will not pity me. (Ibid., i 247)

Many of the same words occur practically unaltered below in saying 19, marking off sayings 14 through 19 as a special unit.

The resignedness of Jesus before the winds of providence is certainly characteristic of Sufism specifically, Islam in general, and of pretty much any and all piety. Thus it does not much help us determine the origin of the saying.

15. God revealed to Jesus: Though thou shouldst worship with the devotion of the inhabitants of the heaven and the earth, but hadst not *love in God and hate in God*, it would avail thee nothing. (Ibid., ii. 119)

Minus the unpleasant note about hating, this saying must be understood as derivative from 1 Cor. 13:1–3, the idea of "worshipping with the devotion of the inhabitants of heaven" echoing "speaking with the tongues of angels" from 1 Cor. 13:1. "Hating in God" may have crept in by assimilation to the next saying, which would in any case be connected by the catchwords "love in God" (saying 15) and "beloved of God" (saying 16). The origin of the saying in a Pauline Epistle rather than the Jesus tradition is attested by the fact that even in its present form it is, again, made a revelation *to* Jesus, not *from* him.

16. Jesus said: make yourselves *beloved of God by hating the evil-doers*. Bring yourselves nearer to God by removing far from them; and seek God's favour

by their displeasure. They said: O Spirit of God, then with whom shall we converse? Then he said: Converse with those whose presence will remind you of God, whose *words* will increase your *works*, and whose *works* will make you desire the next world. (Ibid., ii. 119)

Gone is the "friend of sinners" we are used to from the canonical gospels. This saying originated among monastics, hermits, and ascetics, whether originally Syrian Christians or Muslim Sufis. The difference in attitude between this saying and the gospels mirrors that between the gospels and Christian devotional literature like Thomas a Kempis's *Imitation of Christ*, and for the same reason. À la Mary Douglas, again, we should recognize that for Jesus to be addressed as "Spirit of God" in this context is no coincidence. The expression denotes just the sort of unearthliness we would expect from ascetics.

"Works" links this saying with the first and last of this subsection, 14 and 19.

17. Jesus said to the apostles: What would you do if you saw your brother sleeping, and the wind had lifted up his garment? They said: We should cover him up. He said: Nay, ye would uncover him. They said: God forbid! Who would do this? He said: One of you who hears a *word* concerning his brother, and adds to it, and relates it with additions. (Ibid., ii. 134)

This striking saying, incidentally, deals with the issue of exaggeration in the process of oral tradition! It has the ring of many of the similes attributed to Jesus in the gospels, where he puts forth a laughably absurd course of mundane action which no one would follow, and then directs the hearer to analogous behavior on a spiritual plane in which we habitually engage.

This saying owes its position in the sequence to its use of "a word," reflecting "whose words" in the preceding saying.

18. They say that there was no form of address Jesus loved better to hear than "*Poor man*." (Ibid., ii. 154)

What is said here of Jesus is characteristic, formulaic, of the Sufis and originated with them, or among their Syrian monastic predecessors. The secondary character of the saying is again evidenced by the reluctance of the tradition to make this saying into a saying of, rather than only about, Jesus. Another version makes Jesus himself the speaker, as usual: "Jesus said: I prefer deprivation and despise wealth. When asked which epithet he liked best he replied: Call me, Pauper!" (Makki, *Qut al-qolub*, vol. II, p. 402, Nurbakhsh)

"Poor man" links the saying with the following, number 19, as well as with the first in this linked set of sayings, number 14.

19. When Jesus was asked, How art thou this morning? He would answer: *Unable to forestall what I hope, or to put off what I fear, bound by my works, with*

all my good in another's hand. There is no poor man poorer than I. (Al-Ghazali, *Revival of the Religious Sciences*, ii. 169)

The repetition from saying number 14 rounds off the special unit. Jesus is made to speak as the ideal of the pious person. He has his own karma to worry about, something unthinkable to Christian Christology (at least post-Mark, since Mark apparently had no problem with Jesus appearing to wash away his sins in the waters of John's baptism—Mark 1:4–9).

20. *Satan*, the accursed, appeared to Jesus and said unto him: Say, there is no God but God. He said: It is a true saying, but I will not say it at thy invitation. (Ibid., iii. 25)

Q specialists suggest that the Q narrative of Jesus' three temptations by Satan in the desert may belong to the secondary, Christianized layer of Q. This is because of Satan's opening gambit, "If you are the son of God. . . ." And yet the present sequence of sayings, numbers 20 through 22, also depicts Satan tempting Jesus (or discussing temptation, Screwtape style, with his infernal subordinates, in the wake of Jesus' advent). Here the point is not precisely Christology but rather the use of Jesus as the ideal ascetic. The hearer/reader ought to take Jesus' example. And then we must look back at the threefold Q temptation story. Is it not apparent that the point there, too, is asceticism? The "Son of God" designation in the story may be sapiential in origin and connotation, as in Wisd. of Sol. 2:13, 18, where the persecuted righteous man is God's son. The point is reinforced when we remember that the three quotations Jesus invokes are from Deuteronomy and all deal with how the Israelites should have reacted to trials in the desert. The implication is that of exemplary behavior for the pious, not an exclusive statement about Jesus as the Christ.

In this saying, we have the idea, present in the Q temptation narrative, too, that "even the devil can quote scripture to suit his purpose." We think of James 2:19: "You believe that God is one; you do well. Even the demons believe—and tremble." "God is one" is a quote from the Shema ("Hear, O Israel, the Lord our God is one . . .").

21. When Jesus was born, the demons came to *Satan*, and said: The idols have been overturned. He said: This is a mere accident that has occurred; keep still. Then he flew till he had gone over both hemispheres, and found nothing. After that he found the son of Mary already born, with the angels surrounding him. He returned to the demons and said: A prophet was born yesterday; no woman ever conceived or bare a child without my presence save this one. Hope not, therefore, that the idols will be worshipped after this night, so attack mankind through haste and thoughtlessness. (Ibid., iii. 28)

As elsewhere in Islamic tradition, including the Koran, the Jesus tradition includes material from extracanonical sources. The reference of this saying is to the toppling of the idols of Egypt during the sojourn of the Holy Family there (*Infancy Gospel of Matthew* XXII-XXIII).[11] The notion that Jesus alone was born immaculate, without the presence of Satan, is characteristic of both Islam and Catholic Christianity.

22. Jesus lay down one day with his head upon a stone. *Satan*, passing by, said: O Jesus, thou art fond of this world. So he took the stone and cast it from his head, saying: This be thine together with the world. (Al-Ghazali, *Revival of the Religious Sciences*, ii. 169)

Here we find echoes of diverse ancient traditions. Jesus is like the patriarch Jacob, seeking whatever rest is available upon a stony pillow; only he is not so fortunate as his predecessor in chancing to meet God (Gen. 28:12). This time it is Satan who appears. He challenges Jesus' use of the stone, as Mara the Tempter challenged the right of Gotama the Bodhisattva to sit upon the earth as he sought enlightenment beneath the boughs of the Bodhi Tree. Gotama placed his hand upon the earth and called her to witness, which she did, vindicating his right. But the most relevant parallel is that of Diogenes, when he who had believed himself divested of all but bare necessities, felt shame at seeing a dog lapping the water and cast his wooden drinking bowl away. The version in saying 65 is even closer. Here is a striking Cynic parallel such as Downing, Mack, and others have compiled for Q. As such, it may have arisen anywhere and more than once, along the course of the evolution of Cynic, Christian, and Sufi asceticism.

23. Jesus was asked, Who taught thee? He answered: No one taught me. I saw that the *ignorance* of the fool was a shame, and I *avoided* it. (Ibid., iii. 52)

Frequently, "revealed" religions represent their founders as unlettered and therefore humanly incapable of authoring their ostensible revelations. The claim has been made for Jesus, Peter and John, Muhammad, and Joseph Smith. But that seems not to be the point this time. The contrast is not Christological (Jesus as divine revealer versus human erudition, as in Matt. 11:25–27), but rather Cynic in nature: One hardly needs the sophistical training of philosophers to recognize fundamental wisdom, that foolish behavior brings shame.

24. Jesus said: Blessed is he who *abandons a present pleasure* for the sake of a promised [one] which is absent and unseen. (Ibid.)

Again, Jesus is made to speak the maxims of popular philosophy, this time not Cynic but Epicurean (and remember, Epicureanism was itself a kind of asceticism, the "pleasure" it sought being that of mental tranquillity and physical self-control).

Saying 24 follows number 23 because of the parallel between "avoiding ignorance" in the one and "abandoning pleasure" on the other.

25. Jesus said: O company of apostles! Make *hungry* your livers, and bare your bodies; perhaps then your hearts may see God. (Ibid., iii. 65).

This sounds like a paraphrase of Thomas, saying 27: "Unless you fast from the world you shall not find the kingdom; unless you keep the Sabbath as Sabbath, you shall not see the Father." If, as Stephen J. Patterson[12] has argued, Thomas stems from the same sort of proto-Christian itinerant charismatics as Q does, we may make the same suggestion of this sort of material in the Sufi source used by al-Ghazali.

26. It is related how Jesus remained sixty days addressing his Lord, *without eating*. Then the *thought of bread came into his mind*, and his communion was interrupted, and he saw a loaf set before him. Then he sat down and wept over the loss of his communion, when he beheld an old man close to him. Jesus said unto him: God bless thee, thou saint of God! Pray to God for me, for I was in an ecstasy when the thought of bread entered my mind, and the ecstasy was interrupted. The old man said: O God, if thou knowest that the thought of bread came into my mind since I knew thee, then forgive me not. Nay, when it was before me, I would eat it without thought or reflection. (Ibid., iii. 67)

The catchword phrase "without eating" obviously connects this saying with the one before it, with its "make hungry your livers."

The issue of meditative absorption in God, undisturbed by even a single thought, is vintage Sufism. Thus the saying is probably Sufi in origin. The point of it seems to be much the same as Martin Luther's commonsense advice to those who worried unduly about thoughts of temptation. Luther said, roughly, you may not be able to stop a bird from lighting on your head, but you sure can stop it from building a nest in your hair!

But notice that the old man outdoes Jesus himself: Even when eating his concentration on God is not interrupted.

27. Jesus said: Beware of glances; for they *plant passion in the heart*, and that is a sufficient temptation. (Ibid., iii. 81)

The planting of passion in the heart in this saying is the link to the previous saying with its lament of hunger's power to distract the ascetic from God. There it was the sudden appearance of the passion of hunger that was bemoaned. Otherwise we may simply note that saying 27 appears to be a paraphrase of Matt. 5:28, "Everyone who looks at a woman lustfully has already committed adultery with her in his heart," though it might be an independent saying to the same effect.

28. Jesus was asked by some men to guide them to some course by which they might enter Paradise. He said: *Speak not at all*. They said: We cannot do this. He said: Then *only say what is good*. (Ibid., iii. 87)

Like Mark 10:17–22, this saying is a classic aphophthegm, common to ancient wisdom literature. Like the Markan saying, but especially in its slightly modified Matthean form (Matt. 19:23–30), it seems to offer a counsel of perfection, implying that a lesser standard is nonetheless acceptable. It is best to divest oneself of all wealth, but it will do to keep the commandments. Likewise, one is on safest grounds forswearing all speech (cf. James 3:2, "If anyone makes no mistakes in what he says, he is a perfect man"), but speaking only the good will do.

29. Jesus said: Devotion is of ten parts. Nine of them consist in *silence*, and one in solitude. (Ibid.)

The catchword "silence" links this saying to the one before. The enumeration of the elements of piety is a common Sufi device, though hardly unique to Sufism. Again, the piety commended here is more in tune with *The Imitation of Christ* than with that in the gospels.

30. Jesus said: Whosoever *lies much*, loses his beauty; and whosoever *wrangles* with others, loses his honour; and whosoever is much troubled, sickens in his body; and whosoever is *evilly disposed, tortures himself*. (Ibid., iii. 92)

Though if this saying had been included among canonical scripture we can be sure some would appeal to it as a prophetic anticipation of the discovery of psychogenic illness (e.g., worrying yourself into a case of cancer), in fact the saying is a fine illustration of how wise sayings embody homespun observational wisdom. Popular wisdom has always been able to observe the physical effects of a contentious personality, just as people knew to call cigarettes "coffin nails" long before the surgeon general caught up with them.

Incidentally, it is worth asking if, in light of this saying, we ought to recognize a similar point in the Q saying Matt. 6:22–23/Luke 11:34–35, "The eye is the lamp of the body. So, if your eye is sound, your whole body will be full of light; but if your eye is not sound, your whole body will be full of darkness. If then the light which is in you is darkness, how deep is that darkness!" The soundness of the eye may refer to generosity as opposed to the "evil eye" of stinginess (Matt. 20:15, "Is your eye evil because I am good?"). We might expect that the eye, being the window of the soul, would be spoken of as symptomatic of one's soul or heart or life. But instead we read of the eye indicating the state of the *body*. Is the point the same as in the Sufi saying, that the attitude determines the body's health? (And if the Q material stems from wandering preachers, we can well imagine them warning how their audiences' stinginess might backfire!)

30a. John the Baptist asked Jesus what was the most difficult thing to bear. The latter replied: The wrath of God. Then, asked John, *what serves most to bring down God's wrath? Your own anger*, answered Jesus. And what brings on one's own anger? asked John. Jesus said: Pride, conceit, vainglory and arrogance. (Ibid., p. 183)

Again, as in the preceding saying, the irony is that you have only yourself to blame for your torment, whether in this world or in the next, since "God's wrath" toward you is only a magnification of some attitude of your own.

Note how this saying presupposes but surpasses the canonical gospel tradition: Here John is no rival of Jesus, nor even merely his forerunner, but actually Jesus' disciple. Here we even see the ostensible origin of the theme of John's preaching, the coming of the wrath of God (Matt. 3:7) and how it may be averted in the same way one first attracted it to oneself, by one's moral behavior, then sinning, now repenting (Matt. 3:8).

31. *Jesus, passing by* a swine, said to it: Go in peace. *They said*: O Spirit of God, sayest thou so to *a swine*? He answered: I would not *accustom my tongue to evil*. (Ibid., iii. 94)

As in number 28, the point is "if you can't find anything nice to say, don't say anything at all." So why does not Jesus simply keep silence in the presence of the unclean pig? If he had, we would have no aphophthegm! Of course, the evil-speaking rejected here is of a piece with the wrangling and lying of the previous saying, accounting for their juxtaposition.

Does the abhorrence of swine mark the saying as stemming from a Jewish context, and hence possibly from the *Sitz-im-Leben Jesu*? Not necessarily: Remember, Muslims abjure pork as well.

32. Jesus said: One of the greatest of sins in God's eyes is that a man should *say God knows what He knows not*. (Ibid., iii. 107)

Here is more evil-speaking, or at least the condemnation of the same. Those who take God's name in vain by swearing a false oath, "God knows I didn't steal your donkey!" (which in fact he *doesn't* know, since you *did* steal it) are "accustoming their tongues to evil."

33. Malik, son of Dinar, said: *Jesus* one day walked with his apostles, and they *passed by* the carcass of a dog. *The apostles said: How foul* is the smell of this dog! But Jesus said: How white are its teeth! (Ibid., iii. 108)

This saying shares with number 31 before it and number 34 following it the setting in which Jesus' remark is prompted by a "passing sight" (as Buddhism calls them). In all three he might have been expected to make a negative remark but makes a positive one instead. In saying 31, the sight is that of an unclean hog; in 33 it is that of a reeking dog carcass. This story works a bit better in that

Jesus' remark, superfluous in itself, is motivated by the previous remark of the apostles. Jesus would have kept silent if they had, but as long as they are going to say something bad, he must counter it with something good.

Why is the saying preceded by an attribution, like the *hadith*, traditional anecdotes of the Prophet Muhammad? Perhaps because of the tinge of silliness, which might strike some as irreverent unless vouched for by a person of well-known piety.

34. *Christ passed by* certain of the Jews, who spake evil of him; but he spake good to them in return. *It was said to him:* Verily these speak *ill* of thee, and dost thou speak good? He said: Each gives out of *his store*. (Ibid., iii. 134)

This third version of the tradition seen also in sayings 31 and 33 is the most sober as well as the most enlightening. It seems to connect two gospel ideas in such a way as to make one explain the other. The advice of Luke 6:28 is to "bless those who curse you." The Q saying Luke 6:45/Matt. 12:34b observes: "Out of the abundance of the heart the mouth speaks. The good man out of his good treasure brings forth good, and the evil man out of his evil treasure brings forth evil." What is the connection? The good-hearted person does not have to reign himself in when insulted, choking back a stinging rejoinder. No, it is simply *not in him* to unleash invectives, even when deserved. He will no more respond with harsh words than he will initiate them.

35. Jesus said: Take not the *world* for your lord, lest it take you for its slaves. Lay up *your treasure* with him who will not waste it, etc. (Ibid., iii. 151)

"Your treasure" in this saying accounts for its appending after the previous one with its mention of the treasure of the heart. Saying 35 recalls Matt. 6:19–21, 24: "Do not lay up for yourselves treasures on earth, where moth and rust corrupt, and where thieves break in and steal, but lay up for yourselves treasures in heaven, where neither moth nor rust corrupts and where thieves do not break in and steal. For where your treasure is, there your heart will be also." "No one can be slave to two masters; for either he will hate the first and love the second, or he will love the first and hate the second. You cannot serve both God and Mammon." (Mammon means money as a god, the Almighty Dollar). As if this Q saying (see also Luke 12:33–34) were not already ascetic enough in its thrust, forbidding the amassing of wealth on earth, the Sufi version accentuates the asceticism: If you make worldly success your ultimate concern, money will cease being a convenience, no longer making things easier. Soon it will bind you and limit your freedom. It is the wealthy who lie awake at night fearing the thief. The poor man is free of such fretting. Note also, the Sufi version has replaced the perils of moth, rust, and burglars with that of profligate stewards, as in Luke 16:1–8. I would guess we have here either an abridging of the parallel gospel texts through memory quotation or an independent saying based on the same traditional motifs.

36. Jesus said: Ye company of apostles, verily *have I overthrown the world* upon her face *for you*; raise her not up after me. It is a mark of the foulness of this world that God is disobeyed therein, and that the *future world* cannot be attained save by abandonment of this; pass then through this world, and linger not there; and know that the root of every sin is love of the world. Often does the pleasure of an hour bestow on him that enjoys it long pain. (Ibid.)

Here someone is remembering the gist of John chapter 16, part of John's Farewell Discourse of Jesus to his disciples, where Jesus warns of the enmity of the world after his imminent departure from it (here: "after me"). But they are not to be intimidated: "In the world you have tribulation, but be of good cheer: I have overcome the world" (John 16:33). But, in accord with its ascetical bent, we are not surprised to read in the Sufi saying a warning, not against persecution, but against worldliness, being at ease in Zion.

The mendicant wandering motif appears again here, as does a reflection of the Cynic saying "The love of money is the mother city of all evils." (Cf. 1 Tim. 6:10, "The love of money is the root of all evils.") The theme of momentary pleasure costing too much in the long term is an Epicurean truism.

37. He said again: *I have laid the world low for you*, and ye are seated upon its back. Let not kings and women dispute with you the possession of it. Dispute not the world with kings, for they will not offer you what you have abandoned and their world; but guard against women by fasting and prayer. (Ibid.)

We have no trouble recognizing here another version of the saying just discussed, and the recurring features supply the catchwords leading to the present arrangement. Added to the Johannine basis of the saying, however, seems to be the same sentiment we find in the Gospel of Thomas, saying 21: "Mary said to Jesus: Who are thy disciples like? He said: They are like little children who have installed themselves in a field which is not theirs. When the owners of the field come, they will say: Release to us our field. They will take off their clothes before them to release it to them and to give back their field to them. Therefore I say: If the lord of the house knows that the thief is coming, he will stay awake before he comes and will not let him dig through into his house of his kingdom to carry away his goods. You then must watch for the world, gird up your loins with great strength, lest the brigands find a way to come to you, because they will find the advantage you expect."

This passage in Thomas is in turn derived from a vague memory quotation of two canonical gospel texts. The first is the parable of the wicked tenants in Mark 12:1–9 ("A man planted a vineyard . . . and let it out to tenants, and went away into another country. When the time came, he sent a servant to the tenants, to get from them some of the fruit of the vineyard . . ."). The second is the parable of the unfaithful steward toward the end of the Markan Apocalypse, 13:34–37, which ends with the exhortation, "Watch therefore, for you do not know when the master of the house will come . . . , lest he come suddenly and find you asleep." Thomas' version makes the tenants into the disciples rather than the enemies of Jesus and bids them acknowledge the claim of the field's/vineyard's true owner (perhaps Satan or the Gnostic Demiurge). Likewise, the owner of the house has become, not the one whose coming is awaited, but rather the one who awaits the coming of another—a thief. Again, the allegorical counterparts have shifted roles. One awaits not God but the devil (cf. Mark 4:15). The Sufi version garbles things further, adding to the general ascetic horror of the alluring world a specific warning against the delights of women.

38. He said again: The world seeks and is sought. If a man seeks *the next* world, this world seeks him till he obtain therein his full sustenance; but if a man seeks this world, the next world seeks him till death comes and takes him by the throat. (Ibid.)

This is an alternative version of Matt. 6:31–33/Luke 12:29–31. Luke's version, closer to the common Q original, reads, "Do not seek what you are to eat and what you are to drink, nor be of anxious mind. For all the nations of the world seek these things; and your Father knows that you need them. Instead, seek his kingdom, and these things shall be yours as well." The Father's kingdom is, of course, the "next world" of the Sufi version. Precisely in abstaining from the pursuit of worldly necessities, the pious man becomes a magnet for these very provisions, thanks to the providence of God. This is the faith not of the conventionally religious householder, but of the wandering brethren of the Son of Man who have no guaranteed place to lay their heads (Matt. 8:20/Luke 9:58), who are thus dependent upon strangers to provide for them (Luke 10:7). The second part of the saying, the corollary, recalls the Lukan parable of the Rich Fool (12:16–20), in which we read of a man caught up in pursuit of worldly security, until the Grim Reaper stops him short on the eve of retirement.

39. Jesus said: The love of this world and of *the next* cannot agree in a believer's heart, even as fire and water cannot agree in a single vessel. (Ibid., iii. 152)

Again, indentured service to two competing masters simultaneously just will not work, as in Matt. 6:19–21, and in saying 35. This saying owes its position after number 38 to the recurrence here of the phrase "the next (world)."

40. Jesus being asked, Why dost thou not take a house to *shelter* thee? said: The rags of those that were before us are good enough for us. (Ibid. iii. 153)

Again, the Son of Man (and those who appeal to him as their exemplar) has no sure place to rest his head. It is good enough not to have to go naked. Actually, some Cynics and Digambara ("sky-clad") Jainist ascetics did go around naked, weather permitting. And the reference to wearing the rags of our forbears in the faith would ideally fit the early Buddhist practice of appropriating the shrouds of the disintegrated dead for clothing. But the reference is most likely to the hand-me-down patched robes of the Sufis, and the saying will then have arisen among their ranks.

41. It is recorded that one day Jesus was sore troubled by the rain and thunder and lightning, and began to seek a *shelter*. His eye fell upon a tent hard by; but when he came there, finding a woman inside, he turned away from it. Then he noticed a cave in a mountain; but when he came thither, there was a lion there. Laying his hand upon the lion, he said: My God, thou hast given each thing a resting place, but to me thou hast given none! Then God revealed to him: Thy resting-place is in the abode of my mercy; that I may wed thee on the day of judgment . . . and make thy bridal feast four thousand years, of which each day is like a life-time in this present world; and that I may command a herald to proclaim: Where are they that fast in *this world*? Come to the bridal feast of Jesus, who fasted in this world! (Ibid.)

The first part of this saying, connected to the previous one by the shelter motif, may be regarded as a narrative padding out of the previous saying, as well as of Matt. 8:20/Luke 9:58. Note that, as a good ascetic, Jesus is less afraid of physical danger, the lion, than of moral, the woman.

The second part, the promise of Jesus' millennial recompense by God, may come from Rev. 19:1–9 ("Blessed are those [celibate ascetics—14:1–5] who are invited to the marriage supper of the lamb!") combined with the parable of the Great Supper (Matt. 22:1–10/Luke 14:16–24), especially Matthew's version, in which the banquet is a wedding reception for a king's son.

41a. 'Ammar ebn Sa'd relates that Jesus arrived at a village where the inhabitants were all lying dead in the pathways and around the houses. O company of disciples, he declared, this community has been destroyed by the wrath of God; otherwise, they would have been properly buried. O Spirit of God, they urged, let us have news of what has happened to them! So Jesus invoked God's name, and a revelation came, whereby God told him to call out to the villagers after nightfall to obtain the answer. When night came, Jesus went up on a hill and hailed the dead populace, and one of the villagers answered up: At your service, O Spirit of God! Jesus asked what had happened to them. The reply came: we spent a peaceful night and woke up in the morning to find ourselves in the pit of Hell. Jesus asked why. Because we loved *the world*, came the answer, and obeyed the behest of sinful people. In what way did you love the world?, queried Jesus. The way a child loves its mother, was the reply. Whenever it came to, we were happy, and whenever it went away, we became sad and wept. Then Jesus asked, Why do your comrades not speak up? Harsh and brutal angels have clamped red hot bits on their mouths, the voice answered. Then how is it you are able to speak? countered Jesus. I was not of them, said the other, even though I was with them. When the torment descended, I remained amongst them. At present, I am at the edge of Hell, not knowing whether I shall be saved or cast down into the infernal depths. At this point Jesus turned to his disciples and told them: Eating barley bread with rock salt and wearing sackcloth and sleeping on dunghills in squalor is more than enough to assure one's well-being in *this world* and the next. (Ibid., iv. p. 562)

The theme of "this world" continues unabated. This saying and the following have been bracketed together by their common use of the motif of the revelation of the doom to come to sinners. In the present saying, it is the disciples of Jesus who are shown the postmortem fate of the worldly, potentially including themselves unless they watch their step. In the next saying, their fate is revealed to those sinners at death.

This saying is a kind of miniature apocalypse on the order of the Apocalypse of Paul or the Apocalypse of Peter, where the disciples are vouchsafed a terrifying vision of sinners finally getting their just rewards.

42. Jesus said: Woe unto him who hath *this world*, seeing that he must die and leave it, and all that is in it! It deceives him, yet he trusts in it; he relies upon it, and it betrays him. Woe unto them that are deceived! When they shall be shown what they loathe, and shall be abandoned by what they love; and shall be overtaken by that wherewith they are threatened! Woe unto him whose care is *the world*, and whose work is sin; seeing that one day he shall be disgraced by his sin. (Ibid.)

This threat of hellfire and worldly vanity follows the previous saying because of their common use of the phrase "this world."

43. Jesus said: Who is it that builds upon the waves of the sea? Such is *the world*; take it not for your resting-place. (Ibid.)

The image is adapted from that in Matt. 7:24–27/Luke 6:47–49. That it is not rather an alternative, parallel, and independent saying is evident from the more far-fetched character of the metaphor. While no one could ever imagine building on the sea, it is barely possible that someone might be stupid enough to build upon sandy ground, as envisioned in the Matthean version. Whence the sea waves of the Sufi version? The inrushing waves of the Q version which destroy the poorly grounded house have become themselves the poor foundation of the house in the Sufi version. It is a case of garbled memory quotation.

This saying has been joined to the previous one by their common use of "the world."

44. Some said to Jesus: Teach us some doctrine for which God will love us. Jesus said: Hate *the world*, and God will love you. (Ibid.)

A third saying featuring "the world" has been appended here. The saying sets up a straw man, the erroneous assumption that God's favorites are those who happen to believe a certain creed. With this false assumption is swept away the depiction of Jesus as primarily a revealer of doctrines. Do we read in too much if we see here the relegation of theological niceties as a part of that worldliness which God and his loved ones alike despise?

It is tempting to make the saying late because of the possible reflection of that Sufi ecumenism that saw all positive religions as mere cocoons for the spirituality concealed within, an ascetic spirituality, of course. But on the other hand, the world-negation motif is quite old, as witness 1 John 2:15: "Love not the world, nor the things in the world, for if any man love the world the love of the Father is not in him."

45. Jesus said: Ye company of apostles, be satisfied with a humble portion in *this world*, so your faith be whole; even as the people of this world are satisfied with a humble portion in faith, so *this world* be secured to them. (Ibid., iii. 154)

This is a parallel with the independent ascetical saying Luke 16:8b, "For the sons of this age are more shrewd in dealing with their generation than the sons of light." Likewise, if one's attention is preoccupied with seeking the next world, one simply will not be competent to deal with worldly affairs, and vice versa.

46. Jesus said: O thou that seekest *this world* to do charity, to abandon it were more charitable. (Ibid.)

This saying, like the last one, refers to "this world"; hence their linking here.

What is the intention Jesus rebukes? Apparently, the person in view does not want just to give charity in this world, but to gain the wealth of the world so as to have something to give to charity. And why is utter abandonment of the world (of possessions and society) a superior course? One might answer that the self-mortification of the ascetic wins the ascetic himself more merit than almsgiving would. But that is not the point. Rather, abandonment of the world is said to be better *for the world*, not for the ascetic. He is doing the world more of a favor than the worldly philanthropist. Why? Perhaps because to give alms contributes to the delusory optimism that the ills of the world are susceptible to remedy within the world. The ascetic knows that is tantamount to rearranging the furniture aboard the *Titanic*. It is the living lesson of the one who has renounced the world that alone will awaken worldly sufferers to their true plight, just as it was the sight of a wandering monk that galvanized Prince Siddhartha to renounce hearth, family, and throne to seek the true Dharma. Could he not have stayed in power and used his wealth to ameliorate the sufferings of those like the old man and the sick man he had seen, which so tormented him? Yes, but this would have been false hope, since the human malady goes much deeper. He wound up doing the world a greater service by discovering the radical surgery necessary to deal with the problem.

46a. Jesus said: *The world* and the hereafter are like two women which a man is trying to please at the same time; when one is pleased, the other is annoyed. (Ibid., Nurbakhsh)

This saying is a better version of Matt. 6:24: "No one can serve two masters, for either he will hate the first and love the second, or he will be devoted to the first and despise the second. You cannot serve God and Mammon." Loving and hating two slave masters seem somehow beside the point. And if the point is not to try to serve two objects of potential devotion, why say the slave must love the one and despise the other? If you hate the one, your mind's made up: your affections are *not* divided. The Sufi version is clearer: The lover of two women sees no more conflict in loving both than the rich religious person sees in loving both God and money. It is not that he loves either object less, but rather that his two-timing annoys both of *them*. Even so, we must imagine that it is God and Mammon (the Buddhist Mara) who despise the would-be slave of both, not the slave who despises one of them while loving the other. If he did the latter, whence the conflict in the first place?

This saying has been placed after the preceding because the compiler shrewdly recognized the notion of gaining wealth in order to give (part of) it to charity (see Nurbakhsh's translation: "O you who seek after worldly goods, in order to do good works. . . .") as a self-deceptive excuse to become or remain wealthy while claiming piety. The strategy is thus an attempt to court both God and Mammon, foolishly imagining that neither will mind.

46b. Jesus said: *This world* is a bridge. Pass over it. Do not linger upon it. (Ibid., Nurbakhsh)

Famously, this saying cannot go back to Jesus, nor even to the early Palestinian community, since there were no bridges in ancient Palestine!

The catchwords connecting this saying to the previous three are "this world."

47. Jesus used to say: My condition is hunger, my inner garment is fear, and *my outer garment* wool. I warm myself in winter in the sun; my candle is the moon; my mounts are my feet; my food and dainties are the fruits of the earth; neither at eventide nor in the morning have I aught in my possession, yet no one on earth is richer than I. (Ibid., iii. 159)

Here is a progammatic statement of Cynic/Christian monastic/Sufi self-sufficiency. There is a hidden and ironic truth in the apparently extravagant promise that God will provide all necessities: The truth is that the ascetic learns to do without whatever is not provided him. What others deem necessities, he has learned to dismiss as luxuries. And thus God has taken care of him by teaching him to do without. The promise is not one of miraculous providence but rather of lowered expectations.

The Sufis take their name from the Arabic word for wool, referring to the humble garments they wear, a practice going all the way back to the first followers of Muhammad in Mecca, who included both the voluntarily and involuntarily poor. There is no reason to think that Muslim ascetics were innovators in this regard, so this saying, which depicts Jesus as a good wool-wearing ascetic, may stem from pre-Islamic Christian monasticism, but there is no particular reason to press further back into religious history.

48. *The world* was revealed unto Jesus in the form of an old woman with broken teeth, with all sorts of ornaments upon her: How many husbands hast thou had? She said: I cannot count them. He said: Hast thou survived them all, or did they all divorce thee? She said: Nay, I have slain them all. Jesus said: Woe unto thy remaining husbands! Why do they not take warning by thy former husbands? Thou hast destroyed them one after the other, and yet they are not on their guard against thee. (Ibid. iii. 161)

This wonderful allegory trades on Old and New Testament images like that of Tob. 2:7–8 (the demon Asmodeus kills Rachel's husbands, seven of them one after the other, before she can consummate marriage with them), Mark 12:20–23 (one woman marries seven brothers, one after the other, because each dies before he can beget children for her), and John 4:16–18 (the Samaritan woman has had five husbands and now lives with a sixth man without the pretense of wedlock). We are also reminded of the conservative Dean Inge's quip that "He who marries the spirit of the age will often find himself a widower"—to which one might answer: It is better than the alternative of necrophilia.

Why has this saying been arranged to follow the one before it? The link is between "my outer garment" in number 47 and the woman's gaudy "ornaments" here in number 48.

49. Jesus said: Of a truth I say unto you, even as the sick man looks at the food, and does not enjoy it, owing to the violence of his pain; even so the man

of *this world* takes no pleasure in worship, neither tastes its sweetness for the love of this world which he feels. And of a truth I say unto you, that even as a beast, if he be not ridden and exercised, becomes intractable and changes his character; even so, if the heart be not softened by the thought of death, and the fatigue of devotion, it becomes hard and rough. And of a truth I say unto you, that even as a *bottle*, so long as it is not rent nor dry, is fit to hold honey; even so the heart, as it is not torn by passion, nor befouled by desire, nor hardened by comfort, shall become a *vessel* for wisdom. (Ibid., iii. 161.)

This set of three similitudes is linked with the preceding saying by the presence in both of the "world." Beyond this, the saying is perhaps remarkable for its unusual anticipation of Schleiermacher's aesthetic approach to religion, "a sense and taste for the Infinite."

The (to us morbid) meditation upon death, urged here, is shown practiced by Jesus himself in sayings 75 and 76.

50. Jesus said: He that seeks after this world is like one that drinks sea-*water*: the more he drinks, the thirstier he becomes, until it slay him. (Ibid.)

This excellent similitude is linked to the previous sayings by the mention in number 48 of "vessel" and "bottle," while number 49 mentions drinking. The ascetic counsel here, as often in Sufism, sounds almost Buddhist: It is, with tragic irony, the very thing one desperately seeks for sustenance that will poison one.

51. The apostles said to Jesus: How is it that thou canst walk upon the *water*, whereas we cannot? He said unto them: What think ye of *the dinar and the dirham*? They said: They are precious. He said: But to me they are equal with the dirt. (Ibid., iii. 175)

Walking upon the water is a favorite Sufi theme, and some Sufi mystics have claimed to be able to do it. This saying presupposes the same link we find in the Apocryphal Acts of the Apostles between docetic Christology and ascetical practice. How has Jesus managed to defy gravity, or in other words to take on the insubstantiality of a ghost (cf. the address "O Spirit of God") so that mere water holds him up? He has parted company once and for all with both the denarius and the drachma. These, in the pockets of others, would act as heavy anchors dragging them down beneath the waves.

52. Jesus said: There are three dangers in *wealth*: First, it may be taken from an unlawful source. And what if it be taken from a lawful source? they asked. He answered: It may be given to an unworthy person. They asked: And what if it be given to a worthy person? He answered: The handling of it may divert its owner from God. (Ibid., iii. 178)

Saying 52 is joined to 51 above because "wealth" here reflects "the dinar and the dirham" (Roman coins) there.

53. Jesus said: Store up for yourselves something which *the fire* will not devour. They said: What is that? He answered: Mercy. (Ibid., iii. 184)

In view here is an eschatological scene like that in 1 Cor. 3:13: "Each man's work will become manifest; for the Day will disclose it, because it will be revealed with fire, and the fire will test what sort of work each one has done." Paul warns that wood, hay, and straw cannot survive such temperatures, while gold, silver, and gems will prove lasting investments. What heavenly treasures might correspond to these goods? Here Jesus answers: mercy. And how will one have been able to stockpile that commodity? By showing mercy to others: "Judge not that ye be not judged, for with that judgment that ye judge, ye shall be judged" (Matt. 7:1–2). This treasure, which one is advised to "store up," serves to connect the saying with the two preceding ones.

54. We are told that Jesus said: Ye evil scholars, ye fast and pray and give alms, and do not what ye are commanded, and teach what ye do not perform. Evil is *your judgment*! Ye repent in words and fancy, but act according to your lust. It avails you not to cleanse your skins, when your *hearts* are foul. Verily I say unto you, be not like the sieve, whence the good corn goes out and the husks remain. Even so with you: ye cause the judgment to issue from your mouths, while the mischief remains in your *hearts*. Ye slaves of this world, how shall he win the next world who still lusts after this world, and yearns after it? Verily I say unto you, that your *hearts* shall weep for your actions. Ye have set the world under your tongues, and good works under your feet. Verily I say unto you, ye have spoiled your future, and the prosperity of this world is dearer unto you than the prosperity of the next. Who among mankind is more unfortunate than you, if you only knew it? Woe unto you! How long will ye describe the path to them that are in earnest, yourselves standing still in one place like those that are bewildered; as though ye summoned the inhabitants of the world to leave it to you? Stay, stay! Woe unto you! What does it profit a dark house that a lamp be set on the roof thereof, when all is dark within? Even so it profits you not that the light of the world should be upon your mouths when your *hearts* are destitute thereof. Ye slaves of this world, who are neither faithful slaves nor honorable freemen!, soon will the world pull you out by the root, and cast you on your faces; and then your sins shall take hold of your forelocks, and push you from behind, till they hand you over naked and destitute to the Royal Judge; then He shall show you your wickedness, and make you ashamed of your evil deeds. (Ibid., iii 198)

Has someone recollected there being a long denunciation by Jesus of the scribes and Pharisees such as we find in Matt. 23 and John 5, but couldn't remember it? This sounds like a kind of pastiche, drawing on some New Testament materials, to be sure. "Your judgment" serves to link the saying with the preceding one's reference to the refining fire of Judgment Day, just as the repeated references to the "heart" link this one with the second saying following this one.

54a. Jesus told his disciples: Whenever one of you should fast, he should smear grease on his hair and face and lips, so that no one is aware of his fasting; and when he gives with his right hand, his left hand should not know what his right hand is doing; and when he prays, he should draw a curtain across the doorway; for God metes out his blessings as he apportions his provender. (Ibid., p. 811)

That there is some relation between this saying and the complex in Matt. 6:1–18 is clear enough, but is the Sufi version to be judged merely a loose memory quotation of Matthew's, or is it rather possibly an independent version? I would guess the latter. As often in the Gospel of Thomas, we find here marks of a more primitive version. Note the lack of a "Matthean antithesis" between the "hypocrites" or Pharisees and the disciples, as well as the lack of the characteristically Matthean refrain, "Your Father who sees in secret will reward you." We also miss the Matthean digression lampooning Gentile Christian glossolalia (Matt. 6:7–8, literally, "Do not say '*Bata.*' "), which interrupts the triptych of secret pieties, as does Matthew's insertion of the Q Lord's Prayer at this point. The Sufi-preserved version, then, gives us evidence that Matthew did not make up his version out of whole cloth, as we would otherwise be tempted to conclude. He had a traditional basis for it, whatever its ultimate origin.

The theme of secret piety connects nicely with the preceding saying, especially if the compiler had Matt. 6:1–18 in mind, since then he must have taken this parallel as applying to the same "evil scholars." The element of modesty in the display of religion connects the saying with the next one, too, with its warning against pride.

55. Christ said: Blessed is he whom God teaches His book, and who does not die *proud*. (Ibid., iii. 256)

Here is a mercifully shorter complaint against evil scholars, those who are learned in the teaching of scripture but are puffed up with conceit over their learning.

The note about pride, added to the references to "the heart" in the preceding saying, serves to link both sayings 54 and 55 with numbers 56 and 57, in which both terms appear.

Nurbakhsh's translation, "Blessed is he who surrenders as God's book guides, for he will not die as an oppressor," gives a very different sense, one parallel to Col. 4:1.

55a. God revealed to Jesus: "When I bestow upon you a blessing, receive it with *humble* gratitude, that I may lavish upon you my entire bounty." (Ibid., 14, p. 945, Nurbakhsh)

The sentiment is an old one, going back at least as far as Deut. 8:17–18, "Beware lest you say in your heart, 'My power and the might of my hand have gotten me this wealth.' You shall remember Yahve your God, for it is he who gives you power to get wealth."

Note the occurrence of the adjective *humble* in this saying, as of *proud* in the one before it, since both will reappear in the following saying.

56. Christ said: The reed grows in the plain, but does not grow on the rock. Even so, wisdom works upon the *heart* of the *humble*, but does not work upon the heart of the *proud*. See ye not, that if a man lifts his head to the roof it wounds him, whereas if he bow down his head the roof shelters him? (Ibid. iii. 261)

Again, note the catchword theme of pride in the heart.

57. Jesus said: Beautiful raiment is *pride* of *heart*. (Ibid. iii. 269)

This sentiment, though reasonable enough, seems contradictory to the Matthean theme of hidden piety whereby one ought not to allow inward piety to be reflected in outward demeanor. For Matthew's Jesus, a public display of piety is a greater temptation for pride than a public display of wealth and beauty (Matt. 6:16–18).

58. Jesus said: Why come ye unto me with the garments of monks upon you, while your hearts are the *hearts of ravening wolves*? Put on the robes of kings, and mortify your hearts with fear. (Ibid.)

In view are the *wool* garments of the Sufis (or Syrian Christian monks) and withal the traditional warning against wolves in *sheep's* clothing. Also, the catchword connection with "heart" is carried still further. Now we do hear something like Matthew's hidden piety, in that pretenders to piety are rather to don impious garb until their self-mortification entitles them to the woolen habit of the true penitent.

59. It is narrated that there was a robber among the children of Israel who had infested the highway forty years, when Jesus passed by him with a pious Israelite, who was an apostle. The robber said in his heart: Here is the Prophet of God passing with his apostle by his side; what if I come out and make a third? Coming forth, he tried to approach the apostle, all the while despising himself and magnifying the apostle, and thinking that such as he was not worthy to walk by the side of that righteous man. The apostle perceived him, and said to himself: Shall such a man walk by my side? and gathering his

skirts together, he went and walked by the side of Jesus, so that the robber remained behind. Then God revealed unto Jesus: Say unto them, they must begin their work from the beginning, for I have canceled their previous deeds; I have canceled the good deeds of *the apostle for his self-conceit*, and the evil deeds of the other for his self-abasement. Then Jesus told them of this, and took the robber for his companion in his pilgrimage, and made him one of his *apostles*. (Ibid. iv. 120)

This tale essentially recasts the parable of the Pharisee and the Publican (Luke 18:9–14), Christianizing it. Note that the theme of the apostle's self-conceit matches that of the hypocritical monks in the previous saying.

60. It is recorded that Jesus said: *Ye company of the apostles* fear transgression, but we the Prophets fear unbelief. (Ibid. iv. 135)

The address to "the company of apostles" here links the saying with the reference to apostles in the previous one, as well as with the next saying.

61. Christ said: *Ye company of apostles*, the fear of God and love of Paradise give patience in tribulation and alienate men from the world. Verily I say unto you, that the eating of barley-bread and *sleeping* with dogs upon a dunghill in the search for Paradise are a little thing. (Ibid. iv. 143)

We are far from the Son of Man who came eating and drinking, who could be plausibly accused of being a drunk and a glutton (Matt. 11:19)! The neurotic voice of monastic extremism meets us here.

62. Christ passed in his wanderings by a man *asleep*, wrapped in a robe. He woke him, and said: O thou that sleepest, rise and make mention of God. He said: What wilt thou of me? Verily I have left the world to them that are *of the world*. He said unto him: Then sleep on, my beloved. (Ibid. iv. 152)

What seemed to be indolence turned out to be the sleep of the just. A somewhat similar anecdote occurs in Codex D, in place of Luke 6:5: "On the same day he saw a man performing a work on the Sabbath. Then he said unto him: Man! If thou knowest what thou doest, thou art blessed. But if thou knowest not, thou art cursed and a transgressor of the law." Appearances are insufficient; motives are what matters, something the sometime libertine Sufis urged their contemporaries to keep in mind.

The mention of "sleep" here matches that in the preceding saying, where ascetics are advised not to think twice about sleeping with the dogs.

63. Christ said: Look *not* unto the *wealth* of the people *of this world*; for the glitter of their wealth takes away the light of their faith. (Ibid. iv. 157)

The mention "of this world" here answers to the phrase "of the world" in the previous saying.

64. Christ said: Four things can be attained only with toil—silence, which is the beginning of devotion; humility; constant prayer; and *poverty*. (Ibid. iv. 173)

Here is the customary Sufi enumeration of the aspects of piety. The element of "poverty" accounts for the placement of the saying directly after number 63, with its admonition "Look not unto . . . wealth."

65. Jesus used to take with him nothing but a comb and a pitcher. One day, seeing a man comb his beard with his fingers, He *cast away the comb*; another day, seeing a man drink out of the river with his hands, He *threw away the pitcher*. (Ibid. iv. 182)

The poverty of the ascetic is absolute, demanding the renunciation of everything that pretends to improve on nature (as the Cynics put it) or on providence (as the Sufis put it), which are in the final analysis deemed to be the same thing. This story follows up the note of "poverty" in the preceding saying with concrete examples of it. The story is an exact parallel to the famous anecdote of Diogenes, considered below.

66. Jesus was asked, Why dost Thou *not buy an ass* to ride? He answered: I am too precious with God for Him to let an ass interrupt my thoughts of Him. (Ibid. iv. 256)

Is property a convenience, as most of us think? Or rather perhaps an inconvenience? If even the most rudimentary possession of a donkey distracts one from contemplation, it has become an inconvenience rather than a convenience. This saying has been grouped with number 65 as yet another example of basic possessions renounced.

67. Jesus passed by a man who was blind, leprous, crippled, paralyzed on both sides, and with his flesh scarred from elephantiasis, but was saying: Praise be to God, who has kept me free from that wherewith he hath afflicted many of his creatures. Jesus said unto him: Sir, what form of affliction is that which has been kept away from thee? He answered: O Spirit of God, I am better off than those *into whose hearts* God has not put that knowledge of himself which he has put into mine. Jesus said: Thou hast spoken truly; give me thy hand. He gave his hand, and straightway became the fairest and best-looking of men, for God had healed him of his afflictions. So he accompanied Jesus, and shared his devotions. (Ibid., iv. 272)

The point is obvious enough. Suffice it to note that here, conspicuously in a story which underlines the irrelevance of the outward man, Jesus is addressed again as "Spirit of God."

68. Jesus asked the children of Israel: Where does the seed grow? They answered: In the mold. He said: Of a truth I say unto you, wisdom grows not save *in a heart* like the mold. (Ibid., iv. 279)

The catchword here is "in a heart," matching "into whose hearts" in number 67.

69. Ibn El-Jala said: God revealed unto Jesus: When I examine *a man's heart*, and find *not therein any love for this world or for the next*, I fill it with *love of me* and sedulously guard it. (Ibid., iv. 281)

We must suppose that Jesus is imagined to have passed along the revelation vouchsafed to him here, but since the maxim is a direct revelation from God, like the Koran, instead of a saying of Jesus himself, the accredited transmitter, Ibn El-Jala almost takes the place of Jesus as the speaker of the saying.

The phrase "a man's heart" provides the catchword connection with the previous two sayings.

70. Jesus was asked: What is the best of works? He answered: Resignation to God, and *love of him*. (Ibid.)

Asked about good deeds, Jesus responds instead with a pair of dispositions, which are therefore more important. A similar contrast appears in John 6:28–29: "What must we do to be doing the works of God? Jesus answered them, This is the work of God: that you believe in him whom he has sent." Only here the virtue is not the Christian one of believing in Jesus but rather the Islamic one of submission to the will of Allah.

"Love of him" in this saying points back to "love of me [God]" in the previous saying.

71. Jesus said: Blessed is the eye that sleeps and thinks no evil, and wakes unto sinlessness. (Ibid., iv. 284)

One wonders if perhaps this saying originally followed immediately after number 62, in which case it would have perpetuated the catchword "sleep." It may have been omitted from the sayings collection by a copyist error, since the catchword principle itself invites accidental omission: A scribe's eye may return to the last word he remembers, but the wrong instance of it. Thus he skips a saying. Perhaps a proofreader noticed the omission and copied it into the margin, from whence the next scribe returned it to the body of the text, only he was perhaps oblivious of the catchword sequence and put the marginalized saying back in the wrong place. Or perhaps al-Ghazali himself departed in this instance from the order of sayings in the source.

72. The apostles asked Jesus: What *action* is just? He answered: That of him who works for God *without desiring that any one should praise him for it*. (Ibid., iv. 298)

This saying shares with number 69 the element of disinterested love of God with neither hope nor expectation of heavenly reward.

73. Jesus said: *Actions* are of *three sorts*—those which are evidently right, which ye should ensue; those which are evidently wrong, which ye should eschew; and those which are doubtful, which are to be referred to those who know. (Ibid., iv. 313)

"Actions" here follow up the previous saying's scholastic positing of the best pious "action" (cf. Mark 12:28-34).

74. On the authority of Ta'us: The apostles asked Jesus, Is there anyone on *earth* today like Thee? He answered: Yea; whosoever has for his *speech* prayer, and for his *silence* meditation, and for his *vision* tears, he is like me. (Ibid., iv. 332)

Is the attestation of the anecdote by Ta'us needed because it is not Jesus who initiates the saying? No such need was felt in other similar cases. At any rate, the saying appears after number 73 because that saying spoke of three sorts of action, and so does this one: prayer, meditation, and penitence.

74a. It is said that Jesus once sat down by an old man who was digging the *earth* with a spade. Said Jesus: O Lord God, take away his hope, and the old man put down his spade and lay down. After an hour had passed, Jesus said: O Lord God, restore hope to him, and he arose, and set about his task. And when Jesus asked him concerning what had transpired he said: While I was at work my soul said to me, How much longer shall you labor, now that you are an old man? so I cast aside my spade and lay down. Then it said to me, By God, you must *live out that which is left to you*. So, I arose and took up my spade once more. (Ibid., Winter trans.)

The reference to "digging the earth" provides the link with the previous saying and its use of the phrase "on earth." The contemplation by the old man of his allotted lifetime links the saying to the next one.

74b. Said Jesus: Pay no attention to your provisions for tomorrow, for if tomorrow is to be part of *your lifetime* then your provisions will come with it, whereas if it is not to be, then you should pay no attention to the lifetimes of others." (Ibid., Winter trans.)

Whereas this saying advises us not to worry about possible future perils, the next one inculcates, by example, the contemplation of death. If the two sentiments seem contradictory, the fact only underlines the nature of the catchword connection principle: The same theme is enough to link two sayings, whether the treatment of that theme is consistent between the sayings or not.

75. When Jesus thought on *death*, His skin dripped blood. (Ibid., iv. 354)

The last three items raise the same question that the presence of Matt. 10:38/Luke 14:27 ("Whoever does not bear his own cross and come after me cannot be my disciple") does in Q: Is there an implicit reference to the death of Jesus? Does the Q saying presuppose the famous death of Jesus on the cross and call the faithful to emulate him if necessary? Or are we reading into it a reference to the crucifixion of Jesus because it is so overwhelmingly familiar to us? The issue is quite important since Q contains no other reference to the death of Jesus, implicit or explicit, which implies the death of Jesus formed no part of the faith of whoever, whatever movement, compiled Q. Strikingly, the same ambiguity meets us in this "Sufi Q."

First, does the relegation of the three "death" sayings to the end of the sequence imply that everyone knew a "gospel," even a nonnarrative sayings gospel like Q (or Thomas) or the Sufi sayings source used by Al-Ghazali, ought to end with a Passion narrative, or at least the nonnarrative equivalent to one? Maybe, but then again it is obvious that material dealing with "the last things" should be placed last! The presence of the three "death" sayings does not need to be a reference to the fact of Jesus' (redemptive) death.

Second, we must remember that morbid introspection about one's own eventual death was a common spiritual exercise for Sufis (and others), as witness saying 49. There need be no reference to the Passion of Jesus, though the sweating of blood has crept into some manuscripts of Luke (Luke 22:44) from some apocryphal tradition—like *this* one! It made perfect sense to Sufis to read this anecdote as describing Jesus' proper pious anxiety about death with no reference to his own crucifixion—since, as Muslims, they believed Jesus had not been crucified!

76. Jesus said: Ye company of apostles, pray unto God that this cup may be easy for me; for I fear *death* with a terror which is like the pains of death. (Ibid., iv. 362)

The parallels to the Gethsemane story are obvious: "Father . . . remove this cup from me . . ." (Mark 14:36). "My soul is exceedingly sorrowful, even unto death" (Mark 14:34). But, again, no reference is actually made to Jesus' dying, though it is assumed that, like all mortals, one day he will. Is it possible that such a saying as is preserved here first formed the basis for the Gethsemane passages just quoted? It would not be the only instance of the gospel tradition taking a saying that originally pertained to the common human lot in a proverbial fashion being subsequently worked up into a narrative about Jesus in particular.

77. Jesus, passing by a skull, kicked it with His foot, and bade it speak by the will of God. It said: O Spirit of God, I was a king in past time. One day, when I was seated in my kingdom on my throne of state, with my crown on my head and my armies and my courtiers around me, the Angel of *Death* appeared to me. Then each of my members fell apart, and my spirit went forth to him. Would that all those armies had been but one troop! Would that all that dense company had been solitude! (Ibid., iv. 363)

The fact that it is not even Jesus' own death in view in this final saying rules out the possibility that the three "death" sayings were intended as the equivalent of a Passion story.

The skull already bore mute witness to the futility of worldly striving. Jesus just makes that silent testimony explicit. Indeed, the point is exactly that of Shelley's great poem "Ozymandias." The king should have done what Prince Siddhartha did: renounce the transitory glory of the kingdom in favor of a life of mendicant meditation, but for him, alas, it was too late.

I wonder: Is it possible to catch here an echo of the famous scene in the Theravada Buddhist text *The Questions of King Milinda*, in which a Buddhist monk explains to the Hellenistic King Menander the anatta (no soul) doctrine by disassembling a chariot piece by piece, asking which particular piece is the "chairot"? Even so, the "soul" is nothing but a superfluous, hypostatizing word better dispensed with. Does Jesus here converse, as the Buddhist once did, with King Menander? Is it the dharma of Buddhism the dead king wishes he had heeded? And was it the "members" of his royal chariot which "fell apart," teaching him a truth ignored at eternal peril?

77a. Said Jesus: How many a healthful body, a graceful face, and a skillful tongue, shall tomorrow be woeful among the tiers of *Hell*! (Ibid., Winter trans.)

We are not told that the possessors of these various excellences are using them for sinful ends. The point seems rather to be that one ought not to be blinded by today's sunlight to tomorrow's possible darkness. One must not put off contemplation of death and thus of repentance.

The fact that the focus is definitely not on Jesus' own death implies that the earlier anticipations of it were aimed at spurring the reader/hearer to contemplating his own.

In retrospect, the thing that jumps out at the reader of Margoliouth's set of sayings of Jesus from Sufi sources is how, once we get into the Jesus traditions from Al-Ghazali's *Revival of the Religious Sciences*, we find a virtually uninterrupted sequence of catchword connections denoting an originally orally transmitted collection of Jesus materials. As I studied Margoliouth's list, I wondered if the catchword sequence might prove an illusion dispelled once I restored the sayings skipped by Margoliouth, but in fact their restoration only served to continue and strengthen the pattern. On the other hand, the first six sayings in Margoliouth's list display no sign of catchword connection, as indeed we should expect, since Margoliouth chose them from disparate written sources. If Al-Ghazali had similarly drawn on disparate sources available to him, we should likewise expect no particular connecting thread. But that is just what we do in fact find. This leads me to the conclusion that Al-Ghazali had before him a written document, a collection of Jesus traditions exactly analogous to Q and to the Gospel of Thomas. Like Q, and as many believe, like Thomas, this document must have been a compilation of orally transmitted sayings and anecdotes. Of course, I infer that Al-Ghazali used the sayings in their original order, thus to some extent structuring his massive work *Revival of the Religious Sciences* around this document, much as the wide-ranging treatise of Shankara on nondualism is structured around the cryptic aphorisms of the *Vedanta Sutras* of Badarayana, or Madame Blavatsky's *The Secret Doctrine* around the terse texts of the *Stanzas of Dzyan*. Though this hypothesis must past muster before the tribunal of scholars of Islam, I offer it here at least as a provisional suggestion which, if valid, is quite significant.

This reconstructed Sufi Q would function as the Gospel of Thomas has ever since its discovery in 1945, as a kind of corroboration of the Q hypothesis. Thomas is an actual example of the kind of document Q was hypothesized to be, as is the Sufi sayings document. Can we suggest a date? No, not really. Very little of it could be construed as specifically Islamic or Sufistic. The developed signature doctrines and practices of Sufism occur in the Sufi Q as little as Gnostic distinctives occur in Thomas. Most scholars who have examined the sayings have deemed it likely that many of them may be hundreds of years older than the twelfth century, when Al-Ghazali wrote, and that many may be pre-Islamic, drawn from Syrian monastic tradition. And then we are talking about Christian agrapha or Apocrypha, something very much like Thomas.

And as I have anticipated, this Sufi Q would tend to increase the plausibility of Burton Mack's profile of the proto- or pre-Christians behind Q. For the compilers of Q, Thomas, and Sufi Q, Jesus was a Cynic-like teacher of wisdom. His death was not apparently part of their faith. They may not even have known what happened to Jesus. Sufi Q strengthens Mack's argument that if the Q community believed the death of Jesus was important, they had a funny way of showing it. Yes, they might have cherished beliefs they did not include in what appears to be a charter document, but what evidence could we point to that they believed what is unattested? But the Sufi Q has been transmitted to us by a community whose beliefs we know. As Muslims, *they certainly lacked any and all belief in Jesus' death or resurrection.*

THE BIG BANG VERSUS THE BIG MACK

Burton Mack bids us dare to part with the traditional model of Christian origins, shared by Bultmann and other supposed radicals, which has it that Jesus was crucified under Pontius Pilate, and that three days later the disciples experienced visions of the Risen Christ. Perhaps the resurrection was a hallucination; no matter. It was the "Big Bang" from which all the diverse forms of Christianity (Gnostic, Catholic, Ebionite-Jewish, and so on) emerged by hook or by crook. All forms of Christianity would have represented various ways of interpreting this "Christ event." So say most scholars, whether conservative or liberal. But not Mack. He suggests instead that what we have all been doing is gullibly adopting the foundation myth of *one* of the many kinds of early Christianity. Since there is no reason to believe the Q community (or that which produced the similar Gospel of Thomas) had the slightest interest in or knowledge of a Passion, why should we assume that the Q document or the Q community stems from such an ostensible death and resurrection? No, Mack says, it is time to recognize that the resurrection was one of many origin myths cherished by but one of a wide diversity of Jesus movements and Christ cults all over Palestine and Syria.

As discussed in earlier chapters, Mack sets forth a typology of the various Jesus movements and Christ cults to which we owe various segments and strata of the New Testament writings. He ultimately seems to leave open the question whether these very different Christianities stem from a common origin point in the historical Jesus. If they did, we might call this common genesis a "Little Bang," since it would be the man Jesus himself, not the theological supernova of the resurrection, that would be the primordial singularity. But it seems hard to imagine that Mack would be willing, in effect, just to push the traditional single-origin concept back a few steps. Though he hesitates to say so, he seems to be implying a multiple-origin theory. Christianity grew from several roots, not one. À la Koester and Robinson, if we plot the trajectories of Christian evolution through the New Testament documents as Mack does, we will come up with multiple Christianities *all the way back*, the gradual federation and assimilation of disparate Christ mystery cults and Jesus movements which *at first had nothing to do with each other*.

We would, in other words, have a situation exactly analogous to that of the ancient Israelite tribal league (or *amphictyony*). It has been clear for some time that Israel initially formed as a confederation of separate tribes, many of them named for their traditional totems or gods (e.g., Zebulon, Asher, and Gad), others for their homeland (Ephraim for the people on Mt. Ephrath; Benjamin for sons of the south, as in Yemen) or occupation (Issachar for burden bearers). Like six- or twelve-tribe leagues all over the ancient Mediterranean, these tribes adopted a common god (Yahve) in addition to "state and local" deities, and each tribe took its turn taking care of the central shrine (Gilgal, Shechem, and Shiloh at different times) for one (or two) months a year. Once the twelve tribes of Israel had come together, they sealed their bond by positing a mythical eponymous ancestor, Israel/Jacob, whose twelve sons were imagined as the progenitors of each tribe. Each tribal patriarch was accorded the name of one of the tribes, even though some were not even personal names.

Implicit in Mack's alternative to the Big Bang model of Christian origins would seem to be what we must call the *Big Mack* model: an assembling of various ingredients to make one big, oozing *melange* of Christianity. And Jesus would be the analogue, in the Big Mack model, to the eponymous mythical patriarch Israel/Jacob. And such a Jesus figurehead would fit perfectly with the composite figure of the gospels who seems to be an amalgam of ill-fitting pieces from Old Testament proof texts and borrowings from contemporary messiahs and prophets. His patchwork character derives from the conflationary nature of the movement for which he serves as eponymous figurehead.

WHO IS THIS BROKEN MAN?

Let me hasten to point out that a multiple-root origin theory for Christianity would not automatically mean there had been no original historical Jesus. Indeed, Mack certainly holds for, so to speak, at least one historical Jesus, the sage whose sayings have been collected for our edification in Q1. But I wonder if Mack's work does not set loose implications that he himself does not yet appreciate. Let me outline three factors that would imply that Q1, far from allowing us access for the first time to the historical Jesus, is instead inconsistent with a historical Jesus.

First, do we receive from the Q1 sayings and anecdotes a striking and consistent picture of a historical individual? Mack thinks we do. There is a sly sense of humor coupled with common sense and prophetic anger. There is a definite outlook on life. And thus, one might think, a definite personality, a real character! But no. The problem is that once we discern the pronounced Cynic character of the sayings, we have an alternate explanation for the salty, striking, and controversial "personality" of the material. It conveys not the personality of an individual but that of a movement, the sharp and humorous Cynic outlook on life. What we detect so strongly in the texts is their Cynicism. The fact that so many Q1 sayings so strongly parallel so many Cynic maxims and anecdotes proves the point for the simple reason that *the Cynic materials used for comparison stem from many different Cynic philosophers over several centuries!* If they do not need to have come from a single person, neither do those now attributed to Jesus which parallel them. Let me illustrate my point by supplying here the text of the hypothetical Q1 (minus a couple of sayings Mack and others feel entitled to add from Luke, unparalleled by Matthew, but which I regard as Lukan redaction), with parallels from contemporary Cynic-Stoic popular philosophy (gleaned from F. Gerald Downing's exhaustive compendium *Christ and the Cynics*.[13]

Q1

Blessed are the poor, for theirs is the kingdom of God.
> *Only the person who has despised wealth is worthy of God.* (Seneca)
> *We should not get rid of poverty, but only our opinion of it. Then we shall have plenty.* (Epictetus)

Blessed are those who hunger, for they shall be filled.
> *People used to see Diogenes shivering out in the open, often going thirsty.* (Dio)
> *Herakles cared nothing about heat or cold, and had no use for a mattress or a woolly cape or a rug. Dressed in a dirty animal skin, living hungry, he helped the good and punished the wicked.* (Dio)

Blessed are those who weep, for they shall laugh.
> *"Don't you want to know why I never laugh? It's not because I hate people, but because I detest their wickedness. . . . You are astonished because I don't laugh, but I'm astonished at those who do, happy in their wrong-doing when they ought to be dejected at failing to do what's right.* (Pseudo-Heraclitus)

I say to you, love your enemies.
Bless those who curse you.
Pray for those who mistreat you.
> *A rather nice part of being a Cynic comes when you have to be beaten like an ass, and throughout the beating you have to love those who are beating you as though you were father or brother to them.* (Epictetus)
> *How shall I defend myself against my enemy? By being good and kind towards him, replied Diogenes.* (Gnomologium Vaticanum)
> *Someone gets angry with you. Challenge him with kindness in return. Enmity immediately tumbles away when one side lets it fall.* (Seneca)

If someone slaps you on the cheek, offer him the other also.
If someone seizes your cloak, offer him your tunic as well.
> *Musonius said he would never indict anyone who'd injured him, nor would he advise anyone else to, not anyone who wanted to be a proper philosopher. . . . Well, if a philosopher cannot despise a slap or abuse, what use is he? . . . People sin against you. You take it without going wild, without harming the offenders. Instead you give them cause for hope of better things.* (Musonius Rufus)
> *If you're inclined to be quick-tempered, practice putting up with being abused, refusing to get cross at insults. You'll be able to go on from that to taking a slap and saying to yourself, I seem to have got entangled with a statue.* (Epictetus)

Give to anyone who asks of you, and if someone seizes your belongings, do not seek them back.
> *If there is a requisition and a soldier seizes {your donkey}, let it go. Do not resist or complain; otherwise you will be first beaten, and lose the donkey after all.* (Epictetus)

Don't get cross when wise people ask you for a tribol, for it's not yours, it's theirs, and you're giving it back to them. . . . For everything belongs to God, friends have everything in common, and the wise are the friends of God. (Pseudo-Crates)

Diogenes used to say we should hold out our hands to our friends palm open, not tight-fisted. (Diogenes Laertius)

What we have now is enough for us, but you take whatever you want of it. (Dio)

Treat others as you would have them treat you.

Take care not to harm others, so others won't harm you. (Seneca)

Let each one here reflect how he feels towards those who try to do him down. That way he'll have a fair idea of how others must feel about him, if that's how he behaves. (Dio)

If you love those who love you, what credit is that to you? Do not even tax-collectors love those who love them? If you greet only your brothers, what more are you doing than others? Does not everyone do likewise? If you lend only to those you expect to pay you back, what credit is that to you? Even evil-doers lend to their fellows expecting to be repaid.

I never did a kindness to win a testimonial or to gain gratitude or any favor in return. (Dio)

. . . as though it were the done thing to be stingy and tight-fisted with impoverished strangers, but to be generously welcoming with hospitable gifts only to the wealthy, from whom you clearly expected much the same in return. (Dio)

No, love your enemies, do good, and lend without expecting repayment. Your reward will be great, and you will be children of God. For he makes the sun rise on the evil and the good; he sends rain on the just and the unjust alike.

By and large only humankind among living creatures is an image of God. . . . As God is . . . high-minded, beneficent and humane (that's how we conceive him to be), so we must think of human beings as his image, so long as they live according to nature, and are eager to. . . . (Musonius)

Diogenes said good men were images of the gods. (Diogenes Laertius)

The whole human race is held in high regard—and equally high regard—by God who gave it birth. (Dio)

Be merciful, even as your Father is merciful.
Judge not, lest you, too, be judged.
For you will be judged by the same standard you apply.

Someone asked how he could master himself. Diogenes replied, "By rigorously reproaching yourself with what you reproach others with." (Stobaeus)

Can a blind man lead a blind man? Will they not both fall into a pit?

Some people prefer to be provided with a blind guide rather than a sighted one. They're bound to take a tumble. (Philo)

You can no more have a fool as king than a blind man to lead you along the road. (Dio)

A student is not better than his teacher. It is sufficient that he should be like his teacher.

When Diogenes saw a boy eating a savory snack, he rightly slapped the slave looking after him; for the fault lay with the one who'd failed to teach rather than with the one who hadn't learned. (Plutarch)

How can you look for the splinter in your brother's eye while there is a two-by-four in your own eye? How can you say to your brother, "Let me remove the splinter from your eye," when you are not aware of the two-by-four in your own eye? Hypocrite! First take the two-by-four out of your own eye, and then you will be able to see to remove the splinter in your brother's eye.

And you, are you at liberty to examine others' wickednesses, and pass judgment on anyone . . . ? You take note of others' pimples when you yourself are a mass of sores. . . . It's like someone covered in foul scabs laughing at the odd mole or wart on someone of real beauty. (Seneca)

When the Athenians do philosophy in your way they are like people promising to heal others of ills they've not managed to cure in themselves. (Pseudo-Diogenes)

A good tree does not bear bad fruit. A bad tree does not bear good fruit. Do they gather figs from thistles, or thistles from figs? Every kind of tree is recognized by its fruit.

Who would think to be surprised at finding no apples on the brambles in the wood? or be astonished because thorns and briars are not covered in useful fruits? (Seneca)

The good man brings forth good things from his treasury; the evil man evil things. For the mouth speaks from what fills the heart.

Evil no more gives birth to good than an olive tree produces figs. (Seneca)

Why do you call me, "Lord, lord," and not do what I say? Everyone who hears my words and does them is like a man who built his house on a rock. The rain fell, the flood broke against the house, and it did not fall, for it had a solid foundation. But everyone who hears my words and does not do them is like a man who built his house on sand. The rain fell, the flood broke against it, and it fell, and it was a total ruin.

Diogenes described himself as a hound of the kind much praised, but which none of its admirers dared to take out hunting. (Diogenes Laertius)

It was mostly people from a distance away who came to talk with Diogenes . . . the common motive was just to have heard him speak for a short while, so as to have something to tell other people about . . . rather than look for some improvement for themselves. (Dio)

If you are in good health and think yourself at last fit to be your own man, I am pleased. The distinction will be mine if I can pull you away from where you are floundering in the waves. But, my dear Lucilius, I'm begging you as well as exhorting you to put down philosophical foundations deep in your heart. Then test your progress! But not by words that you speak or write. To see what strength of mind you have gained, and what unruly desires you've shed, you must test your words by your deeds. (Seneca)

A man said to him, "I will follow you wherever you go." Jesus said to him, "Foxes have holes, and birds of the air have nests, but the sons of men have no place to lay their heads [for the night]."

According to Theophrastus Diogenes had watched a mouse running around, not bothering to find anywhere for its nest, not worrying about the dark, showing no particular desire for things one might suppose particularly enjoyable. It was through watching this mouse that he discovered the way to cope with circumstances. (Diogenes Laertius)

No city, no house, no fatherland, a wandering beggar, living a day at a time. (Diogenes Laertius)

The whole earth is my bed. (Pseudo-Anarcharsis)

I've no property, no house, no wife nor children, not even a straw mattress, or a shirt, or a cooking pot. (Epictetus)

I have traveled around for so long, not only without hearth or home, but without even a single attendant to take round with me. (Dio)

Another man said to him, "First let me go and bury my father." Jesus said to him, "Let the dead bury their dead."

Though the mass of people want the same results as the Cynics, once they see how difficult the way is, they steer well clear of those who propose it. (Pseudo-Crates)

Someone wanted to do philosophy with Diogenes. Diogenes gave him a tunny-fish to carry around and told him to follow him. For shame the would-be disciple threw it down and left. Some time later Diogenes met him. "Our friendship was broken up by a tunny fish," he said with a laugh. (Diogenes Laertius)

Someone said to Diogenes, "I'm yours to command." He took him along and gave him a half-obol's worth of cheese to carry. He refused. "Our friendship's been shattered," said Diogenes, "by a piece of cheese costing all of a half-obol." (Diogenes Laertius)

It's not how you think it is. . . . You say, "I wear an old cloak already—I'll go on doing that. I sleep on a hard bed now, and I shall still. I'll get myself a satchel and staff, and I'll wander around, begging from the people I meet. . . ." If you think that's how it is, stay well clear of the whole business; there's nothing in it for you. (Epictetus)

If you die without a servant to wait on you, who will take you away to bury you? Whoever wants the house, said Diogenes (Diogenes Laertius)

Diogenes was harsher. . . . In Cynic style he spoke more crudely, giving orders that he was to be thrown out without burial. His friends asked, "For the birds and wild animals?" "Certainly not. You're to put a staff near me to drive them off with." "How could you?" they asked. "You'll be past all feeling." "Well, what harm is there in being torn to pieces by wild beasts if I'm past all feeling?" (Cicero)

A little while before Demonax died someone asked, "What instructions have you given about your burial?" "No need to fuss," he said. "The stink will get me buried." (Lucian)

There's no need to thank your parents, either for your birth, or for being the sort of person you are. (Pseudo-Diogenes)

Obeying your father, you're obeying the will of a fellow human being. Doing philosophy, you're obeying Zeus. (Musonius)
If you're not accomplishing anything, there was not much point your coming in the first place. Go back and look after things at home . . . you'll have a bit more pocket money, and you'll look after your father in his old age. (Epictetus)

He said, the harvest is abundant, but the laborers are few; therefore, beg the master of the harvest to send out more laborers into the harvest.
The problem may well lie with the so-called philosophers. Some of them refuse point-blank to face crowds, just won't make the effort. Perhaps they've given up hope of improving the masses. (Dio)
A true Cynic will not rest satisfied with having been well-trained himself. He must realize he's been sent as God's messenger to his fellow humans to show them where they are going astray over what is right and what is wrong . . . (Epictetus)

See, I send you out as lambs amid wolves.
Crates said that people living with flatterers were in as bad a way as calves among wolves. (Diogenes Laertius)

Do not carry money, or a pouch, or sandals, or a staff.
And according to Diocles Antisthenes was the first to double his cloak, and use just that, and carry a staff and a satchel. (Diogenes Laertius)
According to some, Diogenes was the first person to double his threadbare cloak, because he had to use it to sleep in, and he carried a satchel for his bread . . . but he took to carrying a staff for support only when he became infirm. (Diogenes Laertius)
When I'd chosen in favor of this Cynic way, Antisthenes took off the shirt and the cloak I was wearing, put a doubled threadbare cloak on me instead, slung a satchel on my shoulder, with some bread and other scraps of food, and put in a cup and a bowl. On the outside of the satchel he hung an oil flask and a scraper, and then, finally, he gave me a staff, too. (Pseudo-Diogenes)
Wearing only ever one shirt is better than needing two, and wearing just a cloak with no shirt at all is better still. Going bare-foot, if you can, is better than wearing sandals (Musonius)
By now Peregrinus had taken to long hair and a dirty threadbare cloak and a satchel, with a staff in his hand. (Lucian)

And do not greet anyone on the road.
Seek out the most crowded places, and when you're there, keep to yourself, quite unsociable, exchanging greetings with no one, neither friend nor stranger. (Lucian)

Whatever house you enter, say, "Peace be to this house!" And if a man of peace is there, your protection will rest upon him. But if not, let your blessing return to you.
"A good daimon {spirit} has come to stay in my house." {Diogenes' host speaking of his arrival} (Diogenes Laertius)

"Is it really necessary to have something written over your doorway?" "Yes, it is." "Then how about this? 'Poverty lives here, evil is debarred.' " (Pseudo-Diogenes)

Don't beg your necessities from everyone, and don't accept unsolicited gifts from just anyone, either. It's not right for moral virtue to be fed by wickedness. Ask and accept only from people who've accepted an invitation into philosophy themselves. (Pseudo-Crates)

And remain in the same house, eating and drinking whatever they provide, for the laborer is worthy of his wages.

You're not asking for a free gift, still less for some worse bargain, but for a contribution to the well-being of everyone . . . you are able to give back something very much better than what you got. (Pseudo-Diogenes)

A good soldier is never without someone to reward his efforts, nor is a laborer or a cobbler. Do you think it's any different for a good human being? Do you think God cares so little for the servants and witnesses he's had so much success with? (Epictetus)

Do not go from house to house.

It looks to me as though what you really want is to go into someone's house and stuff yourself with food. (Epictetus)

If you enter a town and they receive you, eat what is set before you. Heal the sick and say to them, "The Kingdom of God has come near you."

A Cynic's friend must share the Cynic's scepter and his royal rule and be a worthy servant. (Epictetus)

Let me enjoy the wealth that is really mine. I have experienced the great and invincible kingdom of wisdom. (Demetrius, quoted by Seneca)

It is Zeus who first and foremost knows how to rule—and shares his knowledge with whom he will. (Dio)

But if you enter a town and they do not receive you, as you leave, shake the very dust from your feet and pronounce against them, "Nevertheless, know this: the Kingdom of God has come near you!"

Diogenes the Cynic Dog to you so-called Hellenes, Be damned to you . . . you lay claim to everything, but you actually know nothing. (Pseudo-Diogenes)

To some Diogenes seemed quite mad; lots despised him as a powerless good-for-nothing. Some abused him and tried insulting him by throwing bones at his feet as you do to dogs. Others, again, would come up and pull at his cloak. . . . Yet Diogenes was really like a reigning monarch walking in beggars' rags among his slaves and servants. (Dio)

When you pray, say:
    Father, May your name be kept in reverence.
    May your kingdom come.
    Give us each day our daily bread.
    Cancel our debts, for we cancel the debts owed us.
    And do not bring us to the test.

> For everyone and for ever and always there is the father who cares for them. Why, to Odysseus, it was no hearsay matter, that Zeus is the Father of humankind, for he always thought of him as Father, and addressed him as Father, and did everything he did with him in mind. (Epictetus)
> Some people do not hesitate to address {Zeus} as Father in their prayers. (Dio)
> God . . . who gives us what we need to live, and life itself, and everything good, the common Father and savior and guardian of human kind . . . is addressed as King because he rules in power, and as Father, I take it, because of his care and gentleness. (Dio)
> Another takes care to provide us with food. (Epictetus)
> With peace proclaimed by God through reason . . . now no evil can befall me. (Epictetus)

Ask and it shall be given you.
Seek and you shall find.
Knock, and the door shall be opened to you.
For every one who asks receives,
and the one who seeks finds,
and the door is opened to the one who knocks.
> *Seek and you will find.* (Epictetus)

Which of you fathers, if his son asks for bread, will give him a stone, or if he asks for fish, will give him a snake? Therefore, if you, being evil, know how to give good gifts to your children, how much more will the Father in heaven give good things to those who ask him!
> *And our parent has put close to hand whatever is going to be to our good.* (Seneca)
> *People blame the gods because they don't make them rich with lots of nice things—but they don't blame their own disposition to stupidity. They must be blind to refuse the really good gifts the daimon gives.* (Pseudo-Heraclitus)

Nothing is hidden that will not one day be made known, or secret that will not eventually come to light.
> *The Cynic . . . ought to have nothing of his own that he wants to hide. Otherwise . . . he's started to be afraid about externals, he's begun to feel the need for concealment. And he couldn't possibly keep anything concealed even if he wanted to. Where or how could he possibly hide himself?* (Epictetus)

What I tell you in the dark, speak in the light. And what you hear whispered in your ear, shout it from the housetops.
> *I shall remain for as long as there are cities and inhabited countries, my learning assuring that I never fall silent.* (Pseudo-Heraclitus)
> *Diogenes lit a lamp in broad daylight and went around with it, saying, "I'm looking for an honest man."* (Diogenes Laertius)

Do not fear those who can kill the body, but cannot kill the soul.
Free under Father Zeus and afraid of none of the great lords. (Pseudo-Diogenes)
What tyrant or thief or court can frighten anyone who does not care about his body or its possessions? (Epictetus)

Are not five sparrows sold at market for two cents? Yet not a single one of them falling to the ground escapes God's watchful eye. The very hairs of your head each has its number. Therefore, do not fear. You are worth more than many sparrows.
Isn't God such that he oversees everything, and is present there with everything, and is able to be in touch, in some way, with everything? (Epictetus)

Therefore I tell you, have no anxiety over your life, what you will eat, or about your body, what you will wear. Is not life more than food, and the body more than clothing? Consider the ravens. They neither sow nor reap nor gather into barns, and God feeds them. Are you not worth more than the birds? Which of you can add a single hour to your life by worrying about it? And why worry about clothing? Consider the lilies of the field, how they grow. They neither toil nor spin: yet I tell you even Solomon in all his finery was not arrayed as one of these! If God clothes the grass of the field in this manner, though it is in the field today, only to be thrown into a furnace tomorrow, will he not clothe you, you of little faith?
Hunger, cold, contempt? Poverty doesn't necessitate any of these. Not hunger, for lots of things grow from the earth and can satisfy hunger; for the dumb beasts go without clothes and don't feel it. (Pseudo-Diogenes)
"Good God, that's all very well, but I'm a poor man without property. Suppose I have lots of children, where am I going to get food for them all?" "Well, where do the little birds go to get food from to feed their young, though they're much worse off than you are—the swallows and nightingales and larks and blackbirds . . . ? Do they store away food in safe-keeping?" (Musonius)
Why not consider the beasts and the birds, and see how much more painlessly they live than humans do, how much more pleasantly and healthily. They are stronger, each lives the longest possible span for their kind—despite lacking hands or human intelligence. . . . They have one enormous advantage to counter-balance any ills they may suffer—they are free of property. (Dio)

Therefore I tell you, do not worry, saying to yourselves, "What shall we eat?" or "What shall we drink?" or "What shall we wear?" For the nations do that, and your Father knows you need these things. Instead, seek his kingdom, and all these things will be provided as a matter of course.
Since I keep my time clear of the things others busy themselves with, come to me, if you need anything I have to offer. I'll refund you generously for all the gifts you currently take so much pleasure in. (Pseudo-Anarchasis)
"What's going to become of me? Is it impossible to find a traveling companion {through life} who's strong and totally reliable?" Then you think to yourself, "If I commit myself to God, I'll make the journey in safety." (Epictetus)

We make a fuss about our little bodies, about our piffling property, about what Caesar thinks of us. And about what's going on inside us? Not a thought! (Epictetus)

The philosophic wise man . . . without being concerned or anxious about more than the bare necessities, will give his stomach and back what's due to them. Carefree and happy, he'll laugh at people busy with their riches, and at others scurrying around trying to get rich, and he'll say, "Why postpone being yourself into the distant future?" (Seneca)

Sell your possessions and give [the proceeds] to the poor.

Crates sold up all his property—he was from a prominent family—and realized about two hundred talents. This he shared among his fellow citizens. (Diogenes Laertius)

I gather that you brought all your wealth to the civic assembly and handed it over to your native city. Then, standing in the middle, you shouted out, "Crates, son of Crates, sets Crates free!" (Pseudo-Diogenes)

Do not store up for yourselves treasures on earth, where moth and rust corrupt and thieves break in and steal. But store up for yourselves treasure in heaven, where moths and rust do not corrupt and thieves do not break in and steal. For where your treasure is, your heart will be there also.

Our soul knows, I tell you, that wealth does not lie where it can be heaped together. It is the soul itself that we ought to fill, not our money-chest. It is the soul that we may set above all other things, and put, god-like, in possession of the universe . . . when it has taken itself off to the great heights of heaven. (Seneca)

Someone who is eager for riches is also fearful for them. But no one stops to enjoy such a worrying gain; they're always at pains to add something more. (Seneca)

Where the "I" and the "mine" are, that's the direction in which the living being is bound to incline. If they're in the flesh, that's going to dominate; if they're in one's moral choice, that's dominant. (Epictetus)

He said, What is the kingdom of God like? To what can one compare it?

{Pheidias the sculptor claims he has tried to represent something of the accepted character of God} to the extent that a mortal man can understand and represent the inconceivable nature of God. (Dio)

It is like a grain of mustard seed which a man took and sowed in his garden. It grew and became a tree, and the birds of the air made nests in its branches.

These words should be scattered like seeds. However small a seed is, once it's sown in suitable ground, its potential unfolds, and from something tiny it spreads out to its maximum size . . . I'd say brief precepts and seeds have much in common. Great results come from small beginnings. (Seneca)

Once a man gave a great banquet and invited many. When time came for the banquet he sent his slave to say to those who had been invited, "Come, for everything is now ready." But they all alike began to make excuses. The first said to him, "I have bought a farm, and I must go and look it over. Please have me excused." Another said, "I have bought five pair of oxen, and I need to inspect them. Please have me excused." Another said, "I have just married a wife, and I cannot come." The slave came and reported this to his master. Then the owner said in anger, "Go out quickly into the streets of the town and bring in as many people as you find." And the slave went out into the streets and brought in everyone he could find, till the house was filled with guests.

We've no end of excuses ready for our base behavior—it's our children, our mother, our brothers. (Epictetus)

He who does not hate his father and mother cannot be my disciple.
He who does not hate his son and daughter cannot be my disciple.

If you'd seized his property, Diogenes would have let it go rather than follow you for it. If you'd seized hold of his leg, he'd have let that go—and his . . . body, his family, his friends, his native land. . . . (Epictetus)

He who does not carry his cross and follow me can not be my disciple.

If you want to be crucified, just wait. The cross will come. If it seems reasonable to comply, and the circumstances are right, then it's to be carried through, and your integrity maintained. (Epictetus)

He who tries to preserve his life will lose it;
but whoever loses his life on account of me will preserve it.

Socrates cannot be preserved by an act that is shameful. . . . It is dying that preserves him, not fleeing. (Epictetus)

Salt is good but if the salt loses its savor, how can it be salted again? It is good neither for the land nor for the manure heap, and they throw it out.

Why have you made yourself so useless and worthless? . . . When some household article has been thrown out intact and serviceable, anyone who finds it will pick it up and prize it. But no one will do that with you. Everyone will think you a dead loss. (Epictetus)

THE AUTHOR AS TITLE

Additionally, I would suggest that the very nature of Q1 (or Q *period,* for that matter) as a sayings collection would imply that the name to which the maxims are attributed is a fictive figurehead, like King Solomon in the Book of Proverbs, the Wisdom of Solomon, and Qoheleth/Ecclesiastes (to say nothing of the Odes of Solomon, the Psalms of Solomon, the Song of Solomon, the Testament of Solomon, or the Key of Solomon!). The Wisdom of Jesus ben-Sira is only an apparent exception since, while the whole collection may well come from the pen of Jesus son of Sirach, we must imagine him as a collector of traditional wisdom, that is, of the venerable sayings of other, anonymous sages before him.

Indeed, the attribution of a collection of maxims to an authoritative name betrays a long subsequent stage of "canonical" anxiety when scribes or theologians have forgotten just what a maxim, a proverb, is. To ascribe the saying to a "big name" implicitly assumes that the credibility of the saying depends upon the authority from whom it stems. You are to take Jesus' or Solomon's or Abe Lincoln's word for it. This mode of thinking I call "canonical," because it presupposes a mindset characteristic of theologians working with a sacred canon of writings which have been theologically homogenized at the expense of finer genre distinctions. "Big name" attributions originated with prophecies and revelations, assertions that could not be empirically verified and so rested upon the prior credibility of the revealer. This is, of course, why the apocalyptic writers all wrote under the names of ancient authorities like Enoch or Moses. But such attributions are in the nature of the case foreign and irrelevant to the maxim genre. Proverbs enshrine wisdom, not revelation. They crystallize insights about life that immediately ring true to experience once we hear them, though chances are we ourselves would never have thought of them. If their truth resonates deep inside us, they have, as it were, their own empirical verification and do not rely upon the authority of a great name. It is only later, once scribes seek extraneous theological legitimation for a collection of sayings, in a theological context, that the sayings collection comes to be judged and legitimated by analogy to revelations and prophecies. It might take the authority of Jesus to make one believe that one's own generation would live to see the Last Judgment, but it would not require anyone's say-so to convince one that "he who hesitates is lost." Thus, again, the Q1 material originally must not have had the name "Jesus," or any other name, on it.

Think of the rabbis whose sayings are preserved in the Pirke Aboth. Most of these great figures are credited with one or two memorable sayings apiece. (We will be considering a number of them, paralleling the gospel sayings attributed to Jesus, in chapter 8.) The blithe complacence with which Christian scholars have credited Jesus with such a huge store of wise sayings only reveals anew the implicit theological bias of supposedly critical scholars. They have just assumed that Jesus was Wisdom incarnate, and that therefore an infinite number of wise and pithy sayings might be attributed to him, while only one or two came from mere mortals like the rabbis or the Greek philosophers.

As for the sheer number of miracle healings attributed to Jesus, the only serious competitor would be Asclepius, son of Apollo and patron of numerous healing spas around the Mediterranean. The great number of Asclepius stories stems from the great number of Asclepius franchises, each of them generating advertising propaganda in the form of testimonials of satisfied customers. By analogy, the great volume of healing and other miracle stories about Jesus stems not from recollections of an historical individual but rather from multiple centers of evangelistic and healing propaganda in the name of the healing god Jesus. In other words, churches.

The same goes for the remarkable volume of wise sayings attributed to Jesus: The name denotes the figurehead for the particular wisdom tradition (as in *Poor Richard's Almanac*), not that of a historical individual. Another analogy would be all the six hundred thirteen laws "of Moses" in the Hebrew Scripture. Does any historian think Moses wrote all or even most of them? It is a good question whether he wrote a single one.

CRUCIFIED SOPHIST

Those who contend that Jesus himself was the Cynic-like fountainhead of the Q1 material presuppose that Cynicism would have been readily available to Jesus given the cosmopolitan Hellenism of Galilee in the first century C.E. But the point has occasioned much debate. There seems to be no decisive evidence either way. Downing is content to argue, not unreasonably, that since we do know Cynicism was widespread in the general time period and in the general area (e.g., Meleager the Cynic, active in nearby but thoroughly Gentile Gadara, died in 50 B.C.E.) the burden of proof is on the one who would exempt Galilee from being afloat on the winds of doctrine sweeping the Hellenistic world. And besides, reasons Downing, the sayings themselves constitute the strongest possible evidence that Cynicism had penetrated Palestine, since there is just no minimizing the Cynic character of them.

But E. P. Sanders and Richard A. Horsley[14] are pretty confident they can shoulder the burden of proof Downing assigns them. Sanders makes a good case that in the first half of the first century C.E., Palestine, including Galilee, was thoroughly resistant to Hellenization, outside of the several new cities Herod the Great had built and settled with Gentiles. One might sum up the gist of Sanders's argument by pointing out that if Meleager's presence in Gadara is normative for Galilee in Jesus' day, then pig herding might as well have been, too (Mark 5:11 ff.). But it wasn't. It is a difficult issue, one not to be resolved here. But suppose Sanders is right, that Galilee in Jesus' day was *not* where one might run into Cynics and Cynic philosophy. What does one do with Downing's evidence of the Cynic coloring of the gospel sayings? Well, they do not suddenly start sounding less Cynic, more apocalyptic or rabbinical. Have we reached an impasse?

Not at all. The answer is clear, though some will not like the sound of it: The sayings of Q1 are Cynic all right; *they just don't come from Jesus*. If we must locate Cynicism elsewhere in the Mediterranean world, and if Q1 bears ample marks of Cynic origin, then Q1 must come from somewhere else in the

Mediterranean world. Why not view it as a collection of originally anonymous Cynic sayings only later attributed to Jesus, just as the Cynic Epistles contain numerous Cynic teachings only subsequently given the names of famous Cynics including Crates, Socrates, and Diogenes?

As Abraham J. Malherbe has demonstrated,[15] the Pauline Epistles give ample evidence of Christian interaction with Cynic, Stoic, and Epicurean competitors. Thus why not assume that Q1 comes from the same areas as the Epistles? All we need to suppose is what we know from other sources anyway, that some Cynics were attracted, for reasons of their own, to the Christian movement. In his ruthless lampoon of Proteus Peregrinus, Lucian of Samosata (ca. 150 C.E.) tells us that Proteus, a Cynic, had also joined the Christian community in Palestine and at length rose to such prominence in it that he became revered almost as a second founder of the Christian movement, held in reverence only below "the crucified sophist" himself. Lucian goes on to say that Proteus had written books that became accepted as Christian scripture (*The Passing of Peregrinus* 11). The only scholarly attempt to make sense of this last note that I know of was the theory of Daniel Völter that Proteus was the pseudonymous author of the Ignatian Epistles. At any rate, Lucian's report attests the plausibility of supposing that Cynics could become Christians and contribute to Christian literature writings still manifestly Cynic in content.

Someone might object, pointing to the Jewish terms and concerns presupposed in various Q sayings. But all we need to assume is that Cynicism came into Hellenistic Christianity by way of the God fearers attached to the margin of Hellenistic Jewish synagogues. Philo was, after all, deeply influenced by Platonism and Stoicism. Jewish elements in Q1 hardly demand that the sayings in question originated with Jesus.

I have already suggested in chapter 2 that Q is a late deposit of the teachings of the Q itinerants. This would hold even for the prechristological Q1. Now I would go further and propose that at first Q consisted solely of aphorisms and proverbs with no narrative introductions, in other words, no apophthegms, no pronouncement stories, no *chreias*. All these sayings, then, would have been unattributed, or else (perhaps subsequently) ascribed to the Wisdom of God, the speaker we can still glimpse behind the saying Matt. 23:34–39/Luke 13:34–35; 11:49–51. Remember Noth's redundancy principle: Since, as we now read the saying, Jesus is the star of the show, what is the Wisdom of God doing there (Luke 11:49, omitted by Matthew's redaction) at all—unless she had first been at center stage and was only subsequently shoved aside? In the Gospel of Thomas the refashioning of Wisdom into Jesus has been much smoother, though also more overt.

On what basis can I suggest that an earlier version of Q lacked any of the narrative setups for the sayings? Simply that, as Bultmann[16] showed long ago, the story portions of the pronouncement stories often do not quite fit the punch lines they ostensibly lead up to, and thus must have originated as exegetical guesses at the meaning of the sayings. (That there was in some quarters an urgency to get them right can be discerned in the first saying of the Gospel of Thomas: "Whoever finds their meaning shall not taste death.") For instance, in Mark 2:15–18, we read that the Pharisee scribes carped at Jesus' practice of dining with sinners. Yet one may ask how they knew this without committing the same sin, being present on the scene themselves? Likewise, Mark 2:23 ff has the scribes objecting that Jesus allowed his disciples to glean grain on the Sabbath. What were they doing, hiding behind the hedgerows, spying? The worst is the cumbersome scene in Luke 7:36–50. In it Jesus forgives a sinful woman who nonetheless showed great love and justifies his leniency with a parable that shows instead that great love is the result, not the occasion, for great forgiveness.[17] The fit of question to answer seems forced in these and other cases, implying somebody has got the cart before the horse.

Picture the early church exegete pondering, "What's the point here? What issue is this saying supposed to be a comment *on?* Well, suppose the saying was a comment on *A*, a response to *B*. Then it would have meant *C*." It would be like the television game show *Jeopardy*, where the contestant is given an answer, and he must supply a relevant question to which the answer would correspond. In exactly the same fashion did the original aphorisms become pronouncement stories. To illustrate the point, I will take one gospel aphorism that somehow never attracted a narrative setup, Matt. 7:6: "Do not give dogs what is holy; and do not throw your pearls before swine, lest they trample them under foot and turn to attack you." I will supply a few lead-in stories, each of which would cast a significantly different light on the saying. I will be recapitulating the role of the ancient gospel tradents.

1. The chief priests and the scribes came to him, seeking to dispute with him, but he would not. And when he was alone with his disciples, they asked him about it. He said, "Do not give dogs what is holy, and do not throw your pearls before swine, lest they trample them under foot and turn to attack you."

2. And as they were eating, he took bread, and blessed and broke it, and he gave it to them, saying, "Take: this is my body." And he took a cup, and he gave it to them, saying, "Drink ye of it: this is my blood." Peter said to him, "Lord, is this remembrance for us, or for all?" Jesus answered him, "Do not give dogs what is holy, and do not throw your pearls before swine, lest they trample them under foot and turn to attack you."

3. All this Jesus said to the crowds in parables. And when he had dispersed the crowds, those who were about him with the disciples asked

him concerning the parables. And he said to them, "To you it has been given to know the secret of the kingdom of God, but for those outside all is in parables. Do not give dogs what is holy, and do not throw your pearls before swine, lest they trample them under foot and turn to attack you."

4. Jesus sent out the Twelve, charging them, "Go nowhere among the Gentiles, and enter no town of the Samaritans, but go rather to the lost sheep of the house of Israel. Do not give dogs what is holy, and do not throw your pearls before swine, lest they trample them under foot and turn to attack you."

5. At this time many of his disciples withdrew and no longer went about with him. Peter said to him, "Lord, it has happened to them according to the proverb, The dog turns back to its own vomit, and the sow is washed only to wallow in the mire." And he had compassion upon them. But Jesus rebuked him, saying, "Do not give dogs what is holy, and do not throw your pearls before swine, lest they trample them under foot and turn to attack you."

6. And from that time on, many sought to kill them. And the disciples were gathered together with the doors locked, and they asked him, "Shall we bear witness even to the death?" And Jesus answered, saying, "Do not give dogs what is holy, and do not throw your pearls before swine, lest they trample them under foot and turn to attack you."

The first version would make the saying warn against getting involved in contentious debate with those who do not appreciate one's beliefs, much in the spirit of Titus 3:9–11: "Avoid stupid controversies, genealogies, dissensions, and quarrels over the law, for they are unprofitable and futile. As for a man who is factious, after admonishing him once or twice, have nothing more to do with him, knowing that such a person is perverted and sinful; he is self-condemned."

The second would apply the saying to the practice of secrecy surrounding the eucharist. The nonbaptized were not to be admitted.

The third applies the saying to the guarding of elite *gnosis* so that the unenlightened will not hear it, be alarmed, and persecute the *illuminati*. The point is the same as in saying 13 of the Gospel of Thomas: "When Thomas returned to his companions, they asked him, 'What did Jesus say to you?' Thomas said to them, 'If I tell you one of the things he said to me, you will pick up stones and throw them at me.'"

The fourth version would reinforce the early Jewish-Christian reluctance to share their gospel among non-Jews: "Now the apostles and the brethren in

Judea heard that the Gentiles also had received the word of God. So when Peter went up to Jerusalem, the circumcision party criticized him, saying, 'Why did you go to uncircumcised men and eat with them?'" (Acts 11:1–3).

The fifth setup makes the saying advocate the Donatist-style intolerance many Christians felt toward those of their number who had denied their faith under threat of persecution. To hell with them!

The sixth lead-in makes the saying advocate the prudent dissimulation certain sects have always practiced during persecution: Why admit your belief when the persecutor cannot possibly be expected to understand you? You know he will jail or kill you, and you could have prevented it! It will be your fault. So keep mum.

Mack points out that it was common in Hellenistic secondary education for students to illustrate their grasp of the characteristic style and thought of a famous sage by fabricating a pronouncement story starring that sage. He ventures that various gospel apophthegms originated this way. Probably so. I have just engaged in a similar exercise, one which Bultmann imagined early Christian exegetes practicing. He was probably right, too.

The brief narrative introductions would have entered the Q tradition only once the Q collection had come to replace the Q itinerants/sages themselves, just as the Koran came to replace the living voice of the Prophet Muhammad. Had the Q sages themselves been on hand, they could have, as once they no doubt had, explained their enigmatic sayings in person. Thus the inclusion of the lead-in stories must be later additions. And it was only once the sayings expanded into pronouncement stories that Jesus seemed to become a historical figure in the situations described in the pronouncement stories. Just as the situations are "ideal" situations, imaginary, "hypotheticals," as in a law class, so the sage Jesus is an ideal figure.

NOTES

1. William Wrede, *The Messianic Secret*, trans. J. C. G. Greig (Altrincham: James Clarke, 1971). Schweitzer saw the alternatives for life-of-Jesus studies as posed between his own "thoroughgoing eschatology" and Wrede's "thoroughgoing skepticism." In our day, Burton Mack comes close to being a skeptic in Wrede's mold, while there are certainly many scholars who still accept Schweitzer's sketch of the apocalyptic Jesus, including A. J. Mattill Jr., who is pretty much an unreconstructed Schweitzerian. Evangelical apologist N. T. Wright claims to follow in Schweitzer's train, but this is merely strategic pretense. Like those Schweitzer criticized, Wright refuses to take Jesus' apocalyptic sayings with any sort of literalness. Wright, like a whole generation of post-Schweitzer, postliberal retrenchers, has merely used Schweitzer's Jesus as a cloak to sneak reformed theology back into the mouth of the "historical Jesus" ventriloquist dummy.

2. Charlotte Allen, "The Search for a No-Frills Jesus," *Atlantic Monthly* (December 1996): 67.

3. Leif E. Vaage, "The Son of Man Sayings in Q: Stratigraphical Location and Significance," in *Semeia 55, Early Christianity, Q and Jesus* (Atlanta: Scholars Press, 1991), pp. 103–30; John S. Kloppenborg, *The Formation of Q: Trajectories in Ancient Wisdom Collections*. Studies in Antiquity and Christianity (Philadelphia: Fortress Press, 1987); Burton L. Mack, *The Lost Gospel: The Book of Q and Christian Origins* (San Francisco: HarperSanFrancisco, 1995), pp. 105–10 ff.

4. George A. Wells, *The Jesus Myth* (Chicago: Open Court, 1999), p. 102–103.

5. Mary Douglas, *Natural Symbols: Explorations in Cosmology* (New York: Pantheon Books, 1982), p. 162.

6. D. S. Margoliouth, "Christ in Islam: Sayings Attributed to Christ by Mohammedan Writers," *The Expository Times*, vol. 5, 1983–1894, pp. 59, 107, 177–78, 503–504, 561; Javad Nurbakhsh, *Jesus in the Eyes of the Sufis* (London: Khaniqahi-Nimatullahi Publications, 1983); Al-Ghazali, *The Remembrance of Death and the Afterlife*, book 40 of *The Revival of the Religious Sciences,* trans. T. J. Winter (Cambridge: The Islamic Texts Society, 1989).

7. Norman Perrin, *Rediscovering the Teaching of Jesus* (New York: Harper & Row, 1976), pp. 39–43.

8. William Morrice, *Hidden Sayings of Jesus: Words Attributed to Jesus Outside the Four Gospels* (Peabody: Hendrickson, 1997), p. 192.

9. Stevan L. Davies, *The Gospel of Thomas and Christian Wisdom*, (New York: Seabury Press, 1983), pp. 81–99.

10. *Jesus and the Constraints of History* (London: Duckworth, Philadelphia: Westminster Press, 1982), p. 100, quoted in Craig Blomberg, *The Historical Reliability of the Gospels* (Downers Grove: InterVarsity Press, 1987), p. 91.

11. Usually called "The Gospel of Pseudo-Matthew," as if we had any reason to believe the writer of the canonical gospel was actually Matthew, or that the writer of this infancy gospel was trying to impersonate the canonical author.

12. Stephen J. Patterson, *The Gospel of Thomas and Jesus* (Sonoma: Polebridge Press, 1993).

13. F. Gerald Downing, *Christ and the Cynics: Jesus and Other Radical Preachers in First-Century Tradition*. JSOT Manuals 4 (Sheffield: JSOT Press, 1988).

14. E. P. Sanders, "Jesus in Historical Context," *Theology Today* 50, no. 3, (October 1993): 429–48; Richard A. Horsley, *Archaeology, History and Society in Galilee: The Social Context of Jesus and the Rabbis* (Valley Forge: Trinity Press International, 1996).

15. Abraham J. Malherbe, *Paul and the Popular Philosophers* (Minneapolis: Fortress Press, 1989).

16. Rudolf Bultmann, *History of the Synoptic Tradition*, 2d ed., trans. John Marsh (New York: Harper & Row, 1968), pp. 39–40.

17. See Robert M. Price, *The Widow Traditions in Luke-Acts: A Feminist-Critical Scrutiny*. SBL Dissertation Series 155 (Atlanta: Scholars Press, 1997), pp. 101–103.

Chapter 6

SACRED SCAPEGOAT

RENÉ GIRARD: DOING SACRED VIOLENCE TO THE TEXT?

A form-critical study of dust jacket blurbs and book reviews might reveal that the most often used concluding line is: "Even if one finds he cannot agree with Dr. Frankenstein's thesis, one must take it seriously." A rhetorical analysis would make it plain that such a line is a euphemistic damning with faint praise. The point seems to be, "He's crazy, but he *did* put a lot of work into it." And yet when one reads Burton Mack's assessment of the work of René Girard, "Many biblical scholars will be troubled by Girard's theory. . . . But none will be able to . . . avoid his challenge,"[1] one cannot help feeling that this time he means it. In Lukan terms, Girard's theory of mimetic violence and the scapegoat mechanism has become "a sign spoken against . . . that thoughts out of many hearts may be laid bare." His hermeneutic of suspicion forces us to rethink the basic character of religion itself, and not just of conventional interpretations of texts. Indeed the challenge of Girard is so wide-ranging that I can take up but the tiniest fragment here. The rest I will gladly leave to the ranks of dissertation writers.

What I intend to do is, first, to summarize Girard's main thesis in broad outline, then to indicate where his own application of it to the gospels seems to go astray, and finally to suggest some results of a consistent application of the Girardian paradigm to the gospels. In Girard's own terms I will be engaging in a mimetic rivalry with Girard himself as my rival, seeking to emulate his method but to do his trick better than he does.

LET NOT YOUR LEFT HAND KNOW . . .

René Girard's theories are set forth in a series of books including *Deceit, Desire, and the Novel* (originally published in French, in 1961), *Violence and the Sacred* (1972), *Things Hidden Since the Foundation of the World* (1978), *"To Double Business Bound"* (1978), *The Scapegoat* (1982), *Job, the Victim of his People* (1985), and *Violent Origins: Ritual Killing and Cultural Formation* (with Walter Burkert and Jonathan Z. Smith, edited by Robert G. Hamerton-Kelly, 1987). For the beginning Girardian, *Violence and the Sacred* or *The Scapegoat* ought to be adequate to give a good, detailed impression of the theory. His hypothesis is that all culture, civilization, political order, cultural forms, and most especially all religion began with the violent resolution of a primordial Hobbesian "war of all against all." That resolution took the form of the collective murder of an arbitrarily chosen scapegoat upon whom all hatred and blame might be focused and so eliminated. "Cast out the scorner, and dissension will go out" (Prov. 22:10). This originary act of violence may be repeated as needed when the social/religious order created after the first scapegoat murder begins to weaken and give way in a time of "sacrificial crisis." Order will then be restored or reinforced, chaos held at bay. And though the saving act of murder is ever and again presented in the form of ritual sacrifice, the true nature of the deed as the frenzy of a lynch mob will be hidden away under various mythic and theological veils. The one sacrificed becomes a divine savior whose death was voluntary obedience to the divine plan. In this way violence is reified and mystified. Girard stands in the tradition of Durkheim, who characterized religion as simply a mystification of social existence. The mystification provides a transcendent sanction for the society's laws and mores. Both the carrot and the stick are made more effective in this way. Girard has, so to speak, taken Durkheim's theory farther in explaining how social systems began and why it should be that religion is the fright mask society wears. Concrete fears of mundane dangers are here magnified to the proportions of Rudolf Otto's "numinous" fear of the *Mysterium Tremendum*, fear of the dissolution of all things. If the sanctions of the Sacred are not obeyed, the dam will collapse and Chaos and Old Night will rampage again.

Though Girard is unclear about the conditions obtaining before the initial crisis, his theory seems to imply that most primitive collectivities began as peaceful anarchies. But probably before too long, trouble began, as the Cain and Abel myth indicates. The trouble was mimetic desire. Girard theorizes that desire is always a function of one's imitation of another as a model. One begins wanting to emulate another, perhaps a parent. Naturally, one begins to desire what the model desires, simply in order to be like the model. One imitates the tastes and the values of the model. But at some point the object of desire becomes an obstacle between model and imitator (or "disciple"). They cannot both have it. And at that point model and imitator become rivals. Soon the desired object becomes irrelevant, because the focus again becomes obviously what it already was implicitly: It is the model himself that the imitator covets. Casting aside his own being, the disciple seeks to gain justification, real being, from the model who already has it.[2] The disciple seeks no longer to be *like* the model but actually to *become*, to *supplant*, the model. Striking contemporary examples of this phenomenon would be the many cases of a fan who idolizes a celebrity to the point of stalking him or her and finally killing the celebrity, as if in so doing, the fan could supplant the idol/rival. Mark David Chapman was the mimetic rival of John Lennon. Or think of Rupert Pupkin in *The King of Comedy*, or of Edward Nigma, mimetic rival/double of Bruce Wayne in *Batman Forever*.

As already anticipated, such mimetic conflict rapidly becomes violent. Sometimes violence thus spreads throughout society, and we have the war of all against all. Bergman's film *Shame* illustrates this condition. So do current events in Bosnia and Serbia. In any case of mimetic violence, whether between two antagonists or between whole countries, the mimetic rivals lose any real distinction from one another. They become mimetic twins. No one is any longer in the right or the wrong. Bosnia seems to us more sinned against than sinning, but one must admit they have their own record of atrocities to place beside Serbia's. Who could support either the Sandinistas or the Contras with a clear conscience?

Since reciprocal violence has leveled the playing field, it becomes not only impossible but also meaningless for either party to admit to being at fault. So how can the turmoil cease? The crowd suddenly seizes on someone, either a third party, someone marginal to the society, or any one of the faceless figures in the general melee, and puts him or her (or them—it might be a minority ethnic or religious group) up as the secret culprit. This scapegoat has become the "monstrous double" of all involved in the conflict. In this figure they see their own rage and culpability, and they see it writ large. And since all distinctions have been obliterated, they are not, strictly speaking, wrong in seeing the guilt anyplace, in any face, they look. But the person chosen must be marginalized or otherwise insignificant since otherwise the victim's partisans will take revenge for his death, and the cycle of reciprocal violence will continue unabated.

The antagonists call a halt to the fighting, forming a united front against the one now perceived as the real culprit. The hapless scapegoat takes the blame. (One might understand Mahatma Gandhi to have acted as a self-chosen scapegoat when he undertook a "punishing" hunger strike to stop the Hindu-Muslim rioting in newly independent India.)

The scapegoat must have created the whole mess by some secret and insidious means, an apple of discord tossed in when no one was looking, a poisoner of the well of good will. If the evil schemer can be done away with, everything ought to return to normal. He dies. It does. The crashing silence of newly won equilibrium seems almost miraculous. Everyone takes a second look at the scapegoat. He must have been a powerful being indeed, not only to bewitch everyone in the first place, but now to heal everyone by his stripes as well! A single death brought peace, demolished the dividing wall that had kept us apart (Eph. 2:14). Whereas before the victim was judged a maleficent magician, now he is seen as a beneficent savior. The scapegoat is retroactively exonerated.

But where does the guilt then go? Perhaps to the members of the community itself, having acted in tragic ignorance. "We esteemed him stricken of God and afflicted, but it was our transgressions that he bore" (Isa. 53:4–5). But that is a hard thing to accept. So a secondary scapegoat may be identified. And all blame is put on him. *He's* the one who deceived us into slaying the savior! Off with his head! (Or it may be that, as Hyam Maccoby suggests in *The Sacred Executioner*, the secondary scapegoat will receive exoneration, too.)

The community owes its peace and order, the restoration of pecking orders, social classes, and boundary lines, to the death of the scapegoat. So the scapegoat is forever after venerated by repeated sacrificial anamnesis. All we like sheep had gone astray (Isa. 53:6), but the savior brought us back together in one fold as a compassionate shepherd who gave his life for his sheep (John 10:14–16). The "surrogate victim" employed may be another human or an animal substitute, but either way he is an actor in a Passion play. By this expedient of repeated sacrifice the danger of chaos is recalled as well as the means of its stemming. The social order is periodically reinforced, and people are warned never to rock the boat again.

Only the saving deed is recalled in a mythically revised form, one in which no real blame is attached to the community, at least not for the arbitrary act of mob violence that put out the fire. It must be so, because if the facts were to become known, the illusion of mystification would be stripped away. All transcendent reference, with its powerful sanctioning function, would be gone. There would not be sufficient fear if the sacred categorical imperative were to be reduced to a merely prudential hypothetical imperative. The Nation of Islam has more spectacular success in getting people off drugs than do humanistic secular agencies. "Pay no attention to the man behind the curtain." So the effectiveness of the whole system depends on the participants and beneficiaries not knowing how and why it works.

But Girard knows how it works. And he believes he is able to discern in various myths and rituals the effaced signs of the originary mob violence that secretly makes the system work. He is able to disclose "the figure in the carpet" (Henry James) by a sharp-eyed scrutiny. As Elisabeth Schüssler

Fiorenza[3] says, Girard has learned to listen to the silences of the mythic texts, aware that they are often more eloquent than the words. "There is no speech, nor are there words; their voice is not heard, yet their voice goes out through all the earth, and their words to the end of the world" (Ps. 19:3–4).

In his analyses of myths Girard is aided by insights derived from two other genres, the classical tragedy and the persecution text. A persecution text is the record of scapegoating written by the persecutors in historical times (his favorite example is Guillaume de Machaut's *Judgment of the King of Navarre*, fourteenth century). It may credulously record how the plague was brought to a halt by a pogrom, or how the burning of witches put an end to an epidemic. The "double transference," whereby the scapegoat is first laden with the guilt of the community and then rehabilitated as a savior after his death, is represented in persecution texts only up to the second transfer. The writer of a persecution text still deems the Jew, the witch, the heretic as the guilty party. Good riddance! So such texts offer us only a half-parallel to what Girard envisions going on in myths. But, as far as it goes, Girard feels that the persecution text does attest to the historical reality of the basic scapegoating mechanism. By definition, the persecution text can go no further toward depicting the second stage of transference than it does.

And yet we may wonder whether Girard does not undermine his own case when he suggests that we lack historical texts depicting the second stage of transference because "mythological persecutors [are] more credulous than their historical equivalents" and thus the latter are not to be expected to be sufficiently cowed by the scapegoat's effectiveness as to deify and worship him.[4] This observation implies that we perhaps ought not to seek any historical analogy to the postmortem transformation of the scapegoat, that no historical plausibility attaches to this element of the myths.

(This is a significant and embarrassing lacuna. But perhaps it may yet be filled. There might be recent historical texts which do attest the second transformation, though of course then they would no longer be persecution texts, not that it matters. For instance, a Calvinist record of repentant Calvinists erecting a monument to Michael Servetus, the nontrinitarian reformer whom Calvin burned at the stake, might qualify: Servetus, once a detestable heretic, had now taken on the halo of a martyr even in the eyes of those whose forbears had hounded him to death.)

Classical tragedies help to decode myths because the dramatists have themselves begun to interpret the myths and to rehistoricize them. It is they who fill in background detail and color, including sociopolitical and religious factors to supply verisimilitude for their audiences. The tragedies, even when they involved supernatural beings, had to seem plausible as happening in the real world. In reconstructing, for example, the political tensions surrounding the tribulations of Oedipus, Sophocles was able, if not to restore the actual events surrounding the originary act of violence Girard postulates, then at least to tell us the *kind* of thing that would have surrounded such events in his world. And once we learn what sort of realities are apt to lie behind the myths, we can extrapolate in the cases of those myths to which no dramatic counterpart survives. We will know what to look for, what counts as a clue.

The actual process of reconstructing the violent events underlying a myth involves a considerable amount of cutting and pasting, juggling and reversing, and supplying elements implicit in the myths. "They must be treated like pieces of a puzzle which is the mimetic theory itself, once the correct arrangement has been found."[5] If Girard here sounds a bit like Claude Lévi-Strauss, he sounds even closer to him when he advises us to disregard the original diegetic order of events in the myth:

> The relationship is then reversed. Differences cancel each other out; a symmetry is constantly generated, invisible in each synchronic moment taken separately but visible in the accumulation of moments. . . . The same details are reiterated throughout the story . . . , but never simultaneously.[6]

> Mythology is a game of transformations. Levi-Strauss has made a most important contribution in revealing this. . . . After shuffling his cards, the magician spreads them out again in a different order. At first we have the impression that they are all there, but is it true? If we look closer we shall see that there is actually always one missing, and it is always the same one, the representation of collective murder.[7]

> To be sure, there are many details of the generative event that have dropped out, many elements that have become so warped, misshapen, and transfigured as to be unrecognizable when reproduced in mythical or ritualistic form.[8]

We recall both Lévi-Strauss, with his paradigmatic approach, and Vladimir Propp, with his syntagmic approach, when we read Girard's analysis of Oedipus' actantial equivalence to other characters in his story:

> All the episodes of the Oedipus myth are repetitions of one another. . . . Oedipus, naturally, is a monster [a parricide and engaging in incest], but Tiresias is a monster, too: as a hermaphrodite. . . . The sphinx is a monster . . . with its woman's head, lion's body, [etc.]. On first glance there is a radical difference between this imaginary creature and the human protagonists, but this difference vanishes on closer inspection. The sphinx plays the same role in relation to Oedipus as do all the human figures. . . . Like Laius, like the drunken Corinthian earlier in the story and Creon and Tiresias later, the sphinx dogs Oedipus's tracks—whenever, that is, Oedipus is not dogging the sphinx's tracks. Like the others, the sphinx catches Oedipus in an oracular trap; in short, the episode of the sphinx recapitulates the other episodes. The sphinx appears as the incarnation of maleficent violence, as Oedipus himself will appear later on. The sphinx has been sent by Hera to punish Thebes, just

as the plague is visited upon the city by order of Apollo. . . . The episode of the sphinx shows Oedipus in the role of monster-killer or executioner. Later a monster himself, he will assume the role of surrogate victim. Like all incarnations of sacred violence, Oedipus can and does play every part in succession.[9]

Indeed, this is just the type of thing we ought to expect in what Todorov calls a "narrative of substitutions" following "ritual logic," one based on a sacred ritual, where there is no linear development, only cyclical repetition. "The origin of the rite is lost in the origin of time."[10]

Two examples highlighted in *The Scapegoat* provide a good picture of Girard's methods in action. The first is the Norse myth of the death of Balder. So beloved is the bright hero of Asgard that his mother Frigga seeks to ensure his safety by persuading every living thing never to harm Balder. They readily agree. Unfortunately, Frigga has neglected to secure the oath of a young sprig of mistletoe, which seemed already too harmless to threaten the divine prince. One day the mischief maker Loki beholds his fellow Aesir at sport. They circle the laughing Balder, throwing all manner of spears, swords, and javelins at him. But all alike turn away at the crucial moment, since the bits of wood in their construction remain unable to break their vow of harmlessness. Loki dislikes to see such a spectacle and calls for it to stop. Unheeded, he departs and wheedles from Frigga the secret of the lone mistletoe sprig. This he finds and fashions into a deadly dart. Placing it in the hand of Balder's blind brother Hother, Loki guides his cast to its fatal target. Of course the myths of Siegfried and Achilles come readily to mind.

But Girard smells something amiss. Like a detective he is sure there is more than meets the eye here at the crime scene. There must have been an earlier version of the myth in which the encircling crowd of gods executed Balder, whom they regarded as a culprit, by means of their firing squad. An initial clue is that in the extant version Loki first tries to halt the game, as if he anticipates a danger the others do not see. How then has he become the villain of the piece? Note, too, the various "distancing devices."[11] We seem to have not only a primary scapegoat, Balder, but a secondary scapegoat as well, Hother. And yet Hother himself is exonerated, first, since he is blind, and thus may have landed the dart accidentally; second, since he is ignorant, not knowing the secret of the sprig until too late; and third, in a subsequent retelling, since it was the pestiferous Loki who put him up to it. Loki then becomes a tertiary scapegoat!

The Greek myth of the infant Zeus and the Curetes presents basically the same scenario. In it, the godling is in danger from his hungry father Cronos. To hide him from the devourer, the Curetes, fierce warriors, form a circle around the child. This protective gesture, however, is enough to frighten baby Zeus, so he begins to cry. To drown out the sound, the Curetes start crashing their spears against their shields, raising a terrible din that frightens the baby even more. The louder he bawls the louder they get, until Cronos goes to find some peace and quiet elsewhere. Girard suspects that such a commotion would be rather odd as a camouflage strategy. Originally it must have meant something quite different. Of course, it must have been a scene in which the Curetes themselves surrounded the divine babe and closed ranks, slaughtering him. But later piety could not brook this, so Cronos was brought on stage as the villain, while the Curetes became an honor guard for the godling, surely a picture more in keeping with the divine dignity.

But is such a myth of the collective slaughter of a divine child really likely? Indeed it is, replies Girard, since we have precisely such a myth still extant, in which the evil Titans surround baby Dionysus ("young Zeus")[12] and dismember him. Later Zeus takes revenge on the Titans and resurrects Dionysus in another form. Perhaps this rescue is simply an alternative way of cleaning up the deicidal myth. Here the original (human) lynch mob has been translated into a group of culpable divinities. In the myths of Zeus and the Curetes, the solution is the docetic one familiar from early Christianity: There was no death. But Girard knows better. It is written plainly between the lines. Perhaps in an intermediate version of the myth the Curetes were trying to protect him, but Zeus *was* killed, with Cronos as the secondary scapegoat, the noisy ruse having failed. ("Hey! What in Hades is going *on* over there? Well, what have we *here?*") In the same way, in the Balder myth the original human slayers of the original human scapegoat were, like the Titans, made into divinities, but innocent ones. Hence the need for a secondary (and tertiary) scapegoat.

. . . WHAT YOUR RIGHT HAND IS DOING

The examples cited and discussed by Girard are plentiful and well argued. I find myself largely convinced in most cases. At least I am eager to try the paradigm on for size. Thus, again, I will not seek to defend the approach here. My goal is more modest. I want to venture a consistent application of the Girardian paradigm to the gospel Passion texts. I find Girard himself coming up short at this point. At the end of *Violence and the Sacred*, he writes, "No attempt will be made here to consider the Judeo-Christian texts in the light of this theory, or vice versa; that must be left to a future study. However, I hope to have suggested here the course that such a project might take."[13] Though the anticipated study might have taken the direction implied in *Violence and the Sacred*, in fact it did not. Indeed, when one ventures into the pages of *Things Hidden Since the Foundation of the World* and *The Scapegoat*, one feels one has made a wrong turn somewhere, or that Girard has. In these books Girard unfurls the banner of Christian apologetics, specifically what I call dissimilarity apologetics.

We are told that the canonical gospels have once and for all called the bluff of the scapegoat mechanism on which all previous religion rested, which all previous mythology had embodied. It has done this by the simple expedient of depicting Jesus as innocent, as being railroaded into his scapegoat death. The very opposite of a persecution text, the gospels are written from the standpoint of the victim. Jesus even attacks the scapegoating mechanism head-on, by damning the Jewish sacrificial system and calling for the end of violence and counterviolence in favor of turning the other cheek and loving the enemy. Jesus thus called for the end of the mystification of violence as the Sacred. Granted, he sometimes had no choice but to employ violent and sacrificial metaphors in order to have any common ground with his hearers, and granted, this may be why it has taken anyone this long to see what Jesus and the gospels were getting at. But there it is. And if we deny the results of Girard's exegesis, we are only continuing the conspiracy of sacred silence and forgetfulness that has kept the cycle of controlled religious violence going all these ages.

A growing group of Girardian disciples has fanned out through the towns of academic Israel to spread this word. Books written from Girard's perspective, promoting his version of the nonviolent gospel, include Raymund Schwager, *Must There be Scapegoats?*, James G. Williams, *The Bible, Violence, and the Sacred: Liberation from the Myth of Sanctioned Violence*, Robert G. Hamerton-Kelly, *Sacred Violence, Paul's Hermeneutic of the Cross* and *The Gospel and the Sacred, Poetics of Violence in Mark*, and Gil Bailie, *Violence Unveiled, Humanity at the Crossroads*.[14] Burton Mack and Lucien Scubla have both undertaken detailed though somewhat limited analyses of Girard's gospel exegesis and found it severely wanting.[15] I agree: The gospels seem to say what Girard says only if the reader already belongs to that community of interpreters[16] infatuated with the Girardian kerygma. Hamerton-Kelly's exegesis of Mark seems almost parodic, a case of hermeneutical ventriloquism at its worst. Page after page of his work (and that of other Girardians) brings inevitably to mind the *pesher* exegesis of the Dead Sea Scrolls. Like scribes trained unto the kingdom of heaven, they are bringing altogether new goods out of the old storehouse (Matt. 13:52).

Indeed, as in Girard's own theory, there is a crucial fact concealed from these exegetes which alone makes their enterprise possible. They are like the Process Theologians of the 1970s who proclaimed Jesus the Christ because he had disclosed the vision of what God is up to in the world: creative transformation. The irony was, they had the wrong messiah. Surely Alfred North Whitehead deserved the diadem! Surely it was he, and not Jesus, who first set forth the view they espoused. No one would ever get Process Christology from the gospels as David Griffin and John Cobb[17] did unless Whitehead had provided the esoteric key. In the same way, the revealer of the scapegoat mechanism is none other than René Girard. Like the early Christian prophets posited by Bultmann, Girard has put his own oracles on the lips of the historical Jesus. Jesus remains the ventriloquist dummy of Christian dogma, though the script is updated now and then.

DISSIMILARITY APOLOGETICS

I have called Girard's handling of the gospels "dissimilarity apologetics." Here is what I have in mind. Norman Perrin dubbed a widely used form-critical tool the "criterion of dissimilarity." That is, the critic cannot be sure of the authenticity of a gospel logion unless it contradicts the beliefs of both contemporary Judaism and the primitive church. Though Jesus may have overlapped at many points with his Jewish contemporaries, and though the early Church may actually have taken him seriously here or there, we will not know what was unique to the message of Jesus unless we employ the criterion of dissimilarity. Behind this assumption lurks the orthodox belief that Jesus must have had startlingly innovative things to say since he was a divine revealer. And, not surprisingly, Perrin and his colleagues tended to exaggerate the differences between Judaism and Jesus, making of Judaism an absurd caricature in the process (as when Gerhard Ebeling imagines that the simple preaching of a loving God would have so infuriated religious Jews as to goad them into executing Jesus! These are the horned Jews of the Oberamergau Passion play).

One can detect the same dissimilarity apologetics in play today in two of the "hottest" subfields of New Testament scholarship: feminist and social scientific criticism. Jewish views and practices concerning women are distorted by selective proof-texting of the Mishnah so that Jesus appears by contrast to have been a radical protofeminist. The gospel evidence certainly shows that Jesus was not a fanatical misogynist, for what that's worth. But it is not hard to see him as fitting in with ordinary Judaism at this, as so many other points. Why should this more modest verdict disappoint? I suspect because the scholars in question think of Jesus as the divine revealer, so he must have been at least as enlightened as themselves. The approach is not unlike fundamentalist efforts to show that Genesis 1 *really* foretold the Big Bang or the sphericity of the earth if you just read it the "right" way.

Social science critics take great pains to construct a paradigm of Mediterranean peasant culture which they assume must have held sway in Jesus' day. Once this paradigm is employed in gospel exegesis, many things are seen in a new light. But what do you know? It turns out that Jesus "radically reversed" or "radically transcended" this or that social more. Just what one would expect of the divine revealer. Someone has forgotten what it means to use a paradigm. Paradigms are "surprise-free."[18] If there is seemingly anomalous data that the model cannot account for or would not have predicted, it must mean the paradigm needs adjustment or replacement, or that we are misinterpreting the evidence. One cannot use the paradigm against itself, as if a futurologist should be so surprised at the appearance of an unforeseen trend as to declare there had been a divine intervention in history. In my view, Girard and his mimetic doubles have pulled the same cheat as these other "dissimilarity apologists." If the gospels appear to defy the type of analysis Girard insists can decode all other supernatural tales as scapegoat myths, then I am willing to bet that either Girard has buckled his paradigm too tightly, or he is giving preferential treatment to a particular set of myths—which just happen to be the scriptures of his own personal religious faith.

It is a simple matter of shaving with Occam's razor: If we find that the gospel tales can after all be easily accommodated by the method Girard uses to such effect on the myths of Balder, Oedipus, the Curetes, and the infant Dionysus, then why look any further? And it would seem that the gospels fit the pattern quite well. Yes, Jesus is depicted as innocent from the start, rail-roaded and exploited as a scapegoat. But this is simply because scapegoat myths are just the opposite of persecution texts. Persecution texts only go up to the first transformation (that of the innocent into the "monstrous double") because they are written by the persecutors who still view the persecuted as the real culprits. But scapegoat myths do not provide both stages of transformation, as Girard implies, but rather only the second. They do presuppose the first, but then that is what Girard says we must coax out. The first transformation is never depicted as such in the myths. Indeed, that is his whole point. What is (at least sometimes) depicted is the subsequent transfiguration of the "evil" scapegoat into a sanctified savior.

But often there is not even an initial period of genuine culpability because the retroactive sanctification of the scapegoat has completely permeated the myth. Here one thinks of Hans Küng's schema whereby the resurrection of Jesus transformed him retroactively from a false prophet to the Messiah.[19] Girard even recounts a number of instances from current field observation in which sacred tribal kings and condemned prisoners treated as kings for a day are venerated and accorded special privileges even while they are blamed for all the community's ills. This ambivalence, he explains, is the result of the retrojection of their still-future sanctification into the present.[20] How much more natural for this retrojection to occur in the retelling of a myth?

> As a community moves away from its violent origins, . . . moral dualism is reinforced. . . . There comes a time . . . when men want only models of morality and demand gods purified of all faults. . . . [Such desires] reflect the disintegration of the primitive notion of the sacred, the tendency toward dualism that only wants to maintain the beneficent aspect of the gods. . . . The tendency to idealize transforms or effaces all the stereotypes: the crisis,

the signs that indicate a victim, collective violence, and of course the victim's crime. This can be seen clearly in the myth of Baldr. The god who is not collectively killed cannot be a guilty god. He is a god whose crime has been completely effaced, a perfectly sublime god, devoid of all fault.[21]

So why consider the Jesus story substantially different from the Balder story? In both the divine hero is unambiguously good and then slain by the machinations of a secondary scapegoat figure.

"A guilty conscience is its own accuser." Just so, Girard himself anticipates our protest: "The uprooting [of the scapegoat mechanism] in the gospels bears the same relationship to the mythological conjuring tricks of a Baldr or the Curetes as the complete removal of a tumor to a village quack's 'magnetic' tricks."[22] And yet on which side of this analogical ratio does Jesus belong? Perhaps not the side Girard intends. "Jesus . . . does as expected of a wandering magician."[23] Girard seems to have learned a few Mesmeric conjuring tricks of his own. Though he himself remarks, "Too great an effort to hide something always reveals the deception,"[24] there are many who do take Girard's special pleading seriously, as we have seen. To them the difference between scapegoat myths and the gospels is (to borrow Hamerton-Kelly's telling phrase) "stupefyingly clear."[25] Just as trivialities seem profound to one under the influence of marijuana, so those under Girard's spell have no trouble plumbing a difference where others may not see a distinction. In fact, elsewhere in the vast Passion megatext, Hyam Maccoby is able to show startling parallels between the Jesus and Balder Passions even to the details. For instance, in one version of the *Toledoth Yeschu*, Judas has to display the dead body of Jesus on a huge cabbage stalk instead of a cross or a tree—since the sorcerer Jesus had, like Frigga, made all trees swear an oath never to act against him! It is as if some recessive gene shared by the two myths had at long last surfaced.[26] Maccoby performs much the same sort of operation on the gospel story of Jesus on the analogy of Balder that we should have expected Girard to perform.[27] Mack does something similar: Though he does not see Jesus as a Girardian scapegoat, at length he concludes that the gospels are persecution texts scapegoating Jews.[28]

Unlike Burton Mack, I do see the gospel Passion as a Girardian scapegoat myth. And while I agree with Hyam Maccoby's analysis as far as it goes (and it does say the most important thing), I will attempt to supply what the disappointed reader of Girard has missed: a scrutiny of some specific features of the Passion à la Girard's ingenious exegesis of the various pagan scapegoat myths.

THE RIGHT MAN AT THE RIGHT TIME

How does Jesus measure up as a Girardian scapegoat? Does he betray any of the classic "signs of the victim"? It seems he is quite suitable for the role. The scapegoat must have an ambivalent relationship to the community. If he is not a member, he cannot bear their guilt as a representative (cf. Anselm's Satisfaction theory of the atonement). On the other hand, he must be somehow on the fringes of the community so as to be safe to pick on. His collective murder must not engender reprisals or the cycle of reciprocal violence will only continue. As we have seen,[29] Jesus is consistently depicted in the gospels as an itinerant preacher after the manner of Elisha or the Cynics. He had no home or family, no possessions, roots, or vested interests. Girard mentions how the scapegoat "passes freely from the interior to the exterior and back again. Thus the surrogate victim constitutes both a link and a barrier between the community and the sacred."[30] Stevan L. Davies sums up the social position of itinerants like Jesus: They visited settled communities but their preaching contained no help for communities since the itinerant's ethos inculcated individualistic asceticism. Such preaching would undermine the community or fall on deaf ears. Thus itinerant prophets were marginalized even among their own supporters.[31] That pretty well fits Girard's characterization of the scapegoat.

Scott D. Hill[32] demonstrates how itinerant holy men have throughout history served as community mediators and arbiters since people regarded them as both divinely inspired and impartial, having no worldly interests (cf. Luke 12:13–14; Mark 12:14). In this they were much like the living Bodhisattvas of Mahayana Buddhism, whose sublime disinterest enabled them to have divine compassion on all beings without favoritism. Girard shows how the scapegoat, while still a "kind of pariah, assumes the role of supreme arbiter. In the event of an irresolvable struggle he is called upon to 'differentiate' the irreconcilable antagonists, thus proving that he incarnates the sacred violence that is sometimes maleficent, sometimes beneficent."[33] And yet it is this very marginality that makes him the perfect choice for the scapegoat: He belongs to neither side in the great crisis, so his murder will not require retaliation. In a sense, as Girard implies, his eventual death as a scapegoat is a kind of logical extension and completion of his role as marginalized arbiter between two disputing factions. Again, Jesus fills the role remarkably well.

There are more obvious marks of a scapegoat. "We need only think of those social categories and individuals that provide the victims in scapegoat rites—vagabonds, beggars [both of these fit an itinerant prophet], cripples—to recognize that derision of one form or another plays a large part in the negative feelings that find expression in the course of the ritual sacrifice and that are finally purified and purged by it."[34] Recall the Hunchback of Notre

Dame.[35] To these categories we might add membership in a minority or foreign group. The crowd begins to intimidate Peter once they catch his Galilean accent (Mark 14:70; Matt. 26:73). Jesus, too, was a Galilean in Judea. Was he a cripple? Eastern Orthodox tradition made him hobble, one leg being shorter than the other.

Girard does not limit massive outbreaks of mimetic violence, requiring the antidote of collective murder, to the dawn of human civilization. He says they continue to erupt repeatedly throughout history whenever the sacrificial system established by the previous crisis begins to break down. Violence is no longer being "managed" in the proper sacerdotal channels. The difference between "good" violence (that which proceeds along authorized channels and at the hands of duly designated functionaries) and "bad" violence (personal vendettas, rioting) has broken down. Girard recognizes that sacrificial crises played an important role in the history of biblical Israel.

> Amos, Isaiah, and Micah denounce in vehement terms the impotence of the sacrificial process and ritual in general. In the most explicit manner they link the decay of religious practices to the deterioration of contemporary behavior. Inevitably, the eroding of the sacrificial system seems to result in the emergence of reciprocal violence. Neighbors who had previously discharged their aggressions on a third party, joining together in the sacrifice of an "outside" victim [i.e., the sacrificial animals], now turn to sacrifice one another.[36]

Signs of sacrificial crisis are abundant in the gospels (and this much, of course, Girard would by no means deny). We can see this most clearly in terms of the Jerusalem temple cultus. Speaking of the sacrificial crisis in general, Girard explains, "If the gap between the victim and the community grows too wide, all similarity will be destroyed. The victim will no longer be capable of attracting the violent impulses to itself; the sacrifice will cease to serve as a 'good conductor,' in the sense that metal is a good conductor of electricity."[37] Bruce Chilton argues that what so disturbed Jesus about the temple sacrifices was the fact that people no longer brought their own animals from home to be sacrificed, but rather simply paid money for "government inspected meat" once they got to the temple.[38] And it wasn't even their own money they used to pay for it! They had to change "idolatrous" Roman coins for *un*filthy lucre, without images. (I think it most likely that Jesus refers to this practice when he dismisses the issue of whether paying Roman tribute represents religious compromise, since the coin used to pay the tax was a Roman coin that couldn't be used to buy animals in the temple. Since you couldn't render your denarius to God anyway, why *not* render it to Caesar?) Chilton has described precisely a situation in which the distance between the offerer and his sacrifice had grown too great for the sacrifice to be meaningful. Sacrificial crisis, here we come.

Girard goes on to add: "On the other hand, if there is *too much* continuity the violence will overflow its channels. 'Impure' violence will mingle with the sacred violence of the rites, turning the latter into a scandalous accomplice in the process of pollution, even a kind of catalyst in the propagation of further impurity."[39] I suspect this is the issue underlying the two tales in which Saul disappoints his patron Samuel (1 Sam. 13:5–15; 15:1–35). For Saul, his hands full of Philistine blood, to have taken on himself the task of offering priestly sacrifice was to trespass the boundary between profane and holy violence. It was for the same reason that Yahve would later forbid the red-handed David to build his temple (1 Chron. 22:8, a priestly redactional development of 1 Kings 5:3, where David had simply not had time during his busy battle schedule to build the temple). And when Saul had offered all the Amalekites as human sacrifices to Yahve, thus fulfilling a duty of sacred violence, he yet spared the life of King Agag, presumably to use as some sort of diplomatic ace in the hole, and gave the captured livestock to his men. Samuel was displeased because all alike should have been offered up. To make exceptions out of worldly considerations was to compromise the purely sacred character of the violence. One may imagine poor Agag following this theological debate with keen interest, though he probably was disappointed with the outcome.

Do we see anything of the kind in the gospels? Indeed we do. At least presupposed in the gospels is the fact of quisling compromise between the temple authorities, especially the High Priest (like the Russian Orthodox Patriarch appointed by the KGB) and the Romans/Herods.[40] The hypocrisy did not escape the people. Like the priests of Matt. 27:6–7 who piously scruple over whether ritually impure bounty money may go back into the temple treasury or should go for a charitable secular contribution, the temple authorities strained out a gnat and swallowed a camel when they took care to exclude heathen denarii from the temple while getting in bed with Caesar and his flunkies to keep their privileged position. Again we may imagine the disgust of Jesus in the "render unto Caesar" scene. The confusion between sacred and profane violence in the temple finally led to the cutting off of the sacrifice for Caesar at the hands of the antipriestly Jewish rebels, signaling the ruinous war with Rome. Likewise, the story of Jesus' "cleansing of the temple" must be seen (or at least Girard would surely see it) in the context of impending sacrificial crisis.

The root problem in a time of sacrificial crisis is the breaking down of traditional class, gender, race, and social boundaries. We witness the same sort of thing today in the fundamentalist panic over gay rights, women's equality, and even the theory of evolution which seems to them to erode the wall between animals and humans. Every culture is defined by where it draws its lines. And when the lines start to be erased, there is going to be trouble, including vigilante violence. When people lose confidence in the proper channels for mediating violence, when, as in our society, they feel the justice system coddles criminals (thus expunging the difference between innocent and guilty), then people begin to take the law into their own hands, and chaos erupts. If the proper channels for violence are sacrificial and ritual in character, then the breakdown or compromise of this system will result in chaos as we have just seen.

> The primitive mind . . . has no difficulty imagining an affiliation between violence and nondifferentiation and, indeed, is often obsessed by the possible consequences of such a union. Natural differences are conceived in terms of cultural differences, and vice versa. . . . Because there is no real difference between the various modes of differentiation, there is in consequence no difference between the manner in which things fail to differ; the disappearance of natural differences can thus bring to mind the dissolution of regulations pertaining to the individual's proper place in society-that is, can instigate a sacrificial crisis.[41]

We see something of this erosion of traditional differences in the gospels, too. But the interesting thing is that Jesus himself is depicted as the chief culprit in erasing those lines! If we take seriously recent work by Elizabeth Schüssler Fiorenza, John Dominic Crossan, Werner Kelber, and others, Jesus appears to have proclaimed a "discipleship of equals" between men and women, welcomed the Untouchables as Gandhi did, received despised Gentiles into fellowship, accepted tax collectors and associated with sinners to the puzzlement of the traditionally pious. Jesus, as painted by Schüssler Fiorenza, Richard A. Horsley, Crossan, and others, even sought to abolish the patriarchal family (Matt. 10:34–36; 23:9). Hamerton-Kelly finds in Mark an idyllic picture of "the confraternity of the kingdom. Within this new context, the traditional family is an anachronism. The new radical fatherhood of God relativizes the claims of earthly parents and family obligations, which were in any case organized for the most part according to the forms of sacred violence."[42]

While this whole raft of politically correct exegeses might be challenged, a greater problem in attributing such notions to the historical Jesus is that saying after relevant saying has long ago been shown to be a redactional composition or a community formation. Horsley in particular seems fully as credulous about the accuracy of the gospels as Girard himself. But let us suppose the exegesis of the passages is correct, though their attribution to Jesus is not. What we are left with is a collection of socially disruptive sayings falsely ascribed to Jesus so as to pin the blame for the current social/sacrificial crisis squarely upon him! Here think also of the impression given in the gospels that Jesus single-handedly sparked the temple crisis. Neither the sacrificial program of Jesus educed by Chilton nor the sociopolitical background of priestly compromise reconstructed by Horsley is given explicitly in the gospel texts. Why not? The larger social conditions have been mythically transformed, wider problems attributed to one man alone: the scapegoat.

Up to this point I have been willing to grant for the sake of argument that Girard is correct in seeing Jesus portrayed as unambiguously innocent in the gospel accounts. Even if that were so, we need simply conclude that the gospels represent an advanced stage of morally dualistic rewriting of the earlier version of the scapegoat myth. "I implied that an original 'criminal' Baldr must have existed in a more primitive version of the myth."[43] I suggest that, in Girardian terms, the revolutionary rhetoric of Jesus in the gospels constitutes surviving vestiges of the earlier version of the Passion tale in which there was a "criminal" Jesus. Think also of the discomfort of the various evangelists over what to do with the "false" charge that Jesus had threatened to destroy the temple (Mark 14:57–59; Matt. 26:59–61; Acts 6:12–14; John 2:18–22). John in particular makes it clear his exonerating rationalization occurred to him long after the fact, a perfect example of Girard's retroactive rehabilitation of the criminal scapegoat.

Can Jesus really have been single-handedly responsible for the sacrificial crisis of his day? Not likely. Girard's explanation of the Oedipus myth fits just as nicely here:

> If the crisis has dropped from sight, if universal reciprocity [of violence] is eliminated, it is because of the unequal distribution of the very real parts of the crisis. In fact, nothing has been truly abolished, nothing added, but everything has been *misplaced*. The whole process of mythical formulation leads to a transferal of violent undifferentiation from all the Thebans to the person of Oedipus. Oedipus becomes the repository of all the community's ills. In the myth, the fearful transgression of a single individual is substituted for the universal onslaught of reciprocal violence. Oedipus is responsible for the ills that have befallen his people. He has become a prime example of the human scapegoat.[44]

So has Jesus. Girard ought to have seen that.

I AM HE AS YOU ARE HE AS YOU ARE ME AND WE ARE ALL TOGETHER

As we have seen, another major sign of the rise of reciprocal violence to crisis proportions is the appearance of doubles or twins. This is a term Girard employs in several related ways. First, in the process of mimesis, when one individual models himself upon another, the model and the imitator are mimetic twins. Second, Girard speaks of the two sides of any struggle, whether individual or collective, as doubles or mimetic twins, indicating that any significant difference between the two has been lost. Reciprocal violence levels the playing field until people may even forget what the violence was all about. Third, in this process, or as the occasion of this process, all traditional differentiations are lost, as we have seen. In this case everyone has become everyone else's twin or double. In fact, since everyone, like Hawthorne's Young Goodman Brown, has come to see the fiend in every face, everyone has become everyone else's "monstrous double." Fourth, often this sort of collective doubling will appear in myths reduced symbolically to a pair of matched characters, usually antagonistic brothers or twins.

Fifth, once the mass settles on a hapless victim to serve as its scapegoat, this unfortunate becomes the blotter to soak up everyone's guilt and paranoia, and he or she becomes the monstrous double of the society. This is the first act of transference. With the second act, the scapegoat is sanctified and idealized as a savior. But what is to be done with the guilt previously attributed to him? Sixth, it is projected onto a secondary scapegoat. If this happens, then we may speak of the new scapegoat as the monstrous double of the first, rehabilitated scapegoat. Given the return of dualist moralism after the crisis subsides, the scapegoat is thus bifurcated, and his evil twin may be a second scapegoated individual (or group: Jews, according to both Mack and Maccoby) or a mythic creation (adding Loki alongside Hother).

I want to focus here on the appearance in the gospels of matched/opposing pairs of characters whose function is to symbolize and concretize the mimetic doubling of the larger society in the real crisis the myth reflects, the fourth use of the doubles metaphor. Evident literary doubles of Jesus include John the Baptist and Lazarus, but I must leave them aside here. I will consider Simon Peter as a double of Jesus, then Judas Iscariot as another.

Girard is quick to note it when pairs of mimetic twins in a myth have equivalent names or different versions of the same name. In the Passion of John the Baptist, every named character save for the baptizer himself is named Herod: Herod Antipas, Herodias, and (implicitly) Herod, the brother from whom Herod Antipas had wooed away Herodias. Similarly, Romulus and Remus are variants of the same name. We might also think of the punning resemblance between Jacob and the name of the river whose resident god he wrestles, the Jabbock. And the rivals Evodia ("Successful") and Syntyche ("Lucky") in Phil. 4:2–3, who are to be reconciled with the help of none other than Syzygus ("Yokefellow")! Maccoby explains why in such cases the names indicate the splitting of an originally single character. As the various transferences and bifurcations occur during the evolution of the myth, traits and functions of the original character come to be multiplied or substituted. There are too many actantial roles for a single character to play any more. So the character is multiplied, all keeping the same name as a vestige of their original identity.[45]

Simon Peter, Jesus' number-one disciple, might, seen through Girardian lenses, betray a considerable resemblance to Simon the brother of Jesus mentioned in Mark 6:3. Though it is possible that this list of names once functioned like the list of the Twelve in Mark 3:14–19—that is, as an official list of the authoritative Heirs of Jesus—it is difficult to see much reason for mentioning them by name—unless someone has passed along a fossilized hint of Simon being Jesus' mimetic twin. He functions in the gospels as a sounding board to amplify Jesus' teachings, since, like Holmes's Doctor Watson, he asks Jesus the question the readers are asking. Thus he is a narrative commentary on the sayings of Jesus. The same point is made in the doctrines of extremist Ismail'is who see Jesus and Peter as distinct syzygies emanated from Allah, Jesus being the "proclaimer" of an exoteric revelation, Peter being the "foundation" who explains the esoteric aspect of the teaching afterward.

More than this, however, Simon Peter seems to be the externalized voice of Jesus' own indecision and doubt. When at Caesarea Philippi Simon voices his opposition to the plan of Jesus' coming death, do we not catch the hint that he has struck a nerve? Jesus turns on him with curses because he himself is thinking the very same thing and is trying to resist the temptation. This is exactly what we see later in the Garden of Gethsemane when Jesus voices overt doubts: If at all possible, cannot Jesus avoid the hemlock cup? Of course Jesus does emerge from the Garden with his resolve intact. He will go the way of the cross in any case. And Simon embodies this, too. For he is also Simon of Cyrene, who carries the cross of Jesus.

And he is Simon the Zealot. Bearing in mind that in the Greek text a "zealous one" and a "jealous one" are the same word, we can see another sign of Peter as a mimetic counterpart of Jesus. We have already seen this in the scene of Peter's confession (where the affirmation of Jesus' identity may thus denote Jesus' *own* realization of his identity) and its aftermath in which Jesus rebukes his own doubt, calling it Satan. We ought also to remember the Last Supper at which Peter accepts that Jesus will have to die but swears he will see him through to the end, his own death as well as Jesus'—for the two are the same. When Jesus questions Peter's ironclad fidelity, is he again questioning his own? But in Girard's terms, does Peter's protest of loyalty denote that Peter has sought to adopt as his own the destiny of his model? In fact, Peter does die by crucifixion in early Christian tradition (beginning with John 21:18–19). Drawing on Basilides' redaction of the myth, we might say that Simon (as Simon of Cyrene) not only shares the fate of his Lord but supplants it, actually taking Jesus' place on the cross. Another set of brothers, James and John, want to mimetically appropriate the destiny of Jesus, too (Mark 10:35–41).

Simon Peter will meet his own double later on in the form of the anti-Simon, Simon Magus, who approaches Peter and asks to duplicate his powers of transmitting the Spirit (Acts 8:18–24). There are still more counterparts to Simon Peter, but we must wait until later to meet them.

JUDAS GOAT

Judas is surely the most complex of Jesus' doubles. We have already noted that he plays the role of the secondary scapegoat once Jesus has been retroactively exonerated. Maccoby develops the idea independently of Girard, though he says precisely what Girard ought to have said on the subject. Maccoby cites numerous myths in which the executioner of the hero is the hero's brother (e.g., Cain and Abel). The point of such a symbol is to bifurcate the original victim so that the executioner may be seen to bear away the evil originally attached to the victim. The original scapegoat has been split into two, one going to Yahve, the other to Azazel.[46] Though Girard cannot bring himself to apply it to Jesus and Judas, he is aware of the same trajectory of mythic evolution:

> Similarly, the Aztec god Xipe-Totec demonstrates the ability of the incarnation of the sacred to assume different roles in the system. Sometimes this god is killed and flayed in the person of a victim offered as substitute for him; at other times the god becomes the executioner, flaying victims in order to don their skin. Evidently religious thought perceives all those who participate in this violent interplay, whether actively or passively, as doubles.[47]

In light of these analyses we can plot out the trajectory of the "Big Bang" that led to the multiplication of Judas figures. Judas is of course "the Iscariot," the False One, the Betrayer. (Here I must side with Bertil Gärtner against Maccoby, who rejects this interpretation in favor of "the Sicarius."[48]) He is the sacred executioner. But to play this role to the fullest, he should be Jesus' brother, too, and he is. He is the Judas numbered among Jesus' siblings in Mark 6:3. More specifically, he is even a *twin* brother, Didymus Judas Thomas, Judas the Twin. And of course Judas must be one of the disciples as well, in order to be within striking distance when the moment comes.

But as Luke knew (and as Schmithals and Günter Klein knew even better), there remains a problem counting out one of the Twelve if there is to be a subsequent college of twelve apostles. How can they all have been appointed by the Risen Jesus (1 Cor. 15:5) if one of them had already hanged himself? Judas was simply bifurcated into "Judas Iscariot" and "Judas not Iscariot" (John 14:22). A few manuscripts omit "not" in John 14:22. If this should chance to be the original reading, suppressed by harmonizing scribes for obvious reasons, then here we would actually be witnessing a stage in the ongoing doubling of Judas. Perhaps the two resultant Judases counted as numbers twelve and thirteen, with Thaddaeus as one of the first eleven. But later, somehow Thaddaeus was assimilated to Judas not Iscariot. This left the famous gap, which Lebbaeus and Nathaniel might have been attempts to fill. Speaking of odd manuscripts, a few have the reading "Judas the Zealot" at Matt. 10:3 (in some Old Latin manuscripts) and at John 14:22 (in some Sahidic manuscripts). This, too, would be significant in the same way "Simon the Zealot" was, the epithet indicating, for neo-Girardian exegesis at any rate, mimetic rivalry: Judas the Jealous.

If twins are literary/mythic personifications of the mimetic doubling in periods of social/sacrificial crisis, Girard observes, the scapegoat (the monstrous double of society as a whole) can just as well be a product of or a partner in incest, just like Oedipus. It is an equivalent image for the horrific effacing of differences and boundaries. We see the logic of the mytheme spinning itself out in the growth of the Judas tradition. Late in the megatext, in The Golden Legend, we find Judas married to his mother, having killed his father,[49] just like Oedipus, and for the same reason. In the thirteenth-century Ballad of Judas he is living incestuously with his sister.[50]

And if Judas is the "monstrous double" of Jesus, we might take a second look at the intriguing guess of some exegetes that the epithet "Son of Perdition" in John 17:12 means the same thing it does in 2 Thess. 2:3. This makes Judas the Antichrist, surely the monstrous double of Jesus! Finally, as a mimetic twin of Jesus, he might be expected to seek the same fate as Jesus. And he gets it. As Maccoby points out, not only does Judas die hanging from a tree like Jesus (Matt. 27:5), but if one factors in Luke's variant in Acts 1: 18–19, where Judas' manner of death is left vague but involves a rain of his blood soaking into the ground, we can hear an echo of the underlying myth on which Jesus' crucifixion was built: the sacrificial deaths of Attis, Abel, (and, one might add, Baal) to fertilize the ground with their blood. (This mytheme is still faintly visible in John 19:41a: "Now in the place where he was crucified there was a garden.") Thus it was not only guilt but telltale mythic coloring that was transferred to Judas the Twin. Could it be that Luke's and Matthew's versions of the death of Judas differ because each has tried in his own way to break the parallel between Jesus and Judas, Luke omitting the hanging (crucifixion) element but retaining the Field of Blood as the place of death, while Matthew retained the hanging but removed the death from the Field of Blood by substituting a different account of the latter, cobbled together from readings of two versions of Zech. 11:13, and with it a different, and safer, etymology?

Some traditions report that it was Judas who died on the cross in Jesus' stead, having been miraculously transformed into his likeness. Abu Ja'far al-Tabari (died 923 C.E.) quoted Ibn Ishaq as relating how "Some of the Christians allege that it was Judas Iscariot who was made [Jesus'] semblance to them and that they crucified him despite his saying, 'I am not one of his companions! I am the one who pointed him out to you!' "[51] It is striking that such Christian docetism survived long enough in remote areas for Muhammad to have picked it up from Christians when they converted to Islam. And so here is a Christian tradition according to which Judas' mimetic rivalry with his Lord came to an ironic fruition. The point is actually rather important. The choice of the scapegoat by the mob is usually random, much like the picking of Simon of Cyrene out of the crowd to carry Jesus' cross (and think again of Basilides' reading: Simon *had* been picked at random to be crucified). It could be anybody because in the crisis of reciprocal violence none is particularly more guilty or innocent than anyone else; indeed, these terms have for the time being lost their meaning. The scapegoat is, however, still falsely accused since he cannot be *totally and uniquely* responsible as charged. But it could as easily be anybody.

And this means it could just as easily have been Judas as Jesus! This is another implication of their being mimetic twins. Girard makes this point in discussing the Oedipus story. Oedipus has concluded that the plague in Thebes is a divine judgment for the murder of Laius, his predecessor on the throne. The task is now to smoke out the regicide and punish him. Of course Oedipus himself is eventually disclosed as the murderer, albeit an unwitting one. But, says Girard, this identification of Oedipus as the culprit was not inevitable, at least not in whatever real set of events the story reflects. The blame for the death circled like a vulture for a while. Initially Oedipus tried to pin the blame on Tiresias and Creon, but he couldn't make it stick. They returned the blame to him, and they did manage to make it stick. Did Oedipus "in fact" commit the deed? He himself was willing to admit he did, but this only means he allowed himself to be persuaded of their version of events. He knew he killed some old man, but at the moment he did not know his identity. It may or may not have been Laius: who knows? But the tail has finally been pinned on the donkey, and that's where it will stay. Oedipus is elected as the scapegoat to save Thebes.

> Having oscillated freely among the three protagonists, the full burden of guilt finally settles on one. It might very well have settled on another, or on none.... The attribution of guilt that henceforth passes for "true" differs in no way from those attributions that will henceforth be regarded as "false," except that in the case of the "true" guilt no voice is raised to protest any aspect of the charge. A particular version of events succeeds in imposing itself; it loses its polemical nature in becoming the acknowledged basis of the myth, in becoming the myth itself.[52]

Judas is forever vilified as a thief (John 12:6), but remember that Jesus was numbered among the thieves (Mark 14:48;15:27), too. And if Judas was called demon-possessed (John 13:27; Luke 22:3), so was Jesus (John 8:48).

Neither set of invectives counts as any more than that. One stuck, the other didn't. Or should we not say, the charges stuck first to Jesus, the primary scapegoat, then were reapplied to Judas, the secondary scapegoat.

To take it one step further, the supposed possession of Judas by Satan may be seen as yet another distancing device to shift some measure of the blame from Judas as the *sacred* executioner. "The condition called 'possession' is in fact but one particular interpretation of the monstrous double. . . . Some presence seems to be acting *through* him—a god, a monster, or whatever creature is in the process of investing his body."[53] Thus Satan becomes the monstrous double of Judas, and a tertiary scapegoat in his behalf. In the Coptic fragments of the Gospel of Bartholomew we read that it was Judas' nagging wife who put him up to his mischief.[54] Another monstrous double.

It only remains to tie up a surprising loose end. If the panicky words of Judas quoted by Ibn Ishaq ("I am not one of his companions!") should remind one of Peter's denials (Mark 14:66–71), this may be no accident, because Peter and Judas would seem to be doubles of one another, too. If Judas Iscariot is Judas the Zealot, and if Simon Peter is Simon the Zealot; if Judas is one of the brothers of Jesus, and if Simon is another, then we might take another look at the epithet "Judas of Simon Iscariot" (John 13:2), which could as easily denote "Judas, brother of Simon" as "Judas, son of Simon."[55] But Simon Peter the False One? Peter Iscariot? That would aptly describe the cowardly denier of Mark 14:66–71 who afterward breaks into weeping just as Judas afterward repented (Matt. 27:3). And compare John 6:66–71 with Mark 8:27–33. In Peter van Greenaway's novel *The Judas Gospel*, a secret Dead Sea Scroll, a Testament of Judas, reveals that it was Peter, not Judas, who sold Jesus out, and that Peter successfully framed Judas for the deed.[56] Is that possible? Was Peter, like Hother, a secondary scapegoat later replaced by Judas, a tertiary scapegoat (like Loki)?

PARTNERS IN MIME

Judas and Simon Peter may be the most obvious cases of mimetic twins among the disciples, but the gospels do not hesitate to cast the whole group of them in the role. Almost like a Greek chorus, the disciples often speak as one with the voice of mimetic desire. They are forever squabbling over who is the greatest, or will be the greatest. And they pin their hopes of greatness on the coat tails of Jesus ("If only I can touch the hem of his garment . . . !"). They generously leave the central throne for Jesus but bicker over the seats of honor alongside him. Mark pictures them always dumbfounded, rebuked for misunderstanding just when they thought they'd got it straight. It all fits Girard's framework perfectly. The mimetic double seeks to be just like his model, but as he closes in, the model tries to keep some distance, sets up some obstacle. "A disciple is not above his teacher, nor a slave above his master; it is enough for a disciple to be like his teacher, and the slave like his master" (Matt. 10:24–25a). "Are you able to drink the cup that I drink, or to be baptized with the baptism with which I am baptized?" (Mark 10:38). And see 2 Kings 4:11–37, Mark 9:14–29, and various tales of Aesclepius, Asclepiades, and Pancrates where the disciples prove utterly incapable of mimicking the feats of the master. Or think of Joshua who first says to the people, "Therefore fear Yahve, and serve him in sincerity and in faithfulness" (Joshua 24:14) and then casts this in their teeth: "You cannot serve Yahve, for he is a holy god; he is a jealous god; he will not forgive your transgressions or your sins!" (Josh. 24:19). The puzzled disciple finds himself in a double bind.[57]

Increasingly frustrated, the imitator gradually slips from adoration of the model into a love-hate relationship with the model, who is increasingly perceived as a competitor and an obstacle, until unalloyed hatred finally emerges.

> By a strange but explicable consequence of their relationship, neither the model nor the disciple is disposed to acknowledge the inevitable rivalry. The model, even when he has openly encouraged imitation ["If any one would come after me, let him take up his cross and follow me"], is surprised to find himself engaged in competition. He concludes that the disciple has betrayed his confidence by following in his footsteps. As for the disciple, he feels both dejected and humiliated, judged unworthy by his model of participating in the superior existence the model himself enjoys.[58]

"Depart from me, O Lord, for I am a sinful man" (Luke 5:8).

"Conflictual mimesis will inevitably unify by leading two or more individuals to converge on one and the same adversary that all wish to strike down."[59] The disciples of Jesus have been imitators of Jesus and thus rivals of one another, and as Jesus continues to frustrate them, what is their next step going to be? Girard should expect them to unite against him. No more bickering about who is to be greatest! We will not have this man to reign over us! They share harmonious fellowship once again as they jointly devour the flesh and blood of their erstwhile master, their scapegoat, the lamb of God who took away their sins. Theodore J. Weeden argued that Mark portrays the disciples finally becoming the enemies of Jesus, betraying, denying, abandoning him, not even visiting his tomb.[60] I believe that a neo-Girardian scrutiny of the Passion will make that description seem mild indeed. In what follows I will attempt to show how Girard's methods should disclose an earlier version in which it was none other than the disciples of Jesus who conspired to kill him.

WE ESTEEMED HIM SMITTEN OF GOD

Sifting through the mosaic tiles of the Passion narratives, I believe the neo-Girardian investigator would have to conclude that it was the anointing in Bethany that proved to be the backbreaking straw. Here the disciples first recognized their idol's clay feet. A shocking lapse convinced them that they held more firmly to his radical ethos than he himself did. The inconsistency? With the inflexible pedantry of the small-minded zealot, "some" (Mark 14:4) on the scene objected to the waste of the fancy oil: "Why was the ointment thus wasted? For this ointment might have been sold for more than three hundred denarii, and [the proceeds] given to the poor" (Mark 14:4b–5). Isn't this the very policy Jesus had urged on so many others? The issue is not quite that they were being holier than Jesus; rather, they were being more like Jesus than Jesus! And consider the resultant double bind. Jesus has been caught out. This discovery convinces them that they are better than Jesus in living out his ethic. Mimesis seems to have gained its object! But in the same moment, they must mourn the loss of their idol. As their idol has proven to be less than perfect, their victory is cheapened by the knowledge that they have only surpassed someone who was really no better than them all along! And so how far have they come? They scorn the model not only for disappointing them but also for depriving them of the goal they thought they had been pursuing and finally gained. "Christlikeness" has been devalued.

But can we be so certain that those objecting from the peanut gallery were disciples? That was apparently Matthew's inference, since his version has "the disciples" as the carpers (26:8). Who else would likely have been present on the scene? Besides, in Mark 6:37, the miraculous feeding, it is also the disciples who speak indignantly about giving something worth great amounts of denarii to the hungry.

It could be that the identity of the critics was known to Mark but that he suppressed it, implying that Judas was the only disciple to take umbrage, since it is he who directly goes to the priests to make his offer. Matthew leaves the disciples as the culprits, but he has tried to soften the blow in another way. Jesus' host on the occasion, according to some source at Matthew's disposal, was one "Simon the leper." By now our Girardian instincts are sufficiently honed to detect here another version of Simon Peter. It is Simon Peter's house. Why disguise him as a leper? Such an identification serves no apparent narrative purpose—unless we are being subtly directed to Numbers 12:1–15, a story in which Miriam and Aaron dare to criticize Moses on account of a woman, his Cushite bride. For her meddling, Miriam is turned into a leper. Is Simon made a leper by Matthew because he dared criticize Jesus on account of a woman? I wouldn't be surprised.

Luke has concealed Simon Peter's identity under a different mask. He has made him into Simon the Pharisee (Luke 7:36–40 ff). Exegetes have noted that this would be the single instance of Jesus addressing a Pharisee or other outsider by name. And yet he elsewhere calls Simon Peter by name (e.g., Luke 22:31; Matt. 16:17; 17:25). While no evangelist minds very much having Jesus rebuke Peter, this time Luke feels things have gone too far: Simon has seemingly lost his faith in Jesus altogether. "If this man were a prophet . . ." So it must be some *other* Simon.

It is by no means difficult to see how the disciples might have taken offense at Jesus' saying "You always have the poor with you, and whenever you will, you can do good to them; but you will not always have me" (Mark 14:7). The heartless arrogance of this saying has always troubled pious readers, all the way back to the late first or early second century, when the Didache warned its readers to eject as a false prophet any itinerant who said under divine afflatus, "Give me money," which is pretty much the same sentiment. The Mark 14:7 saying is only the caption of the scene of extravagant anointing. The actions spoke just as loudly. Note that Luke has clumsily tried to change the subject, redirecting the reader's attention to the supposed bad character of the woman. It becomes an incoherent mishmash of themes from other tales in which Jesus forgives sins. As Girard says, "The only feasible or even conceivable response seems to be that the version of the myth we are analyzing *is not the first*."[61] My Girardian guess is that after this incident, it is not Judas alone who moves to engineer the death of Jesus, but his apostolic compatriots as well.

SCAPEGOATS GRUFF

I would next like to deal with a set of four pericopae which seem perhaps to reflect scapegoat themes, though they do not bear directly on Jesus as the scapegoat. What are they doing here? Perhaps, as elsewhere in the gospels, it was simply a vague but discernible kinship of theme which accounted for them being included in the general vicinity of Jesus' own Passion.

The first episode is that of blind Bartimaeus (Mark 10:46–52). Once we see a crowd menacing a blind beggar, a doubly good choice for a scapegoat, and the beggar calling out for mercy, we know the game is afoot. Who knows but that originally the story told not of the recovery of Bartimaeus' sight, but rather his narrow escape from an angry mob? Like the man in the Garden of Gethsemane who just managed to escape by the skin of his teeth, glad enough to leave his only garment behind, given the alternative (Mark 14:51–52), Bartimaeus pitches aside the superfluous ballast of his threadbare coat to run for his life.

We must cast our net wide: Could it be that the similar story of Jesus' healing a blind man outside of Bethsaida (Mark 8:22–26) was another version of the Bartimaeus tale? "And some people brought to him a blind man." That has an ominous ring about it, reminiscent of the pariah pericope John 7:53–8:11, that of the woman taken in adultery. "The Pharisees brought a woman who had been caught in adultery." They meant to carry her out dead. Is the blind man of Bethsaida being scapegoated, too? If so, somehow he gets off the hook, but Jesus tells him not to take any chances: "Do not even enter the village."

The second adjacent scapegoat episode is Matt. 21:18–20, the cursing of the fig tree, along with 21:33–39, the parable of the Wicked Tenants. It only takes a wee bit of reshuffling to make the parable a story in which strife breaks out among the sharecroppers themselves, who then gang up on a figure marginally associated with the vineyard. The man they kill does not work there but is the son of the absentee landlord. His death puts an end to their strife. He is driven outside the gates to be killed, like the ancient Greek *pharmakos*, or, following Mark 12:8, he is killed and then cast forth. And if we add the story of the fig tree, we might even detect a trace of some earlier version of Jesus' own death in which he was blamed for a wasting agricultural disease à la Joel 1:11–15, where vinedressers and withered fig trees are mentioned in the same breath.

Next we may briefly consider Matthew's parable of the Guest without a Wedding Garment (22:2,11–14). Before the rejoicing of the wedding feast could begin in earnest, had there once been a need to choose someone for a scapegoat, in this case marked out by his poor dress? If so, it would be a reflection of the marriage festival custom of the Niquas in which the marriage is sealed by the scars won by relatives of the bride and groom in a battle during the ceremony. Often the ritual violence culminates in the prearranged death of a slave during the general melee. The slave is a perfect scapegoat to banish the interfamilial tensions since he is helpless and will have no one to avenge his murder.[62] Neither did the poor man in Matt. 22:12, who no doubt wondered why he had been hustled in at the last moment at all. He found out the hard way.

Finally, there is the conundrum put to Jesus by the Sadducees in Matt. 22:23–33, the parable of the woman with seven husbands, if I may venture to call it that. Girardian exegesis, it seems to me, ought to grow suspicious at the picture of the woman surviving when all seven husbands have come to a bad end in rapid succession. Is she Lady Bluebeard? Perhaps the shroud is on the wrong corpse here. We might speculate that in an earlier version, the seven husbands were all very much alive, and it is the death of the woman which is at issue. Instead of bringing this riddle to Jesus, suppose in the original version, it was the woman herself who was brought—by the seven men. Suddenly we are dealing with something that sounds remarkably like the adulteress pericope again. Shrewd popular exegesis long ago suggested that no one took Jesus up on his invitation to cast the first stone, provided one was sinless—because all of them had sinned with her! Plug in here, if you will, the interchange between Jesus and a very similar character in John 4:16–18, " 'Go call your husband and return here.' The woman answered him, 'I have no husband.' Jesus said to her, 'You are right to say, "I have no husband." The fact is, you have had five husbands, and the man you have now is not your husband.' " Perhaps these previous "husbands" were someone *else's* husbands. Perhaps the seven "husbands" of the woman in Matt. 22:25 were not that woman's husbands either. As in the "cast the first stone" pericope, perhaps the group of seven had come to resent one another for their common dalliance with her. The only way to heal the breach between the rivals was to eliminate that which stood between them: her. Just as Girard was able to corroborate his reversal of the myth of the Curetes and baby Zeus (that originally they conspired to destroy him, not to protect him) by comparing it with a surviving parallel in which the Titans do gang up on an infant god to kill him, I have tried to reconstruct an original scapegoat version of the woman with seven husbands by comparing it with the related story of the woman taken in adultery.

ONE LAST MEAL

As to the Last Supper, we can dispense with two notable but fairly simple items quickly. The first is the Words of Institution. It is clear enough, on any critical reading, that here we are dealing with a ceremonial etiology. As Loisy noted long ago, the very words "This is my body, this is my blood" imply a ritual context in which a celebrant explains the meaning of the various items of the liturgy. The case is not entirely closed, as witness Chilton's discussion in *The Temple of Jesus*,[63] but I would see the words as part of a post-Jesus liturgy. The question then becomes, what was the sacrificial violence that first gave rise to this masked liturgical commemoration? Here the veil is rather thin: it is the death of Jesus. But note that it must be the death of Jesus as a collective murder, only later sanctified as a sacrificial ritual. The key is the added word, "Drink ye all of it." Girard explains, "The sacrificial ceremony requires a show of collective participation, if only in purely symbolic form. This association of the collectivity with the sacrificial victim is found in numerous instances—notably in the Dionysiac *sparagmos*. . . . All the participants, without exception, are required to take part in the death scene."[64] The reason, even if no longer understood, is to reflect the logic of the original mob lynching. The entire group must take part, or the violence will remain on the level of "bad"—that is, secular and personal—violence. In concrete terms, a murder in which only some participate would leave itself open for vendetta against the individual killers and their families. But if the whole collectivity has taken part in it, what are you going to do? Vengeance is short-circuited, and peace returns. The direction for all present at the eucharist to commune echoes the unity of the disciples in their murder of Jesus. This may sound farfetched, but as Maccoby says,[65] it remains true today that Christians are quite happy for Jesus to have died, no matter how much they may mourn the same event. But that is the whole logic of the scapegoat, isn't it?

In Luke's version of the Supper scene he has Jesus quote Isa. 53:12 (Luke 22:37), "he was reckoned among the transgressors." Here is the tip of a large iceberg, the early Christian use of the Deutero-Isaianic Servant Song. Let us simply note that one could ask no better evidence, not that the gospels expose and debunk the scapegoat myth as Girard says, but just the reverse, that they embrace it wholeheartedly. This application of Isa. 53 to Jesus plainly presupposes Christians looking back at the days when *they* ("we") acted wrongly, albeit in good faith, thinking Jesus to be a villain condemned by God. It was only later that they "realized" the savior had been innocent all along, that it was the secret plan of God that he should die to bear away the sins of his contemporaries. In the early Christian singing of the Servant Song we see, as Girard should lead us to expect, only the second transfer, that of guilt away from the scapegoat and onto the community of faith who erred in ignorance. Of the first transfer, the attribution of the community's ills to the scapegoat as if they were his, we hear only echoes. Do they yet know that *they* had *victimized* the innocent scapegoat by piling their sins high on his back? No, they know only that they had been wrong in imagining him to be suffering from his own sins. They believe it is only *now, retrospectively*, that the vicarious dimension of his suffering has become known. In other words, the scapegoating character of the act of generative violence has been suppressed and is now safely forgotten.

The designation by Jesus of his betrayer must occupy us next. We usually read John's account of Jesus giving the sop to Judas in answer to the query of the Beloved Disciple and Peter, as if Jesus already knew who would betray him and is telling the secret in pantomime so as to prevent any disturbance. And that is no doubt the Fourth Evangelist's intention. But Maccoby[66] believes he can sniff out an earlier version in which Jesus engineered being handed over to the authorities (much as in Kazantzakis's *The Last Temptation of Christ*). In giving the sop to Judas he was making the decision as to who would do the dirty work. While this suggestion is attractive, I cannot help thinking that for Jesus to hand the sop to Judas, implying that it was Jesus' own decision to make, represents a redactional attempt to cover up an earlier version, still visible in Mark 14:20 ("It is one of the twelve, one who is dipping bread into the same dish with me") and Matt. 26:23 ("He who has dipped his hand in the dish with me, will betray me"), in which Jesus had left it to chance, much as in Acts 1:26, where the apostles cast lots to determine

Judas' replacement. (It is even possible that the Acts scene is a rewritten version of the Last Supper scene.) Since chance, like God, moves in mysterious ways, it is employed like Gideon's fleece to let God express his will (cf. also 1 Sam. 6:7–9). It is to open up a zone of indeterminacy, breaking the link of human cause and effect, so that God may have a window of intervention. "The victim is chosen by lot [whose] expulsion will save the community."[67]

But in Jesus' case it is not precisely the victim who is chosen, but rather the sacred executioner. I suggest, along Girardian lines, that the lot is being cast here (by a method only disclosed afterward so as to prevent any attempt to influence the outcome) in order to choose by divine providence *who is to make the choice of victim*. Again, this would be needful to ensure the victim was taken by surprise and could not flee forewarned, as he could had the lot elected him there on the spot. But wasn't Jesus already the chosen victim of the scheming Twelve who were sick of him? According to my reconstruction of the anointing scene, yes. But as Girard is the first to admit, the same originary event leaves its traces in many and various myths. As de Maupassant observed, it is difficult to keep one's deceptions consistent with one another. And here in the dipping in the dish scene I am wagering that what we have is another version of the story in which mimetic rivalries have developed between the disciples themselves as well as between them and Jesus. In all the bickering over which was the greatest, one might as easily point to James and John (Mark 10:41) as the lightning rods of controversy (Mark 3:17), and thus the best choices for elimination (Mark 10:39). But then there was Peter with his tiresome claims to primacy. Best to cast out *some* scorner so dissension would go out. At the very least it ought to provide a deterrent to further arguing! People still remembered the story of Korah (Num. 16; Jude 11), after all, but maybe they needed a reminder.

It turns out to be Jesus, as he discovers too late in the Garden. "Friend, why have you come?" (Matt. 26:50). Oh, *that's* why. Perhaps Judas himself did not know until that moment. "The one I kiss is the man; seize him" (Matt. 26:48). As many exegetes have noticed over the years, it makes no sense at all to suppose that the guards have come to arrest Jesus not knowing what he looks like! The whole reason for the clandestine arrest is supposed to be that Jesus is so popular that *everyone* knows him! Maccoby takes this incongruity to denote the later and superfluous addition of Judas to a scene in which originally he did not figure. Likely enough. But it could also be that the authorities simply want to make an example of *someone*, and the choice is up to Judas, who can make no choice till the moment comes. When it does, he kisses Jesus, pretty much at random, and the matter is settled.

Why then does the canonical version have both the death of Jesus and the role of Judas in bringing it about preordained, locked into a divine plan? "The original act of violence is unique and spontaneous. Ritual sacrifices, however, are multiple, endlessly repeated. All those aspects of the original act that had escaped man's control—the choice of time and place, the selection of the victim—are now premeditated and fixed by custom."[68] In precisely the same way, the liturgical recitation of the Passion of Jesus came to have a preordained character since everyone already knew what happened, and this expectation entered the story itself, making all the events part of a divine script, both within and without the narrative world.

MESSIAHS BY THE SACKFUL

Medieval Muslim commentators on the Passion of Jesus, which they understood in a docetic framework, had their own clever explanation as to why Judas had to tell the guards which of these men was the notorious Jesus. As soon as Judas and his goon squad arrived, Allah transformed all the disciples into the physical likeness of Jesus! Thus the need to ask, "Will the real Jesus please stand up?" In the confusion, Jesus himself ascended into heaven, leaving only a choice among counterfeits. And it was one of them, in some versions Judas himself, who wound up on the cross.[69] What is interesting about this version from a Girardian standpoint is that it provides an unparalleled example of the mythic concretization of mimetic doubles into literal, physical doubles, and on a large scale. "If violence is a great leveler of men and everybody becomes the double, or 'twin,' of his antagonist, it seems to follow that all the doubles are identical and that any one can at any given moment become the double of all the others."[70] "According to Freud, the crowd of doubles stands in absolute opposition to the absolute specificity of the hero,"[71] but Girard would modify this sketch at a significant point: The hero (actually, the victim) stands opposed to a crowd of doubles who are his *own* doubles as well, since in the crisis of reciprocal violence, all distinguishing marks have faded away. Girard prefers the formulation of Freud according to which we have "A crowd of people all with the same name and similarly attired."[72] That is said strikingly well in the Islamic version of the arrest.

AND SO SAY ALL OF US

But let us hypothesize another version of the arrest in the Garden in which no Judas figures. Judas, after all, would have to be a later addition, as a secondary scapegoat to shift the deicidal blame from the shoulders of the community as a whole. Suppose there was an earlier account in which the disciples simply turned on Jesus *en masse*, ambushing him as the senators did Julius Caesar. Here we must take our hint from Girard's comparison of the

Curetes myth with the myth of the infant Dionysus. The Curetes appear in the extant version as a phalanx of armed warriors forming a circle around the godling to protect him. But comparison with the Dionysus myth, in which the Titans close around Dionysus and dismember him, leads Girard to infer that originally the Curetes did the same. It was only later that the story was cleaned up by the simple expedient of making the Curetes Zeus' bodyguards instead of his assassins.

In the Gethsemane scene we have similar elements. Jesus is with a crowd, his disciples, at least some of whom are carrying weapons. Suddenly Jesus is menaced by a weapon-brandishing crowd. The only ones actually said to employ any weapons in the ensuing melee are Jesus' disciples. Jesus sees that resistance is futile and allows himself to be led away peaceably, though he is stung by the feeling of betrayal. Of course when we fill in specific details the way the evangelists do, we see that the armed disciples only sought to protect Jesus from arrest by an invading second group. But perhaps that is not the only way to fill in the blanks.

Surprisingly little would change if the story were to be rewritten as that of Jesus' being ambushed and apprehended by his own disciples. And as a neo-Girardian, I am suggesting that the alteration went in the other direction. Attackers have been converted into protectors. In Matthew, Mark, and John, there is no preparation whatever for the sudden appearance of the disciples' swords. Presumably this would have fit better a version in which the weapons came as just as much a surprise to Jesus as to the reader. It would make more sense, then, for Jesus to say to the "crowd" *of disciples*, "Have you come out as against a robber, with swords and clubs to capture me? Day after day I *was with you* in the temple teaching, and you did not seize me" (Mark 14:49). Matthew (26:55) has changed the crucial phrase to: "Day after day I sat in the temple teaching," which seems to mean merely, "You knew where to find me." Perhaps Matthew realized Mark's text could be read as meaning something else, something he did not like.

If we picture the group of disciples as the murderers of Jesus, as I believe consistent Girardian exegesis would require, then must we write off the series of trials before the Sanhedrin and Pilate as forming no part of the original? Not quite. As for Jesus' trial (or hearing, or interrogation) before the Sanhedrin, it bears clear marks of having been not invented, but transformed. Most likely, playing by Girardian rules, the group before whom Jesus is brought is once again his own disciples. For one thing, this would at a single stroke rid us of the vexing problem of the Sanhedrin holding a capital trial on Passover eve, an incongruity that already has many scholars willing to dismiss the whole scene as mudslinging fiction anyway.

Is the role of the chief villain Caiaphas a complete fiction, too? Again, no. His priestly miter is on the wrong head, though. His vestments do not quite fit their wearer, any more than Saul's armor fit David. If we lift the turban from over the concealed brows, we recognize a familiar face, for "Caiaphas," at least here, is yet another double of "Cephas," Simon Peter, binding and loosing as he sees fit. The "real" Peter, the Simon Peter persona, who from the standpoint of a later piety cannot be imagined leading a drumhead courtmartial against the Christ, is nonetheless on the scene. He has been moved from center stage, but not very far! We find him only a few yards away, in the high priest's courtyard. But even there he is an understudy, playing essentially the same role, only toned down. He is still among the "wrong crowd," and this much, of course, Girard does see.[73] Eric Auerbach drew the contrast between Jesus on trial inside and Peter on trial (though in a lower court!) outside.[74] But I am urging a comparison between Caiaphas inside and Cephas outside. Just as Caiaphas condemns Jesus to death, so does Cephas: "I do not know the man!" Do we not here catch an echo of Jesus' own sentence of doom upon his enemies? "Depart from me; ye cursed; I never knew you!"

John, trying to supply some narrative verisimilitude, has Peter admitted to the priestly quarters by the Beloved Disciple because the latter is known to the high priest: "It's okay; he's with me." What on earth is going on *here*? Anyone would have to strain pretty far to catch *this* fly ball! C. S. Griffin even identified the Beloved Disciple as Judas himself![75] That would certainly explain the Beloved Disciple's chumminess with the powers that be. But through Girardian lenses, we can spot another intriguing possibility. The detail of the Beloved Disciple whispering to the bouncer is a vestige of the earlier version in which this disciple, simply *as* a disciple, belonged to the group before whom Jesus was being tried, because he was being brought before the disciples!

Similarly, recall how Matthew and John make Joseph of Arimathea a secret disciple of Jesus, John adding Nicodemus to the list. Of course the two evangelists are trying to make sense of what seems to them a contradiction: how could the man anxious to see Jesus properly buried be a member of the group that condemned him? But the incongruity arose only once that group was transformed from the disciples into the Sanhedrin. According to the scapegoat theory, it is quite natural that the crowd of murderers should come to take a more sympathetic view of the scapegoat after his death, since his death did heal their divisions. Joseph was another vestige of the stage when the killers were the disciples. His name even recalls that of another famous biblical scapegoat betrayed by his (nearly a) dozen brethren.

When Jesus is libeled by "false witnesses" who claim they heard him threaten to destroy the temple, most scholars already see something amiss. As noted above, this feature is widely recognized as an attempt to defuse an apologetical bomb. To use Crossan's felicitous term, it is "damage control." Jesus must have said something of the kind, though Christians soon came to wish he hadn't. Or at least they were chagrined that earlier Christians had made Jesus appear to say it. I am suggesting that originally the scene showed the disciples themselves bringing Jesus' words back to haunt him. His words are returning to him worse than void. (Paul also raises the theoretical possibility of apostles being "false witnesses" in 1 Cor. 15:15. In the case of the Pillars, he seems to have deemed it no mere theoretical possibility!)

To these accusations Jesus replies, "Ask those who have heard me, what I said to them. They know what I said" (John 18:21). Presumably they are present to be asked, but not the way the scene reads now. It may once have read differently. Similarly, when Jesus is asked the inquisitor's question, "Are you the Christ, the son of the Blessed One?" and he answers, "You say that I am," is it possible he is answering *Peter*, who indeed *did* say so, back at Caesarea Philippi? That might make more sense than the mess exegesis usually makes of Jesus' answer.

When we read in Mark 14:64 that "they all condemned him as deserving death," I take it to mean all the disciples, and for the reason Girard gives: The murder must be agreed to by all. As Benjamin Franklin said, "Gentlemen, if we do not hang together, we shall all most assuredly hang separately." Mark, a later reteller of the tale, tries to get the disciples offstage before the Sanhedrin scene can begin. He softens "They all condemned him as deserving death" to "They all forsook him and fled" (Mark 14:50), but "they" were simply actors running for their dressing rooms to change for the next scene. And of course he has attributed the condemnation to the disciples' "monstrous doubles," the Sanhedrin. It is the disciples who condemned, and who mocked and beat Jesus (Mark 14:65). The irony is all the more poignant if it is his erstwhile disciples who mock his prophetic abilities and who "received him" (cf. John 1:12)—with their fists.

Was there a second trial, before Pilate? Probably not. As many have noted, the trial as depicted in the gospels is pretty much a doublet of the Sanhedrin trial, and the beating by the guards is the same. So it all reduces to the kangaroo court of the disciples. As outrageous as a neo-Girardian account may seem, remember that the Pilate passages seem to many scholars to invite radical surgery just as urgently as the Sanhedrin texts. If it is hard to imagine the Sanhedrin holding a trial on the eve of Passover, is it any more likely for Pontius Pilate to lift a finger to try to save Jesus, much less to let Barabbas, a known insurrectionist, go free?

It is common to suggest that the blame for Jesus' death has been passed from the Romans, whom Christians thought it best not to offend, to the Jews. But scholars are finding it increasingly difficult to produce a plausible reason that either Jewish or Roman authorities should have wanted Jesus dead. Perhaps that is because *neither of them did*. The Romans may as easily have been the secondary scapegoat used by early Christians to shift the blame from themselves. And that should come as no surprise, the scapegoat game being what it is. Girard remarks that "there is reason to believe that the wars described as 'foreign wars' in the mythic narratives were in fact formerly civil strifes. There are many tales that tell of two warring cities or nations, in principle independent of one another—Thebes and Argos, Rome and Alba, Hellas and Troy—whose conflicts bring to the surface so many elements pertaining directly to the sacrificial crisis and to its violent resolution that it is hard not to view these stories as mythic elaborations of this same crisis, presented in terms of a 'fictive' foreign threat."[76] I suspect that the presence of Roman authority in the Passion is a mythic cover-up of precisely this kind.

BETTER HIM THAN ME

The Barabbas incident, however, demands separate treatment. It does not stand or fall with Pilate's involvement. Hyam Maccoby's reconstruction of the scene, however, does involve Pilate. Maccoby ventures that an earlier version of the story depicted not a weak and vacillating Pilate, trying to pass the buck, but rather a cruel Roman such as we know Pilate to have been. He did not offer a choice to the crowd but only rejected their pleadings—for the release of Jesus! This was in the days before Christians chose Jews to take the blame for Jesus' death. Once Jews were retroactively drafted as Christ-killers, however, the story could not be left showing Jews in a sympathetic light. The solution, Maccoby hypothesizes, was to bifurcate the Jesus character into Jesus the Nazarene and Jesus Barabbas, and to have the Jews ask for the release of the wrong one. The original identity of the two Jesuses is broadly hinted, again, in the coincidence of the two names. In some Old Latin manuscripts, translated from earlier Greek originals than we possess, Barabbas appears in Matt. 27:16, 18 as "Jesus Barabbas," and so the New English Bible renders it. And of course, "Bar-Abbas" looks suspiciously like "Son of the Father."

But there are other possibilities which present themselves once we dissolve the historical character of Barabbas. We would have to ask, on Maccoby's reading, why the "wrong" Jesus is still "Jesus the Son of the Father." This is still too close. Is it possible to take the text as an early piece of docetism? Could it have meant that the *right* Jesus *escaped* crucifixion? The result is not too far from the Christian traditions reported by Ibn Ishaq. But then why would the "wrong" Jesus still be called "the Christ?" Note that Pilate refers to him in Matt. 27:17, 22 as "Jesus who is *called* Christ," a term that admits of some ambiguity, reminiscent of Josephus' reference to "Jesus the *so-called* Christ"; or of Luke 3:23, "the son, *as was supposed*, of Joseph"; or Rom. 8:3, "sending his own son in *the likeness of* sinful flesh." Perhaps this means the same thing the Koran says: "They did not kill him and they did not crucify him but a semblance was made to them" (4:157).

Docetic interpretations of this sort are by no means incompatible with the Girardian perspective. The extant version of the myth of Zeus and the Curetes seems to have undone the death of the god featured in the hypothesized earlier version. Compared with a version of the Akedah Isaac hypothesized by several scholars,[77] in which Isaac actually died and was raised, the present canonical version of Gen. 22 would also qualify as a docetic rewrite in order to protect the sensibilities of later readers.

But there are a couple of other elements in the Barabbas story suggesting a different neo-Girardian version. One is the clear depiction of a crowd howling for the blood of Jesus. Where such a scene meets us, a scapegoat reading cannot be far behind. Maccoby rightly says that later Christians could not brook a scene where Jews clamored for the release of Jesus. My own suggestion that the story depicted Jesus' own disciples calling for his death (whether from Pilate or not) seems equally hard to accept, though for different reasons—except that this has been the traditional reading until recently! Most readers have always understood the ugly crowd at the Praetorium to be the same crowd who had hailed Jesus at his entrance to the city only days before. And this was, as the gospels clearly state, a group of disciples and admirers of Jesus. "Ecumenically correct" exegesis has recently wanted to see the crowd as an unruly bunch of local pool-hall rowdies and hooligans ("base fellows," Judg. 19:22) in an attempt to distance this crowd from Jews or Jerusalemites in general, so as to shield the latter from Matthew's chilling imprecation in 27:25. (Whether this maneuver is motivated by interfaith sensitivity or by face-saving apologetics, I will leave the reader to decide.) Girard himself identifies the Praetorium crowd with that in the Triumphal Entry, but he does not make the final step: It was Jesus' own disciples who put him to death.

The element that Jesus had been "delivered up out of envy" (Mark 15:10) also has Girardian resonances of mimetic desire. Suppose we try one of Girard's reversals and posit that in the earlier version the choice being made here was not which will *live*, but rather which will *die*. And was the choice originally between only two candidates? Not necessarily. The two Jesuses, remember, are mimetic twins, mythic ciphers for a condition where, things having degenerated to a spiral of reciprocal violence, everyone is everyone else's twin. The victim might as well be anyone, chosen from the whole group.

> Everything suggests a crowd whose intentions were initially pacific [as on Palm Sunday-RMP]; a disorganized mob that for unknown reasons (of no real importance to our argument) came to a high pitch of mass hysteria. The crowd finally hurled itself on one individual; even though he had no particular qualifications for this role [i.e., was no more guilty than anyone else], he served to polarize all the fears, anxieties, and hostilities of the

crowd. His violent death provided the necessary outlet for the mass anguish, and restored peace.[78]

KING FOR A DAY

It is in the scene of the mock coronation and veneration of Jesus, and his shameful display before the crowd, that scholars have seen the clearest evidence of Jesus' death as a ritual scapegoat. In the Roman Saturnalia as in the Babylonian Sacaea (and many other such rites all over the world, as Frazer and Girard describe) someone, often a condemned criminal, is chosen to be wined and dined, waited on and honored, as King of the Wood, King of Fools, and so on. After this, he is summarily executed. Girard rejects Frazer's theory that such "corn kings" were meant to mime the passing of the seasons. This imagery did admittedly enter the picture later, as a secondary association, but, Girard says, the origin of the ceremony must have been the act of generative violence, the collective murder of the scapegoat. This is the only way to explain the unique ambivalence of these rites. Why is the mock king venerated as sacred and yet reviled as a criminal and unclean? Girard explains: "the king is both very 'bad' and extremely 'good'; the *historical* alternation of violence and peace is transferred from time to space."[79] That is, the ritual mock king stands for the ancient scapegoat who was regarded simply as a villain at first, and shown no honors, and subsequently venerated posthumously. And just as the slain scapegoat is retrospectively understood as a martyred savior, the later mock king ritual cannot help but view the whole story of the scapegoat retrospectively. Thus they already treat the scapegoat-surrogate with a measure of reverence "up front," before they kill him. Kill him they must, but this time they know who it is they are about to kill.

Now how are we to relate the mock king rites to the mockery of the thorn-crowned Jesus? There are a few options, each with different implications. If we remained blissfully ignorant of the various history-of-religions parallels, we might be satisfied to take the gospels at face value: Jesus has absurdly claimed to be king, and the rowdy guards mean to show him his folly. But the close resemblance of the gospel Passion to the parallels makes this too simple. Are they just coincidence? The mockery of a poor man with delusions of royalty is not unattested. In fact, some source or earlier version of Luke seems to be quoting verbatim from Diodorus Siculus (34:2, 5–8), who has a character mock a slave with royal pretensions: "Remember me when you come into your kingdom." But there is no elaborate mock king charade here.

Not even Philo's account of the mock king Carabbas helps here:

> There was a certain madman named Carabbas . . . , the sport of idle children and wanton youths; and they [the Alexandrian mob], driving the poor wretch as far as the public gymnasium, and setting him up there on high that he might be seen by everybody, flattened out a leaf of papyrus and put it on his head instead of a diadem, and clothed the rest of his body with a common door mat instead of a cloak and instead of a scepter they put in his hand a small stick of . . . papyrus . . . and when he had been . . . adorned like a king, the young men bearing sticks on their shoulders stood on each side of him instead of spear bearers . . . , and then others came up, some as if to salute him, and others as though they wished to plead their causes before him. . . . Then from the multitude . . . there arose a . . . shout of men calling out *"Maris!"* And this is the name by which it is said that they call the kings among the Syrians; for they knew that Agrippa was by birth a Syrian, and also that he was possessed of a great district of Syria of which he was the sovereign. (*Against Flaccus* VI, 36–39)

Insofar as this rowdy display seems to be a spontaneous prank, like that of Jesus' Roman mockers on the traditional reading, it happens not to be directed at any royal claims of poor Carabbas himself, for he made none, but at the actual kingship, just created by Caligula, of Herod Agrippa I. The crowd staged this embarrassment for the benefit of Agrippa who was on his way through Alexandria at the time. And, of course, Carabbas was not killed. Had Jesus' mockery been parallel to that of Carabbas, we should expect the Roman legionaries to have displayed him brazenly before Herod Antipas, whom Luke does place in Jerusalem at the time, to mock *him*. But nothing is said of this.

If one seizes on the eerie similarity of the name Carabbas to that of Barabbas, as some have understandably done, then the only conclusion is that they represent two local variants of the title always given to a mock king in one of those rituals, and that brings us to the next option.

Paul Wendland and Sir James Frazer speculated that the gospel account is substantially accurate, and (implicitly) that Jesus was simply the poor joker pressed into service to play the mock king in a barracks Saturnalia party or to impersonate Hamaan in a hypothetical Purim adaptation of the Babylonian Sacaea festival.[80] Though Christian apologists have bristled over this identification, it is at first hard to see why. One would think the whole argument a member of the same species as that which tries to vindicate Matthew's accuracy by demonstrating that the Bethlehem star was really a supernova or a planetary alignment. The theory would seem only to add historical plausibility to the gospel accounts by providing both historical parallels and a sensible motivation for the soldiers' action. In fact, for some reason not explained very well, Girard himself disdained Frazer's view at least partly because it implied the Passion accounts were firsthand testimony![81] What is so disturbing here?

I suspect the problem is that in this case apologists could no longer argue, as Nils Dahl did,[82] that Jesus must have claimed (at least implicitly) to be the Messiah or he never would have been executed as "king of the Jews." But on the Frazer/Wendland theory, Jesus' death as a mock king would imply nothing at all about any messianic claims of Jesus. The royalty business would simply be a function of the cruel ritual in which he had been forced to participate. Why would this make any difference to Girard either way? Because if Jesus had merely been forced to play a role in a traditional ritual, this would seem to compromise the picture of his death as that of a scapegoat. Girard agrees that Jesus was put to death as a scapegoat; he claims, however, that the gospels do not accept the scapegoat mechanism but rather expose it. The problem is that the mock king ritual is too far removed from the original scapegoating act it commemorates. Its mock king is merely playing the dramatic role of the scapegoat of the past. His own death is not that of an actual scapegoat. Rather, it is the "managed violence" or "sacred," "good violence" of the sacrificial system founded on the originary violence of long ago. And Girard wants Jesus himself to have died as a scapegoat, not just playing one.

Girard's view, as well as his disdain for Frazer's theory, would not exclude the possibility that Jesus actually did die at a time of sacrificial crisis, but that the gospel accounts stem from a subsequent Christian ritual transformation, a Christian mock king ritual. But even on Girard's reading there would appear to be no reason to think Christians ever practiced repeated rites of human sacrifice—other than symbolically in the eucharist, which involves no mock king element. Even the later liturgical Passion plays provide no help, since they are simply dramatizations of the supposed events of the Passion, including the mockery as king of the Jews; that is, they already presuppose the transformation of Jesus' scapegoat death into its disguised form. They do nothing to effect that transformation.

Is there another option? Some of Frazer's contemporary critics reacted to his speculations a bit too vehemently, apparently confusing his ideas with those of the Christ-Myth school. To this Frazer responded thusly: "The doubts which have been cast on the historical reality of Jesus are in my judgment unworthy of serious attention."[83] But it might not be so outrageous to link Girard's theory to the Christ-Myth theory. Girard is happy to cite and to interpret the most ancient and fantastic myths (and the tragedies based on them) as dim reflections of actual scapegoat incidents. He does not for a minute suppose that there was a historical Pentheus, Balder, Oedipus, Romulus, Dionysus, or Zeus lying behind the myths, only that these myths (and dramas) stem ultimately from real events about which we can no longer know anything specific. I am trying to treat the gospels as Girard treats these other sources, especially the dramas. These attempted to rehistoricize their mythic sources in order to provide verisimilitude by showing the *kind* of thing that *might* have happened, drawing on the customs of their own day. Just as Girard imagines that Sophocles may have adapted elements of Athenian *pharmakos* rites to flesh out his Oedipus cycle, the evangelists may be imagined to have borrowed details of current Saturnalia rites to embellish a myth of Jesus the scapegoat savior, since the rite would be known to their readers and was at least the same *kind* of thing. Thus it would have lent a measure of verisimilitude to the dramatized myth.

I should imagine that for the purposes of Girard's methodology, it hardly matters whether there had been a historical Jesus any more than there had been a historical Oedipus. I am not even sure that Girard's actual views of the gospels as a revelation of the scapegoat mechanism (not, as I argue, an example of it) would require a historical Jesus, even though Girard everywhere speaks of Jesus himself as the revealer. I suppose a fictional expose of the scapegoating mechanism would be as genuine a revelation as a historically based one. He says "the revelation of the founding victim was first achieved *in this text*."[84]

BAPTIZED IN THE RIVER LETHE

Girard talks quite a bit about the willful forgetting on which sacrificial religion is built, the suppression of the originary violence done to the scapegoat. He claims that the gospels have at last revealed the ruse, that "to this day . . . that same veil remains unlifted, because only through Christ is it taken away" (2 Cor. 3:14). And yet it seems to me that Girard himself is guilty of trying to draw the veil back over the corpse of the scapegoat, after having stripped it off for a moment, in that he will not see how the gospels embody the scapegoating mechanism instead of exposing and exploding it. Indeed, the religion of the cross and the brutalized victim would seem to be the ultimate epitome and triumph of what one liberal Protestant called "the butcher shop religion of the fundamentalists." And to pervert the scapegoat theory into an apologetic for the very thing it tries to expose is a tragic irony indeed. One might compare Girard with a man who found himself dizzy, teetering on the edge of the yawning abyss he has uncovered, and then carefully backing away. He claimed to have found the abyss and could even point out the location, but as he had been careful to draw the lid back over it, he had made it once again impossible to see—until one fell into it unsuspectingly, as people had for many centuries.

NOTES

1. Burton L. Mack, "The Innocent Transgressor: Jesus in Early Christian Myth and History," *Semeia* 33 (1974), p. 137.
2. Eric Hoffer, *The True Believer: Thoughts on the Nature of Mass Movements* (New York: Harper & Row, 1951), pp. 12–13.
3. Elisabeth Schüssler Fiorenza, *In Memory of Her: A Feminist Theological Reconstruction of Christian Origins* (New York: Crossroad, 1984), p. 41.
4. René Girard, *The Scapegoat* (Baltimore: Johns Hopkins University Press, 1986), p. 50.
5. Ibid., p. 162.
6. René Girard, *Violence and the Sacred* (Baltimore: Johns Hopkins, 1977), p. 245.
7. Girard, *Scapegoat*, p. 73
8. Girard, *Violence and the Sacred*, p. 310.
9. Ibid., p. 252.
10. Tzvetan Todorov, *The Poetics of Prose* (Ithaca: Cornell University Press, 1977), p. 132.
11. Hyam Maccoby, *The Sacred Executioner: Human Sacrifice and the Legacy of Guilt* (New York: Thames and Hudson, 1982), pp. 50, 97.
12. Gilbert Murray, *Five Stages of Greek Religion* (Garden City: Doubleday Anchor, 1951), p. vi.
13. Girard, *Violence and the Sacred*, p. 309.
14. Raymund Schwager, *Must There be Scapegoats? Violence and Redemption in the Bible*, trans. Maria L. Assad (San Francisco: Harper & Row, 1987); James G. Williams, *The Bible, Violence, and the Sacred: Liberation from the Myth of Sanctioned Violence* (Valley Forge, Penn.: Trinity Press International, 1995); Robert G. Hamerton-Kelly, *Sacred Violence: Paul's Hermeneutic of the Cross* (Minneapolis: Fortress Press, 1992); Hamerton-Kelly, *The Gospel and the Sacred, Poetics of Violence in Mark* (Philadelphia: Fortress Press, 1994); Gil Bailie, *Violence Unveiled, Humanity at the Crossroads* (New York: Crossroad, 1995).
15. Mack, "The Innocent Transgressor"; Lucien Scubla, "The Christianity of René Girard and the Nature of Religion," in *Violence and Truth: On the Work of René Girard*, ed. Paul Dumouchel (New York: Athlone Press, 1988), pp. 160–78.
16. Stanley Fish, *Is There a Text in This Class? The Authority of Interpretive Communities* (Cambridge: Harvard University Press, 1980), p. 272.
17. David R. Griffin, *A Process Christology* (Lanham, Md.: University Press of America, 1990); John B. Cobb Jr., *Christ in a Pluralistic Age* (Philadelphia: Westminster Press, 1975).
18. Herman Kahn and Anthony J. Wiener, *The Year 2000—A Framework for Speculation on the Next Thirty-three Years* (New York: Macmillan, 1967); cited in Peter L. Berger, *A Rumor of Angels: Modern Society and the Rediscovery of the Supernatural* (Garden City: Doubleday Anchor, 1970), p. 1.
19. Hans Küng, *On Being a Christian* (Garden City: Doubleday, 1976), pp. 344, 372–73; Wolfhart Pannenberg, *Jesus-God and Man*, 2d ed. (Philadelphia: Westminster Press, 1977), pp. 135–36.

20. Girard, *Violence and the Sacred*, pp. 276–78, 302.
21. Girard, *Scapegoat*, p. 79.
22. Ibid., p. 103.
23. Hamerton-Kelly, *The Gospel and the Sacred*, p. 101.
24. Girard, *Scapegoat*, p. 69.
25. Hamerton-Kelly, *Gospel and the Sacred*, p. 68.
26. Hyam Maccoby, *Judas Iscariot and the Myth of Jewish Evil* (New York: Free Press, 1992), p. 98.
27. Maccoby, *Sacred Executioner*, pp. 49–51, 100–101.
28. Mack, "Innocent Transgressor," pp. 154–57.
29. Gerd Theissen, *Sociology of Early Palestinian Christianity* (Philadelphia: Fortress Press, 1978); Gerd Theissen, *Social Reality and the Early Christians: Theology, Ethics, and the World of the New Testament* (Philadelphia: Fortress Press, 1992); F. Gerald Downing, *Christ and the Cynics: Jesus and Other Radical Preachers in First-Century Tradition*. JSOT Manuals 4 (Sheffield: JSOT Press, 1988); Downing, *Cynics and Christian Origins* (Edinburgh: T. & T. Clark, 1992); John Dominic Crossan, *The Historical Jesus, The Life of a Mediterranean Jewish Peasant* (New York: HarperCollins, 1991).
30. Girard, *Violence and the Sacred*, p. 271.
31. Stevan L. Davies, *The Revolt of the Widows, The Social World of the Apocryphal Acts* (Carbondale: Southern Illinois University Press, 1980), p. 36.
32. Scott D. Hill, "The Local Hero in Palestine in Comparative Perspective," in *Elijah and Elisha in Socioliterary Perspective*, ed. Robert B. Coote (Atlanta: Scholars Press, 1992), pp. 37–74.
33. Girard, *Violence and the Sacred*, p. 262.
34. Ibid., p. 254.
35. Erving Goffman, *Stigma: Notes on the Management of Spoiled Identity* (Englewood Cliffs: Prentice-Hall, Inc., 1963).
36. Girard, *Violence and the Sacred*, p. 43.
37. Ibid., p. 39.
38. Bruce Chilton, *The Temple of Jesus, His Sacrificial Program Within a Cultural History of Sacrifice* (State College: Penn State Press, 1992). For Chilton's analysis of Girard in particular, see Chilton, "René Girard, James Williams, and the Genesis of Violence," *Bulletin for Biblical Research* 3 (1993), pp. 17–29.
39. Girard, *Violence and the Sacred*, p. 39.
40. Richard A. Horsley, *Jesus and the Spiral of Violence: Popular Jewish Resistance in Roman Palestine* (Philadelphia: Fortress Press, 1993), pp. 3–15.
41. Girard, *Violence and the Sacred*, p. 56.
42. Hamerton-Kelly, *Gospel and the Sacred*, p. 83.
43. Girard, *Scapegoat*, p. 79.
44. Girard, *Violence and the Sacred*, p. 77.
45. Maccoby, *Sacred Executioner*, pp. 126–30.
46. Ibid., p. 128.
47. Girard, *Violence and the Sacred*, p. 251.
48. Bertil Gärtner, *Iscariot* (Philadelphia: Fortress, 1971); Maccoby, *Judas*, p. 135.
49. Frank Kermode, *The Genesis of Secrecy, On the Interpretation of Narrative* (Cambridge: Harvard University Press, 1979), p. 95; Maccoby, *Judas*, p. 106.

50. Maccoby, *Judas*, p. 107.

51. Neal Robinson, *Christ in Islam and Christianity* (Albany: State University of New York Press, 1991), p. 131.

52. Girard, *Violence and the Sacred*, p. 78.

53. Ibid., p. 165.

54. Maccoby, *Judas*, p. 91.

55. Ibid., pp. 134–35.

56. Peter van Greenaway, *The Judas Gospel* (New York: Dell Books, 1972).

57. Girard, *Violence and the Sacred*, p. 179.

58. Ibid., p. 146.

59. René Girard, *Things Hidden Since the Foundation of the World* (Stanford: Stanford University Press, 1987), p. 26.

60. Theodore J. Weeden, *Mark: Traditions in Conflict* (Philadelphia: Fortress Press, 1971).

61. Girard, *Scapegoat*, p. 68.

62. Girard, *Violence and the Sacred*, p. 248.

63. Ibid., pp. 150–54.

64. Ibid., p. 100.

65. Maccoby, *Judas*, p. 94.

66. Maccoby, *Sacred Executioner*, p. 125.

67. Girard, *Violence and the Sacred*, p. 314.

68. Ibid., p. 102.

69. Robinson, *Christ in Islam*, p. 127.

70. Girard, *Violence and the Sacred*, p. 79.

71. Ibid., p. 203.

72. Ibid., p. 212.

73. Girard, *Scapegoat*, chap. 12.

74. Eric Auerbach, *Mimesis: The Representation of Reality in Western Literature* (Garden City: Doubleday Anchor, 1957), pp. 35–43.

75. C. S. Griffin, *Judas Iscariot, the Author of the Fourth Gospel* (1892), cited in Maccoby, *Judas*, p. 138; also Kermode, *Genesis of Secrecy*, pp. 91–92.

76. Girard, *Violence and the Sacred*, p. 249.

77. Bin Gorion, *Sinai und Garazim* (1926), cited in Maccoby, *Sacred Executioner*, pp. 74–86; Shalom Spiegel, *The Last Trial, On the Legends and Lore of the Command to Abraham to Offer Isaac as a Sacrifice: The Akedah* (Woodstock, Vt.: Jewish Lights, 1993), p. 57.

78. Girard, *Violence and the Sacred*, p. 131.

79. Ibid., p. 268.

80. R. Angus Downie, *Frazer and the Golden Bough* (London: Victor Gollancz Limited, 1970), pp. 52–53.

81. Girard, *Things Hidden*, p. 169.

82. Nils Alstrup Dahl, *The Crucified Messiah and Other Essays* (Minneapolis: Augsburg Press, 1974), p. 25–26.

83. R. Angus Downie, *Frazer and the Golden Bough* (London: Victor Gollancz, 1970), p. 54.

84. Girard, *Things Hidden*, p. 443, emphasis mine.

Chapter 7

THE CRUCI-FICTION?

In chapter 1, I showed how, thanks to Koester, Robinson, and Talbert, the gospels' similarity to and probable dependence upon the aretalogy genre are being more and more recognized. But something seldom noticed is the striking fact that the gospels also match certain features often found in a related genre, that of the ancient romance novels. This should not surprise us, since these genres (like all genres) are not airtight. The ancient romances and the aretalogies tend to shade over into one another. For example, *The Alexander Romance* and Philostratus' *Life of Apollonius of Tyana* have equal elements of both types. In the present chapter, the similarity of the gospels to the ancient novels will take on striking relevance, for their plot devices mirror at crucial points some of the gospel episodes considered by almost all scholars of whatever theological stripe to be bedrock history. And you know what that means.

Three major plot devices recur like clockwork in the ancient novels, which were usually about the adventures of star-crossed lovers, somewhat like modern soap operas. First, the heroine, a princess, collapses into a coma and is taken for dead. Prematurely buried, she awakens later in the darkness of the tomb. Ironically, she is discovered in the nick of time by grave robbers who have broken into the opulent mausoleum, looking for rich funerary tokens (as in King Tut's treasure-lined tomb). The crooks save her life but also kidnap her, since they can't afford to leave a witness behind. When her fiancé or husband comes to the tomb to mourn, he is stunned to find the tomb empty and first guesses that his beloved has been taken up to heaven because the gods envied her beauty. In one tale, the man sees the shroud left behind, just as in John 20:6–7.

The second stock plot device is that the hero, finally realizing what has happened, goes in search of the heroine and eventually runs afoul of a governor or king who wants her and, to get him out of the way, has the hero crucified. Of course, the hero always manages to get a last-minute pardon, even once affixed to the cross, or he survives crucifixion by some stroke of luck. Sometimes the heroine, too, appears to have been killed but winds up alive after all.

Third, we eventually have a joyous reunion of the two lovers, each of whom has despaired of ever seeing the other again. They at first cannot believe they are not seeing a ghost come to comfort them. Finally, disbelieving for joy, they are convinced that their loved one has survived in the flesh. Anyone who professes not to see major similarities between these novels, long ignored by scholars because of their supposed frivolity, and the gospels either has never read the gospels or does not want to admit the disturbing parallels.

ESCAPING CROSSES, EMPTYING TOMBS

In Chariton's *Chaereas and Callirhoe*, Chaereas is falsely incited to rage against his wife Callirhoe and delivers a kick which seems to kill her. She is entombed alive. Soon pirates (who are virtually ubiquitous in these novels) appear, intent on robbing the tomb. They discover Callirhoe alive, now having revived in the cool of the mausoleum, and they kidnap her to sell her as a slave. In her captivity, Callirhoe pities her doubly vexed husband in terms strikingly reminiscent of the New Testament empty tomb accounts: "You are mourning for me and repenting and sitting by an empty tomb. . . ."[1] But the resemblance to the gospel accounts only grows stronger a little later when in fact poor Chaereas discovers the tomb to be empty.

> When he reached the tomb, he found that the stones had been moved and the entrance was open. [Cf. John 20:1] He was astonished at the sight and overcome by fearful perplexity at what had happened. [Cf. Mark 16:5] Rumor—a swift messenger—told the Syracusans this amazing news. They all quickly crowded round the tomb, but no one dared go inside until Hermocrates gave an order to do so. [Cf. John 20:4–6] The man who went in reported the whole situation accurately. [Cf. John 19:35; 21:24] It seemed incredible that even the corpse was not lying there. Then Chaereas himself determined to go in, in his desire to see Callirhoe again even dead; but though he hunted through the tomb, he could find nothing. Many people could not believe it and went in after him. They were all seized by help-

lessness. One of those standing there said, "The funeral offerings have been carried off [Cartlidge's translation reads: "The shroud has been stripped off"—cf. John 20:6-7]—it is tomb robbers who have done that; but what about the corpse—where is it?" Many different suggestions circulated in the crowd. Chaereas looked towards the heavens, stretched up his arms, and cried: "Which of the gods is it, then, who has become my rival in love and carried off Callirhoe and is now keeping her with him . . . ?"[2]

The parallels to the empty-tomb accounts, especially to John 20:1–10, are abundant and close. Chaereas even suggests that Callirhoe has been (like Jesus) translated to heaven. An almost identical scene is found in Photius' summary of Iamblichus' *Babylonian Story* (all we have left of this romance):

> The grave of the young woman is left empty, and there are left behind several robes that were to be burned on the grave, and food and drink. Rhodanes and his companion feast on the food and drink, take some of the clothing, and lie down to sleep in the young woman's grave. As daylight comes, those who set fire to the robber's house realize that they have been tricked and follow the footprints of Rhodanes and Sinonis, supposing that they are henchmen of the robber. They follow the footprints right up to the grave and look in at the motionless, sleeping, wine-sodden bodies lying in the grave. They suppose that they are looking at corpses and leave, puzzled that the tracks led there. [Cf. Luke 24:12][3]

Back to *Chaereas and Callirhoe*: Later on, Callirhoe, reflecting on her vicissitudes, says, "I have died and come to life again."[4] Later still, she laments, "I have died and been buried; I have been stolen from my tomb." Note the parallel to 1 Cor. 15:3-4, "that Christ died . . . , that he was buried, that he was raised. . . ." Scholars debate whether the "buried" reference in 1 Corinthians means to imply a tomb emptied by the Resurrection. I would venture that the parallel with *Chaereas and Callirhoe* does suggest such an implication, since in the latter, disappearing from the tomb is equal to rising from the dead. Again, towards the end of the novel Callirhoe recounts, not simply her regaining of consciousness, but "how she had come back to life in the tomb."[5]

In Miletus, Callirhoe comes to believe that Chaereas perished while searching for her. To console her and to lay her fond memory of his rival to rest, Dionysius, her new husband, erects a tomb for Chaereas. It lacks his body, but this is not, as all think, because the corpse is irrecoverable, but rather in fact because he is still alive elsewhere. His tomb is empty because he is still alive. Why seek the living among the dead?

But elsewhere poor Chaereas is condemned to the cross!

> Without even seeing them or hearing their defense the master at once ordered the crucifixion of the sixteen men in the hut. They were brought

out chained together at foot and neck, each carrying his cross. . . . Now Chaereas said nothing when he was led off with the others, but [his friend] Polycharmus, as he carried his cross, said: "Callirhoe, it is because of you that we are suffering like this! You are the cause of all our troubles!"[6]

At the last minute Chaereas' sentence is commuted.

Mithridates sent everybody off to reach Chaereas before he died. They found the rest nailed up on their crosses; Chaereas was just ascending his. So the executioner checked his gesture, and Chaereas climbed down from his cross. . . .[7]

As he later recalls, "Mithridates at once ordered that I be taken down from the cross—I was practically finished by then." Here, then, is a hero who went to the cross for his beloved and returned alive. In the same story, a villain is likewise crucified, though since he is gaining his just deserts, he is not reprieved. This is Theron, the pirate who carried poor Callirhoe into slavery. "He was crucified in front of Callirhoe's tomb."[8] We find another instance of a crucifixion adjacent to the tomb of the righteous in *The Alexander Romance*, when Alexander arrests the assassins of his worthy foe Darius. He commanded them "to be crucified at Darius's grave."[9] We cannot help being reminded of the location of Jesus' burial "in the place where he was crucified" (John 19:41).

We meet with the familiar pattern again in the *Ephesian Tale* of Xenophon. The beautiful Anthia seems to have died from a dose of poison but has in fact merely been placed in a deathlike coma. She awakens from it in the tomb.

> Meanwhile some pirates had found that a girl had been given a sumptuous burial and that a great store of women's finery was buried with her, and a great horde of gold and silver. After nightfall they came to the tomb, burst open the doors, came in and took away the finery, and saw that Anthia was still alive. They thought that this too would turn out very profitable for them, raised her up, and wanted to take her.[10]

Later on, her beloved Habrocomes goes in search of her and winds up being condemned to death through a series of misadventures too long to recount here. "They set up the cross and attached him to it, tying his hands and feet tight with ropes; that is the way the Egyptians crucify. Then they went away and left him hanging there, thinking that the victim was securely in place." But Habrocomes prays that he may yet be spared such an undeserved death. He is heard for his loud cries and tears. "A sudden gust of wind arose and struck the cross, sweeping away the subsoil on the cliff where it had been fixed. Habrocomes fell into the torrent and was swept away; the water did him no harm; his fetters did not get in his way. . . ."[11]

At length Habrocomes returns to a temple where, in happier days, he and

Anthia had erected images of themselves as an offering to Aphrodite. Still deprived of Anthia and thinking her to be dead, he sits there and weeps. He is discovered by old friends Leucon and Rhode.

> They did not recognize him [Cf. Luke 24:16; John 20:14], but wondered who would stay beside someone else's offerings. And so Leucon spoke to him. "Why are you sitting weeping, young man . . . ?" [Cf. John 20:13–14; Luke 24:38] Habrocomes replied, "I am . . . the unfortunate Habrocomes!" When Leucon and Rhode heard this they were immediately dumfounded, but gradually recovered and recognized him by his appearance and voice, from what he said, and from his mention of Anthia.[12]

Here I see a striking resemblance to the New Testament empty tomb accounts, where Jesus or an angel accosts a weeping mourner, and a dramatic recognition results; cf. John 20:11–16, where we also have the question "Why are you weeping?" the initial failure of recognition, and the recognition being sparked by the mention of a woman's name. Luke 24:13 is only slightly less close.

In Achilles Tatius' *Leucippe and Clitophon*, the heroine twice appears to be disemboweled in climactic scenes worthy of a Saturday afternoon movie serial. But both times it was sleight-of-hand or mistaken identity. On the former occasion Leucippe had to lie in a coffin until her faked sacrifice. She is warned by her confederate to "stay inside the coffin as long as it was daylight and not try to come out even if she woke up early."[13] And of course she does eventually emerge alive from the coffin, giving us another resurrection scene. Referring later to this scene in a letter to Clitophon, she recalls "For your sake I have been a sacrificial victim, an expiatory offering, and twice have died."[14] Another character marvels over Leucippe's many adventures, including "those sham deaths": "Hasn't she died many times before? Hasn't she often been resurrected?"[15]

Eventually Leucippe must prove her virginity by means of an old local ritual, described thusly:

> If she has lied about her virginity, the syrinx is silent, and instead of music, a scream is heard from the cave. At once the populace quits that place, leaving the woman in the cave. On the third day a virgin priestess of the place enters and finds the syrinx lying on the ground, with no trace of the woman.[16]

On the third day a woman comes to cave in which someone was *entombed* but now *finds no trace of a body*!

In Longus' *Daphnis and Chloe* we find only traces of the pattern, but they are worth noting. "He ran down to the plain, threw his arms around Chloe, and fell down in a faint. When he was, with difficulty, brought back to life by Chloe's kisses and the warmth of her embraces. . . ."[17] Later in the tale we hear that in the bleak midwinter Daphnis, deprived of the sight of his beloved Chloe, "waited for spring as if it were a rebirth from death."[18] Later, when some vandalism mars the garden tended by the happy pastoral folk of the story, there is fear of harsh reprisal: " 'There's an old man [the master will] string up on one of the pines, like Marsyas; and perhaps he'll . . . string up Daphnis, too!' . . . Chloe mourned . . . at the thought that Daphnis would be strung up. . . . When night was already falling, Eudromus brought them the news that the old master would arrive in three days' time . . ."[19] but all ends well.

The pattern comes into sharper focus again in Heliodorus' *Ethiopian Story*, where Knemon hides Charikleia, lover of Theagenes, in a cave for safekeeping.

> "Put her in, my friend, close the entrance with the stone in the normal way, and then come back. . . ." This stone dropped effortlessly into place and could be opened just as easily. . . . Not a sound passed Charikleia's lips; this new misfortune was like a deathblow to her, separation from Theagenes tantamount to the loss of her own life. Leaving her numbed and silent, Knemon climbed out of the cave, and as he replaced the threshold stone, he shed a tear in sorrow for himself at the necessity that constrained him, and for her at the fate that afflicted her; he had virtually entombed her alive. . . .[20]

There are two more cases of apparent death and resurrection in *The Story of Apollonius, King of Tyre*. The king's wife seems to expire during childbirth while on a sea voyage, though the text baldly says, "she suddenly died."[21] They secure her body in a carefully sealed coffin and commit her to the sea. *"Three days later waves cast up the coffin."*[22] A medical student examines the body and is able to tell from subtle indications that she still lives. He manages to revive her, though it will be years before her loved ones learn she is not dead after all.

The baby daughter grows up and is committed to the care of foster parents by the grief-stricken Apollonius. Out of envy for her royal possessions, her foster mother conspires to have young Tarsia assassinated. The hired killer cannot bring himself to commit the crime, but instead sells her into a brothel as a slave. Meanwhile, the wicked foster mother, thinking Tarsia dead, trumps up a false story of how she died and builds an "empty tomb"[23] to honor her memory. Tarsia contrives to maintain her virginity even in the midst of a brothel and is eventually hired to visit a despairing old man (Apollonius, of course) to cheer him up. This she tries to do with nothing more salacious than moral exhortations, bidding him to "come out of the darkness and into the light."[24] When the two recognize one another, he says, "my hope has been brought back to life."[25] The townspeople, learning of Tarsia's identity, avenge the outrage perpetrated upon royalty, killing the pimp whose slave Tarsia was. Apollonius responds, "Thanks to you, death and grief have been shown to be false."[26] Once he has also been reunited with his wife, who has in the meantime become a priestess of Diana, Apollonius prays to Diana, thanking her that "you restored me to life."[27]

Iamblichus, in his *Babylonian Story*, features not only an empty tomb story, as we saw above, but yet another apparent death. The maid Sinonis is missing. Her father discovers a half-devoured female corpse and hastens to the conclusion that it is that of his lost daughter. He hangs himself on the spot, but not before inscribing in blood, "Lovely Sinonis lies buried here." Arriving on the scene not long afterwards, Sinonis' lover Rhodanes despairs and is about to stab himself, but another woman appears and shouts, "It is not Sinonis lying these, Rhodanes."[28]

A friend of the two lovers, Soraechus, "is condemned to be crucified," but while "being led away to be crucified," Soraechus is rescued by a band of soldiers who drive away his guards. But in the meantime, Rhodanes, too,

> was being led to and hoisted onto the cross that had been designated for him by a dancing and garlanded Garmus, who was drunk and dancing round the cross with the flute players and reveling with abandon. While this is happening, Sacas informs Garmus by letter that Sinonis is marrying the youthful king of Syria. Rhodanes rejoices high up on the cross, but Garmus makes to kill himself. He checks himself, however, and brings down Rhodanes from the cross against the latter's will (for he prefers to die [seeing that his beloved is to marry another])[29]

Apuleius' *The Golden Ass* contains two scenes which bear an uncanny resemblance to the gospels' scenes at the empty tomb of Jesus, though neither is exactly analogous to them. First is a scene of forbidden necromancy. Those assembled seek to interrogate the shade of a murdered man in order to discover the identity of his slayer.

> "Behold here is one Zatchlas, an Egyptian, who is the most principal prophesier in all this country, and who was hired of me long since to bring back the soul of this man from hell for a short season, and to revive his body from the threshold of death for the trial hereof," and therewithal he brought forth a certain young man clothed in linen raiment. . . .[30]

The dead man is briefly reanimated and supplies the desired information. I have thus far omitted the occasional scenes of actual raising of corpses for purposes of necromancy. We find it occasionally in the novels, but I include this one because of the association with a resurrection of a young man in white as in Mark 16:5.

Second, in the romance of *Cupid and Psyche*, interpolated into the larger unit of *The Golden Ass*, we find a scene in which Psyche's sisters seek her out, fearing her dead.

> After a long search made, the sisters of Psyche came unto the hill where she had been set on the rock, and cried with a loud voice and beat their breasts,

in such sort that the rocks and stones answered again their frequent howlings: and when they called their sister by her name, so that their lamentable cries came down the mountain unto her ears, she came forth, very anxious and now almost out of her mind, and said: "Behold, here is she for whom you weep; I pray you torment yourself no more, and dry those tears with which you have so long wetted your cheeks, for now may you embrace her for whom you mourned."[31]

A typical sham death and resurrection due to poisoning meets us later in the novel. An evil stepmother has sought from a doctor poison with which she intends to dispatch her stepson, who has rebuffed her illicit advances. But the doctor, suspecting some chicanery, sells her only a potent knockout formula. So in the midst of the inquest, he leads everyone to the coffin where a surprise awaits them (though by now *we* know full well what to expect).

Every man had a desire to go to the sepulchre where the child was laid: there was none of the justices, none of any reputation of the town, nor any indeed of the common people, but went to see this strange sight. Amongst them all the father of the child removed with his own hands the cover of the coffin, and found his son rising up after his dead and soporiferous sleep: and when he beheld him as one risen from the dead he embraced him in his arms; and he could speak never a word for his present gladness, but presented him before the people [cf. Luke 7:15] with great joy and consolation, and as he was wrapped and bound in the clothes of the grave [cf. John 11:44], so he brought him before the judges.[32]

The stepmother is exiled, her henchman "hanged on a gallows," or literally, crucified. Again we have the immediate association of crucifixion with an empty tomb.

Petronius's *Satyricon* repeats a widely disseminated tale which juxtaposes the same two features again, and in a striking fashion. A woman of Ephesus is so devoted to her late husband that she resolves to enter the tomb with him, there to starve herself to death and so join him in the great beyond. A servant keeps vigil with her. Meanwhile a company of thieves is crucified nearby.

Next night the soldier who was guarding the crosses to prevent anyone removing one of the corpses for burial noticed a light shining among the tombs and, hearing the sound of someone mourning, he was eager to know ... who it was and what was going on. Naturally *he went down into the vault and seeing* a beautiful woman, at first stood rooted to the spot *as though terrified* by some strange sight.[33]

The soldier brings some food and urges her to eat. He seeks to comfort her in her loss. The servant accepts the food and begins to join in the soldier's urgings. "What good is it . . . for you to drop dead of starvation, or *bury yourself alive . . . ? . . .* Won't you *come back to life?*" This counsel proves persuasive. In fact, not only does the widow refresh herself with the food, but she is so infused with the *joi de vivre* that she fornicates with the soldier right there in the tomb. "*The doors* of the vault *were* of course *closed*, so if a friend or a stranger came to the tomb, he thought that the blameless widow had expired over her husband's body."[34]

While all this is going on, the family of one of the crucified thieves, noticing that the crosses are unattended, "took down the hanging body in the dark and gave it the final rites." The soldier finds one cross empty and knows what must become of him for failing his post. [Cf. Matt. 28:11–14] He is about to kill himself when his new lover suggests he "take the body of her husband from the coffin and fix it to the empty cross." This is what he does.[35]

Here a dead man exits his tomb only to be crucified and thus save the life of the soldier and to bring a new lease on life to his no longer grieving widow! Here the elements of the story of the crucified and resurrected savior in the gospels are reshuffled but all present. There is even the element of a crucified dead man disappearing despite the posting of guards, somewhat recalling Matthew's empty tomb account!

Another Matthean peculiarity finds its parallel in an account in book 4 of Philostratus' *The Life of Apollonius of Tyana*. In chapter 16, the divine sage makes a pilgrimage to the tomb of Achilles. He calls out, like Jesus to Lazarus,

> "O Achilles, . . . most of mankind declare you are dead, but I cannot agree with them . . . show . . . yourself to my eyes, if you should be able to use them to attest your existence." Thereupon a slight earthquake shook the neighborhood of the barrow [cf. Matt. 28:1–2], and a youth issued forth five cubits high, wearing a cloak of Thessalian fashion . . . but he grew bigger, till he was twice as large and even more than that; at any rate he appeared . . . to be twelve cubits high just at that moment when he reached his complete stature, and his beauty grew apace with his length. [Cf. the gigantic risen Jesus in the Gospel of Peter] (Book IV, XVI, Loeb)

THE STUMBLING BLOCK OF THE CROSS?

As Charles H. Talbert has shown, the canonical gospels, even in their present form, would not have been hard for an ancient reader to recognize as official (and fictive) hero biographies compiled by a philosophical movement to glorify their founder.[36] It seems to me that Mack, Koester, and Robinson would all shy away from such a conclusion, given the prominence of the Passion story in the canonical gospels. The notion of an atoning death does not seem to fit the picture of the philosophical aretalogy. But it is hardly clear, at least in Mark and Luke, that the idea of an atonement has much to do with it. It may be Helmut Koester's Lutheran background that tempts him to read a theology of the cross into Mark, when only two brief texts could even possibly be read that way (Mark 10:45 and 14:24), and Luke chops even these (compare his versions, Luke 22:27 and 22:18)!

As Mack notes (in company with John Dominic Crossan and others), the story of Jesus' arrest, humiliation, and crucifixion seems to be derived from a whole different cluster of ideas than that of an atonement theology. Rather, the story is probably intended as a typical story of the wise man who endures all the depredations of the wicked, to whose sin he is a living rebuke. Such a righteous one is always either saved in the nick of time or glorified after death.[37] It is easy to see Jesus' crucifixion account in these terms. And this is the sort of thing we would expect to find in a community like the Q partisans, as Mack understands them. The Q community could easily have produced such a hero biography, such a novelistic aretalogy, issuing in the persecution and deliverance of their hero, the wise man/sophist Jesus, without actually knowing *what* had happened to the historical Jesus, a question the Q sayings, after all, leave wide open.

But didn't the story of the persecuted wise one usually end with the *rescue* of the hero (Joseph, Daniel, Aniqar, and so forth)? Yes, though Mack and Crossan apparently feel that a *posthumous* reward would not violate the logic of the story. It would be a natural variation on the theme. But would it? The notion of the wise man having the last laugh at the expense of his enemies boils down to the fundamental idea that "wisdom is the best policy," that "nice guys finish first." Wisdom is implicitly enlightened self-interest, the Socratic dictum that if people knew better, they would always do the virtuous thing—because they would see that it is always in their own best interests. Not, "Do the right, and let the chips fall where they may," but rather, "Here's how to succeed." The Book of Proverbs wasn't asking anybody to be a martyr. No, the idea was, if you were wise you would ultimately escape the fowler's snare of the wicked.

But maybe the aretalogy of Jesus *did* fit the pattern anyway. Remember, the literary devices of the ancient novel included people surviving crucifixions and people getting entombed alive! What if an earlier version of the Passion narrative pursued the logic of the tale of the wise sufferer to the letter—and had Jesus survive crucifixion, appearing *still* alive, not alive *again*? Even in the canonical gospels there are striking hints of a barely erased precanonical version that must have read precisely this way. Muslim interpreters of the gospels have seen some of these hints, but it is only with the advent of modern narrative criticism that the clues have become visible to any of the rest of us.

For instance, why does Mark 14:35–36 show Jesus asking his father to allow him to escape death on the cross in Gethsemane? This is an exceedingly odd, even an offensive, thing to write if the goal of this narrative is to have

Jesus die after all. But I suspect the writer is planting a seed that will blossom rather differently later in the story. Likewise, for Mark 15:34 to have Jesus repeating Psalm 22, a prayer anticipating final deliverance even at the last moment (Ps. 22:22–24), creates all manner of problems unless this prayer, too, is to be answered by story's end. Did Jesus think his God had forsaken him? No, of course not. As Heb. 5:7 says, his loud cries and tears were *heard*, his prayer for deliverance from death *answered*. The irony of the bystanders' taunt, "Let the Christ, the King of Israel, come down now from the cross, that we may see and believe" (Mark 15:32), lies in the fact that this is precisely what is about to happen, though they will not recognize it. And, otherwise, what is the point of the strange detail of Pilate marveling that Jesus was dead after a mere six hours (Mark 15:44), when it ought to take days for the cross to kill? As Chekov said, if a writer says somebody drove a nail into the wall, he'd better make sure to hang something from it later in the story! And, obviously, the payoff would have been that Jesus had fallen into a coma, which ironically, providentially, resulted in his being removed from the cross in time for him to survive.

And why does Matthew have Joseph of Arimathea bury Jesus in Joseph's own tomb (Matt. 27:57–60)? And why does Matthew add the note that Joseph was rich (27:57)? Why, simply to provide narrative motivation for tomb robbers to come and open the tomb, as in the ancient romances, and find Jesus alive! The fainting of Matthew's guards (27:4) probably reflects the terror of the superstitious tomb robbers, finding a living man but no treasure. And then, in Luke 24:36–43, when Jesus appears to his bereaved disciples who assume he is dead and cannot believe their eyes, what does he say to reassure them? Like Apollonius of Tyana says in a similar scene, after a miraculous escape from the treacherous designs of Domitian, he bids his friends to behold his living physical body, to convince themselves that he has not risen from the realm of the dead, he is no ghost, but rather, as his solid corporeality attests, he is still alive.

> Damis' grief had just broken out afresh, and he had made some such exclamation as the following: "Shall we ever behold, O ye gods, our noble and good companion?" When Apollonius, who had heard him—or as a matter of fact he was already present in the chamber . . . —answered: "Ye shall see him, nay, ye have already seen him." "Alive?" said Demetrius, "for if you are dead, we have anyhow never ceased to lament you." Whereupon Apollonius stretched out his hand and said: "Take hold of me, and if I evade you, then I am indeed a ghost come to you from the realm of Persephone, such as the gods of the under-world reveal to those who are dejected with much mourning. But if I resist your touch, then you shall persuade Damis also that I am both alive and that I have not abandoned my body." They were no longer able to disbelieve, but rose up and threw themselves on his neck and kissed him, and asked him about his defense. (*Life of Apollonius*, VIII, XII)

John knew that people understood the story of Jesus' passion, this way, which is why he adds two items unprecedented in any other gospel: the nailing of Jesus to the cross (often people were simply tied to the cross), not narrated but assumed in John 20:25, and the spear-thrust in John 19:34. He protests too much (John 19:35), in the style of the writers of apocrypha (cf. 2 Pet. 1:16–18), that he was there and saw the blood flow. In his version, Jesus shows not his solid hands and feet (as in Luke 24:39), but rather his *wounded* hands and *side* (John 20:20). John doesn't want anyone thinking Jesus survived the cross and went to preach among the Greeks (John 7:35).

But the original tellers of the aretalogical tale had no concern for an atoning death. And Q, remember, does not even say that Jesus died! In the conspicuous absence of any statement that he died, one can well imagine that the Q-sophists or the communities that revered them would make Jesus shrewdly avoid death. Once a belief in the martyr death of Jesus entered the picture from another quarter of the patchwork quilt of Jesus movements, the aretalogy was reedited to make Jesus good and dead. The Passion predictions in Mark (8:31; 9:12, 31; 10:33–34) are obviously artificial "prolepses" (flash-forwards)[38] ruining the narrative tension of the original, pre-Markan version, which craftily dropped hints of what would happen to Jesus and kept the reader guessing. The result, in the gospels as we now read them, is a wooden "plot of predestination,"[39] whereby narrative suspense is exorcised and each successive episode is a redundant rehearsal of the one before, as all alike seek to drive home a single monotonous point to the reader viewed as a catechumen. "Did you get it last time? Just in case, here it is again: Jesus died in Jerusalem; everything was leading up to that, nothing else matters much." The so-called Narrative Critics, New Testament scholars like Jack Dean Kingsbury, Werner Kelber, and Mark Allan Powell,[40] for all their self-professed expertise in narratology, fail to perceive that the narrative of the gospels works best only when one uncovers its original, theologically obscured outlines. But it is no surprise, because in the hands of these churchmen-scholars, the "literary" study of the gospels has served from the first as a diversionary route of escape from engagement with the troubling questions of genuine historical criticism.

NOTES

1. Chariton, *Chaereas and Callirhoe*, trans. B. P. Reardon, in *Collected Ancient Greek Novels*, ed. B. P. Reardon (Berkeley: University of California Press, 1989), p. 37.

2. Ibid., p. 53; as far as I know, the first one to recognize the relevance of this ancient text as a parallel to the gospel resurrection accounts was Johannes Leipoldt in 1948. An English translation of his seminal article appeared nearly fifty years later: Johannes Leipoldt, "The Resurrection Stories," *Journal of Higher Criticism* 4, no. 1 (spring 1997): 138–49, trans. Darrell J. Doughty.

3. Iamblichus, *Babylonian Story*, trans. Gerald N. Sandy, in *Collected Ancient Greek Novels*, p. 787.
4. Chariton, *Chaereas and Callirhoe*, p. 62.
5. Ibid., p. 111.
6. Ibid., p. 67.
7. Ibid., p. 69.
8. Ibid., p. 57.
9. *The Alexander Romance*, trans. Ken Dowden, in *Collected Ancient Greek Novels*, p. 703.
10. Xenophon, *Ephesian Tale*, trans. Graham Anderson, in *Collected Ancient Greek Novels*, pp. 151–52.
11. Ibid., p. 155.
12. Ibid., p. 67.
13. Achilles Tatius, *Leucippe and Clitophon*, trans. John J. Winkler, in *Collected Ancient Greek Novels*, p. 220.
14. Ibid., p. 242.
15. Ibid., p. 262.
16. Ibid., p. 273.
17. Longus, *Daphnis and Chloe*, trans. Christopher Gill, in *Collected Ancient Greek Novels*, p. 315.
18. Ibid., p. 319.
19. Ibid., p. 336.
20. Heliodorus, *Ethiopian Story*, trans. J. R. Morgan, in *Collected Ancient Greek Novels*, p. 375.
21. *The Story of Apollonius, King of Tyre*, trans. Gerald N. Sandy, in *Collected Ancient Greek Novels*, p. 752.
22. Ibid., p. 753.
23. Ibid., p. 758.
24. Ibid., p. 763.
25. Ibid., p. 767.
26. Ibid., p. 769.
27. Ibid., p. 770.
28. Ibid., p. 791.
29. Ibid., p. 793.
30. Lucius Apuleius, *The Golden Ass*, trans. William Adlington, rev. Harry C. Schnur (New York: Collier Books, 1962), p. 62.
31. Ibid., p. 118.
32. Ibid., p. 241.
33. Petronius, *The Satyricon*, and Seneca, *The Apocolocyntosis*, trans. J. P. Sullivan (Baltimore: Penguin Books, 1977), p. 120.
34. Ibid., p. 121.
35. Ibid., pp. 120–22.
36. Charles H. Talbert, *What Is a Gospel? The Genre of Canonical Gospels* (Philadelphia: Fortress Press, 1977).
37. George W. E. Nickelsburg, "The Genre and Function of the Markan Passion Narrative," *Harvard Theological Review* 73 (1980): 153–84.

38. Gerard Genette, *Narrative Discourse: An Essay in Method*, trans. Jane E. Lewin (Ithaca: Cornell University Press, 1983), p. 40.

39. Tzvetan Todorov, *The Poetics of Prose*, trans. Richard Howard (Ithaca: Cornell University Press, 1977), pp. 53–65, 120–42.

40. Mark Allan Powell, *What Is Narrative Criticism?* Fortress Guides to Biblical Scholarship, New Testament Series (Minneapolis: Fortress Press, 1990).

Chapter 8

THE HISTORICIZED JESUS?

CHRIST EVOLVING

The mainstream of critical New Testament scholarship today embraces a theory of the evolution of Christology that strikingly parallels the ancient christological doctrine of Adoptionism. Ancient Adoptionists, including the Jewish-Christian Ebionites, believed that Jesus was a natural man, completely human and mortal, not an incarnate god or demigod. As recognition and reward of a life of righteousness and a ministry of costly faithfulness culminating in martyrdom, Jesus was exalted to the rank of Messiah and royal son of God, a kind of honorary divinity like that predicated of the ancient kings of Judah who also were called Messiah and son of God (Ps. 2:2, 7). Few Christian scholars would embrace this notion as their own personal creed; they do not believe this is what actually happened to Jesus. But most would say that the development of Christian thought about Jesus was in a sense "adoptionistic" in that the whole process began with a historical prophet named Jesus who did not claim godhood in the manner of some demagogues ancient and modern, but was nonetheless later magnified by his admirers to such a degree that shortly he was believed to have been an incarnation of the very Godhead.[1] Into this theological mix there entered all manner of Hellenistic mythemes as well as philosophical concepts (such as the Philonic doctrine of the Logos).

Such an opinion about the history of belief in Jesus was once itself a controversial and heretical view, since the sheer recognition of a development in Christology was seen to undermine that Christology. As Nietzsche and Foucault have shown, the delineation of a history, a "genealogy" of thought, is itself a deconstruction of that thought, since it shows any belief to be the product of a process of human fashioning, not a full-blown fact of nature (or of revelation). But scholars, to their great credit, found that their zeal for understanding the text and the history of Christianity was greater than any loyalty to an ecclesiastical party line.[2] They stuck to their guns, and the view I have just outlined has become something like critical orthodoxy. One may suspect that another reason for the eventual triumph of the "adoptionistic," evolutionary theory of christological origins was that it was at least not as disturbing as an even more radical view, the pure Christ-Myth theory: that there had never been a historical Jesus at the root of the full-blown mythical Christology. According to the Christ-Myth theorists, Jesus had first been regarded in the manner of an ancient Olympian god; he had supposedly once visited the earth and died and been raised from the dead, like Hercules and Asclepios. The imagined incarnation, death, and resurrection would have occurred in the hazy zone of mythic time, as Paul Veyne describes it in *Did the Greeks Believe in their Myths?*[3] not in the historical time of chronologies and dates. Hercules was not popularly imagined to have existed in the same sort of past as Pericles. Neither, at first, was Jesus. It was only subsequently, says the Christ-Myth theory, that the incarnation, death, and resurrection of Jesus was rendered historical, datable, a piece of recent worldly history. Christianity, then, would have begun with a "high" Christology, but with no historical grounding (hence one might call it "docetic"), whereas the "adoptionistic" theory of mainstream scholars holds that Christians first held a "low" Christology, placing Jesus on our level, not God's, only later yielding to a process of mythification of the historical man Jesus of Nazareth. The choice is between a historical Jesus mythicized and a mythic Jesus historicized. Are there grounds for preferring one to the other? I would like to explore that question in the present chapter. First, I will consider the possibility that there was a historical Jesus who was rapidly glorified to mythic heights. I will appeal to historical analogies usually overlooked, arguing that the whole notion is by no means implausible, though whether the gospel data are best interpreted this way is a separate question.

LUBAVITCHERS AND NAZOREANS

I believe we can postulate a scenario of development from a mortal, a Jewish rabbi, to the status of a god underlying the Gospel of John. It will be helpful to compare the stages and factions involved in the hypothesized process with analogous factors in the recent case of Rabbi Menachem Mendel Schneerson and the Lubavitcher movement in Hasidic Judaism. First, let us presuppose a historical Jesus pictured as a rabbi with halachic opinions sufficiently distinctive to have made him the center of a formal or informal school after his death. We would then be able to place the traditions culminating in the Gospel of John among the Jesus partisans in what Burton Mack calls the Synagogue Reform Movement. Like Rabbi Schneerson, it would have been Jesus' charisma of holiness and piety, as well as his persuasive wisdom and legal rulings that led his disciples to identify him with the coming Messiah. Perhaps like Lubavitcher sectarians, they did not believe their master had already risen from the dead, but expected that he soon would, at the general resurrection of the just, when he would inherit his due messianic dignity. From this initial period of Johannine faith (as I will call the religion of the movement that ultimately produced the Gospel of John) we have the echo that some were willing to admit that Jesus was "a teacher sent from God, for no one can do the signs that you do unless God is with him" (John 3:2). These "signs," or signifying miracles, might have functioned as what Gerd Theissen calls "rule miracles." This means Jesus might have been believed to have settled matters of scribal debate by resort to miracles (as in Mark 2:8–12). God must be on his side. As Jacob Neusner has shown, the later mainstream of rabbis shied away from the notion that points of Torah or doctrine might be settled by signs and portents.[4] Consider the following Mishnaic anecdote, set amid the halachic debates among the rabbis at Yavneh after the fall of Jerusalem. Rabbi Eliezer is firm in his insistence on his opinion in the face of a united front of his fellow scribes, whose consensus, as in Islam, must decide the question.

> On that day, Rabbi Eliezer replied with every legal argument in the world, but the rabbis would not accept them. Thereupon, he said to them, "If the halachah is on my side, let that carob tree show it." The carob suddenly uprooted itself and flew through the air one hundred cubits. They said to him, "No bringing of proof from a carob tree!" He said to them, "If the halachah is on my side, then may that stream of water show it!" The stream of water turned around and flowed backward. They said to him, "No bringing of proof from streams of water!" He turned and said to them, "If the halachah is on my side, may the walls of the house of study we are in show it!" The walls of the house of study leaned inward as if about to fall. Rabbi Jehoshua rebuked the walls, saying to them, "If the sages battle each other over halachah, why do you interfere?" They did not fall out of honor for Rabbi Jehoshua, nor did they straighten up out of honor for Rabbi Eliezer; they continue crookedly standing to this day. Again Eliezer said to them, "If the halachah is on my side, let Heaven show it!" A voice from Heaven cried out, "What do the rest of you have against Rabbi Eliezer? The halachah is on his side in everything!" Rabbi Yehoshua leaped to his feet and quoted [Deut. 30:12], "It is not in heaven.'" What did Yehoshua mean by saying, "It is not in heaven'?" Rabbi Yeremiah explained, "Since the Torah

> has already been given from Mount Sinai, we do not pay heed any longer to a heavenly voice. You yourself, O Lord, wrote in the Torah given at Mount Sinai, 'Turn aside after the multitude.' " Later Rabbi Nathan happened to see the Prophet Elijah. He asked him, "What did the Holy One, Blessed be he, do when we did not pay heed to any of Rabbi Eliezer's miraculous proofs, or the heavenly voice?" Elijah replied, "What did he do! God said, 'My sons have defeated me! My sons have defeated me!' " (*Baba Mezia* 59b)[5]

Does this cast doubt on the likelihood that Christian Jews could have made any headway by making such appeals, to Jesus' rule miracles? No; it is entirely possible that Christian claims helped turn the rabbis in the direction they took. Note that Eliezer does what Jesus tells the disciples they can do in Luke 17:6, "If you had faith as a grain of mustard seed, you would say to this mulberry tree, 'Be uprooted and planted in the sea!' and it would obey you." Eliezer also duplicated the feat promised by the messiah Theudas, that, like Joshua, he would make the Jordan turn round so his followers might cross dryshod (Josephus, *Antiquities of the Jews* XX, V, 1). Similarly, Eliezer performed a version of the miracle promised by the Egyptian messiah mentioned by Luke (Acts 21:38) and Josephus (*Antiquities* XX, IX, 6), who told his followers he would, again like Joshua, cause the walls of Jerusalem to fall down like those of Jericho.

From some of the healing stories in the Gospel of John (5:8–10; 9:13–14 ff) we might deduce that, as in the Synoptics, Jesus' rulings on what types of action were permissible on the Sabbath were rather liberal and offended some. It is interesting that, though legal appeal to miracles carried no weight in emerging rabbinism, a more liberal, Hillelite view of many issues, such as Jesus is shown advocating in the gospels, became the mainstream. And this is something worth remembering in what follows.

At this early stage, the Johannine Christians would have had a strong sense of group identity, and that would have included their heritage as Jews, as members of the synagogue. Their reformist activities, pursuing their halachic agenda, signify both a strong subgroup identity and a strong sense of belonging to the larger synagogue identity. Rather than splitting off, which would mean a higher valuation of subgroup identity, they sought to influence a larger group for which they still felt proprietary responsibility. And yet, to use Mary Douglas's terms, the Johannine group would also have been considered "low grid," i.e., governed by a fairly loose set of codes, rules, taboos.[6] The walls between them and other groups were not very high or thick. Movement between the Johannine Jewish Christians and outsiders was still readily possible. They did not regard those without loyalty to Jesus as unbelievers or "the unsaved." Nor would they have been regarded as heretics or apostates by those not of their number. All would have seen themselves and their rivals as good Jews, even if out-of-step.

Not surprisingly, the same situation exists in the Lubavitcher movement. The demographics are different in one sense, since the believers in Rabbi Schneerson's messiahship form the majority of Lubavitch. But a diversity of belief does exist in this single movement of pious hasidim who credit one another as good Jews and can tolerate a difference of opinion on even so large a matter as the messianic claim. Despite outsiders' predictions that upon the Rebbe's death the movement would fragment, it has not happened, though trouble has begun to brew with increasing tensions, sometimes actual fistfights, between Schneerson messianists and other Lubavitchers. And there have already been minor offshoots. If history is repeating itself, the Lubavitcher movement would seem to be in the transitional state Christianity was in just before the split between Jews and Christians.

We find another relevant parallel in the situation of Rabbi Akiba, who endorsed Simon bar-Kochba as Messiah about a century after Jesus. Even though history judged him to have been in error, his reputation as one of the very greatest rabbis was not much tarnished. And while his hopes for messianic redemption were still alive, he presumably did not write off fellow Jews who had their doubts about Simon; rather he must have imagined they would be mildly chagrined and pleasantly surprised once Simon bar-Kochba had ushered in the Kingdom of God. And though the Johannine faction must have cherished their own Jesus-derived halachah, since their halachah were more liberal it is not they who would have felt themselves separated from other Jews. It is usually the stricter party that wants separation, and it is thus no surprise that the Johannine Christians might have eventually found themselves on the receiving end of excommunication.

But that seems not to be what happened. As I mentioned above, the positions ascribed to Jesus in the Gospel of John, centering on "healing by incantation" (as it is called in the Mishnah), appear to be in harmony with the positions taken in the Mishnah: Only the paid medical practice of professional physicians was forbidden on the Sabbath, and that only when life was not at stake. And the same is true on other halachic issues advocated by Jesus in the Synoptic gospels. Thus, Jesus' practice could not have been that controversial among the scribes as it seems in retrospect in the gospels, distorted by later Jewish vs. Christian rancor. Either that, or Jesus' liberality must have been part of a general liberal-leaning movement in scribalism which eventually prevailed, as Harvey Falk argues in *Jesus the Pharisee*.[7] Either way, it must not have been the legal interpretations of the Johannine group that finally got them excommunicated. What then was it?

The more similar two religious groups or subgroups are, the more accentuated their remaining differences become, even should those differences be fairly trivial. If the Christian claims for Jesus are the wedge of separation, we should expect that the claims for Jesus will become more and more controversial. Jesus will grow closer and closer to godhood. The more elevated his status, the greater the alienation between Jews and Christians, and in turn, the status of Jesus will climb yet higher. Accordingly, when the halachic issues are no longer paramount, the leftover issue is that of Jesus himself. What about that business about him as Messiah? Two new subgroups would have emerged at this point. The character Nicodemus represents those inclined to accept the halachic positions of the Johannine faction ("Rabbi, we know you are a teacher sent from God. No man can do the signs you do unless God is with him," John 3:2), but they are wary of messianic claims made on Jesus' behalf. The Nicodemus types would find their modern-day counterparts in one faction of Lubavitchers. Menachem Brodt, spokesman for the Lubavitcher organization Israel Habad, refers to the late Rabbi Schneerson as simply "the rebbe," not as the Messiah. He asked reporter Herb Keinon, "Why do you make the connection between the rebbe and the Moshiah? First and foremost he is the rebbe." Some are not so outspoken. Keinon says that the smallest of four factions in the movement is that which "believe[s] the rebbe was a great man, but no Messiah."[8]

Joseph of Arimathea ("being a disciple of Jesus, but in secret, for fear of the Jews," John 19:38), on the other hand, represents those in the synagogue who do accept Jesus as Messiah but fear to say so publicly as these claims become more controversial. These, too, have their counterpart in the Lubavitcher movement because of the similar group dynamics, but the shoe is on the other foot given the demographics, since most of the movement accepts the messiahship of Rabbi Schneerson, unlike the Johannine party which existed as a minority within synagogue Judaism. One prominent hasidic leader who would not allow reporter Keinon to use his name, bemoaned, "I sit at Habad gatherings, and hear people talk about the rebbe being the Moshiah, and just keep quiet. What am I going to do, argue with them? It is difficult to fight the flow." Keinon says this man believes that "many who say Schneerson will be resurrected and revealed as the Messiah do not really believe it. 'Many times people utter slogans, because they feel they must, or because of pressure from the community they are a part of, even though they don't really believe them.' "[9] John's Nicodemus-types felt the same pressure, only, given that they were in the minority in a group that did not affirm Jesus' messianic identity, it was their messianic faith, not the lack of it, that they felt pressure to keep secret.

The Gospel of John contains stories designed to encourage both subgroups to go all the way to public confession of Jesus as Messiah. In John chapter 3, Nicodemus no sooner makes his affirmation of faith in Jesus as a divinely commissioned teacher than the Johannine Jesus brings him up short, sweeping his confession aside contemptuously, demanding the rebirth of baptism ("Amen, amen, I say to you: unless a man be born from above he cannot see the Kingdom of God," 3:3). We think of John the Baptist's blistering rejoinder to those complacently religious who naively imagined themselves his supporters, yet remained on the sidelines, crisp and dry, smiling on the poor sinners who emerged dripping from the Jordan: "Do not begin saying to yourselves, 'We have Abraham as our father,' for I tell you, God can raise up children to Abraham from these stones" if that's all he wants (Matt. 3:9).

The man born blind and healed by Jesus at the Pool of Siloam in John chapter 9 is upheld as the example for the Joseph of Arimathea types. Despite threats of excommunication from the synagogue (9:22; cf. 16:2, "They will make you outcasts from the synagogue"), they are encouraged to take a stand. In the face of opposition, itself perhaps sparked by increasingly strong claims for Jesus, the Johannine group had strengthened their distinctive group identity, their allegiance to Jesus taking precedence over their loyalty to the synagogue (now that push had come to shove), and their grid factor had risen: Faith in Jesus as Messiah had become paramount. It is the shibboleth required of "believers," "the saved." "Unless you believe that I am he, you will die in your sins" (John 8:24). In the same way, in October 1997 one group of Lubavitcher rabbis issued a legal ruling requiring all Jews to accept Rabbi Schneerson as Messiah.[10] By contrast, David Berger, Orthodox rabbi and president of the Association for Jewish Studies, opined that "belief in the rebbe as Messiah is sufficient to exclude someone from Orthodox Judaism."[11]

It is only once the Johannine Christians had been excommunicated from the synagogue that they developed their doctrine of Jesus as the *true* vine of Israel (John 15:1 ff), the *true* Hanukkah light (8:12), the *true* door through which the flock enters the divine presence (10:7 ff., cf. Psalm 100), the wine that deepens the empty water jars of Jewish ritual (John 2:1–11), and so forth. Such metaphors denote the separation of devout Jews from the Jewish community. They exactly parallel the piety-in-exile of the Dead Sea Scrolls sect, priests who repudiated the Jerusalem temple because of what they perceived as the ritual laxness of the temple establishment. For these sectarian separatists the true sacrifices to God were prayer and piety offered from a sincere heart. Such sentiments, which rightly strike the modern reader as a spiritualizing advance over actual animal sacrifice, were nonetheless born as virtue of necessity. The Johannine "spiritualization" of Judaism originated in the same way: a sour grapes theology. Deprived of the rituals and sacraments of the Jewish community, they created spiritualized counterparts. Thus free of the theological restraint of Judaism, Christology could rise higher and higher, to measure the widening gap between the Johannine sect and Judaism, partly due to new, non-Jewish influences hitherto shunned.

As elsewhere in the New Testament, the decisive break between a Christian faction and its Jewish parent quickly led to a redirection of evangelistic outreach to groups traditionally outside Jewish religious boundaries. We observe the same process loud and clear with the Jewish-Christian Matthean community (compare Matt. 10:5–6 with Matt. 28:19–20 and Matt. 21:43) and in Acts 13:46 ("It was necessary that the word of God should be spoken to you first; since you repudiate it, and judge yourself unworthy of eternal life, behold, we are turning to the Gentiles"); 18:6 ("Your blood be on your own heads! I am clean. From now on I shall go to the Gentiles"); and 28:28 ("Let it be known to you therefore, that this salvation of God has been sent to the Gentiles, and they will listen"). Romans chapter 11 deals at length with the same issue. Even so, the Johannine sect turned to both Gentiles (John 10:16: "I have other sheep that are not of this fold; I must bring them also and they shall hear my voice; and they shall become one flock with one shepherd.") and Samaritans (John chapter 4, in which the mission to the Samaritans is read back into the time of Jesus, for purposes of dominical authorization). These groups were ritually unclean in the eyes of Jews, as the Gospel of John itself makes clear ("For Jews and Samaritans do not use the same dishes in common," John 4:9), and this onus of impurity would have passed to the Johannine sect which was now willing to deal with them. They were shunned all the more as a result. The famous Johannine texts about God's love for *the whole world* (e.g., John 3:16) would stem from this period, the point being the same as in Rom. 3:29: "Or is God the God of Jews only? Or is he not the God of the Gentiles too?"

My guess is that it was this contact with Gentiles and Samaritans that resulted in the assimilation of theological and mythological themes from these traditions, both as Johannine missionaries accommodated their message to the categories of their hearers and as Samaritan and pagan converts brought favorite beliefs and mythemes, even unwittingly, into their new religion. Thus in the Gospel of John Jesus repeats the water-to-wine miracle of Dionysus (2:1–11) and describes himself, like Dionysus, as the life-giving grapevine (15:1–10). (Of course the Synoptics bear many of the same traces of Dionysus influence: Jesus' blood is wine, his flesh bread, since he is a Dionysian corn king.) Thus also in John's Gospel Jesus is explicitly and overtly identified with the Samaritan Taheb, their counterpart to the Jewish, Davidic Messiah (John 4:25–26). It seems to me that John's debates between Jesus and those who falsely value their descent from Abraham reflect the struggles in Romans and Galatians over who is the true seed of Abraham: Jews or Christian Gentiles. Like Mark, John's Gospel also disparages the brothers of Jesus (7:5), probably because of their opposition to, or interference in, the Gentile mission (cf. Gal. 2:11–14 ff; Acts 11:1–3). Of course, this opposition from the Heirs of Jesus or Pillars of Jerusalem might have stemmed from their fear of the very syncretism that resulted in Johannine Christianity.

The same fears, and the same alarm at the reality once it appeared, must also have led to the falling away of a group from within the Johannine movement itself. Many found the assimilation, e.g., of the Mystery Religion sacrament of divine flesh and blood, outrageous to Jewish sensibilities, including theirs. And as we might expect, the more controversial this sacrament became among the Johannine sectarians themselves, the more exaggerated it became in importance, just as Jesus' own messianic role was the more magnified the more it became a bone of contention between Jews and Johannine Christians. The result is that the eucharist became needful for salvation. Speaking to Jews who are ostensibly his followers, Jesus requires the eucharist for salvation (John 6:53: "Amen, amen, I say to you, unless you eat the flesh of the Son of Man and drink his blood, you have no life in you"). This denotes a higher grid requirement within the Johannine community, and a further weeding-out process, as well as a fortress mentality. Significantly, while the theological grid had remained low, open to the invasion of foreign mythemes, the sacramental grid was raised. This makes sense, since the controversial sacrament was itself a major piece of such syncretic assimilation, and it is no surprise that such an innovation would be defended to the hilt in direct proportion to the controversy it generated. Such is human nature.

Those within the Johannine community who could not brook the new influences packed up and left (for Judaism? for another Johannine or other Christian faction?). They were bade good riddance by their erstwhile compatriots. The heavenly Father must never have truly drawn them to him anyway ("No one can come to me unless the Father draw him," John 6:44). They were never really members of Jesus' flock anyway, and were thus incapable of hearing his voice (John 10:26–27). These developments led to the next stage, where God was pictured no longer as loving the world but as sending his son to redeem his elect out of the world. The sectarian walls were rising.

As Jerome H. Neyrey argues in a fascinating yet sadly neglected monograph[12] from which the present analysis has drawn much inspiration, the Johannine elevation of Jesus to a status of "equal to God" (John 5:18) represents a full and intentional severance from Judaism. Christianity had by this token become a new and separate religion. We read in the Gospel of John Gnostic-like sneers at Jewish rituals, pedigrees, and scriptures ("your law," John 10:34).

To cross-reference the Lubavitchers once more, it is striking to read that Rabbi Shaul Shimon Deutsch, who broke with the Lubavitch sect to found his own Liozner Hasidic movement, felt the need to split with the parent body once he saw signs that some were deifying Rabbi Schneerson. "Lubavitch has gone off course. You have a situation where kids at one of the central schools, Ohalei Torah, are kissing the rebbe's picture. This is not Judaism, but the beginning of a new religion. At one point we had to stand up and say that something is terribly wrong."[13] He decided to pack up and leave his Habad neighborhood "when my daughter, who was six at the time, came home and asked me if the rebbe is God. I thought to myself this is going off course, and it is time to get out." In January 1998 David Berger, an Orthodox rabbi, charged that for the Lubavitch mainstream, "The Lubavitcher rebbe is becoming God." He pointed to Lubavitch writings calling Rabbi Schneerson the "Essence and Being of God enclothed in a body, omniscient and omnipotent." Another proclaimed of the rebbe that "his entire essence is divinity alone."[14] Sure enough, Berger then called for the excommunication of any Lubavitchers who espoused such views.

When the figurehead of a movement becomes God, it means he has become the object of faith of a whole new self-contained communal and symbolic world in which his adherents live. A savior Christology implied redemption of the world, what H. Richard Niebuhr called a "Christ transforming Culture" model,[15] but a creator-God Christology means the public world has been abandoned for a sheltered sectarian subworld ("If anyone is in Christ, there is a new creation; old things have passed away. Behold, new things have come," 2 Cor. 5:17). The community has retreated to radical isolation, loving neither the world nor the things in the world (1 John 2:15). Wayne Meeks made this point well in his monograph, "The Man from Heaven in Johannine Sectarianism."[16] The elevation of Jesus to the status of a God come down from heaven ("You are from below, I am from above; you are of this world; I am not of this world," John 8:23) denoted a community fundamentally alienated from the world they knew. Though Meeks does not appeal to the parallel, his sketch of the Johannine sect mentality rings all the more true for its similarity in this respect to today's flying saucer religions who avidly look for otherworldly deliverance at the Parousia of the Mother Ship, most notably the extinct Heaven's Gate sect.[17] The same sort of image, saviors from space, denotes the same social sectarian dynamic. J. L. Houlden shows how Johannine ethics (in 1 John) smacks of the worst kind of sectarian infighting, despite its (selective) talk of love.[18]

At this stage, rituals ironically became less important since, as Neyrey reasons, they hadn't guaranteed true faith (i.e., didn't prevent dropouts). Or, more generally, the rituals (like baptism, though probably not the Eucharist) were held in common by two groups who found occasion to differ over other matters. Thus rituals were taken for granted, stopped functioning as the shibboleth, and receded in importance. The new shibboleth was doctrinal. "Unless you believe that I Am . . ." (John 8:24). Accordingly, "spiritual" language predominates. This is probably why, in John chapter 6, after it has been made inescapably clear that one must partake of the sacramental flesh and blood of Jesus, we are suddenly taken aback to read, "It is the spirit that gives life; the flesh counts for nothing. The words which I have spoken to you are spirit and are life" (John 6:63). I take this comment to be an interpolation made at this stage, to devaluate the sacraments in favor of correct belief.

Coincident with this further spiritualization there emerged yet another new phase in the evolution of the Johannine movement and its Christology. Itinerant Johannine prophets (of whom we read in the Johannine Epistles: "Many false prophets have gone out into the world," 1 John 4:1), speaking, as they suppose, by the afflatus of the Paraclete (John 16:12–13), were receiving new Gnostic and docetic revelations, denying "that Jesus Christ has come in the flesh" (1 John 4:2). These new teachings tended toward the concomitant emphases on the only *apparent* reality of the fleshly form of Jesus and the need for ascetical mortification of the flesh by the Christian. In both cases "the flesh counts for nothing." As Stevan L. Davies[19] has seen, the apocryphal Acts of John enshrines the legendary aretalogies of these docetic, ascetic Johannine itinerants, and the mini-gospel contained in this document ("John's Preaching of the Gospel") is the most explicitly docetic account of the life and death of Jesus in all surviving Christian texts. In it we read that Jesus left no footprints in the sand, appeared differently to different people at the same moment, only pretended to eat, was alternately intangible or hard as steel, and appeared to John in a cave on the Mount of Olives during the crucifixion, denying his identity with the form on the cross!

JOHANNINE DOCETISM

We are close to such a phantom Jesus at numerous points in the Gospel of John. As soon as we are assured in the prologue that "the Word was made flesh" the assertion is qualified: He only "pitched his tent among us" (John 1:14), leaving the same impression as Charles Wesley's implicitly docetic Christmas carol "Hark, the Herald Angels Sing": "*Veiled* in flesh the Godhead see." In John chapter 4, we are told it is antidocetic for John to show Jesus tired, parched, and hungry (4:6–8), yet as soon as his disciples return with food and urge him to partake, he refuses: "I have food to eat that you know not of. . . . My food is to do the will of him who sent me, and to accomplish his work" (4:32, 34). Hold that burger! At the grave of Lazarus, Jesus appears to be moved by the human tragedy of death, weeping with fellow-feeling (11:35–36). But, no, he knows Lazarus will be back momentarily, so it is all a sham. The charade is only made more gross when Jesus prays before he works the miracle, noting aloud that the prayer itself is but a stage whisper, as someone has said, for the benefit of the crowd ("Father, I thank you that you heard me. And I knew that you hear me always, but I said it because of the people standing around, that they may believe that you sent me," 11:41–42). The Moonies call it "heavenly deception," but we could just as easily call it Docetism. Jesus' arrest in the Garden of Gethsemane is sheer farce, too. At a single word from Jesus, and that a double entendre discernible only by the

Christian reader, the arresting party falls flat like a bunch of bowling pins. They get up, brush themselves off, and proceed as if nothing has happened! The point is precisely the same as in Philostratus' *Life of Apollonius of Tyana*, in a scene in which Apollonius awaits his trial before Domitian, where his disciple expects he will be martyred. No, Apollonius reassures his disciple Damis,

". . . no one is going to kill us." "And who," said Damis, "is so invulnerable as that? But will you ever be liberated?" "So far as it rests with the verdict of the court," said Apollonius, "I shall be set at liberty this day, but so far as depends on my own will, now and here." And with these words he took his leg out of the fetters and remarked to Damis: "Here is proof positive to you of my freedom, so cheer up." Damis says that it was then for the first time that he really and truly understood the nature of Apollonius, to wit, that it was divine and superhuman, for without any sacrifice,—and how in prison could he have offered any?—and without a single prayer, without even a word, he quietly laughed at the fetters, and then inserted his leg in them afresh, and behaved like a prisoner once more." (IV:44, Loeb)

Docetism, no? On the cross Jesus cries out to be relieved of thirst—not because he is actually thirsty, but simply to fulfill scripture (19:28). Raised from the dead, Jesus invites Thomas to probe his wounds, surely a piece of antidocetic polemic—but then Thomas doesn't! Merely seeing the Risen Lord overwhelms him. Jesus tells the adoring Magdalene. "Touch me not, for I have not yet ascended to the Father. But go to my brethren and say to them, 'I am ascending to my Father and your Father, to my God and your God'" (John 20:17). Randel Helms[20] suggests that the scene is based on a similar leave-taking in the Book of Tobit, where the angel Raphael is poised to return to God in heaven and explains, "Even though you watched me eat and drink, I did not really do so; what you were seeing was a vision. So now get up off the ground and praise God. Behold, I am about to ascend to him who sent me" (Tob. 12:19–20). In the Bible, angels, being pure spirits, cannot eat (cf. Judges 13:15–20). If the author of the corresponding passage in John did indeed have this passage in mind, as seems likely, then Jesus' command, "Touch me not," is probably meant to denote his intangibility. Again, Docetism.

There are passages in the Gospel of John that "realize" eschatology, that is, that teach that no literal, physical resurrection or final judgment is to be expected, contrary to popular opinion. "Amen, amen, I say to you, he who hears my word and believes him who sent me, has eternal life, and does not come into judgment, but has passed out of death into life. Amen, amen, I say to you, an hour is coming and now is when the dead shall hear the voice of the Son of God; and those who hear shall live" (John 5:24–25) "Jesus said to her, 'Your brother shall rise again.' Martha said to him, 'I know that he will rise again in the resurrection on the last day.' Jesus said to her, 'I am the resurrection and the life; he who believes in me shall live even though he die, and he who lives and believes in me shall never die' " (11:23–26). "Judas, not Iscariot, said to him, 'Lord, what has happened that you will reveal yourself to us, and not to the world?' Jesus answered and said to him, 'If anyone loves me he will keep my word; and my Father will love him, and we will come to him and make our abode with him' " (14:22–23). This deliteralization, or spiritualization, of the traditional future expectation is one of the major characteristics of Gnosticism. These Johannine texts must stem from the schismatic Gnosticizing Johannine faction. Bultmann is no doubt correct in seeing passages like John 5:28: "Do not marvel at this, for an hour is coming in which all who are in the tombs shall hear his voice and shall come forth, those who did the good to a resurrection of life, those who committed the evil to a resurrection of judgment," as later corrections by the more conservative faction.

Returning to our primary concern, the evolving Christology of the Johannine movement, we may observe how the more conservative faction for whom the exaltation of Jesus to the Godhead was a dangerous abomination left their polemical traces in the Gospel of John, too. These are texts which still give Chalcedonian theologians headaches today. The first is John 12:44, "He who believes in me believes not in me but in him who sent me." The point seems to be to reopen a space between Jesus and God, collapsed by the Jesus-deifying faction. The second is John 14:28, "You heard that I said to you, 'I go away, and I will come to you.' If you loved me, you would have rejoiced, because I go to the Father, for the Father is greater than I." The third is a correction added to John 14:7–10: " 'If you had known me, you would have known my Father; from now on you know him and have seen him.' Philip said to him, 'Lord, show us the Father, and it is enough for us.' Jesus said to him, 'Have I been with you so long, Philip, and still you do not know me? He who has seen me has seen the Father' " (verses 7–9). Up to this point, the text delivers the most powerful christological statement in the New Testament, the absolute identification of the Father with the Son (later stigmatized as a heresy called Patripassianism, implying that the Father suffered on the cross). This was the affirmation of the Johannine Christians who made Jesus "equal to God," and meant it. But the more christologically modest faction emended their copy of the gospel with this equivocating addition, "Do you not believe that I am in the Father and the Father is in me?" (verse 10). Readers wishing to glorify Jesus today still read verse 10 as something of a come-down, a disappointment after the much stronger statement of verses 7–9.

I suggest that each faction along this path of historical evolution and mitosis of the Johannine community had its own copy of the Gospel of John. As each new stage emerged, additions were made by each faction to update the text and accommodate it to the current orthodoxy. When, as presumably happened, a copy containing the distinctive themes of one faction came into the hands of a rival faction (for instance, when a scribe switched sides, taking his copy with him), it would receive theological corrections in the margins, which would then be inserted right into the text during the next copying. Finally, once all these debates were dead and forgotten, an eclectic text was produced, harmonizing all the texts the scribes could find. The same thing happened with 1 John which, as a result, juxtaposes Gnostic perfectionism (3:5–10; 5:18) and Catholic antiperfectionism (1:7–10; 5:16–17) side by side.

But Johannine Christology had not done evolving, as we can see when we consult other texts belonging to the Gnostic faction of the Johannine movement, such as the Apocryphon of John, which is even now extant in various manuscript forms reflecting the redactions of various scribes. When the editors of *The Nag Hammadi Library* conflated all three different manuscripts of the Apocryphon of John, they were doing something like I imagine ancient scribes did when they produced our extant, conflated versions of the Gospel of John and 1 John. And in the Apocryphon of John we encounter full-blown Gnosticism, including the belief that the solid earth was created not by the heavenly Father, nor even by his Son the Logos, but by an inferior being called the Demiurge. Christ is a higher entity than the Demiurge, and his mission in descending into this sublunar world was to enlighten the Gnostic elect as to their alien origin and otherworldly destiny in the Pleroma of light. Here, as Hans Jonas discussed in his *The Gnostic Religion*,[21] the alienation of the Gnostic sectarian is radical and complete; he wants nothing more than to escape this vale of tears. This radical world-negation is perfectly mirrored in the full-blown Gnostic Christology. Jesus has become not merely "equal to God," but now actually *greater than God!* That is, greater and higher than the creator. Again, the magnification of Christology has proceeded conjointly with the increasing self-definition by self-isolation of the factions of the Johannine movement. Obviously, we do not know how Christology developed. We can only draw inferences from the (admittedly ambiguous) evidence. But I believe the scenario I have sketched here, based on the work of various scholars, shows the general plausibility of what I have dubbed "adoptionistic" theories of the growth of Christian belief about Jesus, assuming he was a genuine historical figure. It may have happened this way.

ALI AND ALLAH

In the Islamic figure of Ali, cousin and adopted son of the Prophet Muhammad, we have a striking parallel to the Christian Jesus. Matti Moosa bemoans the fact that "Ali became so mythologized that, in many of the anecdotes about him or attributed to him, it is difficult to separate the real Ali from the legendary one."[22] This mythologization occurred with amazing rapidity, beginning already within the very lifetime of Ali and included the notion that Ali was Allah himself incarnate upon earth. It was not long before, under Persian influence, the doctrine of the Ghulat sect of the Nusayri (also called the Alawi, the sect to which Syrian President Hafez Assad belongs) made Ali the ultimate Godhead, the creator of the world. The mythology of Ali has undergone many permutations, including Trinitarianism, Docetism, and the equation of Ali with both the sun and the moon by different factions! And yet there is no particular reason to deny, even to question the historical existence of Ali. One would have to disregard the whole bloody mess of the succession to the Caliphate, in which Ali ascended to the throne following the death of the previous Caliph Uthman, assassinated by partisans of Ali, who believed he should have been the immediate successor of Muhammad. The same tendency toward deification expressed itself in the identification of Ali's martyr son, the Imam Hussein, as the creative Logos of God. In fact, it seems to me we are never far from such idolatrous hero-worship when we meet the standard Jewish veneration formula; "James the Just, [for example,] on whose account heaven and earth were created" (Gospel of Thomas, saying 12). The motivation for the rapid deification of Ali is not far to seek. Ali was of course the fountainhead of the whole Shi'ite movement. As the Shi'ite movement became separated more and more widely from the Sunni mainstream, Ali's own status, like the standard of sectarian battle, was raised higher and higher, precisely as I have suggested we can trace in the case of Johannine Christology.

CHRISTIAN MOSAIC

It must be asked whether we do not have in the case of Jesus just the same sort of historical linkage in secular affairs as we do in the case of Ali, for is not the death of Jesus intertwined with the history and with historical figures of his time, even as Ali's was with Muhammad, Uthman, and the history of the Caliphate? At first glance, we do indeed. But I think there is less than meets the eye, that the linkage of Jesus with the setting of first-century Roman Palestine is more apparent than real. I will try to demonstrate this by a comparison of the events of the gospel Passion with striking historical parallels from contemporary documents which I deem the likely sources of the political coloring of the Passion story.

I suggest that the whole business of Jesus entering Jerusalem as a messianic "king of the Jews" and then being crucified as a messianic pretender is a subsequent layer of reinterpretation, a rewriting of the Jesus story. First, allow me a running start. Burton Mack, John Dominic Crossan, Robert Funk, Marcus Borg, James Breech, and many other scholars today reject the gospel depiction of Jesus heralding the imminent end of the age. All the material in the gospels that gives that impression seems to be secondary. In other words, Jesus himself spoke of the Kingdom of God in much the same terms as the Cynics or even the later rabbis did: God's kingdom was simply God's rules for living a wise and righteous life. Only later, at a time of crisis, did Jesus' partisans start preaching, in his name, an apocalyptic disaster scenario. As Mack and other Q scholars suggest, this crisis may have been nothing else than their frustration at a large-scale rejection of their message.

But, as Mack also notes, Mark seems to have mixed the events of the death of Jesus with those of the fall of the city in 70 C.E.[23] In this way Mark was able to make the fall of Jerusalem the divine punishment for the execution of Jesus. I think he is on to something here but does not pursue it nearly far enough. Crossan sees a few inches beyond Mack, but he doesn't know what to make of it either. What Crossan does see is that certain episodes of the Passion story of Jesus reflect other episodes found in the contemporary Jewish writers Josephus and Philo. We have already seen that Philo describes how, in order to mock the petty kingship of Herod Agrippa, the Alexandrian rowdies prepared a mock reception for him as he was passing through the city on his way home from receiving the crown from Caligula. Here is another glance at the story.

> There was a certain madman named Carabbas ... this man spent all his days and nights naked in the roads, minding neither cold nor heat, the sport of idle children and wanton youths; and they, driving the poor wretch as far as the public gymnasium, and setting him up there on high that he might be seen by everybody, flattened out a leaf of papyrus and put it on his head instead of a diadem, and clothed the rest of his body with a common door mat instead of a cloak and instead of a sceptre they put in his hand a small stick of the native papyrus which they found lying by the wayside and gave it to him; and when, like actors in theatrical spectacles, he had received all the insignia of public authority; and had been addressed and adorned like a king, the young men bearing sticks on their shoulders stood on each side of him instead of spear-carriers, in imitation of the bodyguards of the king, and then others came up, some as if to salute him, and others making as though they wished to plead their causes before him, and others pretending to wish to consult with him about the affairs of the state. Then from the multitude of those who were standing around there arose a wonderful shout of men calling out *Maris*; and this is the name by which it is said that they call the kings among the Syrians; for they knew that Agrippa was by birth a Syrian, and also that he was possessed of a great district of Syria of which he was the sovereign. (*Flaccus* 36–39)[24]

Crossan allows that the strikingly similar mockery of Jesus as king of the Jews by the Roman soldiers might be a fictive borrowing of this well-known tale. The same goes for the tale of another local madman, Jesus ben-Ananias, whom Josephus describes as prophesying the doom of Jerusalem four years before the war with Rome.

> One Jeshua son of Ananias, a very ordinary yokel, came to the feast at which every Jew is expected to set up a tabernacle for God. As he stood in the temple he suddenly began to shout, "A voice from the east, a voice from the west, a voice from the four winds, a voice against Jerusalem and the Sanctuary, a voice against bridegrooms and brides [cf. Luke 17:26–27, "As it was in the days of Noah, so it will be in the days of the Son of Man. They ate, they drank, they married, they were given in marriage, until the day when Noah entered the ark, and the flood came and destroyed them all"], a voice against the whole people." Day and night he uttered this cry as he went through all the streets. Some of the more prominent citizens, very annoyed at these ominous words, laid hold of the fellow and beat him savagely. Without saying a word in his own defense or for the private information of his persecutors, he persisted in shouting the same warning as before. The Jewish authorities, rightly concluding that some supernatural power was responsible for the man's behavior, took him before the Roman procurator. [cf. Luke 23:1, "Then the whole company of them rose and brought him before Pilate."] There, scourged till his flesh hung in ribbons [cf. Mark 15:15; John 19:1], he neither begged for mercy nor shed a tear [cf. Mark 14:61, "But he was silent and made no answer."], but lowering his voice to the most mournful of tones answered every blow with "Woe to Jerusalem!" [cf. Luke 13:34–35, "O Jerusalem, Jerusalem, killing the prophets and stoning those who are sent to you! . . . Behold, your house is forsaken."] When Albinus—for that was the procurator's name—demanded to know who he was, where he came from and why he uttered such cries, he made no reply whatever to the questions [cf. John 19:9, "He entered the Praetorium again and said to Jesus, 'Where are you from?' But Jesus gave him no answer."] but endlessly repeated his lament over the City, till Albinus decided he was a madman and released him [cf. Luke 23:22b, "I will therefore chastise him and release him."]. All the time till the war broke out he never approached another citizen or was seen in conversation, but daily as if he had learned a prayer by heart he recited his lament: "Woe to Jerusalem!" Those who daily cursed him he never cursed [cf. Luke 6:28a, "Bless those who curse you."]; those who gave him food he never thanked [cf. Luke 10:7b, "For the laborer deserves his wages."]; his only response to anyone was that dismal foreboding. His voice was heard most of all at the feasts [cf. John 2:13 ff; 5:1 ff; 6:4 ff; 7:2 ff; 37; 10:22–23 ff; 11:55–56]. For seven years and five months he went on ceaselessly, his voice as strong as ever and his vigour unabated, till during the siege after seeing the fulfillment of his foreboding he was silenced. He was going round on the wall uttering his piercing cry: "Woe again to the City, the people, and the Sanctuary!" [cf. Luke 21:20–21, "But when you see Jerusalem surrounded by armies, then know that its desolation has come near. Then let those who are in Judea flee to the mountains,

and let those who are inside the city depart, and let not those who are out in the country enter it; for these are days of vengeance, to fulfill all that is written. ... For great distress shall be upon the earth and wrath upon this people ... and Jerusalem shall be trodden down by the Gentiles ..."] and as he added a last word: "Woe to me also!" a stone shot from an engine struck him, killing him instantly. Thus he uttered those same forebodings to the very end. (*The Jewish War*, VI, V, 3. G.A. Williamson trans.)

But this is only the beginning. We can parallel Jesus' triumphal entry into the city and cleansing of the temple with that of revolutionary messiah Simon bar-Giora, welcomed into the temple by the priests because he had promised to exterminate the faction of Joseph of Gischala, who had occupied the sacred precinct. They were "brigands," "bandits," as guerrillas were called; thus Joseph's mission was to "cleanse" the temple, which had become a "den of thieves." These phrases, familiar from the gospels, make more natural sense in the context Josephus describes and thus probably originated there.

In order to overthrow John they voted to admit Simon, and olive-branch in hand [Mark 11:8: "And many spread their garments on the road, and others spread leafy branches which they had cut from the fields."] to bring in a second tyrant to be their master. The resolution was carried out, and they sent the high priest, Matthias, to implore Simon to enter—the man they so greatly feared! The invitation was supported by those citizens who were trying to escape the Zealots and were anxious about their homes and property. He in his lordly way expressed his willingness to be their master, and entered with the air of one who intended to sweep the Zealots out of the City, acclaimed by the citizens as deliverer and protector [cf. Luke 19:38, "Blessed is the king who comes in the name of the Lord!"]. (Ibid., V, IX, 11)

Eventually surrendering to the Romans, Simon was taken to Rome and displayed in the triumphal procession, finally to be executed as would-be king of the Jews after suffering abuse by his Roman guards [cf. Mark 15:16–20]. He wasn't crucified, true, but then this portion of the Jesus story recalls Plutarch's account of the death of Cleomenes, the revolutionary king of Sparta, exiled because of his land-reform policies. He was caught fomenting egalitarian revolution in Alexandria, too. Knowing their time was short, most of his compatriots took their own lives.

Fanteus walked over them as they lay, and pricked every one with his dagger, to try whether any was alive [cf. John 19:33–34a, "but when they came to Jesus and saw that he was already dead, they did not break his legs. But one of the soldiers pierced his side with a spear ..."]; when he pricked Cleomenes' ankle, and saw him turn upon his back, he kissed him, sat down by him, and when he was quite dead, covered up the body, and then killed himself over it.... Ptolemy, as soon as an account of the action was brought him, gave order that Cleomenes's body should be flayed and hung up [cf. Mark 15:15b, "and having scourged Jesus, he delivered him up to be crucified."].... A few days later, those that watched the hanging body of Cleomenes saw a large snake winding about his head and covering his face, so that no bird of prey would fly at it [cf. Mark 15:33, 38, "And when the sixth hour had come, there was darkness over the whole earth until the ninth hour.... And the curtain of the temple was torn in two, from top to bottom."]. This made the king superstitiously afraid [cf. Mark 15:44; John 19:8, "When Pilate heard these words he was the more afraid."] and set the women upon several expiations [cf. Mark 16:1–2, "Mary Magdalene, and Mary of James, and Salome bought spices, so that they might go and anoint him. And very early on the first day of the week they went to the tomb."], as if he had been some extraordinary being, and one beloved by the gods, that had been slain. And the Alexandrians made processions to the place and gave Cleomenes the title of hero, and son of the gods [cf. Mark 15:39, "And when the centurion, who stood facing him, saw that in this way he breathed his last, he said, 'Truly this man was the son of God!'"]... (Plutarch's *Lives of the Noble Grecians and Romans, Cleomenes.* Dryden trans.)[25]

The gospels show Pontius Pilate as being desperate to get Jesus released, but as eventually caving in to the threats of the crowd who say they will report him to Caesar if he does not execute the false Messiah Jesus (John 19:12). This seems quite odd to scholars, hardly characteristic of the Pilate known to history as a Jew-baiting tyrant. In fact it sounds like it might be a garbled version of another story Josephus tells on Pilate. It seems the procurator had been informed of a planned rally on Mount Gerizim in Samaria. The Samaritan messiah

> bade them get together upon Mount Gerizim, which is by them looked upon as the most holy of all mountains, and assured them that, when they were come thither, he would show them those sacred vessels which were laid under that place, because Moses put them there. So they came thither armed, and thought the discourse of the man probable; and as they abode at a certain village, which was called Tirathaba, they got the rest together to them, and desired to go up the mountain in a great multitude together; but Pilate prevented their going up, by seizing upon the roads with a great band of horsemen and footmen, that fell upon these that were gotten together in the village, and when it came to an action, some of them they slew, and others of them they put to flight, and took a great many alive, the principal of whom, and also the most potentate of those that fled away, Pilate ordered to be slain.
>
> But when this tumult was appeased, the Samaritan senate sent an embassy to Vitellius, a man that had been consul, and who was now president of Syria, and accused Pilate of the murder of those that were killed; for

that they did not go to Tirathaba in order to revolt from the Romans, but to escape the violence of Pilate. So Vitellius sent Marcellus, a friend of his, to take care of the affairs of Judea, and ordered Pilate to go to Rome, to answer before the emperor to the accusations of the Jews. So Pilate, when he had tarried ten years in Judea, made haste to Rome, and this in obedience to the orders of Vitellius, which he durst not contradict. (*Antiquities of the Jews*, XVIII, IV:1–2.Whiston trans.)

Here are most of the elements in the gospels' Pilate episode, only they are reshuffled. Or have the gospels reshuffled the pieces of an original historical account in which Pilate cruelly crushed a peaceful messiah, was reported by the survivors, and found he had Caesar's ire to face?

JOSHUA MESSIAHS

In Acts 5:35–39, Luke has Rabban Gamaliel lump Jesus together with Judas of Galilee and Theudas the Magician, both revolutionary prophets or messiahs mentioned by Josephus. Theudas had promised his followers that, like the Old Testament "Jesus" (Joshua), he would part the Jordan River.

> Now it came to pass, while Fadus was procurator of Judea, that a certain magician, whose name was Theudas, persuaded a great part of the people to take their effects with them, and to follow him to the river Jordan; for he told them he was a prophet, and that he would, by his own command, divide the river, and afford them an easy passage over it; and many were deluded by his words. However, Fadus did not permit them to make any advantage of his wild attempt, but sent a troop of horsemen out against them; who, falling upon them unexpectedly, slew many of them, and took many of them alive. They also took Theudas alive, and cut off his head, and carried it to Jerusalem. (Ibid., XX, V, 1)

Similarly, Claudius Lysias asks Paul in Acts 21:38 if he is not the notorious Egyptian prophet who organized an army out in the desert some time ago. Josephus mentions this failed messiah, too. The Egyptian had promised he would cause the walls of Jerusalem to fall down like Joshua did the walls of Jericho.

> And now these impostors and deceivers persuaded the multitude to follow them into the wilderness, and pretended that they would exhibit manifest wonders and signs, that should be performed by the providence of God. And many that were prevailed on by them suffered the punishments of their folly; for Felix brought them back, and then punished them. Moreover, there came out of Egypt about this time to Jerusalem, one that said he was

a prophet, and advised the multitude of the common people to go along with him to the Mount of Olives as it was called, which lay over against the city, and at the distance of five furlongs. He said farther, that he would show them from hence, how, at his command, the walls of Jerusalem would fall down; and he promised them that he would procure them an entrance to the city through those walls, when they were fallen down. Now when Felix was informed of these things, he ordered his soldiers to take their weapons, and came against them with a great number of horsemen and footmen, from Jerusalem, and attacked the Egyptian and the people that were with him. He also slew four hundred of them, and took two hundred alive. But the Egyptian himself escaped out of the fight, but did not appear any more. (Ibid., XX, IX, 6)

A few scholars have noted the odd "coincidence" that both Theudas and the Egyptian sought to repeat the ancient feats of Joshua leading his people into the promised land. If they were trying to substantiate their messianic claims by aping Joshua, wouldn't this mean there was some currently available category like a "Joshua Messiah," a "Jesus Christ"? ("Joshua" and "Jesus" are variant forms of the same name.) It seems there was. Samaritans made a great deal of the Deut. 18:18–22 prophecy of the eventual advent of a "Prophet like Moses," and some Samaritan sectarians believed that the Samaritan mage Dositheus (whom the Pseudo-Clementine Homilies make a disciple of John the Baptist who lost out to Simon Magus in a squabble for leadership of the sect after John's death) was the Messiah. Other Samaritans claimed that the future prophetic Messiah was Moses' immediate successor, Joshua. What did they mean by this? As Kippenberg has suggested, the Joshua identification may have intended to stymie any speculation about the identity of a future Messiah and thus nip in the bud any new and dangerous messianic movements.[26] The point would have been the same as when Rabbi Hillel asserted that all messianic prophecies were already fulfilled in the righteous King Hezekiah, so that no future Messiah ought to be expected ("Israel has no Messiah because they already consumed him in the days of Hezekiah," *B. Sanhedrin* 98b, 99a). But Hillel's quip backfired: Some concluded, apparently on the basis of it, that Hezekiah would come *again* as Messiah at the end of the age![27] In the same way, it seems that Dositheus' disciples applied the Deuteronomy prophecy to their master and understood him as the Old Testament Joshua come again![28] And apparently Theudas and the Egyptian made the same claim for themselves, as their Joshua-like messianic programs suggest.[29] Thus, for some Jews and Samaritans, to be Messiah was to be Joshua. To be Christ was to be Jesus.

Luke, the author of Acts 5:35–39, knows it would have been natural for people to confuse Jesus with other infamous figures connected with revolt against Rome. Even more revealing is the warning of Mark's apocalyptic discourse, attributed to Jesus, in chapter 13. He has Jesus warn the readers of the gospel (this is explicit: "Let the reader understand," verse 14) not to confuse Jesus with various prophets and messiahs connected with the fall of Jerusalem (Mark 13:6, 21). No, they are different, though there is a real danger of not being able to keep one's messiahs straight (". . . so as to deceive, if possible, even the elect," Mark 13:22). In plain speech, it seems to me, Mark is letting on that various early Jesus believers unwittingly confused Jesus with people like Jesus ben-Ananias, Simon bar-Giora, Carabbas, "Joshua Messiahs" Theudas and the Egyptian, Jesus ben-Sapphiah the bandit chief, Jesus bar-Abbas the insurrectionist, Elymas bar-Jesus the sorcerer, Jesus Justus, and the martyred Samaritan messiah. The war was over: Mark did not fear that his readers might take up arms against Rome under the leadership of Menahem or Simon. That was in the past. So what sort of confusion might he still fear? Precisely that his readers should have amalgamated features from different heroic but martyred messiahs and prophets together with Jesus, polluting his story with elements from a generation later when messiahs swarmed the land. Such confusion must have been proceeding apace, or there would be no occasion for Mark to warn against it, having Jesus warn against it beforehand. And yet it was far too late; Mark's own story already presupposed a great amount of such conflation.

So I am saying that, insofar as the Jesus movement only later repainted Jesus as an apocalyptic figure, this would most likely have included repainting him as a messianic king entering Jerusalem triumphantly, clearing the temple, being mocked as a pretended king, condemned by an intimidated Pilate, crucified as king of the Jews, and shown by portents at the cross to be the Son of God. All this is quite possibly the result of confusing Jesus with the exciting events of Jewish revolt against Rome. Indeed, as Mack says, Mark had already collapsed the generation separating Jesus from the fall of the city. And if this is anywhere near the mark, then we would have to suppose that the pre-70 C.E. community of the Pillars had understood the absent Jesus in quite a different way, not as a slain king, but perhaps as a hidden Imam, as I have suggested in my earlier speculations about James the Just as the Door of Jesus. But we must raise even more searching questions.

EUHEMERISM

The so-called Apostles' Creed treats almost entirely of invisible, metaphysical matters, supposed events that sound like myths, divine creations and incarnations, a virgin birth, a descent into the inferno, and so on. The sole historical peg upon which it attempts to hang the life of the savior Jesus is his crucifixion in the time of Pontius Pilate. Yet I have just suggested that the connection of Jesus with Pilate may be based on the same sort of garbled speculations that led Luke to connect the birth of Jesus with both Herod the Great and Quirinius' census. Jesus' connection with the Roman governor Pilate on one end of his biography need be no more historical than his connection with the Roman governor Quirinius on the other. Even greater doubt is thrown on the matter by the parallel tradition, still extant but just barely, that Jesus was executed under Herod Antipas! The Gospel of Peter has Herod consult with Pilate but see to the execution himself. And, as Alfred Loisy noted long ago, Luke seems to have had access to a version of the Passion in which it was Herod who had Jesus killed, not Pilate.[30] This becomes evident when one examines Luke's cumbersome and improbable sequence involving Jesus being tried before Pilate, then Herod Antipas, then Pilate again. No one has ever come up with a plausible reason for Pilate remanding Jesus to Antipas, as Luke has him do. Once Jesus gets to Herod's court, it is Herod's troops who mock him, not Pilate's as in the other gospels, implying that Luke was trying to harmonize the Markan Pilate-Passion with another set in Herod's court and had to choose between mockings. The most flagrant mark of indelicate editing is Herod's acquittal of Jesus—then sending him back to Pilate! It is clear Luke must have had one Passion story in front of him, Mark's, in which Pilate ordered Jesus' execution, and another, like that in the Gospel of Peter, in which it was Herod Antipas who condemned him. To use both, he had to change Herod's verdict from guilty to innocent (otherwise, as in the Gospel of Peter, he must have Herod send him to the cross). But instead of having Herod let Jesus go in peace, as an acquittal surely would demand, he has Herod send Jesus back to Pilate—for what? And if Pilate awaited Herod's verdict, why did he not let him go, too, since Herod had acquitted Jesus? Luke has too many cooks in the kitchen, and the stew is spoiled.

But the key question is, if Jesus was known to have been crucified quite recently in dramatic public circumstances, at the behest either of Pilate or of Herod, how on earth could uncertainty over who killed him ever have arisen? If either Herod or Pilate had recently executed him, how could any belief about the involvement of the other have come about? But, on the other hand, if both were merely educated guesses as to who killed Jesus, we can easily see how the confusion arose.

And there is even more confusion over the date of Jesus' death. As G. R. S. Mead[31] pointed out long ago, there is a persistent Jewish tradition to the effect that Jesus died about 100 B.C.E., in the time not of Pontius Pilate, but of Alexander Jannaeus and his widow Queen Salome. This version makes Jesus a "heretical" disciple of Joshua ben Perechiah (just as many critical scholars make Jesus a dissenting disciple of John the Baptist). It is attested in both the Talmud and in the Toledoth Jeschu, the Jewish gospel satire, which as Hugh J. Schonfield convincingly showed, must have been based on an apocryphal Jewish-Christian gospel from no later than the second century C.E.[32]

Christ-Myth theorists from Arthur Drews to George A. Wells have remarked how 1 Cor. 2:8 and Col. 2:13–15 attribute the death of Jesus to no earthly agents but rather to supramundane spiritual entities. Wells and others went on to argue that at some point Christians took to trying to locate the death of their savior in the historical past, finally fixing upon the reign of Pilate, a notorious villain.[33] To have done so would have entailed no risk of Roman disfavor, since as we have seen Pilate was disgraced in the eyes of the Romans. Choosing him would in fact be a way of currying favor with Rome, much as Josephus sought to do by pleading that it was not Rome per se but only the occasional rotten Roman apple that created trouble with Jews.

Such a process of hypothetical historicizing of a god hitherto imagined as living in the vague past would certainly not be without precedent. I find it ironic that in his book *Did the Greeks Believe in Their Myths?* Paul Veyne[34] both scoffs at those who deny the historical existence of Jesus and at the same time implicitly enhances the argument of Christ-Myth theorists. He describes how thinkers of Greek and Roman antiquity, including Diodorus, Cicero, Livy, Pausanias, and Strabo, approached mythic figures such as Theseus, Herakles, Odysseus, Minos, Dionysus, Castor, and Pollux: They readily dismissed the supernatural tales of their heroes' divine paternity and miraculous feats but doggedly assumed there must have been a historical core that had been subsequently mythologized. Their task as historians was to distill the history from the myth and to place the great figures where they must have occurred on the historical time-chart. Herodotus, for instance, tried to determine just when Herakles lived, though he could not quite manage to reconcile the conflicting "information" he derived from Egyptian, Greek, Phoenician, and other sources.[35] The whole approach earned the name of Euhemerism, from Euhemerus who originated it. The idea was to assume that all ancient gods were glorified ancestors or historical culture heroes. Though no mundane, "secular" information about them survived, it had to be assumed that a genuine historical figure lay at the root of the myths.

Unless I am mistaken, this seems to be the approach of the questors for a historical Jesus. Though the gospel story of Jesus matches the pattern of the Mythic Hero Archetype in every detail, with nothing left over, Christian scholars, among whose number we must surely count even Bultmann, simply assume there must have been a historical Jesus at the root of the thing, and this even if, à la Bultmann, we cannot come near to specifying what it was. But just as important, it seems equally to have been the guiding assumption of Christians at some stage of reflection when they felt some need to nail down the earthly appearance of Jesus in, to them, recent history. The Jewish and Jewish-Christian dating of Jesus about 100 B.C.E. may represent one attempt at fixing such a date, the more common Herod Antipas and/or Pontius Pilate date representing another, evidently that of Gentile Christians of some stripe and of a later time.

New Testament scholars are quite accustomed to the basic logic here, only they have not applied it so broadly as the Christ-Myth theorists. For instance, many would agree with Charles Talbert[36] and Elaine Pagels[37] that the spiritual, visionary resurrection of Jesus affirmed by earlier Christians (1 Cor. 15:43-50; 1 Pet. 3:18-19) gave way to "historicized," flesh-and-blood resurrection stories such as we find in Matt. 28:9; Luke 24:36-43; John 20:24-29; Acts 10:40-41) due to an effort by emerging catholic Christianity to combat Gnostics who claimed still to receive visionary apparitions of the Risen One replete with new and "heretical" teachings, of which Gnostic texts like the Pistis Sophia are full. To concretize the nature of the appearances as those of a physical individual, albeit a resurrected one, was to imply a manageable, "canonical" number of them. The same logic underlay the later attempt to delimit the number and character of writings in the New Testament canon. Both were attempts to co-opt and control revelation claims.

Again, many New Testament scholars would agree thus far. Christ-Myth theorists like Drews and Wells make but one natural step farther in the direction thus indicated. The need to concretize and thus to define and control Christian thinking and practice had earlier led to the historicizing of the Jesus figure itself, the result being an earthly "life of Jesus," something the Gnostics never quite accepted, with their docetic Christology, even once they had assimilated the basic Markan story-plot. The more of an earthly establishment Christianity became, the more it felt the need to point to "our founder," a divine figure who had once laid down the law, the canon law, to the exclusion of Gnostic daydreams and hallucinations.[38]

But where, pray tell, had Mark derived his Jesus story line? From the facts? Here we have another case where accepted critical axioms in gospel studies would seem to have much more radical implications than even the most supposedly skeptical critics themselves seem to have realized. One of Bultmann's early colleagues in form criticism of the gospels, Karl Ludwig Schmidt, broke important new ground by, in a sense, pointing out the obvious, namely that the order of events in the gospels is arbitrary.[39] Already in Mark most episodes have no narrative logic interconnecting them, but rather are merely taped together by means of Mark's favorite connective adverb "immediately," as if to say "Next he did this.... Next he went there." The artificiality is evident, for instance, in 2:32 through 3:6, where Mark has grouped anecdotes together topically, for example, Sabbath controversies, or in 9:33-50, a sequence of largely unrelated sayings strung together by the mnemonic device of catchwords. Mark had simply created a schematic framework for his presentation of a great number of hitherto independent stories and sayings which had previously circulated by word of mouth ("oral tradition") one by one. Each story or saying (and many of the stories built up to sayings as their punchline) served a particular purpose, for example, to lay down the Christian law about fasting, prayer, exorcism, church discipline, healing tips or formulae, miracle-mongering propaganda. And these original uses can still be detected despite Mark's working them all up into a story. Indeed, form-criticism was all about reisolating these units from their gospel contexts and figuring out what purpose each must once have served.

In one way, this discovery eased the burden of apologists for gospel accuracy, for it immediately became clear that none of the gospel writers was much interested in chronological sequence. If Matthew and Luke felt free to change the order of events and sayings as they found them in Mark, the exegete could stop barking up the wrong tree, trying to defend the evangelists according to a standard of accuracy they were not even trying to meet. Did John have Jesus cleanse the temple at the commencement of his ministry, while the other gospels placed the event at the close of his public activity? No matter: The difference was merely a rhetorical one, and one might even make homiletical hay of the difference.

After Schmidt, scholars ostensibly recognized that the plot outline of Mark was the evangelist's own creation, a more or less arbitrary string along which to arrange the pearls. This did not, however, stop many or most of them from continuing to take the Markan sequence for granted as an outline of at least the public ministry of Jesus: a "Galilean Spring" of popular acceptance, followed by a cross-shadowed last journey to Jerusalem to face bitter conflict from the establishment, then death. If one did take the form-critical insight seriously, that the Markan plot is but a frame device to showcase a number of originally independent anecdotes and sayings, one might be inclined at the very least to skepticism like Bultmann's: One might give up any idea of writing a biography, however rudimentary, of Jesus. One might, in other words, assume that the events of the life of Jesus, their interconnection both with one another and with outside events and influences, is forever lost to us. Had he served an Essene novitiate? Possibly, not unlikely, but pure speculation. Had he learned Cynic philosophy in nearby Sepphoris? Who knows!

But one's agnosticism might go a good deal further to the conclusion that the very idea of an earthly, itinerant ministry of Jesus as teacher, healer, and exorcist, was a product of Mark's framing device. As the Russian Formalist critic Boris Tomashevsky observed, "The protagonist . . . is the result of the formation of the story material into a plot. On the one hand, he is a means of stringing motifs together; and on the other, he embodies the motivation that connects the motifs."[40] Tomashevsky might almost have had Mark himself in mind! Was Jesus an itinerant? There is no reason to think so. It is the impression created by the choice of placing anecdotes side by side in narrative form. Bruno Bauer once argued that Mark had himself created the Jesus character out of whole cloth. I am saying that it may well be that Mark took preexisting traditions of miracles and wise sayings, some or all of them already attributed to the Christian savior, Jesus, and from them created the idea of a "historical Jesus."

TRUTHS AND TRUISMS

Where did these pre-Markan materials come from? Many of the sayings may have come from anywhere. Bultmann, T. W. Manson, Arthur Drews,[41] and others long ago demonstrated how a huge number of the sayings and parables attributed to Jesus in the Synoptic gospels are even verbally paralleled among the voluminous aphorisms of the rabbis in the Mishnah, as well as among Cynic and Stoic philosophers. Here are several rabbinic parallels.

> I should be surprised if there were anyone in this generation who would accept correction. If one says to a man, "Remove the spelk from your eye," he will reply, "Remove the beam from yours." (Rabbi Tarphon, ca. 100 C.E.; cf. Matt. 7:3–5)
>
> A Jew who has much knowledge of the Law and many good works is like a man who lays stone foundations for his house and builds thereon with sun-dried brick. Though floods may come the house is not affected because its foundations are sound. But the man who has much knowledge of the Law and no good works is like a man who lays foundations of sun-dried brick and builds thereon with stone. If only a small flood comes the house collapses because the foundations are not sound. (Rabbi Elijah ben Abuya, ca. 120 C.E.; cf. Matt. 7:24–27)[42]
>
> No bird perishes without God—how much less a man! (Rabbi Simeon ben Jochai, ca. 150 C.E.; cf. Matt. 10:29–31)
>
> Whoever has bread in his basket and asks "What shall I eat tomorrow?" is none other than those of little faith. (Rabbi Eleazer, 1st century, *Sotah* 48b; cf. Matt. 5:31)
>
> When thou hast mercy upon thy fellow, thou hast one to have mercy on thee; but if thou hast not mercy upon thy fellow, thou hast none to have mercy upon thee. (Tanchuma; cf. Matt. 7:1–2)
>
> He who hates his neighbor, lo he belongs to the shedders of blood. (Eliezer, ca. 90 C.E.; cf. Matt. 5:22)
>
> He who looks at a woman with desire is as one who has criminal intercourse with her. (*Kalla* par. 1; cf. Matt. 5:28)
>
> The yea of the righteous is a yea; their no is a no. (Rabbi Huna; cf. Matt. 5:37)
>
> There were two chambers in the Temple: one the Chamber of Secrets, the other the Chamber of Utensils. Into the Chamber of Secrets the devout

used to put their gifts in secret and the poor of good family received support therefrom in secret. (*Shekalim* 5, 6; cf. Matt. 6:2–4)

It is enough for the servant to be like his master. (Common Jewish proverb; cf. Matt. 10:25)

Whoever gives a piece of bread to a righteous man, it is as though he had fulfilled the whole Law. (*Genesis Rabbah* on Gen. 23:18; Matt. 10:41–42)

> Turn in to me, ye unlearned,
> And lodge in my house of instruction.
> How long will ye lack these things?
> And how long shall your soul be so athirst?
> I open my mouth and speak of her,
> Acquire wisdom for yourselves with money.
> Bring your necks under her yoke,
> And her burden let your soul bear;
> She is nigh unto them that seek her,
> And he that is intent upon her findeth her.
> Behold with your eyes that I laboured but little therein,
> And abundance of peace have I found.
> (Sirach 51:23–27; cf. Matt. 11:28–30)

If two sit together and words of Torah [are spoken] between them the Shekinah rests between them.... (Rabbi Hananiah ben Teradion, died 135, *Aboth* 3, 2; cf. Matt. 18:20)

Like a king who invited his servants to a feast and did not specify a time for them. The astute ones among them adorned themselves and sat at the gate of the palace. They said, "There is no lack in the palace" [so the feast could start any time]. The foolish ones among them went to their work. They said, "There is no feast without preparation" [thus, there is still time to spare]. Suddenly the king asked for his servants. The astute ones among them came into his presence as they were, adorned; and the foolish ones among them came into his presence as they were, dirty. The king was pleased with the astute ones and angry with the foolish ones. He said, "Let these who adorned themselves for the feast sit down and eat and drink. Let those who did not adorn themselves for the feast stand and look on." (Johannan ben Zakkai, *Shabb.* 153a; cf. Matt. 22:1–3a, 11–13)

God does not give greatness to a man till he has proved him in a small matter: only then he promotes him to a great post. Two were proved and found faithful, and God promoted them to greatness. He tested David with the sheep . . . and God said, Thou wast faithful with the sheep; I will give thee my sheep that thou shouldst feed them. And so with Moses, who fed his father-in-law's sheep. To him God said the same. (cf. Matt. 25:14–29)

He that learns from the young, to what is he like? To one that eats unripe grapes and drinks wine from his winepress. And he that learns from the aged, to what is he like? To one that eats ripe grapes and drinks old wine. Look not on the jar but on what is in it; there may be a new jar that is full of old wine and an old one in which is not even new wine. (Rabbi Jose ben Judah of Kefar ha-Babli, *Aboth* 4.20; cf. Mark 2:21–22)

A scholar whose inward (thoughts) do not correspond to his outward (profession) is no scholar. (Raba, died 352 C.E.; cf. Matt. 23:2–4)

Stay two or three seats below thy place and sit until they say to thee, "Go up." Do not begin by going up because they may say to thee, "Go down." It is better that they should say to thee, "Go up, go up" than that they should say to thee, "Go down, go down." (Rabbi Simeon ben Azzai, died. 110 C.E., *Leviticus Rabbah* 1; cf. Luke 14:7–11)

Rabbi Abahu argues that God gives a higher place to repentant sinners than to the completely righteous. (end of third century C.E.; cf. Luke 15:7)

When a man loses a piece of gold, he lights many lamps in order to seek it. If a man takes all this trouble for the sake of temporal things, how much the more should he when there is a question of treasures that keep their worth in the world to come? (*Midrash Schir hashirim* 3, 2; cf. Luke 15:8)

It is to be compared to the son of a king who had removed from his father for the distance of a hundred days' journey. His friends said to him, "Return unto your father," whereupon he rejoined, "I cannot." Then his father sent a message to him, "Travel as much as it is in thy power, and I will come unto you the rest of the way." And so the Holy one, blessed be he, said 'Return unto me, and I will return unto you.' " (Mal. 3:7) (P.R., 184 b and 185a; cf. Luke 15:11 ff)[43]

Two godly men lived in Ashkelon. They ate together, drank together, and studied in the Law together. One of them died and kindness was not shown to him [no one attended the funeral]. Bar-Majan, a tax-collector, died, and the whole city stopped to show him kindness. The [surviving] pious man began to complain; he said, "Alas that no evil comes upon the haters of Israel." In a dream he saw a vision, and one said to him: "Do not despise the children of your Lord. The one had committed one sin and departed in it [which is why he had died unremembered]; and the other had performed one good deed and departed in it [i.e., the well-attended funeral was all the reward he was due]." He had arranged a banquet for the city councilors, but they did not come. So he gave orders that the poor should come and eat it, so that the food should not be wasted. After some days that godly man saw the godly one, his companion, walking in gardens and parks beside springs of water [i.e., in heaven]. And he saw bar-Majan, the publican, stretching out his tongue on the edge of a river; he was seeking to reach the water, and he could not [just like Tantalus in Hades]. (Talmud of Jerusalem, *Hagigah*, II, 77d; cf. Luke 14:16–24; 16:19–31)

To whom shall I liken Rabbi Bon, son of Chaija? To a king that hath hired laborers, among whom was one of great power. This man did the king summon to himself, and held speech with him. And when the night fell, the hired labourers came to receive their hire. But the king gave to the favoured laborer the same hire which he had given unto others. Then they murmured and said, "We have laboured the whole day, and this man hath labored but two hours, yet there is given unto him the same wages that we have received." And the king sent them away, saying: "This man hath done more in two hours than ye have done during the whole of the day." Even so hath the Rabbi Bon done more in the study of the Law in the twenty-eight years of his life than another would have done who had lived in a hundred years. (*Beracoth*. 5.3c; cf. Matt. 20:1–16)

My fathers stored in a place which can be tampered with, but I have stored in a place that cannot be tampered with. (*Baba bathra* 11a; cf. Matt. 6:21)

In my whole lifetime I have not seen a deer engaged in gathering fruits, a lion carrying burdens, or a fox as a shopkeeper, yet they are sustained without trouble, though they were created only to serve me, whereas I was created to serve my Maker. Now, if these, who were created to serve me are sustained without trouble, how much more should I be sustained without trouble, I who was created to serve my Maker! (*Kidushin*. 82b; cf. Matt. 6:26)

Hast thou ever seen a bird or a beast of the forest that must secure its food by work? God feeds them, and they need no effort to obtain their nourishment. Yet the beast has a mind only to serve man. He, however, knows his higher vocation—namely to serve God; does it become him, then, to care only for his bodily wants? (*Kidushin* 4, *Halach* 14; cf. Matt. 6:30–33)

Fret not over tomorrow's trouble, for thou knowest not what a day may bring forth, and peradventure tomorrow he is no more; thus he shall be found grieving over a world that is not his. (*Sanh*. 100b; cf. Matt. 6:34)

He who calls down judgment on his neighbor is himself punished first. (*Rosch hasch*. 16b, second century C.E.; cf. Matt. 7:1–2)

Our rabbis taught: He who judges his neighbor in the scale of merit is himself judged favorably (Shab. 127b; cf. Matt. 7:1–2)

When he knocks, the door is opened for him. (R. Bannajah, ca 200 C.E.; cf. Matt. 7:7)

God says of the Israelites: "To me they are upright as doves, but to the nations they are wise as serpents," (Judah ben Simon in *Midrash on Canticles*. 2:14 (101a); cf. Matt. 10:16)

The Sabbath is given over to you, not you to the Sabbath. (frequently in the rabbis; cf. Mark 2:37)

Is a light of any sort of use save in a dark place? (*Mek*. 60a; cf. Mark 4:21)

A young man deserves praise when he becomes like the children. (*Tanchuma* 36, 4; cf. Matt. 18:2–4)

Whoever humbles himself for love of the Law, the same will be reckoned among the greatest in the kingdom of heaven. (*Baha Mezia* 84, 2; cf. Matt. 18:2–4)

Are you from Pombeditha, where they can drive an elephant through the eye of a needle? (*Baha Mezia* 38, 2; cf. Matt. 19:23)

Do I not number the hair of every creature? (*Pesikta* 18, 4; cf. Matt. 10:30)

Thou shalt not hate, not even internally. (*Menachot*, 18; cf. Matt. 5:22)

Love him that punisheth thee. (*Derech Erez Sutha*, c. 9; cf. Matt. 5:43–44)

Be rather among the persecuted than among the persecutors. (*Baba Mezia*, 93; cf. Matt. 5:10)

If any man demand thy donkey, give him the saddle also. (*Baba Kama*, 27; cf. Matt. 5:40–42)

A muleteer drove twelve span before him, all laden with wine. One of them strayed into the yard of a Gentile. Then the driver left the others and sought the one that had broken loose. Asked how he had ventured to leave the others for the sake of one, he answered: "The others remained on the public road, where there was no danger of any man stealing my property, as he would know that he was observed by so many." So it was with the other children of Jacob [than Joseph]. They remained under the eye of their father, and were moreover older than Joseph. He, however, was left to himself in his youth. Hence the Scripture says that God took special care of him. (*Genesis Rabba*, 86, 84, 3; cf. Matt. 18:12–14; Luke 15:3–7)

A king had appointed two overseers. One he chose as master of the treasure; the other he put in charge of the straw-store. After a time the latter fell under suspicion of unfaithfulness. Nevertheless he complained that he was not promoted to the post of master of the treasure. Then was he asked, in astonishment at his words: "Fool, thou hast incurred suspicion in charge of the stores of straw: how couldst thou be trusted with the treasure?" (*Jalkut Simeoni* 1, 81,1; cf. Luke 16:1–12)

Bultmann noted that in such cases where the saying attributed in the gospels to Jesus closely parallels a rabbinic saying, great doubt must arise as to whether they really go back to Jesus. Likewise with texts in which Jesus is made to quote Old Testament scripture. Why? Bultmann points out that no one ever remembers the Great Man quoting someone else. It is his own quotes that are memorable. It is likely, however, that cliché sayings and truisms will be attributed to a Great Man for want of remembering who did actually say them. Of course, as Jacob Neusner has eloquently argued, the same holds true for Mishnaic sayings attributed to this or that famous rabbi.[44] None can be relied upon for biographical purposes.

HERO STORIES

As for the gospel stories, as distinct from the sayings, Randel Helms[45] and Thomas L. Brodie[46] have shown how story after story in the gospels has been based, sometimes verbatim, on similar stories from the Greek Old Testament, the Septuagint. For instance, the stilling of the storm (Mark 4:35–41) was rewritten from the similar story of Jonah. The resurrection of the son of the widow of Nain (Luke 7:11–17) seems to be another version of Elisha's raising of the Shunnamite's son in 2 Kings 4:32–37. The story of Jesus' appointment of the Twelve, followed by his refusal to receive his mother and brothers (Mark 3:13–21, 31–35), seems to be a negative rewriting of the story of Moses receiving his father-in-law Jethro and his family, followed by his appointment of the Seventy elders (Exod. 18).

In this connection Earl Doherty[47] has taken a second look at New Testament claims that such-and-such happened "according to the scriptures" (1 Cor. 15:3–4) or "in order that the scriptures might be fulfilled" (Matt. 1:22–23; 2:5–6,15,17–18, 23). His conclusion is that, contrary to the conventional wisdom which presupposes a historical Jesus, these formulae denote not attempts to find prooftexts for known events in the life of Jesus, but rather midrashic fictions based on scripture passages. We usually imagine that the question in the minds of the early Christians was, "How do we know the Messiah was supposed to die for sins and rise from the dead, as Jesus in fact did? Because scripture, read the right way, predicted he *would*." But Doherty argues forcefully that they may instead have been thinking, "What happened to Jesus? He must have died for sins and risen from the dead, because scripture, read the right way, says he *did*." This approach certainly comports with the otherwise astonishing fact that even the account of the crucifixion itself is a patchwork quilt of (mostly unacknowledged) scripture citations rather than historical reportage. It is common knowledge that Mark's crucifixion account corresponds verbally with selected lines from Psalm 22, but believers imagine that this is because Mark was seeking to show how closely the events corresponded to their prophetic predictions. However there is no reference in Mark's story to prophetic prediction. It is left to the reader to discover that "My God, my God, why have you forsaken me?" is the opening line of Psalm 22, and so on. Similarly, when Matthew feels inclined to expand the mockery of Jesus' enemies at the foot of the cross (Matt. 27:43), he supplements it not with memories or historical research, but with more scripture quotes, this time from Wisd. of Sol. 2:16–18. Elsewhere Matthew has created whole features in his version of the Passion out of the text of the prophet Zechariah. How did he "know" Judas received the sum of thirty silver shekels? He found it in Zech. 11:12b ("And they weighed out as my wages thirty shekels of silver"). How did he "know" Judas returned this money, throwing it to the temple treasury floor? He derived the "fact" from the Syriac version of Zech. 11:13 ("Then Yahve told me, 'Cast it into the treasury' "). How did he "know" the priests took this money and bought a potter's field with it? The Hebrew version of the same verse, Zech. 11:13 ("Then Yahve told me, 'Cast it to the potter' "), told him so. How did he "know" Judas hanged himself? Well, Matthew reasoned, if it was good enough for Ahithophel (2 Sam. 17:23), who betrayed David, it would be good enough for Judas, Jesus' betrayer.

Other gospel stories, as we have seen, are so close to similar stories of the miracles wrought by Apollonius of Tyana, Pythagoras, Asclepius, Asclepiades the Physician, and others that we have to wonder whether in any or all such cases free-floating stories have been attached to all these heroic names at one time or another, much as the names of characters in jokes change in oral transmission. And this observation leads us to a concluding consideration. It is not only the miracle stories of the gospels that are parallel to the life stories of other heroes. In fact, as folklorist Alan Dundes has shown,[48] the gospel life of Jesus corresponds in most particulars with the worldwide paradigm of the Mythic Hero Archetype as delineated by Lord Raglan, Otto Rank, and others. Drawn from comparative studies of Indo-European and Semitic hero legends, this pattern contains twenty-two typical, recurrent elements.[49] Here is a list, highlighting those present in the story of Jesus:

1. *mother is royal virgin*
2. *father is a king*
3. father related to mother
4. *unusual conception*
5. *hero reputed to be son of god*
6. *attempt to kill hero*
7. *hero spirited away*
8. *reared* by foster parents *in a far country*
9. *no details of childhood*
10. *goes to future kingdom*
11. *is victor over king*
12. marries a princess (often daughter of predecessor)
13. *becomes king*
14. *for a time he reigns uneventfully*
15. *he prescribes laws*
16. *later loss favor with* gods or *his subjects*
17. *driven from throne and city*
18. *meets with mysterious death*
19. *often at the top of a hill*
20. *his children, if any, do not succeed him*
21. *his body is not buried*
22. *nonetheless has one or more holy sepulchres*

Jesus' mother Mary is a virgin, though not of royal descent unless one harmonizes the Lukan and Matthean genealogies to make one of them Mary's. Later apocrypha do make Mary Davidic. Joseph is of course "of the house of David," though not the reigning king—but that's just the point: The king is *coming*. There is no relation between Joseph and Mary. Jesus' conception is certainly irregular, miraculous. Jesus is the son of God, and he is immediately persecuted by the reigning king, Herod. In most hero legends, the persecutor is not only the king but the infant hero's father (as in the Oedipus story). This role has been split in Jesus' case: His earthly father, Joseph, is a royal heir, but not king, so there must also be a king to persecute him. Fleeing the persecution, the infant hero takes refuge in a far country, Egypt, though it is not foster parents who raise him, as usually in hero legends. (And yet Joseph and Mary may be understood as Jesus' foster parents in that his real father is God.) There are no details of Jesus' childhood in three of the gospels, and the one incident in Luke 2:41–52, where Jesus is displayed as a child prodigy, is itself a frequent mytheme in other hero tales not considered by Raglan. Jesus goes to Jerusalem to be acclaimed as king. He does not, however, take military power, so there is no contest with the old king (though one might see a parallel in Jesus' telling Pilate that he is the king of Truth, not of a worldly kingdom like Caesar's—John 18:36–37). Nor does he marry, though he is said to be followed by loyal women, one of them related to royalty (Luke 8:3). Does Jesus have an "uneventful reign, prescribing laws"? Not literally, but the pattern fits anyway, since we see Jesus holding court, for the moment unchallenged, in the temple (Mark 11–12). Instead of binding laws, he issues teachings, parables, and prophecies, which are taken with legal force by his followers. But suddenly the once-ardent crowd of admirers turns ugly and demands his blood, whereupon Jesus is driven forth from the city and crucified, accompanied by supernatural portents, atop Mount Calvary, the hill of Golgotha. He is temporarily buried, but his body turns up missing, leaving an empty tomb, which would seem to be within legitimate variant-distance of the ideal legend type. The holy sepulchre remains a testimony to his resurrection. He has no offspring, but his brother succeeds him as head of his community.

Traditionally, Christ-Myth theorists have argued that one finds a purely mythic conception of Jesus in the epistles and that the life of Jesus the historical teacher and healer as we read it in the gospels is a later historicization. This may indeed be so, but it is important to recognize the obvious: *The gospel story of Jesus is itself apparently mythic from first to last.* In the gospels the degree of historicization is actually quite minimal, mainly consisting of the addition of the layer derived from contemporary messiahs and prophets, as outlined above. One does not need to repair to the epistles to find a mythic Jesus. The gospel story itself is already pure legend. What can we say of a supposed historical figure whose life story conforms virtually in every detail to the Mythic Hero Archetype, with nothing, no "secular" or mundane information, left over? As Dundes is careful to point out, it doesn't prove there was no historical Jesus, for it is not implausible that a genuine, historical individual might become so lionized, even so deified, that his life and career would be completely assimilated to the Mythic Hero Archetype.[50] But if that happened, we could no longer be sure there had ever been a real person at the root of the whole thing. The stained glass would have become just too thick to peer through.

Alexander the Great, Caesar Augustus, Cyrus, King Arthur, and others have nearly suffered this fate. What keeps historians from dismissing them as mere myths, like Paul Bunyan, is that there is some residue. We know at least a bit of mundane information about them, perhaps quite a bit, that does not form part of any legend cycle. Or they are so intricately woven into the history of time that it is impossible to make sense of that history without them. But is this the case with Jesus? I fear it is not. The apparent links with Roman and Herodian figures is too loose, too doubtful for reasons I have already tried to explain. Thus it seems to me that Jesus must be categorized with other legendary founder figures including the Buddha, Krishna, and Lao-tzu. There may have been a real figure there, but there is simply no longer any way of being sure.

NOTES

1. Eg., Reginald H. Fuller, *The Foundations of New Testament Christology* (New York: Scribners, 1965); Maurice Casey, *From Jewish Prophet to Gentile God: The Origins and Development of New Testament Christology* (Louisville: Westminster/John Knox Press, 1991).

2. Mircea Eliade, *Yoga: Immortality and Freedom*, trans. Willard R. Trask (Princeton: Princeton University Press, 1969), p. 4: "The sacrifices that the European philosopher is prepared to make to attain truth in and for itself [include the] sacrifice of religious faith. . . ."

3. Paul Veyne, *Did the Greeks Believe in Their Myths? An Essay on the Constitutive Imagination*, trans. Paula Wissing (Chicago: University of Chicago Press, 1988), pp. 17–18.

4. Jacob Neusner, *Why No Gospels in Talmudic Judaism?* Brown Judaic Studies 135 (Atlanta: Scholars Press, 1988).

5. *Baba Mezia* 59b, trans. David L. Dungan, in *Sourcebook of Texts for the Comparative Study of the Gospels*, ed. Dungan and David R. Cartlidge, 67–68.

6. Mary Douglas, *Natural Symbols: Explorations in Cosmology*, pp. 54–64.

7. Harvey Falk, *Jesus the Pharisee: A New Look at the Jewishness of Jesus* (Mahwah: Paulist Press, 1985).

8. Herb Keinon, "Messiah When?" *Jerusalem Post*, August 30, 1997, p. 20.

9. Ibid.

10. "Lubavitchers Prepare to Answer Charge of Idolatry," *The Forward*, February 6, 1998, p. 14.

11. Ibid.

12. Jerome H. Neyrey, *An Ideology of Revolt: John's Christology in Social-Science Perspective* (Philadelphia: Fortress Press, 1988).

13. "Lubavitchers Prepare," p. 2.

14. Ibid., p. 14.

15. H. Richard Niebuhr, *Christ and Culture* (New York: Harper & Brothers, 1951).

16. Wayne Meeks, "The Man from Heaven in Johannine Sectarianism," *Journal of Biblical Literature* 91 (1972): 44–72.

17. James R. Lewis, *The Gods Have Landed: New Religions From Other Worlds* (Albany: State University of New York Press, 1995).
18. J. L. Houlden, *Ethics in the New Testament* (New York: Oxford University Press, 1977), pp. 35–41.
19. Stevan L. Davies, *Revolt of the Widows: The Social World of the Apocryphal Acts* (Carbondale: Southern Illinois University Press), pp. 30–31.
20. Randel Helms, *Gospel Fictions* (Amherst, N.Y.: Prometheus Books, 1989), pp. 146–47.
21. Hans Jonas, *The Gnostic Religion: The Message of the Alien God and the Beginnings of Christianity*, 2d ed (Boston: Beacon Press, 1963), pp. 320–40.
22. Matti Moosa, *Extremist Shi'ites: The Ghulat Sects* (Syracuse: Syracuse University Press), 1988, p. xvi.
23. Burton L. Mack, *A Myth of Innocence: Mark and Christian Origins* (Minneapolis: Fortress Press, 1991), p. 282. Matthew's redaction carries the same tendency further. In Matt. 23:35, he adds the patronymic "son of Berachiah" to the name "Zechariah" from a Q saying, turning it into an (anachronistic) reference by Jesus *back* to Zechariah, son of Baruch, a victim of Jewish terrorists who had entered Jerusalem just before it fell to the Romans! (Josephus, *The Jewish War* IV, V, 4)
24. Philo, *Flaccus* 36–39, trans. C. D. Yonge, *The Works of Philo* (Peabody: Hendrickson, 1993).
25. Plutarch, *The Lives of the Noble Grecians and Romans*, trans. John Dryden, rev. ed. (New York: Modern Library, n.d.).
26. In Stanley Jerome Isser, *The Dositheans: A Samaritan Sect in Late Antiquity*. Studies in Judaism in Late Antiquity, vol. 17. (Leiden: E. J. Brill, 1976), pp. 66, 130.
27. Raphael Patai, *The Messiah Texts* (New York: Avon Books, 1979), pp. 25–26.
28. A. D. Crown, "Some Traces of Heterodox Theology in the Samaritan Book of Joshua," *Bulletin of the John Rylands Library* 50 (1967), pp. 178–98; in Isser, *The Dositheans*, p. 130.
29. Isser, *The Dositheans*, p. 129.
30. Alfred Loisy, *The Origins of the New Testament*, trans. L. P. Jacks (New York: Collier Books, 1962), p. 192.
31. G. R. S. Mead, *Did Jesus Live 100 B.C.?* (New Hyde Park: University Books, 1968).
32. Hugh J. Schonfield, *According to the Hebrews* (London: Duckworth, 1937).
33. George A. Wells, *The Jesus of the Early Christians: A Study in Christian Origins* (London: Pemberton Books, 1971), pp. 5–6, 92, 242–43, 310–11.
34. Veyne, *Did the Greeks Believe in their Myths?* p. 106.
35. Ibid., pp. 1–2, 13–14, 53.
36. Charles L. Talbert, *Luke and the Gnostics* (New York: Abingdon, 1966), pp. 30–32.
37. Elaine Pagels, *The Gnostic Gospels* (New York: Random House, 1979), pp. 3–27.
38. Arthur Drews, *The Christ Myth*, trans. C. Delisle Burns, 3rd ed. (Amherst, N.Y.: Prometheus Books, 1998), pp. 271–72.
39. Karl Ludwig Schmidt, "Jesus Christ," in *Twentieth Century Theology in the Making, I Themes of Biblical Theology*, ed. Jaroslav Pelikan. Fontana Library of Theology and Philosophy (London: Fontana Books, 1969), pp. 93–120.

40. Tomashevsky, "Thematics," trans. Lee T. Lemon and Marion J. Reis, in *Russian Formalist Criticism: Four Essays* (Lincoln and London: University of Nebraska Press, 1965), p. 90.

41. Rudolf Bultmann, *History of the Synoptic Tradition*, trans. John Marsh, 2d ed. (New York: Harper & Row, 1968); Drews, *The Christ Myth*; T. W. Manson, *The Sayings of Jesus* (London: SCM Press, 1948).

42. Manson's summary of the parable, p. 61.

43. In Solomon Schechter, *Some Aspects of Rabbinic Theology* (New York: Macmillan Company, 1910), p. 327.

44. Jacob Neusner, *In Search of Talmudic Biography: The Problem of the Attributed Saying*. Brown Judaic Studies 70 (Chico: Scholars Press, 1984).

45. Helms, *Gospel Fictions*, 1900.

46. Thomas L. Brodie, "Luke the Literary Interpreter: Luke-Acts as a Systematic Rewriting and Updating of the Elijah-Elisha Narrative in 1 and 2 Kings." Ph.D. diss., Pontifica Universita S. Tommaso d'Aquino [Vatican], 1981; Thomas L. Brodie, "Reopening the Quest for Proto-Luke: The Systematic Use of Judges 6–12 in Luke 16:1–18:8," *Journal of Higher Criticism* 2, no. 1 (spring 1995): 68–101.

47. Earl Doherty, "The Jesus Puzzle," *Journal of Higher Criticism* 4, no. 2 (fall 1997): 68–102.

48. Alan Dundes, "The Hero Pattern and the Life of Jesus," in *In Quest of the Hero*, ed. Robert A. Segal (Princeton: Princeton University Press, 1990), pp., 179–223.

49. Ibid., p. 190.

Conclusion

THE MANY BEHIND THE ONE

Our survey of the early Christianities has indicated that the cherished image of a single early Church untainted by heresy, with everyone of one heart and soul worshipping one Christ, and eventually producing a harmonious canon of scripture speaking a single gospel with a single voice—is a myth. In every case, an earlier diversity has been unsuccessfully hidden away behind a screen of history as the finally dominant faction wished it had been. Even mainstream scholarship, while recognizing a significant degree of diversity and disunity both in the New Testament and among the range of early Christian sects, has been slow to depart from what Burton Mack calls "the Big Bang" model of Christian origins. That is, most scholars have gone on blithely assuming that there was a single Jesus of Nazareth, some sort of prophet and reformer, who was crucified, after which his followers experienced some sort of visions of Jesus as if risen from the dead. Only then, we are told, did the diversity begin, as various people interpreted and symbolized Jesus and his exaltation in terms appropriate to their own cultures.

And yet there were clues that there could have been no primordial zone of oneness even this far behind the scenes. For instance, the current crop of critical lives of Jesus present us with an embarrassment of riches. There are too many plausible portraits, each centering on a different selection of gospel data. None is particularly far-fetched, but neither are they easily compatible. Thus we have the same sort of range of evidence for Jesus that led F. C. Baur and Walter Bauer to deny a single, monochrome early Christianity. In some sense, then, we must reckon with several different Jesuses.

The gospels' Jesuses are each complex syntheses of various other, earlier, Jesus characters. Some of these may have been reflections of various messianic prophets and revolutionaries, others the fictive counterparts of itinerant charismatics, and still others historicizations of mythical Corn Kings and Gnostic Aions. I think it is an open question whether a historical Jesus had anything to do with any of these Jesuses, much less the Jesuses of the gospels. Each is the figurehead, the totem, of a particular kind of Jesus community or Christ cult, and we will never know whether and to what extent each community reflects a remembered Jesus opposed to a Jesus or Christ who is a concretization of its own beliefs and values.

INDEX

Abba (Father), 14, 107
Achilles Tatius, 217, 225
Achtemeier, Paul, 62, 63, 73
Acts of Andrew, 49
Acts of John, 16, 49
Acts of Paul, 49
Acts of Peter, 49
Acts of Thomas, 25, 49
Adonis, 86, 89, 91, 92, 93
Adoptionism, 30, 55, 85, 227, 228
Agnosticism, 10, 16, 17, 252
Akiba, 101, 231
Alawi sect, 241
Alexander Jannaeus, 249
Alexander the Great, 35, 36, 42, 112, 213, 216, 224, 260
Al-Ghazali, 116, 118, 119, 125, 127, 144, 146, 147, 167
al-Hallaj, 82, 94, 120
Ali, 53, 57, 240, 241
Allegro, John M., 52, 72
Allen, Charlotte, 166
Anath, 86, 90
Anaximander, 10
Andrew (disciple), 104
Anthia, 216, 217

Antisthenes of Athens, 114, 155
Apelles, 26
Aphrodite, 11, 86, 89
Apocalypse of Adam, 44, 45
Apocalypse of Paul, 134
Apocalypse of Peter, 134
Apocryphal Acts of the Apostles, 16, 49, 103, 138, 262
Apocryphon of John, 240
Apollo, 35, 161, 175
Apollonius of Tyana, 15, 35, 37, 38, 40, 41, 42, 84, 213, 221, 223, 238, 258
Apollonius of Tyre, 218, 225
Apollos, 49, 84, 103
apologetics, 98, 99, 176, 178, 204
apologists, 10, 11, 88, 91, 98, 103, 104, 106, 166, 179, 206, 252
Apuleius, 219, 225
aretalogy/ical, 35, 40, 42, 43, 49, 103, 213, 221, 222, 224
Arius/Arians, 13, 27
Asclepiades, 192, 258
Asclepius, 32, 38, 39, 161, 192, 228, 258
Athanasius, 13, 26, 32
Athena, 16, 40

INDEX

Attis, 68, 86, 88, 89, 91, 92, 189
Auerbach, Eric, 201, 211

Baal, 86, 90, 91, 189
Bab, 57, 58
Baha'i Faith, 57
Bailie, Gil, 177, 209
Balder, 175, 176, 179, 180, 185, 207
baptism of Jesus, 14
Barabbas, 203, 204, 248
Bardesanes, 24
Barth, Gerhard, 111
Basilides, 26, 27, 187, 190
Bauer, Bruno, 17, 253
Bauer, Walter, 17, 22, 24, 25, 26, 27, 28, 29, 44, 108, 112, 265
Baur, Ferdinand Christian,, 17, 22, 23, 24, 28, 29, 31, 32, 44, 265
Beloved Disciple, 58, 84, 197, 201
Berger, Peter L., 209
Bergman, Ingmar, 171
Bharati, Agehananda, 102, 111
Blavatsky, Madame Helena Petrovna, 147
Blomberg, Craig, 167
Bodhisattva, 32, 50, 82, 94, 126, 181
Book of Thomas the Contender, 25, 34, 35, 43, 72
Borg, Marcus, 241
Bornkamm, Günther, 15, 19, 111
Bousset, Wilhelm, 92, 94
Brandon, S. G. F., 14, 18, 59, 109, 112
Breech, James, 241
Brodie, Thomas L., 257, 263
Brown, Peter, 44, 111
Brown, Raymond E., 89, 95
Buddha/Siddhartha/Gotama, 37, 82, 126, 136, 147, 261
Buddhism, 32, 50, 83, 94, 129, 133, 136, 147, 181
Bultmann, Rudolf, 15, 19, 61, 63, 70, 73, 98, 99, 102, 103, 106, 110, 111, 148, 163, 166, 167, 178, 239, 250, 251, 253, 257, 263
Burkert, Walter, 170

Caiaphas, Joseph, 200, 201
Callirhoe, 214, 215, 216, 224
Calvin, John, 10, 104, 111, 173
Carabbas, 205, 206, 242, 248
Casey, Maurice, 102, 111, 261
Cephas, 49, 53, 84, 103, 201
Cerdo, 25
Cerinthus, 55
Chaereas, 214, 215, 216, 224
Chalcedon(ian), 11, 13
Charikleia, 218
Chariton, 214, 224
Chilton, Bruce, 182, 184, 196, 210
Chloe, 217, 218, 225
Christ-Myth Theory, 85, 115, 166, 207, 228, 250, 251, 260, 263
Cicero, 154, 250
Cleomenes, 244, 245
Clitophon, 217, 225
Cobb, John B., Jr., 177, 209
Collingwood, R. G., 97, 110
Constantine, 12, 24, 32, 56
Coote, Robert B., 210
Couchoud, M., 85, 94
Crates, 158, 159, 162
Cronos, 175, 176
Crossan, John Dominic,, 13, 14, 16, 18, 19, 48, 184, 201, 210, 222, 241, 242
Crown, A. D., 262
crucifixion of Jesus, 9, 14, 47, 55, 56, 76, 77, 78, 114, 146, 148, 149, 189, 196, 207, 215, 216, 221, 222, 228, 245, 248, 249, 258, 260, 265
crucifixions, 42, 187, 189, 214, 216
Cupid, 219
Curetes, 175, 176, 179, 180, 196, 200, 204
Cybele, 86, 87, 92
Cynics/ism, 14, 16, 47, 48, 49, 50, 51, 68, 69, 71, 83, 114, 115, 116, 126, 131, 133, 137, 143, 148, 150, 151, 154, 155, 156, 157, 162, 163, 167, 181, 242, 252, 253

Dahl, Nils, 207, 211

Index

Daphnis, 217, 218, 225
Davies, Stevan L., 45, 49, 50, 71, 167, 181, 210, 237, 262
Dead Sea Scrolls, 14, 18, 31, 32, 59, 60, 72, 115, 177, 191, 233
Demonax, 154
Derrida, Jacques, 11, 12, 18
Descartes, René, 10, 11
Dialogue of the Savior, 33, 34
Diatessaron of Tatian, 24
Didache, 48, 50, 84, 194
Dio Chrysostom, 150, 151, 152, 153, 154, 156, 158, 159
Diodorus Siculus, 205, 250
Diogenes Laertius, 151, 153, 154, 155, 157, 158
Diogenes of Sinope, 69, 114, 126, 143, 151, 153, 154, 155, 156, 160, 162
Dionysus, 68, 86, 87, 92, 93, 176, 179, 196, 200, 207, 234, 250
Docetic, 16, 25, 57, 138, 199, 204, 228, 237, 251
Docetism, 16, 25, 31, 83, 90, 190, 203, 237, 238
Dodd, C. H., 54, 55, 72
Doherty, Earl, 258, 263
Dositheans/ism, 61, 262
Dositheus, 33, 60, 247
Doughty, Darrell J., 34, 35, 45, 224
Douglas, Mary, 115, 124, 166, 230, 261
Downie, R. Angus, 211
Downing, F. Gerald, 14, 48, 71, 114, 126, 150, 162, 167, 210
Drews, Arthur, 17, 94, 250, 251, 253, 262, 262
Druze, 120
Dundes, Alan, 259, 260, 263
Durkheim, Emil, 170

Ebeling, Gerhard, 178
Ebionites/ism, 24, 30, 31, 32, 52, 59, 60, 72, 107, 109, 148, 227
Egyptian, The, 230, 246, 247, 248
Eisenman, Robert, 14, 18, 58, 59, 60, 72, 112
Eisler, Robert, 14, 18, 59

El, 90
Eliade, Mircea, 94, 95, 261
Eliezer ben Hyrkanus, 99, 100, 101, 102, 104, 105, 107, 229, 230
Elijah, 51, 63, 64, 65, 66, 109, 123, 210, 230, 263
Elisha, 63, 65, 69, 181, 210, 257, 263
Elliott-Bins, L. E., 64, 73
Elymas bar Jesus, 248
Empedocles, 35
Encratism, Encratites, 24, 28, 31, 32
Enkidu, 89
Enoch-Metatron, 102, 161
Enosh Uthra, 61, 81
Epictetus, 150, 151, 154, 155, 156, 157, 158, 159, 160
Epicurus/Epicurean, 69, 126, 131, 162
Epistle of the Apostles, 34
Essenes, 59, 60, 61, 252
Eusebius, 21, 24, 27, 28, 58, 108, 109
Eutyches, 13
exorcism, 15, 252
exorcist(s), 14, 15, 108, 252

Falk, Harvey, 14, 18, 111, 231, 261
Firmicus Maternus, 88, 94
Fish, Stanley, 209
Fortna, Robert, 62, 65, 73
Frazer, James, 91, 205, 206, 207, 211
Freyne, Sean, 112
Frigga, 175, 180
Fuller, Reginald H., 261
Funk, Robert W., 72, 241

Gager, John G., 14, 19
Galilean, 14, 16, 79, 107, 108, 109, 182, 252
Galilee, 48, 64, 65, 66, 79, 106, 107, 108, 109, 110, 110, 112, 162, 167
Gamaliel, 100, 246
Gandhi, Mohandas K., 171, 184
Gärtner, Bertil, 188, 210
Gaston, Lloyd, 81, 94
Genette, Gerard, 225
Georgi, Dieter, 49, 71
Gerharsson, Birger, 98, 99, 111

INDEX

Ghulat sect, 241, 262
Girard, René, 17, 169–211
Gnostic, 26, 27, 31, 32, 34, 45, 55, 60, 79, 80, 81, 82, 83, 85, 90, 93, 132, 148, 235, 237, 240, 251, 266
Gnosticism, 24, 32, 33, 45, 80, 81, 82, 83, 84, 239, 240
Gnostics, 27, 28, 32, 61, 82, 83, 84, 94, 120, 251
Goffman, Erving, 210
Goldziher, Ignaz, 72
Gorion, Bin, 211
Gospel according to the Nazarenes, 30
Gospel according to the Egyptians, 26, 30
Gospel according to the Hebrews, 26, 30
Gospel of Bartholomew, 191
Gospel of Peter, 25, 249
Gospel of Philip, 33, 45
Gospel of Thomas the Israelite, 43
Griffin, C. S., 201, 211
Griffin, David, 177, 209

Habrocomes, 216
Hadad, 90
Haenchen, Ernst, 71
Hahn, Ferdinand, 102, 111
halakah, 14, 101, 104, 105, 109, 229, 230, 231, 232
Hamerton-Kelly, Robert G., 170, 177, 180, 184, 209, 210
Hanina ben Dosa, 14, 99, 108
Hanson, Anthony T., 52, 72
Harvey, A. E., 123
Hasidism, 70, 108, 115, 229, 231, 235
Hegesippus, 58, 59
Heirs of Jesus, 52, 53, 54, 57, 58, 62, 75, 107, 108, 187, 234
Held, Hans-Joachim, 111
Heliodorus, 218, 225
Helms, Randel, 238, 257, 262, 263
Herakles, 90, 228, 250
Herod Antipas, 186, 249, 251
Herod the Great, 249, 259
Hesse, Hermann, 100, 111
Hill, Scott D., 181, 210

Hillel, 14, 230, 247
historical Jesus, 9, 12, 13, 14, 15, 16, 17, 19, 21, 84, 117, 149, 208, 228, 250, 253, 258, 266
Hoffer, Eric, 209
Hoffmann, R. Joseph, 44
Honi the Circle-Drawer, 14, 108
Horsley, Richard A., 14, 19, 50, 162, 167, 184, 210
Horus, 86, 90
Hother, 175, 186, 191
Houlden, J. L., 236, 262
Hume, David, 11
Hussein, 241

Iamblichus, 35, 36, 45, 215, 219, 224
Ignatius, 25, 27, 163
Imam, 57, 59, 101, 241, 248
Infancy Gospel of Matthew, 43, 126
Ishtar, 86, 91
Isidore, 26
Isis, 86, 88, 90, 92
Islam, 52, 56, 57, 77, 101, 112, 115, 116, 117, 123, 125, 126, 137, 148, 172, 190, 211, 229
Ismail'is, 187
Isser, Stanley Jerome, 262

Jainists/ism, 133
James the Just, Brother of Jesus, 18, 52, 53, 57, 58, 59, 60, 61, 73, 78, 108, 109, 112, 241, 248
James, son of Zebedee, 16, 52, 53, 187, 198
Jeremias, Joachim, 15, 19, 98, 110, 111
Jesus ben Ananias, 109, 242, 243, 248
Jesus ben Sapphiah, 248
Jesus Seminar, 16, 72
Jews, 30, 31, 32, 58, 65, 66, 68, 76, 78, 87, 97, 105, 110, 111, 130, 173, 204, 230, 230, 231, 232, 233, 242, 244, 248, 253
Johannon ben Zakkai, 97, 98, 109, 254
John the Baptist, 60, 61, 70, 109, 125, 129, 186, 190, 203, 247, 249
John, son of Zebedee, 16, 52, 53, 104, 126, 187, 198

Index

Jonas, Hans, 240, 262
Joseph of Gischala, 244
Josephus, Flavius, 15, 42, 59, 109, 203, 230, 242, 243, 244, 245, 246, 262
Joshua ben Perechiah, 249
Judaism, 14, 19, 29, 30, 32, 67, 69, 76, 77, 86, 93, 97, 99, 104, 105, 106, 107, 112, 116, 178, 229, 233, 262
Judas Iscariot, 186, 188, 189, 190, 191, 193, 197, 198, 199, 210, 211, 258
Judas of Galilee, 54, 58, 246
Justin Martyr, 24, 88

Kahn, Herman, 209
Kee, Howard Clark, 106, 112
Kelber, Werner, 184
Kelber, Werner, 224
Kermode, Frank, 210, 211
Kingsbury, Jack Dean, 224
Klein, Günter, 188
Kloppenborg, John, 79, 113, 166
Knox, John, 80, 94
Koester, Helmut, 17, 25, 28, 29, 33, 42, 43, 44, 45, 84, 149, 213, 221, 222
Koran, 66, 101, 112, 122, 125, 144, 166, 203
Kramer, Werner, 81, 94
Küng, Hans, 179, 209

Law, Torah, 23, 30, 31, 59, 60, 66, 67, 68, 70, 76, 77, 97, 99, 100, 102, 103, 104, 105, 106, 109, 118, 165, 229, 235, 253, 254, 255, 256
Leibniz, Gotthold, 11
Leipoldt, Joahannes, 224
Leucippe, 217, 225
Lévi-Strauss, Claude, 12, 174
Loisy, Alfred Firmin, 196, 249, 262
Loki, 175, 186, 191
Longus, 217, 225
Lubavitchers, 228, 229, 231, 232, 233, 235, 236, 261
Lucian of Samosata, 47, 79, 154, 155, 162, 163
Lüdemann, Gerd, 112
Luther, Martin, 127

Maccoby, Hyam, 14, 18, 172, 180, 186, 188, 189, 197, 198, 203, 204, 209, 210, 211
Mack, Burton L., 14, 17, 28, 43, 44, 45, 47, 48, 49, 50, 52, 54, 56, 58, 62, 63, 64, 67, 68, 70, 71, 75, 77, 78, 79, 93, 104, 107, 110, 111, 113, 114, 115, 126, 148, 149, 150, 165, 166, 169, 177, 180, 186, 209, 222, 229, 241, 242, 248, 262, 265
Magdalene, Mary, 238, 245
magic, 14
magician(s), 14, 16
Mahayana, 32, 82, 181
Malherbe, Abraham J., 162, 167
Mandaeans, 61, 81
Mani, 24, 82, 83
Manicheans/ism, 28, 84
Manson, T. W., 253, 262
Marcion, 27, 29, 30, 44, 80
Marcionites/Marcionism,, 24, 25, 28, 29, 32
Margoliouth, D.S., 116, 147, 166
Matthew (disciple), 25, 167
Mattill, A. J. Jr., 14, 18, 166
McNeile, A. H., 98, 111
Mead, G. R. S., 249, 262
Meeks, Wayne, 236, 261
Melchizedek, 26, 32, 81
Meleager, 48, 69, 162
Menander, 25
Menippus, 48
Meyer, Ben F., 15, 19
Mishnah/Mishnaic, 97, 98, 99, 100, 101, 102, 103, 104, 106, 109, 110, 229, 231, 253, 257
Mithras), 87, 92
Montanists/ism, 27
Moosa, Matti, 240, 262
Morrice, William, 118, 167
Moses, 30, 35, 42, 60, 61, 63, 64, 65, 66, 70, 73, 79, 81, 100, 104, 107, 109, 112, 161, 193, 247, 254, 258
Muhammad, 53, 57, 66, 83, 99, 101, 117, 122, 126, 130, 137, 166, 190, 240, 241

Müller, Max, 92
Murray, Gilbert, 209
Muslim(s), 25, 53, 56, 57, 117, 124, 129, 137, 148, 199, 222
Musonius Rufus, 151, 152, 154, 155, 158
Mystery Religions/cults, 87, 88, 91, 92, 93, 235

Nag Hammadi, 26, 32, 33, 44, 60, 72, 81, 90, 92, 240
Nazarenes, 31, 73, 203
Nazareth, 17, 19, 29, 47, 60, 66, 73, 101, 108
Nazoreans, 31, 60, 61, 66, 73, 83, 84, 85, 107, 109, 228
Nestorius, 13
Neusner, Jacob, 17, 98, 99, 100, 101, 103, 104, 107, 111, 229, 257, 261, 263
Neyrey, Jerome H., 17, 235, 236, 261
Nickelsburg, George W. E., 225
Nicolaitans, 26
Niebuhr, H. Richard, 236, 261
Noth, Martin, 70, 73, 163
Nurbakhsh, Javad, 116, 119, 120, 122, 124, 136, 140, 141, 167
Nusayri sect, 241

Odeberg, Hugo, 111
Oedipus, 173, 174, 179, 185, 189, 190, 207, 208, 259
Oenomaus, 48
On the 8th and the 9th, 32
Osiris, 86, 88, 89, 90, 91, 94
Otto, Rudolf, 170
Overman, J. Andrew, 112

Pagels, Elaine, 251, 262
Pannenberg, Wolfhart, 209
Papias, 53
Patai, Raphael, 262
Patterson, Stephen J., 127, 167
Paul, 23, 24, 25, 27, 29, 30, 48, 49, 55, 59, 71, 80, 81, 83, 84, 88, 92, 103, 107, 112, 139, 202

Pentheus, 207
Peregrinus, Proteus, 47, 155, 162, 163
Perkins, Pheme, 45
Perrin, Norman, 15, 19, 45, 102, 111, 116, 117, 167, 178
Persephone, 89
Perseus, 87
Peter, Simon, 23, 24, 25, 27, 52, 53, 55, 126, 182, 186, 187, 188, 191, 193, 194, 197, 198, 201, 202
Petronius, 220, 225
Pharisees, 14, 31, 43, 59, 60, 66, 67, 68, 70, 97, 105, 106, 107, 110, 121, 139, 140, 142, 163, 194, 195, 231, 261
Philo, 68, 152, 163, 205, 227, 262
Philostratus, 15, 37, 213, 221, 238
Photius, 215
Pilate, Pontius, 14, 39, 148, 200, 202, 203, 204, 223, 243, 245, 246, 248, 249, 250, 251, 260
Pillars, 52, 53, 54, 57, 58, 62, 75, 107, 109, 201, 234, 248
Pistis Sophia, 34, 251
Plato, 10, 32, 68, 163
Plutarch, 45, 152, 244, 245, 162
Polycarp, Epistle of, 25
Powell, Mark Allan, 224, 225
Price, Robert M., 167
Pritz, Ray A., 112
Propp, Vladimir, 174
Psyche, 219
Pythagoras, 35, 36, 45, 258

Q Document, 17, 33, 43, 47, 48, 49, 50, 51, 52, 61, 63, 69, 70, 79, 84, 108, 113, 114, 115, 116, 117, 118, 121, 122, 125, 126, 127, 128, 130, 132, 134, 140, 145, 146, 147, 148, 150, 160, 161, 162, 163, 166, 222, 223, 224, 242, 262
Quirinius, 249

rabbi, 14, 15, 31, 66, 98, 99, 105, 107, 161, 167, 228, 229, 230, 231, 232, 233, 242, 247, 253, 254, 255, 256

rabbinic, 14, 65, 67, 81, 98, 99, 105, 110, 162, 257, 263
Raglan, Lord, 259, 260
Ramakrishna, 102
Ranck, Otto, 45, 259
Reardon, B. P., 224
Reitzenstein, Richard, 32, 73, 92
Remus, 186
resurrection of Jesus, 9, 10, 27, 34, 35, 43, 47, 54, 55, 56, 61, 93, 148, 149, 179, 215, 221, 224, 228, 251, 260, 264
Riesenfeld, Harald, 98, 99, 110
Robinson, James M., 17, 28, 29, 33, 34, 43, 44, 45, 149, 213, 221
Robinson, John A.T., 55, 72
Robinson, Neal, 211
Romans, 14, 15, 28, 40, 47, 52, 63, 67, 79, 97, 105, 110, 182, 183, 202, 203, 205, 206, 210, 242, 243, 244, 246, 249, 261, 262
Rome, 24, 27, 40, 45, 68, 110, 112, 183, 203, 244, 246, 247, 248
Romulus, 40, 186, 207
Rorty, Richard, 10, 11, 18
Rudolph, Kurt, 44

Salome, 249
Samaritans, 31, 60, 64, 65, 66, 79, 107, 109, 137, 234, 245, 247, 248, 262
Sanders, E. P., 15, 19, 162, 167
Sanders, Jack T., 112
Sanhedrin, 14, 97, 109, 110, 200, 201, 202, 247, 256
Satan, 125, 126, 132, 187, 191
Satornilus/Saturninus, 25
Schechter, Solomon, 263
Schleiermacher, Friedrich Daniel Ernst, 138
Schmidt, Karl Ludwig, 251, 252, 262
Schmithals, Walter, 80, 82, 83, 84, 85, 94, 111, 188
Schneerson, Menachem Mendel, 15, 54, 228, 229, 231, 232, 233, 235, 236
Schoeps, Hans-Joachim, 44
Schonfield, Hugh J., 14, 18, 59, 249, 262
Schüssler Fiorenza, Elisabeth, 14, 19, 172, 173, 184, 209
Schwager, Raymund, 177, 209
Schweitzer, Albert, 12, 13, 18, 113, 166
Scubla, Lucien, 209
Segundo, Juan Luis, 14, 19
Seneca, 150, 151, 153, 156, 157, 158, 159, 225
Serapis, 88
Servetus, Michael, 173
Set, 86
Seth, 26, 32, 81
Shankara, 147
Shepherd of Hermas, 27
Shi'ites, 57, 60, 101, 241, 262
Signs Source, 62, 65
Simeon bar Cleophas, 109
Simon bar Giora, 244, 248
Simon bar Kochba, 105, 111, 231
Simon Magus, 33, 60, 81, 82, 187, 247
Simon of Cyrene, 187, 190
Simon the Leper, 193
Simon the Pharisee, 194
Simon the Zealot, 187, 189, 191
Skeptics, 10
Smith, Jonathan Z., 88, 89, 90, 91, 95, 170
Smith, Joseph, 126
Smith, Morton, 14, 18
Socrates, 10, 47, 69, 162, 222
Son of God, 14, 27, 35, 36, 40, 55, 65, 76, 78, 100, 125, 227, 238, 245, 248, 259
Sophia of Jesus Christ, 33, 34
Sophocles, 173, 208
Spiegel, Shalom, 211
Spinoza, Baruch, 11
Stanzas of Dzyan, 147
Stobaeus, 152
Stoics/ism, 78, 162, 163, 253
Strauss, David Friedrich, 60
Strecker, Georg, 44
Sufi Q, 146, 148
Sufis/ism, 82, 115, 116, 117, 118, 119, 120, 123, 123, 126, 127, 128, 131,

132, 133, 134, 135, 136, 138, 141, 146, 147, 148, 167
Sunni Islam, 57, 101, 241

Taheb, 64, 234
Talbert, Charles L., 41, 45, 213, 221, 225, 251, 262
Talmud, 104, 249, 255, 263
Tammuz, 86, 91
Teacher of Righteousness, 59, 60
Teicher, Jacob L., 59, 72
Temple (Jerusalem), 14, 31, 53, 59, 67, 104, 105, 182, 183, 185, 196, 200, 210, 233, 243, 244, 252, 253, 260
Thales, 10
Theagenes, 218
Theissen, Gerd, 48, 50, 71, 72, 83, 84, 94, 103, 111, 112, 115, 210, 229
Theravada, 32
Theseus, 90, 250
Theudas, 15, 230, 246, 247, 248
Thiering, Barbara, 45
Thomas (disciple), 25, 42, 58, 104, 120, 165, 188, 238
Titans, 176, 196, 200
Todorov, Tzvetan, 175, 209, 225
Tödt, H. E., 102, 111
Tomashevsky, Boris, 252, 263
Trinity, 11, 12, 112
Tübingen School, 27
Twelve, the, 23, 24, 30, 53, 80, 110, 164, 187, 188, 198, 258

Ulansey, David, 94
Uthman, 241

Vaage, Leif E., 113, 114, 166

Valentinus/Valentinians, 26, 27, 81, 82, 84, 85
Van Gennep, Arnold, 94
Vedanta Sutras, 147
Vermaseren, Maarten, 91, 95
Vermes, Geza, 14, 18, 102, 108, 111, 112
Veyne, Paul, 228, 250, 261, 262
Völter, Daniel, 163

Weeden, Theodore J., 44, 192, 211
Weiss, Johannes, 15, 19
Welburn, Andrew J., 44
Wells, George A., 115, 166, 250, 251, 262
Wendland, Paul, 206, 207
Whitehead, Alfred North, 177
Wiener, Anthony J., 209
Williams, James G., 177, 209, 210
Williams, Sam K., 76, 78, 79, 94
Wilson, Bryan, 89
Winter, T. J., 116, 145, 147, 167
Wrede, William, 18, 55, 72, 113, 166
Wright, N. T., 166

Xenophon of Ephesus, 216, 224

Yavneh, 97, 98, 100, 109, 229

Zagreus, 87
Zealots, 14, 18, 59, 60, 244
Zeus, 16, 48, 87, 114, 154, 156, 175, 176, 196, 200, 204, 207
Zoroaster/Zoroastrian, 20, 32, 45, 81
Zostrianos, 32

SCRIPTURE INDEX

GENESIS
9:4–6, p. 76
19:30–38, p. 106
chapter 22, p. 204
23:18, p. 254
27:40, p. 108
28:12, p. 126
37:9, p. 66

EXODUS
5:15–19, p. 70
chapter 14, p. 63
chapter 16, p. 63
chapter 18, p. 258
32:32, p. 79

NUMBERS
11:14–15, p. 63
11:18–23, p. 63
11:31–32, p. 63
12:1–15, p. 193
chapter 16, p. 198

DEUTERONOMY
8:17–18, p. 141
18:15–16, p. 64
18:18–22, p. 247
30:12, p. 229

JOSHUA
24:14, p. 192
24:19, p. 192

JUDGES
chapters 6–12, p. 263
13:15–20, p. 238
19:22, p. 204

1 SAMUEL
6:7–9, p. 198
13:5–15, p. 183
15:1–35, p. 183

2 SAMUEL
17:23, p. 258

1 KINGS
5:3, p. 183
7:17–24, p. 63
12:1–20, p. 64
17:8–16, p. 63

SCRIPTURE INDEX

2 KINGS
4:1–7, p. 63
4:11–37, p. 192
4:32–37, p. 257
4:32–35, p. 63
4:42–44, p. 63
5:10, p. 63

1 CHRONICLES
22:8, p. 183

2 MACCABEES
6:18–31, p. 77
chapter 7, p. 77
7:37–38, p. 77

4 MACCABEES
chapters 5–6, p. 77
6:27–29, p. 77

JOB
9:6, p. 52

PSALMS
2:1–3, p. 108
2:2, p. 227
2:7, pp. 55, 227
19:3–4, p. 173
22, pp. 223, 258
22:1, p. 258
22:22–24, p. 223
100, p. 233
110, p. 103

PROVERBS
chapter 8, p. 118
22:10, p. 170

CANTICLES
2:14, p. 256

WISDOM OF SOLOMON
2:13, p. 125
2:16–18, p. 258
2:18, p. 125

SIRACH
51:23–27, p. 254

TOBIT
2:7–8, p. 137
12:19–20, p. 238

ISAIAH
1:10–17, p. 118
29:13, p. 106
chapter 53, pp. 77, 197
53:4–5, p. 172
53:6, p. 172
53:12, p. 197

JEREMIAH
7:21–26, p. 30
8:8, p. 30

EZEKIEL
8:14, p. 86

DANIEL
chapter 7, pp. 54, 103
9:21–22, p. 117

JOEL
1:11–15, p. 195

ZECHARIAH
11:12, p. 258
11:13, pp. 189, 258
chapter 12, p. 103
12:11, p. 86, 90

MALACHI
3:7, p. 255
4:5, p. 64

MATTHEW
1:22–23, p. 258
1:21, pp. 37, 84, 85
2:5–6, p. 258
2:15, p. 258
2:17–18, p. 258
2:23, p. 258

3:7, p. 129
3:8, p. 129
3:9, p. 233
3:12, p. 92
4:9, p. 79
5:10, p. 257
5:17–19, pp. 23, 30, 106
5:19, p. 118
5:20–48, p. 31
5:22, pp. 253, 256
5:23–24, p. 118
5:20, pp. 127, 253
5:31, p. 253
5:37, p. 253
5:40–42, p. 257
5:43–44, p. 257
6:1–18, p. 140
6:2–4, p. 254
6:7–8, p. 140
6:16–18, p. 141
6:19–21, pp. 130, 132
6:21, p. 256
6:22–23, p. 128
6:24, pp. 130, 136
6:26, p. 256
6:30–33, p. 256
6:31–33, p. 132
6:34, p. 256
7:1–2, pp. 139, 253, 256
7:3–5, p. 253
7:6, pp. 120, 164
7:7, p. 256
7:21–23, p. 23
7:24–27, pp. 134, 253
8:5–13, p. 63
8:10, p. 79
8:20, pp. 48, 132, 133
10:3, p. 189
10:5 ff., p. 122
10:5, pp. 31, 66
10:5–6, p. 234
10:5–15, pp. 48, 52
10:12–13, p. 122
10:16, p. 256
10:24–25, pp. 103, 192
10:25, p. 254

10:29–31, p. 253
10:30, p. 256
10:34–36, p. 184
10:38, pp. 47, 145
10:41–42, pp. 50, 254
11:19, pp. 78, 142
11:20–24, p. 108
11:25–27, p. 126
11:28–30, p. 254
12:5–7, p. 106
12:10–14, p. 105
12:34, p. 130
13:24–30, p. 22
13:52, pp. 107, 177
14:13, p. 57
15:17, pp. 23, 107
16:17, p. 194
17:24–27, p. 104
17:25, p. 194
18:2–4, p. 256
18:12–14, p. 257
18:20, pp. 54, 254
19:16–20, p. 119
19:21, p. 119
19:23, p. 256
19:23–30, p. 128
19:28, pp. 24, 53
20:1–16, p. 256
20:15, p. 128
21:18–20, p. 195
21:33–39, p. 195
21:43, p. 234
22:1–10, p. 133
22:1–3, p. 254
22:2, p. 195
22:11–13, p. 254
22:11–14, p. 195
22:12, p. 195
22:23–33, p. 195
22:25, p. 196
chapter 23, p. 139
23:2–4, p. 255
23:2, p. 107
23:6, p. 107
23:8–9, p. 107
23:9, p. 184

23:13, p. 121
23:24–39, p. 163
23:27, p. 121
23:35, p. 262
25:14–19, p. 254
25:31, p. 54
25:31–46, p. 50
26:8, p. 193
26:23, p. 197
26:48, p. 198
26:50, p. 198
26:55, p. 200
26:59–61, p. 185
26:64, p. 58
26:73, p. 182
27:3, p. 191
27:4, p. 223
27:5, p. 189
27:6–7, p. 183
27:16, p. 203
27:17, p. 203
27:18, p. 203
27:22, p. 203
27:25, p. 204
27:43, p. 258
27:57–60, p. 223
27:57, p. 223
28:1–12, p. 221
28:9, p. 251
28:11–14, p. 221
28:16–18, p. 54
28:18–20, p. 40
28:19–20, pp. 31, 234

MARK

1:4–9, p. 125
2:8–12, p. 229
2:15, p. 51
2:15–17, p. 78
2:15–18, p. 163
2:18, p. 60, 70
2:21–22, p. 255
2:23, p. 163
2:24, p. 70
2:25–26, p. 106
2:27, p. 105

2:28, p. 106
2:32–3:6, p. 251
2:37, p. 256
3:13–21, p. 258
3:14, p. 80
3:14–19, p. 187
3:17, pp. 52, 198
3:19, p. 51
3:20–21, p. 54
3:31–35, pp. 54, 258
4:2–9, p. 29
4:12, p. 108
4:15, p. 132
4:21, p. 256
4:35–51, p. 62
4:35–41, p. 257
5:1–20, pp. 38, 62, 63, 109
5:11 ff, p. 162
5:19, p. 110
5:21–23, p. 62
5:25–34, p. 62
5:32–34, p. 63
5:35–42, p. 63
5:35–43, p. 62
6:1–3, p. 108
6:3–6, p. 108
6:3, pp. 187, 188
6:34–44, p. 62
6:45–51, p. 62
6:7, p. 80
6:7–11, pp. 48, 52
6:30, p. 80
6:34–44, p. 62
6:37, p. 193
7:5, p. 70
7:6–7, p.60
7:11–13, p. 104
7:18–19, p. 48
7:19, pp. 23, 107
7:24–30, p. 62
7:27, p. 63
7:32–37, p. 62
7:33–34, p. 63
8:1–9, p. 62
8:1–10, p. 63
8:22–26, pp. 62, 195

8:23, p. 63
8:27–29, p. 51
8:27–30, p. 109
8:27–33, p. 191
8:28, p. 65
8:31, p. 224
8:38, p. 52
9:2–8, p. 66
9:12, p. 224
9:14–29, p. 192
9:33–50, pp. 33, 251
9:41, p. 50
10:17–22, p. 128
10:33–34, p. 224
10:35–41, p. 187
10:38, p. 192
10:39, pp. 53, 198
10:41, p. 198
10:45, p. 222
10:46–52, p. 194
10:47–48, p. 65
chapters 11–12, 260
11:8, p. 244
11:15–18, p. 59
12:1–9, p. 131
12:8, p. 195
12:14, p. 181
12:14–17, p. 104
12:20–23, p. 137
12:28–34, p. 145
12:35–37, p. 65
chapter 13, pp. 109, 117, 248
13:6, p. 248
13:14, p. 248
13:21, p. 248
13:22, p. 248
13:27, p. 54
13:32, p. 117
14:4, p. 193
14:4–5, p. 193
14:7, pp. 50, 194
14:12, p. 53
14:20, p. 197
14:22–25, p. 92
14:24, p. 222
14:34, p. 146

14:35–36, p. 222
14:36, p. 146
14:48, p. 190
14:49, p. 200
14:50, p. 202
14:51–52, p. 194
14:57–59, p. 185
14:61, p. 243
14:64, p. 202
14:65, p. 202
14:66–71, p. 191
14:70, p. 102
15:10, p. 204
15:15, pp. 243, 245
15:16–20, p. 244
15:25, p. 54
15:27, p. 190
15:32, p. 223
15:33, pp. 40, 245
15:34, p. 223
15:38, p. 245
15:39, pp. 40, 245
15:44, pp. 223, 245
16:1–2, p. 245
16:5, pp. 214, 219
16:6–7, p. 41
16:7, pp. 35, 54
16:8, p. 35

LUKE
1:26–38, pp. 37, 117
2:41–52, p. 260
2:46–47, p. 36
2:52, p. 36
3:15, p. 61
3:23, p. 203
5:1–11, p. 35
5:8, p. 192
6:5, p. 142
6:28, pp. 130, 243
6:45, p. 130
6:47–49, p. 134
7:1–10, p. 63
7:5, p. 106
7:9, p. 79
7:11–17, p. 257

7:15, p. 220
7:36–40 ff., p. 194
7:36–50, p. 163
8:3, p. 260
9:1–5, p. 48
9:3, p. 122
9:11–17, p. 38
9:58, pp. 48, 132, 133
10:7, pp. 132, 243
10:10–12, p. 52
10:16, p. 103
10:28, p. 119
10:29, p. 66
11:1, p. 61
11:34–35, p. 128
11:44, p. 121
11:49–51, p. 163
11:49, p. 163
11:52, p. 121
12:13–14, p. 181
12:16–20, p. 132
12:29–31, p. 132
12:33–34, p. 130
13: 34–35, pp. 163, 243
14:1–6, p. 105
14:7–11, p. 255
14:16–24, pp. 133, 255
14:27, pp. 47, 145
15:3–7, p. 257
15:7, p. 255
15:8, p. 255
15:11 ff., p. 255
16:1–18:8, p. 263
16:1–12, p. 257
16:1–8 p. 130
16:8, p. 135
16:19–31, p. 255
17:6, p. 230
17:26–27, p. 243
18:9–14, p. 142
19:38, p. 244
21:14–15, p. 52
21:20–21, p. 243
22:3, p. 190
22:18, p. 222
22:27, p. 222

22:30, p. 53
22:31, p. 194
22:37, p. 197
22:44, p. 146
23:1, p. 243
23:22, p. 243
23:31, p. 92
24:12, p. 215
24:13–35, p. 39
24:13, p. 217
24:16, p. 217
24:36–43, pp. 223, 251
24:38, p. 217
24:39, p. 223
24:45–49, p. 40
24:50–53, p. 42

JOHN

1:6–7, p. 61
1:12, p. 202
1:14, p. 237
1:18, p. 58
2:1–10, p. 92
2:1–11, pp. 233, 234
2:13 ff., p. 243
2:18–22, p. 185
chapter 3, p. 232
3:2, pp. 229, 232
3:3, p. 232
3:16, p. 234
3:28–30, p. 61
chapter 4, pp. 234, 237
4:6–8, p. 237
4:9, p. 234
4:16–18, pp. 137, 196
4:25–26, p. 234
4:25, p. 64
4:26, p. 57
4:29, p. 64
4:32, p. 237
4:34, p. 237
4:42, p. 64
4:46–54, p. 63
chapter 5, p. 139
5:1 ff., p. 243
5:8–10, p. 230

5:18, p. 235
5:24–25, p. 238
5:28, p. 239
6:4 ff., p. 243
6:10, p. 63
6:19, p. 63
6:35, p. 57
6:44, p. 235
6:53, p. 235
6:63, p. 236
6:66–71, p. 191
6:70, p. 53
7:1–7, p. 54
7:1, p. 57
7:2 ff., p. 243
7:5, p. 234
7:35, p. 223
7:37, p. 243
7:52, p. 66
7:53–8:11, p. 195
8:12, pp. 57, 233
8:23, p. 236
8:24, pp. 233, 236
8:48, p. 190
chapter 9, p. 233
9:6, p. 63
9:13–14, p. 230
9:22, p. 233
10:7 ff., p. 233
10:9, p. 57
10:14–16, p. 172
10:16, p. 234
10:14, p. 57
10:16, p. 76
10:22–23 ff., p. 243
10:26–27, p. 235
10:34, p. 235
11:23–36, p. 239
11:25, p. 57
11:35–36, p. 237
11:41–42, p. 237
11:44, p. 220
11:55–56, p. 243
12:6, p. 190
12:24, p. 92
12:44, p. 239

chapters 13–17, p. 34
13:2, p. 191
13:23–25, p. 58
13:27, p. 190
14:7–10, p. 239
14:22–23, p. 239
14:22, pp. 188, 189
14:28, p. 239
15:1–10, p. 234
15:1–6, pp. 92, 233
15:1, p. 57
16:2, p. 233
16:7, p. 58
16:12–15, p. 34
16:12–13, p. 237
16:33, p. 131
17:12, p. 189
18:21, pp. 58, 202
18:36–37, p. 260
18:37, p. 82
19:1, p. 243
19:8, p. 245
19:9, p. 243
19:12, p. 245
19:28, p. 238
19:33–34, p. 244
19:34, p. 223
19:35, p. 214
19:38, p. 232
19:41, pp. 92, 189, 216
20:1–10, p. 215
20:1, p. 214
20:4–6, p. 214
20:6–7, p. 215
20:13–14, p. 217
20:14, p. 217
20:17, p. 238
20:19, p. 41
20:20, p. 223
20:24–29, pp. 42, 251
20:25, p. 223
20:30–31, p. 65
21:1–11, p. 39
21:6, p. 39
21:11, p. 39
21:18–19, p. 187

21:24, p. 214

THOMAS
1, pp. 33, 163
6, p. 21
12, pp. 53, 241
13, pp. 51, 120, 165
21, p. 131
27, p. 127
28, p.118
39, p. 121
60, p. 66
102, p. 121

ACTS
1:4, p. 54
1:6, p. 34
1:9, pp. 40, 42
1:18–19, p. 189
1:26, p. 197
2:36, p. 55
3:1–8, p. 23
3:19–21, p. 55
5:14–16, p. 23
5:35–39, pp. 246, 247
6:12–14, p. 185
6:13–14, p. 68
7:57, p. 29
8:9–24, p. 23
8:18–24, p. 188
9:36–42, p. 23
chapters 10–11, p. 115
10:1–4 ff., p. 106
10:40–41, p. 251
10:41, p. 54
11:1–3, pp. 165, 234
12:1–2, p. 53
12:2, p. 53
12:1–11, p. 23
13:6–11, p. 23
13:33, p. 55
13:46, p. 234
14:8–10, p. 23
chapter 15, p. 107
15:1, p. 107
15:5, p. 106

16:23–26, p. 23
18:6, p. 234
19:11–12, p. 23
20:7–12, p. 23
21:38, pp. 230, 246
24:5, p. 66
28:28, p. 234

ROMANS
1:3–4, p. 55
1:5, p. 24
1:14, p. 24
3:27–4:1–5 ff., p. 23
3:29, p. 234
5:2, p. 78
chapter 8, p. 203
chapter 11, p. 234
chapters 14–15, pp. 106, 107
14:1–15:6, p. 70
15:15–20, p. 24
15:31, p. 52

1 CORINTHIANS
1:11–12, p. 60
1:12, pp. 49, 83
1:12–13, p. 103
2:8, p. 250
3:13, p. 139
7:18, p. 107
7:25, p. 102
chapter 8, p. 92
chapters 8–10, p. 88
8:5, p. 88
8:6, p. 88
12:3, pp. 61, 83
12:12 ff, p. 103
13:1–3, p. 123
13:1, p. 123
15:3–11, p. 54
15:3–4, pp. 215, 258
15:4, p. 54
15:5, p. 188
15:15, p. 202
15:20–23, p. 54
15:43–50, p. 251

2 Corinthians
2:14, p. 47
3:1–2, p. 49
3:14, p. 208
5:17, p. 236
11:4–5, p. 23
11:5, p. 83
11:13–15, p. 23

Galatians
1:6–9, p. 23
chapter 2, p. 107
2:7–9, p. 24
2:9, p. 52
2:10, pp. 31, 52
2:11–14 ff., p. 234
2:12, p. 107
2:14, p. 23
2:21, p. 77

Ephesians
2:14, p. 172
4:16–17, p. 103

Philippians
2:6–11, pp. 54, 85
4:2–3, p. 186

Colossians
2:8, p. 119
2:13–15, p. 250
4:1, p. 140

2 Thessalonians
2:1, p. 54
2:3, p. 189

1 Timothy
6:10, p. 131

Hebrews
5:7, p. 223
11:35, p. 77

James
1:22, p. 119

2:19, p. 125
2:20, p. 23
3:2, p. 128
5:16–18, p. 123

1 Peter
2:7–8, p. 108
2:10, p. 77
3:18–19, p. 251

2 Peter
1.16–18, p. 223
3:15–16, p. 24

1 John
1:7–10, p. 240
2:15, pp. 135, 236
2:27, p. 81
3:5–10, p. 240
4:1, p. 237
4:2, p. 237
5:10, p. 10
5:16–17, p. 240
5:18, p. 240

2 John
10, p. 50

3 John
10, p. 50

Jude
11, p. 198

Revelation of John
1:17, p. 54
chapters 2–3, p. 51
2:9, p. 78
3:14–22, p. 108
3:20, p. 54
7:4–8, p. 23
7:17, p. 52
11:15, p. 54
14:1–5, p. 133
14:4, p. 26
19:1–9, p. 133

19:19, p. 54
21:12, p. 23
21:14, p. 23